KING, PRIEST,
AND PROPHET

Easter Season 2004

Bob —

In sincere appreciation of your
collegiality, faithfulness, and support.

Warmest thanks,

Bob

Theology for the Twenty-first Century is a series sponsored by the Center of Theological Inquiry (CTI), an institute, located in Princeton, New Jersey, dedicated to the advanced study of theology. This series is one of its many initiatives and projects.

The goal of the series is to publish inquiries of contemporary scholars into the nature of the Christian faith and its witness and practice in the church, society, and culture. The series will include investigations into the uniqueness of the Christian faith, but it will also offer studies that relate the Christian faith to the major cultural, social, and practical issues of our time.

Monographs and symposia will result from research by scholars in residence at the Center of Theological Inquiry or otherwise associated with it. In some cases, publications will come from group research projects sponsored by CTI. It is our intention that the books selected for this series will constitute a major contribution to renewing theology in its service to church and society.

WALLACE M. ALSTON JR., ROBERT JENSON,
and DON S. BROWNING
Series Editors

What Dare We Hope?
by Gerhard Sauter

The End of the World and the Ends of God
edited by John Polkinghorne and Michael Welker

God and Globalization, Volume 1:
Religion and the Powers of the Common Life
edited by Max L. Stackhouse with Peter J. Paris

God and Globalization, Volume 2:
The Spirit and the Modern Authorities
edited by Max L. Stackhouse with Don S. Browning

God and Globalization, Volume 3:
Christ and the Dominions of Civilization
edited by Max L. Stackhouse with Diane B. Obenchain

Redemptive Change:
Atonement and the Christian Cure of the Soul
by R. R. Reno

King, Priest, and Prophet:
A Trinitarian Theology of Atonement
by Robert Sherman

KING, PRIEST, AND PROPHET

A Trinitarian Theology of Atonement

Robert Sherman

T&T CLARK INTERNATIONAL
A Continuum imprint
NEW YORK • LONDON

T & T Clark International
Madison Square Park, 15 East 26th Street, New York, NY 10010

T & T Clark International
The Tower Building, 11 York Road, London SE1 7NX

T & T Clark International is a Continuum imprint.

Design: Corey Kent

Library of Congress Cataloging-in-Publication Data
Sherman, Robert J.
  King, priest, and prophet : a Trinitarian theology of atonement /
Robert J. Sherman.
      p. cm. — (Theology for the twenty-first century)
Includes bibliographical references and index.
  ISBN 0-567-02560-8 (pbk.)
  1. Trinity. I. Title. II. Series.
BT111.3.S53 2004
232'.3—dc22
                                                          2003022129

Printed in the United States of America
04 05 06 07 08 09   10 9 8 7 6 5 4 3 2 1

For Carol

Contents

Preface

Books are written for multiple and sometimes competing reasons. This book intends to serve the church and its mission of communicating the good news of Christ's atoning work to the world. So its primary and intended audience is Christian ministers, whether they be ordained clergy, seminary students seeking to become such, or lay leaders. To be sure, I am an "academic theologian" and the book exhibits a number of standard academic trappings (about which more below), but my motivation for writing is pastoral. I am convinced that theology written for the academy—or, more pointedly, just for other academic theologians—misses its original and true calling. That calling is to serve the church by helping it better understand the full meaning and implications of the gospel it proclaims in its preaching, liturgy, counseling, catechesis, and evangelism. I offer this book in hopes that it may make certain biblical themes and theological traditions more accessible and powerfully present for ministers in their diverse pastoral work, to the end that the church's work may be faithfully enriched and strengthened.

That said, one of the book's academic trappings is that it spends a considerable amount of time setting the stage before starting the show. To begin with, chapters 1 and 2 concern themselves with presenting a thesis, surveying some theological literature, establishing the theological method to be used, and offering some historical background. Necessary material all, but not yet dealing with the heart of the matter. To further fill in the background, chapter 3 sketches in broad strokes the trinitarian character of God's dealings with the faithful by examining a variety of telling New Testament texts. Only in chapters 4, 5, and 6 do the main themes of Christ as King, Priest, and Prophet make their full entrance, although they have been anticipated earlier. The upshot of all this is that some readers may want to engage the book in a different order than that presented. Those who are most concerned with the practical and pastoral implications of my book may want to start with chapter 3, or perhaps 4. Indeed, they may profit by reading first the last sections of chapters 4, 5, and 6, along with the final chapter. By so doing, they can quickly learn the practical and pastoral pay-off of my work, which should then help clarify the reasons for the exegetical and theological positions I stake out. If, on the basis of these positions, readers gain a new appreciation of key parts of the Christian tradition or are prompted toward some new theological connections of their own for their pastoral work, then this book will certainly have served its purpose.

Writing a book is almost never an undertaking of one person alone, and especially the writing of one in Christian theology, which is never properly an individualistic exercise, but always one in conversation with the community of faith. This book is certainly the product of such conversations, as well as the support of such a community. So I am grateful to many different people, and want to express that gratitude openly. First, I want to thank my students at Bangor Theological Seminary, because the kernel of the book originally germinated in the give-and-take of the classroom. I especially want to thank those members of a particular Christology course I offered some years back who were the first to hear, appreciate, and respond to the approach eventually embodied in this book. They were Beverly Blaisdell, Brian Grover, Alan Manwiller, Chad Poland (who also served as a research assistant), John Titus, and Brenda Wesselink. My appreciation goes as well to Iain Torrance, whose support in publishing an article-length precursor of this work in the *Scottish Journal of Theology* indicated it could be of value to a wider audience.

Of course, scholarly projects often do not come to full flower unless there is ample time to nurture and cultivate them. So I also have a special word of appreciation for the sabbatical opportunity afforded me during the 2000–2001 academic year by the President of Bangor Theological Seminary at that time, Ansley Coe Throckmorton, and to the Seminary's Board of Trustees. In addition, I am grateful to my faculty colleagues, who took up a number of additional responsibilities during my yearlong absence. Thanks as well to the Louisville Institute and its Executive Director James W. Lewis, whose Christian Faith & Life Sabbatical Grant helped support my family and me. Indeed, the fact that we were a family in two places for six months of my sabbatical was finally only manageable because of the generosity of this support. I also want to express my sincere appreciation to all those connected with the Center of Theological Inquiry in Princeton, New Jersey, where I was a member-in-residence during the first half of 2001. I specifically want to acknowledge the gracious support of its Director, Wallace M. Alston, Jr., and its Senior Fellow for Research, Robert W. Jenson, as well as staff members Kathi Morley, Marion Gibson, Maureen Montgomery, and Mary Rae Rogers. I also owe a debt of gratitude to all of my fellow members-in-residence, whose comments, critiques and support were such a boon to my thinking and writing. In particular, I want to thank Ellen Charry, Beverly Gaventa, Ann Jervis, Lois Malcolm, and Philip Rolnick, whose doors were always open when I needed a conversation partner to work through a variety of exegetical or theological challenges.

I want to thank as well those pastors who read through the entire manuscript and met with me several times to offer their pastoral evaluations and very practical advice. These included the Reverend Robert Carlson, the Reverend Renee U. Garrett, the Reverend Dr. James Haddix, the Reverend Kevin Holsapple, and the Reverend Dr. Carol Sherman.

My appreciation also extends to Henry Carrigan, Jr., of T & T Clark International, whose support and editorial guidance has made this a better book. Thanks, too, to Amy Wagner who helped shepherd things along expeditiously and courteously.

Finally, an additional word to one of the pastors just mentioned, who also happens to be my wife: Carol, for your unflagging support, good cheer, countless words of encouragement and wisdom, sustaining prayers, kindness and love, I am ceaselessly amazed and grateful. While it is only a small token of the gratitude I have for all you have given me, I dedicate this book to you.

The 4th Sunday of Advent 2003

1

Why Bother with a Trinitarian Theology of Atonement?

Why should the church—her pastors and teachers, her deacons or presbyters, her laymen and women, her priests, her vestry and committee members, her confirmands and Sunday school students—concern herself with a trinitarian theology of the atonement? Why should the church bother to let her theological reflection and pastoral practice be guided, indeed, grow out of such an obscure-sounding theme? Because such a theology points to the very source of her existence as church and elucidates the fundamental purpose to which God calls her. Because such a theology offers Christians of all sorts the spiritual and pastoral resources to deepen their own faith and extend a hand to those outside the church, offering them new hope, a new identity, a new sense of meaning and new courage in a world filled with uncertainty, coarseness, danger, and death. Because it explains in a deep and rich and practical way what it actually means to make the seemingly simple claim that "Jesus saves." The rather awkward rubric, "a trinitarian theology of the atonement," connects the God whom the church invokes, worships, and petitions with what it is that this God actually accomplishes for the reconciliation and restoration of the world. Without such a recognition of who God truly is and what he has done and continues to do, the church's sacraments become merely human ceremonies, her prayers merely human pleading, her preaching merely human opinion and exhortation, her consolation merely wishful thinking, and her service merely human moralism and social work. But with such a recognition, the church learns the world's God-given origin and end, and her own true purpose in fulfilling God's commission. With such a recognition, the church may finally escape the mundane banality that so often passes for a contemporary vision and reclaim its transcendent birthright: a powerful and multifaceted trinitarian life, imagination, and vocation.

Such a reclamation is indeed an urgent need. For in the twilight of the millenium just ended and the dawn of the millenium now upon us, God offers the church of Christ an age of renewed opportunity and challenge in proclaiming and enacting the gospel. Especially in its North American context, the church is now encompassed by a culture newly receptive to matters of spirituality, yet still—and perhaps even more than past eras—resistant to "organized religion" and its faith traditions. The tide of secularity that swept American culture in the 1960s (a tide the origins of which, of course, are centuries older) no longer seems so irresistible or desirable, even as the individualistic claims of moral and spiritual autonomy have only increased since that decade. As certain observers have noted, the question a generation ago was, "Would religion even survive in an age of increasing secularization?" But now, secularism itself seems on the wane in the face of the astounding popular interest in matters of "spirit." Yet in this context the current interest in spirituality seems shaped more by the individual tastes and eclectic preferences of religious consumers than the teaching and commitments of historic religious communions, whether Christian or some other faith. Perhaps this is to be expected, for not since the early centuries of the church's existence have Christians had so much competition in the "marketplace of religions." But in contrast to those early centuries, Christianity is no longer the new and different faith that might by that very fact move modern people to give it the benefit of the doubt. This is quite a hindrance in an age conditioned by advertising, the entertainment industry, and even so-called high culture to desire the new and different, the cutting edge, and that which "pushes the envelope." Moreover, the church is burdened by the specter of its own very real inadequacies, excesses, corruption, and oppressions accumulated over the millennia. It is also burdened by the fact that most people assume that they already know—whether accurately or not—what Christian faith actually entails.

All this means that even in those remaining contexts in which the church may reasonably think of itself as "established" (by social and cultural habit, if not legally or politically), it is increasingly clear that its traditional faith is by no means secure. Especially in the old-line denominations, but also in more evangelical churches, eclecticism often reigns. A sense of continuity with the historic Christian faith and a sense of accountability to that faith in presenting Christian belief to a new age in a coherent, complex, vital, and faithful manner is often simply absent. Even though Jesus as a figure remains popular, this tendency toward eclecticism typically produces works and perspectives of varying sophistication and depth. Jesus makes regular appearances on the covers of weekly newsmagazines as a perennial topic of interest and he serves as a recurring subject of contemporary movies and television dramas. The former generally offer stories recounting the "latest" scholarly theories and opinions (an approach that often tends to produce either a bland or fragmented picture of Jesus). The latter generally display more coherence, but also idiosyncrasy. If all these descriptions of the context in which the church finds itself are indeed the case, then the challenge to, and opportunity for, all Christians—and not just the church's pastors, teachers, and theologians—should be obvious.

So as a theologian deeply committed to the Christian faith and fully convinced of its truth and continuing relevance for our current age, I am motivated to write by two complementary concerns. On the one hand, I want to open up and represent the riches of the Christian tradition regarding God's atoning work in Christ through the Spirit in a way that is faithful and fair to its scripturally described nuance and diversity. On the other hand, I want to take seriously the challenges and complexity of contemporary life, on its individual and collective levels. I am convinced that the resources of the Christian faith, if rendered in a serious and dynamic manner, can still help awaken persons to the gift of God's grace: the offer of true liberation, deep solace, authentic challenge, and the power to transform lives.

What leads me to suppose that I can successfully address these twin concerns of representing classic Christian understandings of the atonement in a way that addresses the complexity of contemporary life? What concrete resources will I have to bring to bear? First, I should simply point out that I am not starting from scratch. There is deep, serious, and systematic theological work being done nowadays, in a manner that was not always promoted or appreciated several decades ago.

And this is true not just in the realm of academic theology, but at a more popular level for the churches and the culture at large.[1] In this context, I am convinced that the rich theological traditions that have emerged over the centuries may still be fruitfully cultivated today. I believe this is especially true with the basic models of the atonement, which, far from being dated and irrelevant, I will argue are in fact essential to contemporary Christian life and faith. Properly understood and employed, doctrine is a boon, not a barrier, to practical spirituality. And the doctrine of the atonement stands at the heart of the Christian message, so it should be at the heart of one's everyday faith. Yet what, precisely, is the content of this doctrine? Theological proposals have varied over the centuries, so there is no one unequivocal answer to this question.

Second, I want to take constructive advantage of the fact that the church has never insisted upon one orthodox understanding of the Christ's work, as it did an understanding of his person. This circumstance has been pointed out before, and taken as an opportunity by numerous theologians before me.[2] Given this doctrinal room to maneuver, I want to overcome the unfortunate but all-too-common tendency in the history of Christian thinking to view the various understandings or models of the atonement as generally exclusive of one another. True, the typical recounting of that history suggests that such a conclusion is inevitable. As students of theology are often taught, Anselm offered his understanding of the atonement at the turn of the first millenium as an alternative to notions prevalent in the church since the earliest centuries. In turn, Abelard's theory was a self-conscious reaction against Anselm's view, and the reemergence of exemplarist models during the Enlightenment and the nineteenth century were seen by their proponents as necessary modern corrections to the presumed superstition and immorality of substitutionary atonement models. I will argue, however, that such polarization is

---

1. Regarding the former, see the reference to the analysis of Gabriel Fackre below, note 30. Regarding the latter, consider, for example, that in addition to his many weighty academic works, Anglican bishop and biblical scholar N. T. Wright also publishes numerous books aimed at a thoughtful lay audience, under the name "Tom Wright." See Wright's *The Meal Jesus Gave Us: Understanding Holy Communion* (Louisville, Ky.: Westminster/John Knox Press, 2003) and *The Original Jesus: The Life and Vision of a Revolutionary* (Grand Rapids, Mich.: Eerdmans, 1997).

2. Among modern theologians see, for example, Michael Winter, *The Atonement* (Problems in Theology; Collegeville, Minn.: The Liturgical Press, 1995), 59, who cites B. Studer's observations in *Handbuch der Dogmengeschichte* (vol. 3; Freiburg, 1978), 2a, 224–25 and J. N. D. Kelly, *Early Christian Doctrines* (5th ed.; London, 1976), 163.

neither true to Scripture nor theologically necessary. Moreover, it does not serve, but actually impoverishes, the resources available for the practical life of faith. I believe the basic witness of the Bible and the church's theological tradition (in its Spirit-guided collective wisdom, if not the intention of its individual authors and theologians) actually offers several diverse but complementary understandings of the atonement. As such, this witness enables far more flexibility, sensitivity, and integrity in the church's pastoral responses to the diverse circumstances of the human condition than it would were there only one understanding, or an arbitrary and entirely open-ended pluralism of understandings.

For example, as a theologian educating future pastors and teachers in a particular church milieu, I am concerned that too many of my students make no greater claim of Christ than that he was a "spirit person,"[3] and construe his work as some variation on personal spiritual mentoring. Whatever their source, such minimalist views can only weaken the church's pastoral ministry and the Christian life. Such an image of Christ may be appealing to a certain middle-class sensibility, but how can it offer anything of real depth and substance should a truly serious personal or historical crisis arise? Such an image is not very demanding—no doubt, one of the reasons for its appeal in everyday circumstances—but in turn, it also seems incapable of having any serious demands placed upon it. In times of trial, people need something with more substance and depth. Of course, I am also well aware that in other church circles, the predominant image of Christ is far different from this one of "spirit person." Some Christians can think of Jesus in no other terms than as the one punished in their place. Such an image may effect a sense of gratitude at God's grace. Yet if it is not enriched and complemented by other understandings of Jesus' place and significance, it may also evoke images of a wrathful Father, misplaced feelings of guilt and inadequacy, or a preoccupation with one's individual salvation at the expense of one's God-given responsibilities in the larger world. Additionally, such a view of Christ's work may serve to make demands or place burdens where the gospel has actually removed them.

Fortunately, in addition to this proliferation of "Jesus options," two other theological trends have emerged that can supply helpful resources for a more nuanced and responsible response. First, interest

---

3. The phrase is Marcus Borg's. See his *Meeting Jesus Again for the First Time* (New York: HarperCollins, 1995), 31ff. I will discuss this more below, in chapter 6.

in the doctrine of the Trinity has reappeared, across the theological spectrum. One need only observe the number of recent journal articles, multiple articles in one issue, indeed, whole journal issues dedicated to the topic.[4] As for the variety, consider that in the last decade or so major books on the Trinity have emerged from a liberation theologian, feminist theologians, a Catholic theologian seeking to bridge ecumenical divides, theologians with "neo-orthodox" sensibilities, an Episcopal theologian with Liberal Protestant sensibilities, a theologian concerned with a dialogue with the natural sciences, and evangelical theologians, to name just a few.[5] Other books are less easy to pigeonhole according to theological perspective precisely because they offer creative syntheses and new perspectives.[6] In the face of such fecundity, various books have appeared striving to summarize the variety of viewpoints now current, typically taking the form of either a one-author survey or an anthology of essays.[7]

---

4. Among those with multiple articles or whole issues on the Trinity, consider *The International Journal of Systematic Theology* 5 (March 2003), *Modern Theology* 18 (October 2002), *The Living Pulpit* 8 (April–June 1999), *Word & World: Theology for Christian Ministry* 18 (Summer 1998), *Modern Theology* 2 (April 1986), and *Theology Today* 54 (October 1997).

5. See Leonardo Boff, *Trinity and Society* (Maryknoll, N.Y.: Orbis Books, 1988), Catherine Mowry LaCugna, *God for Us: The Trinity and Christian Life* (New York: HarperCollins, 1991), Elizabeth Johnson, *She Who Is: The Mystery of God in Feminist Theological Discourse* (New York: Crossroad, 1992), David Coffey, *Deus Trinitatis: The Doctrine of the Triune God* (New York: Oxford University Press, 1999), T. F. Torrance, *The Trinitarian Faith* (Edinburgh: T&T Clark, 1988), Colin E. Gunton, *The Promise of Trinitarian Theology* (Edinburgh: T&T Clark, 1991 [1st ed.], 1997 [2d ed.]), Robert W. Jenson, *The Triune Identity: God According to the Gospel* (Philadelphia: Fortress Press, 1982) and *The Triune God* (vol. 1 of *Systematic Theology;* New York: Oxford University Press, 1997), David S. Cunningham, *These Three Are One: The Practice of Trinitarian Theology* (Challenges in Contemporary Theology, eds. Lewis Ayres and Gareth Jones; Oxford: Blackwell Publishers, 1998), Ted Peters, *God as Trinity: Relationality and Temporality in Divine Life* (Louisville, Ky.: Westminster/John Knox Press, 1993), Ben Witherington III and Laura M. Ice, *The Shadow of the Almighty: Father, Son, and Spirit in Biblical Perspective* (Grand Rapids, Mich.: Eerdmans, 2002), and Peter Toon, *Our Triune God: A Biblical Portrayal of the Trinity* (Wheaton, Ill.: Victor Books, 1996).

6. Consider, for example, Kathryn Tanner, *Jesus, Humanity, and the Trinity: A Brief Systematic Theology* (Minneapolis: Fortress Press, 2001), S. Mark Heim, *The Depths of the Riches: A Trinitarian Theology of Religious Ends* (Sacra Doctrina: Christian Theology for a Postmodern Age; Grand Rapids, Mich.: Erdmans, 2001), Bruce D. Marshall, *Trinity and Truth* (Cambridge Studies in Christian Doctrine; Cambridge: Cambridge University Press, 2000), and Paul S. Fiddes, *Participating in God: A Pastoral Doctrine of the Trinity* (Louisville, Ky.: Westminster/John Knox Press, 2000).

7. See, for example, John Thompson, *Modern Trinitarian Perspectives* (New York: Oxford University Press, 1994), Christoph Schwöbel, ed., *Trinitarian Theology Today*

Other works are using the Trinity as the lens through which historical investigations are undertaken or topical issues explored.[8] Moreover, a number of books have been published seeking to explain the importance of the Trinity to a student or lay audience.[9]

Second, a similar if somewhat less prolific flow of new discussions and books has emerged around the doctrine of the atonement. Many books seek simply to explain and make accessible a more or less traditional understanding of this doctrine.[10] Other writers are less satisfied with the tradition, and seek to offer new construals.[11] Several well-publicized alternate proposals have come from two members of the Jesus Seminar, of which one promotes a prophetic/political model and the other a more "spiritual" one.[12] Yet another productive source of current writing stems from explicit feminist critiques of sacrificial and vicarious substitution

---

(Edinburgh: T&T Clark, 1995), Kevin J. Vanhoozer, ed., *Trinity in a Pluralistic Age* (Grand Rapids, Mich.: Eerdmans, 1997), and Stephen Davis, Daniel Kendal, and Gerald O'Collins, *The Trinity* (New York: Oxford University Press, 1999).

8. For example, Samuel Powell, *The Trinity in German Thought* (New York: Cambridge University Press, 2001), Paul M. Collins, *Trinitarian Theology, West and East: Karl Barth, the Cappadocian Fathers, and John Zizioulas* (Oxford: Oxford University Press, 2001), and Eugene F. Rogers, *Sexuality and the Christian Body: Their Way into the Triune God* (Oxford: Blackwell, 1999).

9. Three good examples include Roger E. Olson and Christopher Hall, *The Trinity* (Guides to Theology Series; Grand Rapids, Mich.: Eerdmans, 2002), Philip W. Butin, *The Trinity* (Foundations of Christian Faith; Louisville, Ky.: Geneva Press, 2001), and Millard J. Erickson, *Making Sense of the Trinity* (Grand Rapids, Mich.: Baker Books, 2000). A lesser effort is Lynne Faber Lorenzen, *The College Student's Introduction to the Trinity* (Collegeville, Minn.: Liturgical Press, 1999). See also William LaDue's *The Trinity Guide to the Trinity* (Harrisburg, Penn.: Trinity Press International, 2003).

10. See, for example, Stephen Sykes, *The Story of Atonement* (Trinity and Truth Series; London: Darton, Longman, and Todd, 1997), Geoffrey Wainwright, *For Our Salvation: Two Approaches to the Work of Christ* (Grand Rapids, Mich.: Eerdmans, 1997), and Paul S. Fiddes, *Past Event and Present Salvation: The Christian Idea of Atonement* (London: Darton, Longman, and Todd, 1989), as well as the hyper-traditionalist text of Gordon H. Clark, *The Atonement* (2d ed.; Hobbs, N.M.: The Trinity Foundation, 1996).

11. Consider, for example, Anthony W. Bartlett, *Cross Purposes: The Violent Grammar of Christian Atonement* (Harrisburg, Penn.: Trinity Press International, 2001), J. Denny Weaver, *The Nonviolent Atonement* (Grand Rapids, Mich.: Eerdmans, 2001), C. J. den Heyer, *Jesus and the Doctrine of the Atonement* (Harrisburg, Penn.: Trinity Press International, 1998), and the already cited book by Michael Winter, *The Atonement* (1995).

12. Consider John Dominic Crossan's Jesus as wandering cynic philosopher/civic agitator and Marcus Borg's "inclusive" Jesus. As I point out above, Borg is the one who describes Jesus as "spirit person." While I obviously think this is an inadequate characterization of Jesus, I appreciate Borg's desire to make Jesus accessible to contemporary culture. His work may also serve as a catalyst for developing a more adequate understanding of Jesus.

theories,[13] which in certain cases include the retrieval and updating of older traditions.[14] Such critiques have predictably served as a catalyst, both directly and indirectly, for responses and yet more alternate proposals.[15] And, of course, the ferment has not just produced books, but journal consideration as well. Indeed, the theological journal *Interpretation* devoted its January issues of both 1998 and 1999 to the theme of atonement, "because of the signal importance of the symbol of the cross and because of the present controversy surrounding the suitability and meaning of atonement language."[16] At a more popular level, during Lent 2001 the *Christian Century* published a two-part set of articles by S. Mark Heim inquiring into why Jesus' death matters and seeking to rethink the meaning of his sacrifice.[17] The articles elicited some very strong, even heated, responses.[18] Clearly, the atonement is something people care about.

In the context of this ferment regarding both the doctrines of the Trinity and atonement, I have set as my task the integration of the two, grounding the latter in the former, and seeking to offer a proposal that is coherent, rich, useful, and faithful. In so doing, I am motivated less by the desire to produce theological innovation than to demonstrate the theological integrity and pastoral value of several classic Christian

---

13. Such critiques have taken academic and more public forms. Of the former, consider Dorothee Sölle, *Suffering* (trans. Everett R. Kalin; Philadelphia: Fortress Press, 1975), 22–32, Joanne Carlson Brown and Carole R. Bohn, *Christianity, Patriarchy, and Abuse: A Feminist Critique* (New York: Pilgrim Press, 1989), 26ff., and, woven through her new proposal for understanding communion, June Christine Goudey, *The Feast of Our Lives: Re-imaging Communion* (Cleveland: The Pilgrim Press, 2002). Of the latter, consider the much publicized rhetoric of the Re-Imagining Conference held in Minneapolis in 1993. The comment of Delores Williams was frequently quoted as representative: "I don't think we need folks hanging on crosses and blood dripping and weird stuff." See *Christianity Today* 38 (April 4, 1994): 74. In December 1994, the *Christian Century* named the conference the second top story in religion in the past year. See the *Christian Century* 111 (December 21–28, 1994): 1211.

14. Darby Kathleen Ray, *Deceiving the Devil: Atonement, Abuse, and Ransom* (Cleveland: The Pilgrim Press, 1998).

15. See, for example, Joel B. Green and Mark D. Baker, *Recovering the Scandal of the Cross: Atonement in New Testament and Contemporary Contexts* (Downers Grove, Ill.: InterVarsity Press, 2000), and Colin E. Gunton, *The Actuality of Atonement* (Edinburgh: T&T Clark, 1988).

16. See *Interpretation* 52 (January 1998): 4.

17. See *Christian Century* 118, no. 8 (March 7, 2001): 12–17, and 118, no. 9 (March 14, 2001): 19–23.

18. See *Christian Century* 118, no. 15 (May 9, 2001): 28–29.

traditions. Specifically, I will offer a constructive theological proposal connecting the Trinity with the rubrics of prophet, priest, and king to help explain Christ's diverse atoning work. My thesis is this: One can understand adequately neither Christ's multifaceted reconciliation of a complex humanity to God nor that reconciliation's fundamental unity as God's gracious act apart from the Trinity. Without this framework one will likely stress one person of the Trinity, one aspect of God's reconciling work, and/or one understanding of the human predicament to the exclusion of the others and the detriment of theology, both systematic and pastoral. As one faithful and useful way to guard against such tunnel vision, I suggest that theology should recognize a certain correspondence and mutual support between the three persons of the Trinity, the three offices of Christ, and the three commonly recognized models of his atoning work.

To be sure, in making this proposal, I am not claiming that Christ's threefold office of prophet, priest, and king necessarily exhausts the biblical and traditional images of Christ's atoning work. The roles of king, priest, and prophet certainly served a central mediatorial function in God's relation to Israel, and as such, I would argue they retain a certain priority when interpreting Christ as the divinely incarnate Mediator. Still, the New Testament witness suggests that other titles or "offices" might with equal justice be ascribed to him (e.g., Son of Man, Shepherd, or Teacher), titles which might help explain Christ's atoning work in different directions. Of course, some of these additional rubrics may be subsumed under one of the threefold offices. For example, in the Old Testament the role of "shepherd" was often associated with the king's rule over the people of Israel (see, e.g., 2 Sam 5:1–4, Ps 78:70–71, Isa 44:28, Jer 23:3–5, and Ezek 37:24). And, as I will argue in chapter 6, the role of teacher may be subsumed under the broader role of prophet. The point is, that while my constructive use of the threefold office will not claim to be the only way of describing the trinitarian nature of the atonement, I do assume it represents a particularly appropriate way of describing that work. On the one hand, I believe it serves a practical function, not the least of which is enabling us to discover meanings and relations we might otherwise miss. On the other, I believe it will better do justice to the multiform witness of Scripture, better address concerns for systematic coherence, and better serve the diverse needs of pastoral ministry and the Christian life than most current approaches.

Outline of the Problem

In order to continue, some basic definitions need to be provided. To begin with, what exactly do I mean by "atonement"? Students of theology know that it is a word employed by William Tyndale for his 1526 English translation of the New Testament, to correspond to the Greek word meaning "reconciliation" *(katallage)*.[19] Tyndale's use refers to the "at-one-ment" effected by God in Christ, and it was his usage which apparently initiated its role as a technical theological term. Since that time, the word has come to be associated in the minds of many with what Christ effects more particularly through his death on the cross.[20] I propose, however, that we employ the term in a more general sense to refer to the salvific "bringing together" of the human to the divine that God the Father effects in Christ the Son through the power of the Holy Spirit. While Tyndale used the term as a translation for a particular Greek word, I am convinced that Scripture describes this "bringing together" in diverse ways, each of which deserves more precise labeling and discussion. Yet because this "bringing together" is the work of the one God directed toward all humanity, it is still theologically appropriate and practically useful to have one word that can describe this work and its effects as a whole. "Atonement" as a term may be taken as pointing to *what* has occurred between humanity and God, but on its own does not necessarily connote *how* it has occurred.

Of course, to say that God has effected a "bringing together" presupposes that some sort of separation or estrangement or alienation divides humanity from God, a condition that needs to be overcome or eliminated before the true and proper relation between them may be restored. So the question that logically precedes "What is atonement?" must be "What is the problem of humanity's alienation or estrangement or separation for which Christ's atoning work is the solution?" Now, in answering my first question with another question, I may be accused of a certain circularity or evasiveness. That is not my intent, and would point to the experience that sometimes questions only become clear when one is confronted by an answer. In this case, an accurate sense of the true character of our human problem often only emerges in retrospect from

---

19. For example, 2 Cor 5:18: "God . . . hath geven unto us the office to preache the atonement." *Oxford English Dictionary* (1971), s.v. "Atonement."

20. Not without reason, as Rom 5:10 straightforwardly indicates and 2 Cor 5:18–21 may be read as implying, especially in light of 2 Cor 5:14–15.

perceptions of the messianic intervention. Yet in the history of the Christian church, and in the writings of her theologians, it appears that there have also been a number of different answers to a number of different questions. One can begin to make sense of this apparent circularity and multiplicity if one distinguishes between what I call the "order of experience" and the "theological order." I see the former as more particular and occasional, the latter as more comprehensive and enduring. On the one hand, the character of the divine-human separation and reconciliation may be experienced in diverse ways, ways that may entail only an aspect of, or appear to reverse the order of, a theologically structured description of their relation. Such experiences simply happen the way they happen, based on the particular situations of the persons involved. There is no one way this experience "ought" to unfold. On the other hand, the theological ordering seeks to discern the internal dynamics and connections between "the human problem" and "Christ's atoning solution" in a comprehensive manner, according to the internal logic of what is revealed by Christ.

Why is it important to recognize such a distinction? Because pastoral theology must always be sensitive to the order of experience, in a very practical sense "starting where the person is," and bringing the gospel message to her or him at that place. Systematic theology, by contrast, concerns itself with the "theological order." It is obliged to discern, based on the witness of Scripture, a broader and more detailed understanding of "the human problem" and "Christ's atoning solution." In that sense, it starts with the gospel message, and brings the person's experience to it, offering him or her a fuller framework of explanation and understanding. A major concern of this book will be to offer a systematic account of the triune God's work of atonement that is pastorally useful. That is, I hope to facilitate a reengagement between systematic and pastoral theology, and to foster discernment and sensitivity in how and when to apply the resources and lessons of the former to the concrete situations of the latter.

With these observations in mind, then, I return to the second of my original questions, the one that is presumably most immediate to common experience: What is the "human problem"? The Christian tradition speaks of humanity's "fall" and of original sin, but what does this mean? The fundamental problem can be described or evoked in manifold ways, and a presupposition of this book is that no single definition describes it adequately. One long and influential strand of the Christian tradition has understood our problem as concupiscence, an inordinate and misplaced craving for that which cannot finally fulfill us. Made to be fulfilled through our relation with God, we seek our fulfillment in things that are not God. Pride has also often been blamed, which may be further described as the human desire to play God. Using language less traditional and ecclesial but perhaps more evocative, mystery writer and Christian apologist Dorothy Sayers spoke of "the idea that there is a deep interior *dislocation* in the very centre of the human personality."[21] It is also common in the modern Western context to speak of human existence as displaying a fundamental undercurrent of alienation, anxiety, or angst. One classic and popular work of modern theology, Paul Tillich's *The Courage to Be,* described three forms of anxiety: the anxiety of death, the anxiety of condemnation, and the anxiety of meaninglessness.[22] While persons in all ages have felt all three forms (in that sense they are simply a corollary of human existence, hence the label "existential"), Tillich also believed that each of the three predominated at different times in Western history: "At the end of ancient civilization ontic anxiety is predominant, at the end of the Middle Ages moral anxiety, and at the end of the modern period spiritual anxiety."[23] I commend his recognition that the human problem cannot be reduced to a single cause or characterization, although I doubt that the spiritual ethos of entire eras can be so neatly categorized. Still, one could more modestly claim that a diversity of descriptions stems not just from the variety of forms the human problem takes, but from the fact that these forms ebb and flow over time. Indeed, I assume they shift, mutate, and overlap in ways that are difficult to distinguish, on an individual as well as social level. To generalize, acknowledging some such diversity and fluidity seems inevitable if one is to reflect concrete human experience accurately—not to mention follow the varied descriptions and implications of Scripture.

All of this suggests it is best to think of "the human problem" within a kind of variable grid, one with generally different but interacting categories. Thus, from one perspective, the problem "happens" to us: we are captive, creatures of our environment or upbringing, held in bondage by powers in some sense external to us and greater than we are. Or we may be held in bondage to our own desires or fears, our subconscious

---

21. Dorothy L. Sayers, *Creed or Chaos?* (New York: Harcourt, Brace, & Co., 1949), 38, italics mine.

22. Paul Tillich, *The Courage to Be* (New Haven, Conn.: Yale University Press, 1952), 40ff.

23. Ibid., 57.

self-centeredness or our lack of a "self." Additionally, the "our" that this captivity binds may refer to our nation or culture, our historical moment or place, our race, sex, or ethnicity. Alternately, this captivity may be more individual. It may bind given persons psychologically, emotionally, or genetically. And of course, the broader corporate and narrower personal forms of this captivity typically interact and reinforce one another in such a manner that the whole is greater than the sum of the parts. Thus, the ultimate cause of our victimization becomes impossible to discern. The Bible describes the root of the human problem understood in this sense variously as bondage (e.g., to Satan or "the principalities and powers"), slavery (to "sin" or "the flesh"), or captivity, each and all of which separate us from God and God's will for us. I will say much more about this complex of themes in chapter 4.

From another perspective, the human problem may just as well arise as a result of our own willful irresponsibility, choices, and actions. We are not so much victims of evil as perpetrators of evil—and this is what separates us from God. Again, this may be corporate or it may be individual. The hurtful word, the conscious lie, the insatiable consumption, the intentional apathy, the rationalized selfishness, the vicious attack, the uncaring exploitation—the list could be expanded indefinitely with little difficulty. We are separated from God due to our own sin. Yet even as it remains undeniably ours, it also takes on a life and power of its own, which we unleash and rationalize in myriad ways, both individually and corporately. A person or group acts in a corrupt or evil manner (and are undeniably responsible) and yet say (perhaps with some justification, but perhaps only as a rationalization) that they were led to it by the corrupt or evil circumstances in which they found themselves. Perhaps the only responsible choice was to choose the lesser of two evils—but this means the choice is still evil. The root and character of the human problem understood in this sense has been dealt with perhaps most extensively by the Western Christian tradition in its understanding and application of the notion of "original sin." Recalling the discussion above, its root has been described variously as pride, or inordinate desire, or a will to power. None of these is incorrect, but neither are any of them sufficient to explain fully why the human problem remains in certain respects our own fault and something for which we are culpable, even as it transcends its origins. I will say more about this complex of themes in chapter 5.

From yet another perspective, the human problem seems less the result of a moral fault, whether imposed upon us from without or arising from our own misdeeds, and more simply the inevitable result of our finitude as creatures, especially given our "fallen" context. In this view, the human problem does not so much require the assignment of culpability as it does the recognition of our unavoidable and ultimately tragic limitations. We are temporal and spatial beings, restricted by our age, place, and bodily existence, and limited in our power, knowledge, passion, and imagination. We may have inherited a fallen world, and yet we also sense that in certain instances an existential "statute of limitations" must take effect. That is, we recognize our disordered and flawed circumstances, but acknowledge that in certain instances it would actually be unjust to think in terms of blame, let alone consider assigning it. Yet even with this acknowledgment, the sense of yearning for something more and higher remains, even as it seems impossible to attain. The problem is not so much a moral one as it is an ontological one. We recognize what is apparently a natural desire that seems incapable of natural fulfillment. Conditions seem out of sync. We sense that the way things are (as good as they may be) is not they way they should be—or were intended to be. Even those who have enjoyed a "good" life may be nagged by the question, "Is that all there is?"

Sometimes, an intuitive sense of the human problem, of life's fundamental disorder, emerges in the simple feeling or experience of the asymmetry between creation and destruction. What takes painstaking labor or ages to create can be destroyed in the blink of an eye. A trivial decision or a moment of inattention or distraction, so often occurring without consequence, results this time in the death of a child. Individual actions that in themselves may be quite understandable, even excusable, perhaps even justifiable precipitate into a collective horror. Why is it that such devastating consequences can result from seemingly inconsequential causes? Why can an event of a mere moment have such irreversible finality, determining conditions or a course of events ever after? Persons lacking the social safeguards that the middle and upper classes of the Western world typically know well the asymmetry of life, of the suffering that can arise as easily from petty thoughtlessness as from malevolent intent, of the devastation that can occur from otherwise innocent decisions made half a world away. But even those usually insulated from a seemingly arbitrary fate may feel its impact in a career of hard work and sincere effort producing only the ephemeral, in the senseless suffering of a loved one from cancer, or even in the affliction brought upon oneself that is nevertheless entirely disproportionate to one's actual and acknowledged misdeed. A sense of life's asymmetry or disjunction is probably something that most all persons feel at one time or another, whether inarticulately or expressly deplored, and regardless of social or cultural location. It seems safe to claim that this sense of asymmetry is simply a given of the human condition. Certainly one can imagine how it might threaten any arena of human life, even if one's own life is infrequently burdened by it. Yet the mere recognition of the threat proves the point. In any case, I will say much more about this complex of themes in chapter 6.

With all this in mind, recall my initial question. What does "atonement" mean? To what does Christ's "atonement" refer? In its most basic sense, it *answers* the human problem. It is the activity of God the Father in the Son through the Spirit that overcomes the bondage or desire or pride or dislocation or estrangement or alienation or evil or limitation that separates humanity from God, and thus enables the restoration of the true and proper relation between them. Yet, does it refer to some single act or event in Christ's life—for example, his death on the cross? Does it refer to his life and/or death and/or resurrection as a whole? Or does it refer not so much to an action or event, but to his being or some aspect thereof, such as his "consciousness"? Addressing the matter from a different tack, and returning to the discussion of terms above, does "atonement" refer to the same thing as the terms "salvation," "redemption," or "reconciliation"? These words are often used interchangeably, yet apart from the word "atonement" as a translation for the Greek word for "reconciliation," they stem from different root meanings. Salvation means to rescue or protect, although it also has the association of healing or restoring to health. Redemption means at root "to buy back," to regain possession of something through making a payment or, conversely, to gain a payment by turning over something. It can refer to something as pedestrian as redeeming coupons or bottles at a store or as extreme as paying a ransom to free a hostage. And reconciliation refers to a reuniting, usually with overtones of a return to harmony in a personal relationship. Clearly, these terms all imply a change from an adverse circumstance to an improved circumstance, yet they also vary in their respective construals of the "before and after." Of course, this is only appropriate, because this terminological variety helps reflect the diversity inherent in the human predicament just described, as well as the diversity of scriptural accounts and images.

This background should bring into greater relief some of the connections I will explore more fully in this book. The three commonly cited models of the atonement (some variation on *Christus victor*, vicarious sacrifice, and "moral exemplar," and their corresponding construals of the human predicament) have a respective affinity with the offices of king, priest, and prophet traditionally ascribed to Jesus. From this connection, I will further suggest that it is biblically appropriate, theologically evocative, and pastorally helpful to associate these three models and offices with the Father, Son, and Holy Spirit, respectively. In this, I am building upon the fact that scriptural descriptions of the one God's activity gave rise to the tradition's affirmation that "the external works of the Trinity are undivided" *(opera trinitatis ad extra indivisa sunt)*. In light of my project, this affirmation suggests that from a theological perspective it would be inappropriate to emphasize one of Christ's offices, one model of the atonement, or one person of the Trinity to the exclusion of the others. The prior divine unity—of both being and work—necessarily entails the unity of the models and offices. Similarly, from an anthropological perspective, it would be inaccurate to recognize, and therefore inappropriate to privilege, only one understanding of the human predicament. Whether this predicament is characterized as some form of bondage, or sinfulness, or tragic limitation, human beings usually manifest, both individually and corporately, simultaneous and entwined variations on all three—which is why the atoning work of the gracious trinitarian God occurs in a manifold manner.

To be sure, there is no unanimity that these three particular atonement models represent the only possibilities. Students of theology will recognize that this schema derives from Gustaf Aulén's classic book, *Christus Victor*, which has been very influential in promoting these three basic ways of understanding Christ's reconciling work. Consider, for example, Van A. Harvey's much-used *A Handbook of Theological Terms*, which reflects Aulén's framework.[24] Yet some theologians suggest a different set of three. For example, Colin Gunton sees the metaphors of "victory," "legal justification," and "sacrifice" as determining his ways of explaining atonement.[25] Still other theologians argue that the variety of scriptural metaphors and images—and the ways they often interrelate—suggests Christ's work should be understood in more than just three ways. For example, Alister McGrath recognizes the *Christus victor* and exemplarist approaches, but echoes Gunton by subdividing what I label

---

24. Van A. Harvey, *A Handbook of Theological Terms* (New York: Macmillan, 1964), "Atonement," 34.

25. Gunton, *The Actuality of Atonement*, 143ff.

"vicarious sacrifice" into sacrifice and legal approaches.[26] Edward Yarnold discerned four categories: atonement understood as transaction, as conflict, as enlightenment, and as solidarity.[27] At the end of the nineteenth century, B. B. Warfield wrote that there are five basic types of atonement theory.[28] Stephen Sykes recalls that the Welsh theologian T. H. Hughes surveyed forty-two modern theologians and discerned seven separate categories of atonement theory. Sykes goes on to note that the "sheer quantity and variety of the arguments began to shed doubt on the credibility of the whole enterprise. In the 1950s reaction against theory construction set in."[29] It would appear that the theological options resist easy pigeonholing.

In view of such obvious lack of consensus, why should I propose yet another comprehensive theory of the atonement? Why should I expect my explanation to better serve the rich witness of Scripture, when so many other highly capable theologians have undertaken the same, but apparently futile, task? I could, of course, appeal to the turning of the generational wheel: if reaction against theory construction set in during the 1950s, then it is obviously time to revisit and perhaps reject that reaction. Just as the writing of systematic theologies dropped in the 1960s and early 1970s, but has recently picked up considerably,[30] so too might it be appropriate to resume the writing of comprehensive theories of atonement. This is, of course, a rather superficial argument, for even if times do change, one could argue that the underlying problem remains: that no one theory appears sufficient to explain all the disparate elements of the scriptural witness. Indeed, in some cases the theories seem artificially imposed upon the scriptural witness, with too much remainder left unexplained. And if nothing else, proponents of

---

26. See Alister E. McGrath, "Soteriology," in *The Blackwell Encyclopedia of Modern Christian Thought*.

27. Summarized in Winter, *The Atonement*, 62ff.

28. See Benjamin Breckinridge Warfield, *The Person and Work of Christ* (Philadelphia: The Presbyterian and Reformed Publishing Co., 1950), 356–69.

29. Sykes, *The Story of Atonement*, 8.

30. For a discussion of this phenomenon, see the summary account and interesting observations offered by Gabriel Fackre in "The Revival of Systematic Theology," *Interpretation* 49 (July 1995): 229–41. These systematics are emerging from across the theological spectrum, as Fackre recounts in his survey of "evangelical" (e.g., Henry, Bloesch, Erickson, Boice, Rodman, Grenz, and Conyers), "ecumenical" (e.g., Berkhof, Wainwright, Braaten and Jenson, Peters, Dulles, and Finger), and "experiential" (Radford Ruether, Soelle, Cone, Suchoki, Hodgson, Chopp, and Taylor) theologians.

one theory all too often come across as less than fair to proponents of another. One could be excused for thinking that theory construction is more frequently motivated by particular theological agendas than by a desire to be true to the rich witness of Scripture.

Recall Stephen Sykes and his understanding of what a "theory" of something entails. On the one hand, he suggests that it is a system of ideas held to explain an otherwise seemingly disparate group of facts or phenomena. On the other hand, he also claims that a "theory is an explanation that attempts to reduce surprise."[31] Putting these two parts together, Sykes means that a theory reduces the surprise of bringing disparate elements together in a comprehensible way. I agree with this as far as it goes, and would label my own approach a "theory" in this respect. But in some cases, "reducing surprise" may mean a theory becomes too tidy and predictable, perhaps obscuring things that should be seen. In this case, I would say a *good* theory not only "reduces surprise" by allowing the bringing together of disparate elements, but also "enables surprise" insofar as it is evocative and enables us to discern that which we might not otherwise see. That is, a good theory is able to make sense of new situations, is able to allow one to make connections not made before, is able to help one move beyond the status quo—in a word, good theories are heuristic. I hope that my proposal demonstrates this capacity, because my intention is, in fact, to make it dynamic and adaptable. To borrow a phrase from trinitarian discourse, I intend for my different understandings to be perichoretical, intertwining and interacting, forming a vigorous whole that is not simply a static and arithmetical combination of otherwise discrete parts. For I understand the life of the triune God as giving the theological basis and the three-fold office of Christ the practical form for integrating understandings of the atonement that are too often understood as mutually exclusive or simply thrown together side-by-side. I appreciate, and learn from, the many theories of atonement that have preceded mine and I am not claiming that my exposition under these three rubrics will exhaustively explain the richness of Scripture's atonement imagery. But perhaps part of the problem in the past has stemmed from the habit of developing rather rigid, if not actually closed, theories out of the various and often not-obviously connected metaphors seeking to describe what Christ has done. I hope that my narrative approach and threefold framework will display both sufficient definition and open-endedness such that every

---

31. Sykes, *The Story of Atonement*, 10.

essential aspect of this rich diversity of scriptural images can find an appropriate place somewhere within its dynamic interrelation, even if I do not have time or space to place them there myself.

Consider my approach from a different perspective. Another typical way of classifying and distinguishing understandings of the atonement uses the labels "objective" and "subjective." These labels, too, are often used as much to disparage as describe. I intend my approach to be both "objective" and "subjective." What is meant by these terms? Their usage varies. Generally, the former term refers to theories that stress that God has accomplished something external to the recipient of the benefits of the atonement, something that is real even if particular persons are unaware of it. Objective theories focus on God's initiative, and they typically center their concern in the past event of Christ's life, death, and resurrection. Generally, the latter term refers to theories that focus on the change occurring in the human recipient, such that atonement only really "happens" for a person if that person embraces it in some manner. Subjective theories focus on the human response, and thus typically center their concern in what happens in the present. It is a crude oversimplification to say that any given theory must be one or another. In fact, most traditional understandings have elements of both, although they may lean more toward one than the other. In any case, I intend my threefold approach to be both objective and subjective in each of its parts. In any event, I do not want to surrender to the difficulties of "theory construction" as apparently happened to an earlier generation, but I am also aware of the problems associated with the desire to structure and systematize. Leanne Van Dyk offers some useful cautionary observations:

> Whatever the conceptual benefits that atonement typologies may yield, this particular task of classification and systematization has often turned from an attempt at clarification into a means of testing or measuring for the perceived orthodoxy of the day. Theologians committed to a highly "objective" account of the atonement, for instance, reject those with strong "subjective" interests, and likewise, theologians devoted to "subjective" accounts expel from discussion those who advocate "objective" claims. Literature on the doctrine of the atonement teems with such stereotypic dismissals.[32]

---

32. Leanne Van Dyk, *John McLeod Campbell's Doctrine of the Atonement: A Revision and Expansion of the Reformed Doctrine* (Ph.D. diss., Princeton Theological Seminary, 1992), 140.

I believe my approach will avoid the problems of a tendentiously narrow interpretation of atonement, because I intend a certain flexibility to be built in. Thus, unlike Aulén's approach, I do not offer three models in order to critique two and advocate the third. Rather, I see my three as complementing and completing one another. I take this approach because I am firmly convinced that there is real theological value—systematic certainly, but even more pastoral and catechetical—in such a structured yet flexible threefold approach.

Let me suggest but one example of this value: this threefold framework offers a very helpful tool for theological exegesis. Specifically, I believe it will allow one to approach a variety of scriptural texts with a framework that will allow both multifaceted yet also coherent interpretation. Consider the densely packed passage, Heb 10:12–16:

> But when Christ had offered for all time a single sacrifice for sins, "he sat down at the right hand of God," and since then has been waiting "until his enemies would be made a footstool for his feet." For by a single offering he has perfected for all time those who are sanctified. And the Holy Spirit also testifies to us, for after saying, "This is the covenant that I will make with them after those days, says the Lord: I will put my laws in their hearts, and I will write them on their minds. . . ."[33]

Now the Epistle to the Hebrews is typically understood as *the* locus in the New Testament for a "priestly" and "sacrificial" understanding of Christ's atoning work. This understanding is certainly correct—but it also does not tell the whole story, as the above passage indicates. This pericope refers to all three persons of the later doctrine of the Trinity, points to three interrelated aspects of God's work in reconciling a separated humanity (a sacrifice for sin, triumph over God's enemies, and a writing of the divine law on human hearts), and describes that work—with allusions to Old Testament passages—in ways that correspond to the linked messianic offices of priest, king, and prophet. Clearly, the theological and pastoral value of the passage would be greatly diminished if its meaning were forced into a too-narrow "priestly/sacrificial" interpretive framework or, alternately, understood simply as an arbitrary hodgepodge of images. The threefold framework I am proposing, however,

---

33. Biblical citations are from the NRSV. I will occasionally alter them to reflect the Greek text more accurately.

helps bring out both its richness and its theological coherence. Each aspect helps clarify, and is clarified by, the other, and the whole is richer than its diverse parts.

W. A. Visser 't Hooft makes an observation that speaks to my concern and helps reinforce my approach.

> The three offices are so related to one another that Christ is Prophet in a priestly and royal manner; Priest in a prophetic and royal way; King, but King as priest and prophet. The three offices can be distinguished; they cannot be separated. At every moment Christ acts in all three capacities. . . . It is, therefore, not permissible to emphasize one of the three offices to such an extent that the other two are forgotten.[34]

Many current understandings of Jesus—especially those deemphasizing or denying his divinity—fall into precisely the trap against which Visser 't Hooft warns.

Perhaps this is inevitable if one overlooks the rootedness of Christ's offices in his person and his person in the Trinity. My proposal presupposes an orthodox understanding of Christ. But to affirm Christ's divinity in a trinitarian context cannot mean he only represents one-third of the total divinity of the Godhead! Getting beyond such quantitative subdividing is what finally enabled the Chalcedonian definition of Christ's person to emerge, and the same must apply in trinitarian reflection. To think in quantitative terms, whether in fractions or whole numbers, is simply misguided, if not in fact a category mistake. "For in him the whole fullness of deity dwells bodily" (Col 2:9), which in this light must be read: the whole fullness of *trinitarian* deity. With this scriptural affirmation in mind, recall Athanasius's summary: "When the Father is mentioned his *Logos* is there too and the Holy Spirit who is in the Son, and if the Son is named, the Father is in the Son and the Holy Spirit is not separated from the *Logos*."[35] Consider as well the words of Anselm: "One who sees the Son sees the Holy Spirit, just as he sees the Father."[36] Also notice the statement of Thomas Aquinas: "The whole Trinity is

---

34. W. A. Visser 't Hooft, *The Kingship of Christ* (New York: Harper & Brothers, 1948), 16–17.

35. Athanasius, *Letter to Serapion*, 1.14, as quoted by Jenson, *The Triune God*, 92n.14.

36. Anselm, *De Processione Spiritus Sancti*, in F. S. Schmitt, ed., *S. Anselmi Opera Omnia* (Edinburgh: Thomas Nelson, 1946–61), 2:208, 23–24, as quoted in Marshall, *Trinity and Truth*, 123n.

spoken in the Word. . . ."[37] Finally, consider these words of John Henry Newman (which anticipate the very project I am undertaking): "It will be observed, moreover, that in these three offices [Jesus] also represents to us the Holy Trinity: for in His proper character He is a priest, and as to His Kingdom He has it from His Father, and as to His prophetical office, He exercises it by the Spirit."[38] The second person of the Trinity does indeed have a particular and proper function, which only he can serve based on the fact that he alone was to become the incarnate One. Yet, the orthodox Christian faith has long affirmed that "the external works of the Trinity are undivided."

This book will offer one explanation of what that formula means concretely in relation to one particular doctrine of the Christian faith, the doctrine of the atonement. To put it in a broader context, I can imagine applying a similar trinitarian approach to an exposition of the doctrine of creation or the doctrine of the church and the "Last Things." The former is traditionally associated with the work of the Father, while the latter is typically understood as the arena of the Holy Spirit's fulfilling work. These associations are reflected in, and in part stem from, the three-part division of the creeds and the way they correlate certain works with specific persons of the Godhead. Yet church tradition does not view this correlation in exclusive terms: both the Son and Spirit are involved in creation, and both the Father and Son are involved in the church and Last Things. The interesting question then becomes "In what way is each person present in each act?" In such a schema, the current volume would stand in the middle, and seek to answer the question with reference to the atonement. In any event, I hope to strengthen and expand Visser 't Hooft's warning and his position: it applies not just to the work of Christ, but to the whole of the Trinity.

My overall proposal allows itself to be charted on a grid, to illustrate that its argument is best understood as one woven together—and I hope, mutually reinforcing—and not merely a linear one. The danger,

---

37. Thomas Aquinas, *Summa theologiae* I, 34, 1, ad 3. Also quoted in Marshall, *Trinity and Truth*, 123n.

38. Taken from an Easter sermon entitled "The Three Offices of Christ," in John Henry Newman, *Sermons Bearing on Subjects of the Day* (new ed.; London: Rivingtons, 1871), 55. Intriguingly, Newman leaves this statement dangling, doing nothing to develop the insight. In fact, to my mind, he actually undercuts its force by immediately adding the sentence: "The Father is the King, the Son the Priest, and the Holy Ghost the Prophet." This seems to evacuate the christological claim just made, even as it comes close to implying modalism. I believe my exposition of this framework avoids this problem.

of course, is that such a chart may imply that my approach is too neat and too static. I hope my actual exposition overcomes any such tendency, for I intend to offer a framework that is simultaneously coherent, dynamic, and pastorally useful. The following chart, then, should help illustrate the basic structure of my proposal, if one keeps in mind the vital interrelation of its various parts.

Person of the Trinity	Father	Son	Holy Spirit
Messianic Office	King	Priest	Prophet
(based on NT titles/images of Jesus)	(Lord/King, Shepherd, Exorcist/Healer)	(High Priest, Lamb of God)	(Prophet, Teacher)
Atonement theory	*Christus victor*	Vicarious sacrifice	"Empowering exemplar"/ Revealer
(based on NT view of human separation from God)	(Held captive by unjust "principalities and powers")	(Not giving God his due/ corrupting creation; human sinfulness)	(Ignorance/ Weakness/ Being Lost)

Survey of Some Current Approaches

As I observed above, theologians have demonstrated a renewed interest in the Christian doctrine of the atonement in the past few years. Their contributions have ranged in character from more comprehensive theologies of the atonement to more narrowly focused and critical monographs dealing only with certain aspects of the doctrine. Notably, the work of Anselm and traditional notions of vicarious sacrifice and penal substitution have provoked particular opposition. More has been written than I can hope to consider in the concluding pages of this chapter, but I will review a selection of the writings that engage critically or constructively the interests of my own project. In part, this will situate my work within a broader field of conversations and concerns. But it will also highlight the agendas and strengths of these other works, even as I indicate the shortcomings that make them finally inadequate for the theological and pastoral role they need to play in the church's ministry and life.

I begin by briefly surveying some of the more comprehensive works in recent atonement theology. These books tend to be more traditional in outlook, although each in its own way is both critical and constructive. Their theological orientation and intentions also tend to be more in line with the purposes of this book, so I will use their diverse insights here and there to support my own efforts. They include Paul Fiddes's *Past Event and Present Salvation: The Christian Idea of Atonement*, Stephen Sykes's *The Story of Atonement*, Joel Green's and Mark Baker's *Recovering the Scandal of the Cross: Atonement in New Testament and Contemporary Contexts*, and Geoffrey Wainwright's *For Our Salvation: Two Approaches to the Work of Christ*. Fiddes offers a helpful book, rich in insight and generally balanced in approach. He, too, wants to overcome the tendency of focusing on one understanding of the atonement to the exclusion of others. This tendency misses the fact that various ideas of the atonement "represent responses to types of human experience that can be found in every age," and in fact all "have some grounding in the New Testament documents."[39] He is also concerned to end the polarization between so-called "objective" and "subjective" theories by suggesting that any adequate understanding of the atonement must have both. In fact, this objective/subjective dialectic is represented in his title: the Christian tradition makes certain claims about the objective centrality of the life, death, and resurrection of Jesus Christ, but these can only have significance for Christians if they can become subjectively effective in the present.

So far, so good. Unfortunately, when Fiddes presents his survey of atonement theories and his own constructive comments, he appears to forget his own prior balance. He considers four different approaches to the atonement in his chapters "The Point of Sacrifice," "The Demands of Justice," "The Decisive Victory," and "The Act of Love." While he appreciates the evocative power of "sacrifice" but assumes its objective claims are untenable to the modern mind, his particular *bete noir* appears to be "legalism." This shows up particularly in his treatment, and repudiation, of the penal substitution theory of atonement and his exposition of the *Christus victor* model. Regarding the former, I believe he misunderstands how God must be "bound" in some sense by the constraints of justice (a misunderstanding best illustrated by his misapplication of the

---

39. Fiddes, *Past Event and Present Salvation*, 13.

parable of the Prodigal Son).[40] Regarding the latter, he takes some time describing the "enemies" that Christ's victory overthrows. This is a generally helpful exposition, although it becomes clear that his treatment of the law (or at least Paul's understanding of it in God's plan) falls into certain stereotypical assumptions that do not derive from Paul. In the end, his preferred model appears to be a retrieved and updated version of Abelard's "moral" model, one that stresses not the human subjective response to Christ's death but "the power of divine love to *create* or generate love within human beings."[41] Fiddes's exposition is engaging and offers intriguing food for thought, yet founding his position on a rehabilitation of Abelard makes his claims somewhat tenuous. His basic argument is that an event external to us can serve as a powerful transformative catalyst. True enough, and he offers some psychological explanation as to how this may occur. But he fails to recognize that in such an encounter, the catalyst itself does not change or act. Rather, the actual agent of change remains the "recipient" or observer of the event. Fiddes does suggest (quite properly, in my view) that in the event of atonement, the Holy Spirit should be affirmed as the actual and immediate agent of our human transformation, but he acknowledges that Abelard himself did not make such a connection between the work of the Spirit with the life and death of Christ.

Stephen Sykes's book, *The Story of Atonement*, is theologically helpful and pastorally sensitive, exhibiting faithfulness to the basic Christian tradition and a relevant nuance in his discussion of its claims and implications. The book has the character of both a constructive and an apologetic, practical work. This adds to its richness, although at times, it also makes his train of thought difficult to follow. On the one hand, he presents a study on the atonement after the manner of narrative theology. Thus, he states: "There is a 'story of salvation.' This story, like all narratives, is a combination of character and event in interaction."[42]

---

40. See ibid., 101–2. Fiddes presumes that the parable of the Prodigal Son, with its graciously forgiving father, negates the basic assumption of penal substitution, namely, "that God cannot forgive us until the punishment demanded by justice is exacted." Fiddes fails to recognize that forgiveness is complicated if the grievance is not merely God's but also someone else's. As I will argue more fully in chapter 5, Anselm's theory recognized that the problem lay not just in the fact that human sin failed to give God his due, but also in the fact that it disrupted "the order and beauty of the universe."

41. Ibid., 141.

42. Sykes, *The Story of Atonement*, 12.

Christians see this story as describing a new reality, indeed, the fundamental reality, and understand themselves and all persons as invited to "live in" or "inhabit" it. As with any good story, the story of the atonement is rich, evocative, and complex. As such, it does not lend itself to easy or obvious categorization and summary. Sykes does not present a neat model or systematization of the atonement. On the other hand, Sykes seems very concerned to address the questions often raised nowadays in response to, even reaction against, the Christian story of atonement. This may be seen in part in the many asides and digressions he makes throughout the book. But he also goes so far as to devote one whole chapter to "Salvation and Other Faiths," following it with an "Interlude" on Lessing's parable, *Nathan the Wise*, which offers counsel on how to live faithfully and lovingly in a context of uncertainty and religious pluralism. These are useful sections, yet their presence in his book is less a natural outgrowth of his exposition of the salvation story than a response to separate issues "brought from outside." As a result of the particular way he combines his constructive and apologetic concerns, the flow of his book is often disjointed.

That said, Sykes's book also focuses on Christ's sacrificial death as the central understanding of the atonement, with that sacrifice understood primarily as the means by which God effects his gracious forgiveness of a sinful humanity. To be sure, Sykes remains aware and appreciative of the diverse theories of atonement. Additionally, he uses his narrative approach as a way of maintaining fluidity between the four "idea-complexes" that Joachim Jeremias discerned in the New Testament accounts.[43] Moreover, he suggests we may read in the New Testament an offering of two somewhat different stories: one presents God the Father as "the leading agent," while the other focuses upon "Jesus, the Son of God, who gives or offers himself out of love for humanity."[44] Still, his first chapter begins with a consideration of forgiveness, and his second chapter is devoted to the subject. His last two chapters are also based largely on associations with, and implications drawn from, Jesus' sacrifice and the Christian's "living sacrifice" or "sacrifice of praise." In sum, it is a book of broad theological insight and much practical pastoral value.

---

43. Sykes summarizes these as "the idea of obedience" (contrasting Adam's disobedience to the obedience of the "second Adam"), "the slavery idea" (relating to redemption and liberation), "the judgement idea" (regarding condemnation and acquittal), and "the cultic idea" (relating to Christ's sacrifice). Ibid., 15.

44. Ibid., 21.

The book by Green and Baker, *Recovering the Scandal of the Cross: Atonement in New Testament and Contemporary Contexts,* appears to be motivated by two key concerns. First, it, too, discredits the tendency of focusing on one model or understanding of the atonement exclusively. Given the evangelical setting from which the book arises and to which it speaks, this means specifically that the authors want to overcome the predominant emphasis on penal substitution in evangelical circles. Their justification for countering this habitual emphasis derives from their insistence (correct, in my view) that the New Testament itself presents more than one model. Second, the authors are not so much concerned to offer their own constructive proposal regarding the atonement as they are to establish the assumptions one should have when constructing any such proposal. They display a deep awareness of context, both the context in which past understandings of the atonement arose and the context of current and future construals. They see the different interpretations contained in the New Testament as having emerged from the apostolic impulse to communicate the gospel message effectively by tailoring it to the variety of cultural settings in which it was preached. From this the authors conclude that effective mission requires a preacher to "speak the people's language" by shaping his or her presentation of the atonement to local conceptualities.

As a way of illustrating what this might mean in a concrete sense, the authors devote a chapter to the topic, "Removing Alienating Shame: The Saving Significance of the Cross in Japan."[45] This is an intriguing chapter, which contrasts the Eastern concept of "shame" with the Western notion of "guilt." The authors use it in part to further put the penal substitution model of atonement in perspective and highlight its limitations. But they also use it more positively to suggest that Japanese concepts of honor and shame, with their accompanying constellation of attitudes and communal practices, may actually be closer to Old Testament concepts of holiness and defilement or uncleanness than the more typically Western concepts of innocence and guilt. It is a fascinating and thought-provoking claim. But as intriguing as it is, Green and Baker still do not use this claim, or any other starting point, to present their own constructive theory of the atonement, one that can encompass a variety of understandings while also maintaining scriptural norms. Rather, they remain content to recognize that missionary

---

45. Green and Baker, *Recovering the Scandal of the Cross,* 153–70.

proclamation must be contextually sensitive to be effective, while also stressing that use of cultural images not be taken so far that one is no longer faithful to the biblical witness. Having made this observation, however, they still offer no theological principle or basis for determining in particular cases the proper balancing of these two concerns.

In fact, Green and Baker finally promote open-endedness as a matter of principle, as the concluding statements of their book make clear:

> No one model of the atonement will fit all sizes and shapes, all needs and contexts where the church is growing and active in mission. This means, ultimately, that the next chapter of this book is being written in hundreds of places throughout the world, where communities of Jesus' disciples are practicing the craft of theologian-communicator and struggling with fresh and faithful images for broadcasting the mystery of Jesus' death.[46]

That fresh images are emerging is obvious; the crucial question is, are they in fact faithful? These closing words imply that there can exist as many ways of explaining the atonement as there are cultural contexts. Yet might not the categories, images, or logic of a context be taken too far, overshadowing if not actually contradicting the primary biblical categories, images, or logic? As the authors had earlier acknowledged, becoming Christian must entail some conformity to the "story" and "language" of Zion. Even if that biblical story is multifaceted, it still defines the human condition and God's salvation in particular ways, it still gives a particular framework and presents particular themes and images—and these must remain normative, or else the gospel will lose all definition. In sum, the approach employed by Baker and Green offers a useful corrective to the narrow, even exclusive focus of so many evangelicals on a penal substitutionary view of the atonement. But their alternative is far too ad hoc and open-ended to offer practical, constructive guidance.

Geoffrey Wainwright's *For Our Salvation: Two Approaches to the Work of Christ* is the book that most closely anticipates my project in both theological approach and pastoral sensibility. In particular, the second of his "two approaches" (which comprises the latter half of the book) employs Christ's threefold office as its basic framework. In the first

---

46. Ibid., 221.

chapter of this section (chapter 6, "The Threefold Office in Retrospect"), Wainwright begins with a historical survey of the notion of Christ's threefold office. He acknowledges that it has been employed most commonly within the Reformed theological tradition, but he also examines its occasional appearance in Lutheran and Roman Catholic texts, both at the time of the Reformation and in the modern era. Indeed, because one of his purposes is to employ the threefold office as a framework for ecumenical conversations, he happily cites examples of its use in contemporary documents, including the 1992 *Catechism of the Catholic Church* and modern interpretations of John Wesley's theology.[47]

Wainwright suggests that over the centuries the threefold framework has been used in five different spheres of the church's thinking and practice, influencing its views on Christology, its understanding of baptism, its soteriology, and its ministerial and ecclesiological teachings. In the christological use, the threefold framework helps explain the "identity and dignity" of Jesus Christ. The baptismal use describes the ways in which Christians may be said to share, by means of this sacrament, in Christ's threefold identity and dignity. The soteriological use became prevalent in the Reformation period, with its renewed emphasis on the salvation accomplished by Christ. The ministerial use arose in the Roman Church in the nineteenth century, as a way of further defining the teaching, sacerdotal, and governing role of the bishops and pope. Similarly, the ecclesiological use arose among Catholic theologians as a way of describing the church as an extension of the incarnation, and thus reinforcing the view that the church "shared the prophetic, priestly, and royal character of its Head."[48] Initially, "church" was understood as referring to the Roman hierarchy alone, but Vatican II expanded the definition to include the role of the laity. As this summary suggests, these five uses did not all emerge at the same time in the same way. Nevertheless, Wainwright employs them as five general rubrics to organize his own concrete and practical exposition of Christ's offices and work.

Wainwright then offers his own understanding of Christ's offices, starting with the prophetic (chapter 7), turning next to the priestly (chapter 8), and then considering the royal (chapter 9). He examines each office under five rubrics (the christological, baptismal, soteriological, ministerial, and ecclesiological), as well as under a sixth rubric of his

---

47. Wainwright, *For Our Salvation*, 107–8.
48. Ibid., 115.

own, "the contemporary hermeneutic." His discussion of each office and rubric relies heavily on the exposition of pertinent verses from Scripture and, in a subsidiary manner, the Christian theological and liturgical tradition. As one might anticipate, the christological use serves as the source and shaper of the uses following it (although the "soteriological use" seems at times to supplement the points made under the first rubric). In any case, the logic of Wainwright's exposition moves from a consideration of what God has accomplished through Christ's fulfillment of each office to the practical implications that work has for the Christian life, in its diverse stages and forms. Of course, a discussion of the practical implications of Christ's saving work could be virtually endless, and Wainwright's consideration of a sampling of topics seems somewhat ad hoc, but nevertheless evocative. These include such matters as the responsibility for Christian teaching, the role of prayer, who precisely and appropriately may be called a Christian "priest," the proper understanding of pastoral ministry and authority, and Christian unity, among other topics. Moreover, under the final rubric of chapters 7 through 9, "the contemporary hermeneutic," Wainwright indicates very briefly how Christ's fulfillment of each particular office serves to address a particular human question. In this move, he is following the suggestion of John Henry Newman, who made (but did not extensively develop) the observation that "these three offices seem to contain in them the three principal conditions of mankind,"[49] which Christ took upon himself to redeem. Wainwright discusses this observation in terms relevant to a late modern audience, but seeks to remain true to Newman's basic insight. Specifically, to the human problems of meaninglessness, of alienation, and of power and authority, Wainwright sees Christ as offering, precisely through his three offices, the gifts of meaning, of reconciliation, and of true and perfect freedom.

Wainwright concludes his book with "The Threefold Office in Prospect" (chapter 10). He starts by observing that the unfamiliar and perhaps archaic character of the terms prophet, priest, and king may be precisely what will allow them to function again as needed archetypes for Christian faith and life. To function as such archetypes, however, three conditions must be met. First, the terms must display some relevance to the human condition as that is now experienced. Second, they must cohere with scriptural and other traditional accounts of Christ.

---

49. Ibid., 120. For the original citation, see Newman, *Sermons*, 54.

And third, they must be able to regain a vital place in Christian devotion and liturgy. Wainwright then suggests, in several diverse and brief ways, how the notion of Christ as prophet, priest, and king may indeed accomplish all these things—and in so doing, greatly enrich the church's understanding and praise of Christ and its own worship, witness, and ministry. Again, his remarks are more suggestive than comprehensive, but even in their brevity they offer much that can serve the practical life of faith.

Indeed, in all of these chapters, Wainwright offers much that is theologically stimulating and pastorally useful. I will draw on his observations and wonderfully telling examples repeatedly, particularly as they relate to the ongoing concerns of Christian liturgy and life. That said, there remain some noticeable differences between his work and what I propose in this book. The most fundamental point where Wainwright's approach differs from mine is his understanding of the internal theological basis for stressing Christ's threefold office. In his view, "the systematic integrity of the notion resides in its entire suitability for the doxological and dogmatic description of the Savior and his work, and (derivatively) of the existence of his church before God and in the world."[50] I do not disagree with Wainwright, but I do take matters one explicit step further. That is, I see the integrity of the concept as residing in the way Christ's person and work recapitulate the inner relations and external work of the Trinity. In other words, I see the framework as grounded not just in the doctrine of salvation (and derivatively in ecclesiology), but more fundamentally in the doctrine of God itself. (In this regard, I am closer to the suggestive but undeveloped insight of John Henry Newman than Wainwright[51]—although I assume that Wainwright would find my approach incompatible with his own.) On that trinitarian basis, I then offer a comprehensive discussion of the ways that Christ's fulfillment of his threefold office addresses the breadth of

---

50. Wainwright, *For Our Salvation*, 109.

51. As found in the sermon just cited, entitled "The Three Offices of Christ," and preached on Easter Sunday 1840. See Newman, *Sermons*, 52–62. Newman's comment alluding to the trinitarian connection is limited to the following: "And it will be observed, moreover, that in these three offices He [Jesus] also represents to us the Holy Trinity; for in His proper character He is a priest, and as to His Kingdom He has it from His Father, and as to His prophetical office He exercises it by the Spirit. The Father is the King, the Son the Priest, and the Holy Ghost the Prophet" (55). Scholars with more knowledge of Newman's work than I possess may know if he has developed this theme more fully elsewhere.

the human predicament, tying that work explicitly to the three most common understandings of the atonement.

This survey continues with a fuller consideration of three recent works that are not only opposed to the predominance of the penal substitution model of the atonement, but also seek to eliminate it altogether and replace it with some constructive alternative. These are works exhibiting a more generally negative tone toward the Christian tradition, works that my own proposal will more determinedly seek to counter. So it is fitting that I consider them at somewhat greater length than the books just surveyed. These three books are Michael Winter's *The Atonement,* Darby Ray's *Deceiving the Devil: Atonement, Abuse, and Ransom,* and C. J. den Heyer's *Jesus and the Doctrine of the Atonement.* I will review each in turn, as a way of preparing the stage for my own constructive representation of the church's traditions. Winter's work is the most orthodox of these three, but even as such he shares their common concern that the doctrine of the atonement be explained in terms more plausible to the modern mind. The key concerns and points of his argument may be summarized as follows. As he describes it, he is writing for "mainstream believers . . . for whom the crucifixion of Jesus is a serious difficulty. That is to say, for people who believe in a loving God, and who find it exceedingly difficult to reconcile this understanding of their deity with one who would require the cruel death of Jesus."[52] A different understanding of how Christ actually effects atonement needs to be developed and promoted. How may such an undertaking be justified? Winter appeals to the commonly recognized fact that the church has never formally determined one orthodox dogma regarding Christ's work, as it did his person (46–47). Indeed, various explanations may be found in the writings of the Fathers[53]—a fact that he uses to imply that there should still be room for diverse understandings. And yet, he observes, in the West, Anselm's particular theory of vicarious satisfaction has taken on an informal dogmatic status, and in the process narrowed our theological vision to such an extent that apparently only Christ's death on the cross has anything to do with effecting salvation. But if the church has not, in fact, asserted one orthodox doctrine of the atonement, then, Winter reasons, even such an informal monopoly should be rejected. We should recover the flexibility and richness discernible in the

---

52. Winter, *The Atonement,* 9.

53. The demonstration of which is Winter's primary purpose in his chapter 3, as his second conclusion on pp. 58–59 makes explicit.

Bible and early church tradition. As the reader might expect, I concur with Winter's desire to broaden the church's field of view, because its ministry is better served by having dynamic and diverse understandings of the atonement upon which to draw.

But at this juncture, Winter diverges from the direction the present work will take. For he does not want merely to add other understandings of the atonement next to that of vicarious sacrifice. Rather, he wants to replace it with a different understanding. He justifies this with the (unargued) assertion that the whole ancient thought-world to which the logic of sacrifice was self-evident is no longer our thought-world. He states his basic premise succinctly: "The intrinsic efficacy of sacrifices no longer convinces the modern mind, and contemporary enquirers are entitled to something satisfactory with which to replace the ancient convictions about blood offerings" (30). That is, he simply takes for granted that all the unspoken assumptions and connections that had made the practice of sacrifice itself plausible (regardless of whether one was a Jew, Christian, or pagan) are no longer plausible to the modern mind—and cannot be made so. Indeed, to the modern mind, they are simply repugnant. Hence, given the other options we could legitimately take, and the implausibility and reprehensibility of vicarious satisfaction, Winter argues for another view. Specifically, he proposes that we understand that "Jesus saves" not as a result of his "blood offering," but as a result of his intercession on our behalf. Winter believes this is a more adequate understanding of the atonement for several reasons. First, it is the view most consistent with the fundamental teaching and actions of Christ that forgiveness is available simply for the asking. That is, there are no preconditions one must meet (such as the payment of a debt or the offering of a sacrifice) before one may be reconciled to God. Indeed, forgiveness is so freely offered that the request for it need not be one's own—in fact, we should come to see that Jesus makes the request on our behalf, as our eternal intercessor. Second, this view allows us to recover a fuller sense of where the "efficacy" of Christ's atoning work is located. That is, it is not restricted only to his death on the cross, but relates as well to his life on Earth and his eternal life at the right hand of the Father. The full breadth of the gospel story informs this view, rather than—apparently—just the passion narratives. Third, this intercessory view can be explained in terms that make sense to a modern mind-set, thus avoiding all the problems connected with a no longer plausible view of Christ's atoning work as a vicarious sacrifice. It will allow him to say that "the crucifixion was literally a cause of the atonement, and yet in the last analysis the cruel death was not absolutely necessary" (1).

There is real value and insight in Winter's proposed understanding of the atonement. Part of its value lies in its desire to bring other understandings of the atonement back into the conversation, in order to counter the overwhelming influence of Anselm's theory and thus broaden and enrich the doctrine overall. Another strength consists of its being grounded in the whole sweep of Jesus' life and ministry, and not just his passion and death. A third insight may be found in the way his discussion of "forgiveness without prerequisites" clarifies and develops an important scriptural theme. Still, Winter's proposal also displays some inconsistencies and problems, both in its own inner logic but also in the adequacy of its underlying assumptions. First of all, he tends toward a position that he had earlier noted as problematic (and which, ironically, he commended Anselm for overcoming), namely, that Jesus had in some sense to placate the Father (64–65). Winter's position does not require, and indeed, rejects the notion that Jesus shed his blood to propitiate the Father's anger. And yet his position does seem to suggest that a division of will, attitude, and purpose exists between God the Father and God the Son prior to the latter's intercession. After all, if this were not the case, why would intercession be necessary? That the first two persons (at least) are, in effect, "working at cross purposes" with one another seems implicit in his opening definition of atonement in his description of Christ's intercession on our behalf (2). But cannot God the Father forgive humanity unless the Son, as humanity's representative, asks Him to? Second, Winter's proposal displays a certain inconsistency when he moves from describing the necessary "moral conversion" and sincerity required of the individual in requesting forgiveness to the claim that this request can be made for humanity collectively by Christ solely on the basis of his hypostatic union. Obviously, if Christ can intercede on our behalf strictly on the basis of his divine-human person, then "moral conversion" and "sincerity" on the individual's part are not a prerequisite after all (90–91, 92–93). Finally, having argued against the de facto dominance of the Anselmian tradition by highlighting the diversity of the church's early thinking on the atonement, Winter himself seems to succumb to the "univocal" temptation. That is, he tends to present his view as the one finally adequate and appropriate view, and does not offer a way of keeping the various approaches or theories in any kind of creative and mutually corrective balance. This is so, even when he had earlier acknowledged that Paul and the Letter to the Hebrews theologize the death of Jesus as an expiatory sacrifice (18)—indeed, had acknowledged that Jesus himself most likely applied the idea to his own expected death (25–26). In this regard, his commitment to developing a theory acceptable to "the modern mind" actually causes him to discard views that he recognizes reflect the biblical witness!

In this tendency, Winter displays an all-too-common modernist chauvinism. More precisely, he assumes too quickly that sacrifice and its attendant presuppositions and worldview are irretrievably alien to the contemporary mind-set. At the same time, he assumes too quickly that the only possible response is to alter drastically certain biblical themes to suit that modern mind, rather than to educate and broaden it into the Bible's own perspectives.[54] The crux of the matter is displayed in Winter's tendency either to discard or demythologize the New Testament explanations of Christ's crucifixion. Christ's death is no longer understood as "doing" anything; rather, it represents Jesus' integrity and ultimate dedication to his mission. This distinction lies behind Winter's opening claim that the crucifixion may be said to "cause" the atonement, without being "necessary" for it. It is a martyr's death, in itself no more or less significant or unique than that of Thomas Beckett, Joan of Arc, Thomas More, Gandhi, Martin Luther King Jr., and Archbishop Oscar Romero. The only distinction Winter grants of Jesus' death in comparison to these other martyrs is that his symbolizes the whole of his life and work: "All aspects of the atonement find their maximum actualization and visible symbolic manifestation in the crucifixion. For that reason I feel that one is entitled to speak of the crucifixion as the sacrament of Christ's intercession" (132). Again, one could make a similar statement about any martyr's death, but Winter sees Jesus as a special case, because of the special status of his person. (It is intriguing that Winter feels compelled to demythologize so much pertaining to traditional understandings of Christ's work for the sake of presenting a plausible picture to "the modern mind," yet relies so heavily on a traditional Christology that the "modern mind" would presumably see

---

54. On this issue, Winter may be too dependent upon Raymund Schwager's book, *Brauchen Wir Einen Sündenbock?* (Munich: Kösel-Verlag GmbH, 1978), English translation, *Must There Be Scapegoats?* (New York: Harper & Row, 1987.) This work reads the Bible through the eyes of René Girard's theories on violence and the sacred, rather than through the Bible's (especially the New Testament's) own understanding of sacrifice, "scapegoats," and Jesus' crucifixion. See Winter's statement of his indebtedness on p. 1.

as needing an equivalent demythologization.) Thus, the uniqueness of Jesus' death consists in the fact that it symbolizes and illustrates Christ's life overall (132)—which, according to Winter, includes not just his earthly life but also his resurrection and "intercession in eternity" as the divine-human one, creator of the human race and one person of the Trinity (94). Thus, the death on the cross no longer "causes" the atonement; it only represents in a particularly stark form a causality that has been shifted to Christ's intercession. In this regard, the cross functions derivatively, even if it also serves as a kind of exclamation point, indeed, as a sacrament of that intercession (133). In sum, I believe Winter presents an intriguing, constructive, and pastorally useful addition to atonement theology, but it is unfortunate that he intends it to replace rather than complement earlier traditions. It is also unfortunate that he does so on the basis of a critique that is, from my perspective, inconsistently carried out and too quick to assume the inaccessibility of a biblical worldview to modern Christians.

Darby Kathleen Ray's *Deceiving the Devil: Atonement, Abuse, and Ransom* presents the second recent atonement proposal I will consider. It is a passionate and creative work. Ray's feminist and liberationist commitments are explicit and influential. While she does not work within theological orthodoxy to the extent that Winter does, she nevertheless seeks to maintain a connection to the Christian tradition. She asserts that the atonement orthodoxy most Christians have imbued since birth is "characterized by paternalism, patriarchalism, and militarism," yet she remains convinced that the Christian story at its root offers a basis for a model that encourages "responsibility, compassion, courage, and creativity."[55] In this respect, she differs from feminist theologians who have dismissed the Christian tradition as irredeemable for their purposes. These theologians resolve the perceived tension between their feminism and their inherited Christian faith by abandoning the latter. But Ray, somewhat ambivalently, wants to retain both, so the tension remains. This prods her to ask a collection of questions, which serve to focus how she construes her dilemma and her task:

> How can I, on the one hand, agree with the conviction that traditional construals of the work of Christ constitute theological violence and, on the other hand, maintain that the life *and death* of Jesus has redemptive

---

55. Ray, *Deceiving the Devil*, viii.

efficacy? Why do feminist theologians tend to dismiss all notions of atonement as irretrievably problematic, while most liberationists insist that some such notion is essential to Christian identity and community? Is there a way of thinking about the salvific work of Christ that can satisfy the need of ordinary Christian people for a theology that is both rooted in tradition and open to the transforming winds of the Spirit? (viii)

As these words make clear, Ray sees her task as being both critical and constructive. She employs feminist principles to critique what she views as the most common understanding of the atonement (with its seemingly exclusive emphasis on Christ's self-sacrificial death on the cross). Yet she also employs liberationist sensibilities, on the one hand, to ask if the feminist critique might in some respects go too far and, on the other, to help develop an alternative.

This sets the stage for her own constructive retrieval of what she terms the "patristic model" of the atonement. This is the mythological account of the atonement that sees humanity enslaved by the power of evil, and in which "the devil actually causes his own defeat by overstepping his boundaries" (140). That is, in seeking to "claim" Jesus in death, as if he were any other mortal, the devil is caught on his divinity and inadvertently brings about God's victory. Thus, Jesus' death simultaneously represents the zenith and the unmasking and collapse of the world's oppressive power. Ray summarizes the logic of this understanding in words that apply equally to her own proposed, and demythologized, reformulation: "Its symbolics demonstrate that the collapse occurs at the point of overextension; in this moment, this space, the truth about human evil is revealed. But it is also here that an alternative, a salvific possibility, is manifest" (141). Understood in this way, Ray contends, Jesus' death retains the centrality it has in Christian tradition and liberation theology, even while the very problematic implications of other understandings are avoided. Specifically, Jesus' death is not "required" by God for atonement, nor is his suffering as such viewed as somehow redemptive and virtuous. Instead, Jesus' crucifixion represents the final violent backlash of the powers he had challenged nonviolently throughout his life and ministry. Responsibility for his death must be laid at their feet, not at God's, and suffering should be construed as a likely consequence of such challenge, but not as a good or virtue in its own right. Redemptive power is found in Jesus' life, not in his suffering and death. In making this distinction, Ray seeks to neutralize any attempt to legitimate and perpetuate unjust suffering by saying it represents a praiseworthy "imitation of Christ."

Ray's retrieval and reformulation occupies the final chapter of her book, although her penultimate chapter clarifies many of the attitudes and presuppositions undergirding her specific proposal. While her final position actually retains little of the traditional patristic model (and far fewer of its theological presuppositions, as I will discuss below), it is nevertheless a nuanced and serious proposal. Indeed, one of the strengths of her undertaking is the recognition that if one is to remain within the broad range of the Christian tradition, one cannot simply ignore or wish away the centrality of Jesus' suffering and death. It must be explained in some manner. And this is not the only strength of her book. Another appears in her recognition of the complexity of life, of the ambiguous and insidious nature of evil, and her rejection of any easy dualisms in explaining the source of evil—a tendency she detects as a weakness in the ancient patristic model. She takes evil seriously, but she cautions against letting that seriousness take the form of moral absolutism. Such forms can too easily make redemption a purely cosmic affair (abstracting one from struggles against injustice in this world) and they can too easily identify some outcast group as personifying the demonic (such as Jews, pagans, and dissident Christians). Interestingly, she implies that feminist theology sometimes falls into this dualistic tendency itself,[56] to which her approach serves as a corrective. Another strength of her proposal consists of her affirmation that Jesus challenged unjust powers, but refused to adopt their methods in doing so. Following Jesus' example, Christian resistance to evil must likewise eschew the means of evil, choosing "not coercion but non-violence, not power-as-control, but power-as-compassion" (138). Such a summary contrast certainly corresponds to scriptural accounts of Jesus' methods and interpersonal behavior (although it is less obvious how it might interpret accounts of the power he exercised in exorcisms and his stilling of the sea).

Ray also recognizes, much to her credit, that focusing solely on one model of the atonement is neither sufficient nor desirable. Rather, atonement theology should encourage "a multiplicity of models that can be put into dialogue with one another in a process of ongoing, mutual critique and revision" (116). She shows an accompanying humility

---

56. See her comments on p. 102.

about the limits of her own proposal, which she acknowledges, like all models, is open to perversion, with its appropriateness dependent on the context in which its placed and how it is used. Unfortunately, the trajectory and implicit force of most of her writing undercuts this recognition and acknowledgment repeatedly. That is, concerning traditional models of the atonement, she occasionally recognizes the value they have in certain instances (e.g., her concession that "some *do* find solace" in the Christian admonition to forgive the sins of others).[57] But she tends to qualify such concessions immediately, either with an explicitly critical statement or by returning her focus to the feminist/liberationist alternatives or her own constructive project. Indeed, she typically presents traditional models not as having certain strengths, which, if one is not careful, can be distorted and abused. Rather, she often implies and sometimes states outright that the problem is not the distortion or misuse of traditional doctrines, but the actual doctrines themselves.[58] Thus, when she speaks of the value of a "multiplicity of models," it appears that only one *genre* of model will do, namely, the feminist/liberationist models she has surveyed in her book, which includes her own constructive proposal. She never gives the impression that she would allow traditional models of the atonement to critique, revise, or even complement these more contemporary models. Her advocacy of a "multiplicity of models" remains commendable in theory, but far too limited in practice.

Furthermore, Ray's retrieval and reformulation of the patristic model does indeed represent a creative and nuanced use of the Christian tradition, but in the process she discards or transforms many of that model's key elements, presuppositions, and connected beliefs. On the most obvious level, these changes derive from her efforts to "demythologize" the model. But they also stem from some fundamental theological differences. I will speak to several of these. First, Ray's soteriology and Christology bear little resemblance to that of the Christian tradition. She does not construe Jesus as the unique Redeemer; rather, he is a revealer of a divine power available to all persons. Jesus gives an example, but redemption only comes to other persons if they embrace and act on this example themselves. "In my interpretation, Jesus' life and death are affirmed as the revelation of amazing grace and liberative powers, but their redemptive possibility depends absolutely on their continued

---

57. Ibid., 67. See also her statements about reading traditional models in their original contexts and according to their original intentions, p. 69.

58. See her qualifying and critical statements on p. 69.

instantiation in the concrete acts of historical people, communities, and institutions" (143). She is concerned that the tradition's exclusive focus on Christ as Redeemer fosters a dependency that cannot help but produce an infantalizing passivity. Thus, she emphasizes the need of persons to act to achieve their own redemption. In this sense, all persons are potential "Christs."

Furthermore, Ray does not develop the traditional notion of resurrection. She neither presents it as something possible for humanity generally, nor considers it in reference to Christ particularly. The closest she comes to broaching the issue appears in statements such as the following: "What the powers of evil did not anticipate, what they did not see, was the infinite font of life that spawned Jesus' struggle and that continues to spring forth long after his death" (143). Also: "In this challenge that is life, the story of Jesus' refusal to be inscribed by the forces of evil surrounding him becomes for us a sacred memory that keeps possibility and hope alive, reminding us that because a praxis of resistance was actualized 'once upon a time,' it can be yet again" (137). And on the concluding page of her book: "To call him Christ is to affirm that this way, this possibility, did not die on the cross of violence but is universally available. To call him Christ is to wager that the path of resistance and compassion is a liberative one, reconciling us with the power of life itself" (145). Behind these statements stands a very different conception of God and creation, and therefore God's relation to Jesus, than that found in orthodox Christian tradition. Influenced by Rita Nakashima Brock, Ray identifies God's presence in the world as "erotic power." It "transcends the bound of any one person, activity, community, or institution, and yet it can become concrete only in such ones. . . . It is the pulse of life that pervades all being, the one breath enlivening the embodied billions, luring each toward individual fulfillment within an organic whole . . ." (134). Her evocation of organic images is quite telling, and an organic analogy can help explain both her omission of resurrection and her understanding of Christ. God exists as a kind of underground life-force and root, from which spring many individual shoots. Those shoots will flower, wilt, and die, or be cut off, but the root remains and will continue to send up new shoots. Thus, life goes on, even though individual embodiments of it do not.

Another motivation for Ray's neglect of the doctrine of resurrection lies in the fact that she rejects and resists any move to understand atonement as operating on a cosmic level. She simply assumes that any such other-worldly construal will detract from our focus on, and responsibility for, this-worldly transformation. This concern also lies behind her rejection of the assumption that Christ's atonement in any way defeats evil "once and for all." From her perspective, such an assumption can too easily produce a sense of triumphalism that may blind us to the world's continuing evil—and demoralize persons into passivity when we realize that it has not been defeated. With this in mind, when Ray speaks of Christian hope, she does not describe it as a theological virtue, as an indubitable conviction about an inevitably positive future outcome granted by God. Rather, she describes it in terms of a motivating desire: "We *hope* the good will prevail. Acting on that hope, we theologize and act in certain ways rather than others, knowing that neutrality is never an option," and "it is up to us to keep hope alive by loving and living the good and resisting evil in concrete acts of compassion and celebration" (133). Why does she take this approach? What does it reveal about her underlying and primary concerns? And how should Christians respond?

Throughout the book, Ray consistently focuses on "unjust suffering" and the ways in which theology can be employed to resist and overcome it. Certainly a concern with justice is a dominant theme in Scripture, especially in the witness of the Old Testament prophets. Certainly a concern with humanity's enslavement by the powers of evil is a dominant theme in Scripture, especially as that is exemplified in Jesus' many exorcisms and healings and in the theology of Paul. Yet in her take on this emphasis, Ray's vision remains rather narrow. On the one hand, while having much to say to the victims of unjust suffering, she has almost nothing to say to its perpetrators. And yet, as repellant as our sense of justice may find it, are not Jesus' call to repentance and his radical offers of forgiveness—even, indeed, especially to evil's perpetrators—intrinsic and unavoidable parts of his message? On the other hand, she neglects to address whether there might be suffering that is not qualified as "unjust," but simply exists as a natural and inevitable part of the human condition. Suffering such as that caused by disease, natural disaster, and our unavoidable mortality does not obviously require consideration in moral categories. To be sure, some "natural" suffering is fostered by preventable causes, in which case a certain moral responsibility should come into play. But it is impossible to imagine (and would require overweening hubris to even entertain the possibility) that the world could be made entirely safe from all such forms of natural suffering. Accidents still happen, disasters still strike, we all still die, and perhaps more often than our sense of loss would like, assigning blame is simply beside the point. One way of posing the issue would be to suggest that traditional notions of the atonement were better suited to dealing with this kind of suffering, while Ray's understanding is more explicitly designed to address the problem of unjust suffering. In this way, they should be understood as complementary, rather than mutually exclusive. As noted above, she herself recognizes the desirability of having multiple views (for such multiplicity enriches the theological resources available and serves a mutually corrective function), and yet her proposal does not really act on this awareness. I believe her own constructive position would be strengthened were she more open to the ways in which her views might complement, and be complemented by, the traditional positions she critiques.

Finally, I want to comment on Ray's methodology, especially in regard to the critical aspects of her work. Her constructive proposal demonstrates both creativity and nuance, even if one might disagree with many aspects of it on theological grounds. However, the critical segments of her book, especially those dealing with the "Anselmian" and "Abelardian" models, are far less persuasive and nuanced. To be sure, she approves of the Anselmian model insofar as it takes sin very seriously and of the Abelardian model insofar as it interprets Jesus' death through the lens of his life—and she sees her approach as incorporating both of these assumptions. But apart from that, the objects of her criticism tend to be more caricatures than fair summaries of positions understood on their own terms. Of course, the "hermeneutics of suspicion" common to feminist theology assumes that the *real* meaning of a traditional position never resides in what a text presents "on its own terms." And Ray seems to concur with this approach when she states that from feminist theologians she has "become convinced that theology was at heart a discourse about power" (118). Still, the question arises: In presenting these criticisms, to what extent is Ray presenting her own views? Much of that criticism is presented via summaries of the critiques made by other feminist theologians; as a result, one cannot always know the extent of her agreement with them. For example, in an earlier section of the book, she discusses, and appears to share, feminist concerns that the death of Jesus is overemphasized, indeed, dangerously exalted in traditional views. She cites, among others, the critical views of Mary Daly and actually borrows Daly's phrase as a rubric for the section, "Necrophilic Theologies" (55–57). Such use naturally suggests that Ray sees the phrase as somehow accurate. And yet much later she writes: "The logic that uncritically reduces Christianity to patriarchy, or atonement to necrophilia, is a logic that eschews complexity, fragility, and conflict" (102). Does this mean Ray has certain reservations about Daly's analysis and characterization? Might it suggest she has reservations about other feminist theologians whose logic might stray into uncritical reductionism? It is hard to say based on the tenor and extent of most of what she has written. Yet at infrequent but seemingly crucial points, her own voice seems to come through clearly, and it gives the impression that were she to follow her own best instincts, she would present a much more nuanced and fair critique than many of the thinkers she summarizes.

Last of all, consider C. J. den Heyer's *Jesus and the Doctrine of the Atonement*. Den Heyer, professor of New Testament at the Theological University of the Reformed Churches in the Netherlands, has written what is finally a melancholy book. It is the least traditional of these three critiques of traditional atonement theology, and it presents the least robust constructive alternative. Perhaps den Heyer wishes he could still believe the traditional teachings of the church, but his particular study of the Bible has made him unable to maintain a classic Christian faith in either the person or work of Christ. Jesus has become for him at most an "exemplary" and "inspiring" man, but hardly the saving Christ of Christian tradition. He signals what his approach and findings will be from the very outset of his work. His preface offers significant clues about his method, his presuppositions, and his conclusions. He intends to undertake a purely historical analysis of Jesus, as a follow-up to his earlier work entitled *Jesus Matters*, but it is clear that this approach describes not only his practical method but also his ideological assumptions. He sees the results of historical investigation as undermining and ultimately antithetical to the Christian dogmatic tradition, as indicated by these words: "Those who engage in an intensive investigation of the historical Jesus find it increasingly difficult to accept christological dogma."[59] Clearly, this is an autobiographical description of his own experience over the years, but he presents it as simply axiomatic. It is easy enough to refute by thinking of those scholars whose historical investigations into Jesus have *not* produced this difficulty (e.g., Luke Johnson, N. T. Wright, and Raymond Brown). Be that as it may, den Heyer's own naturalistic conclusion stands out clearly: "Jesus was a human being among other human beings" (ix). On this basis, it comes as no surprise when he continues by saying that Jesus' "humiliating death on the cross can be explained historically in every respect" (x). Indeed, the most that he can claim of Jesus is this: "His faith in God is 'exemplary' and inspires people, sometimes hesitantly

---

59. Den Heyer, *Jesus*, x.

and sometimes enthusiastically, to take the way of reconciliation."[60] It is a rather minimalist claim. In other words, den Heyer presents a Jesus who stands in stark contrast to the Christ of the church's tradition—and even that of Winter and Ray.

However, this does not mean den Heyer avoids making any theological claims. But he does so in a fashion actually quite common in certain circles of "historical Jesus" scholarship. That is, he reconstructs what he sees as the most accurate historical picture of Jesus, and then engages in his own theological reflection on that reconstruction. In other words, he wants to leap over the nearly two thousand years separating us from Jesus and "think for himself," rather than accepting the church's doctrinal conclusions and language about Jesus. He is quite explicit about his undertaking: "Here I shall be doing precisely what the early Christian community also did: looking for words, images and metaphors which express [the significance of the life and death of Jesus of Nazareth]. We live almost two thousand years later. We have to look for new words, images and metaphors" (xi). Note the historicist assumptions, assumptions that one might conclude are actually in tension with one another— a tension den Heyer does not recognize. That is, on the one hand, in spite of his earlier caveats regarding the limits of historical reconstruction, den Heyer nevertheless assumes he can recreate Jesus in enough detail so as to have an object of theological reflection equivalent to what the early church had. On the other hand, we live nearly two thousand years later, and must "look for new words, images and metaphors"— statements that suggest a gulf in mental worldview and outlook so great between our age and that of the early church as to be unbridgeable. But if that is the case, how can we be sure we have an accurate picture of the "historical Jesus"? More pointedly, if the gulf is so great, how could this historical Jesus, himself a product of that nearly two-thousand-year-old culture, have anything relevant to say to us? Is den Heyer following the lead of scholars such as Harnack, Bultmann, and McFague? That is, does he strip away what he views as historical accretions from Jesus to get to some presumed kernel or essence, which he will then reclothe with his own more contemporary images and metaphors? If this is the case, then it represents at best a special pleading for the enduring power of some presumed essence and at worst a final failure of nerve in one's historicist assumptions. Yet later in the book, he apparently repudiates even a sense

---

60. Ibid., 135. This is, in fact, the concluding sentence of his book, the context and substance of which I will discuss more fully below.

of some enduring essence. With regard to the letters 1 and 2 Peter and Revelation, den Heyer discusses the changing context, and draws a very pointed conclusion:

> Unavoidably the picture of the "historical" Jesus began to fade. That was not such a bad thing as it might perhaps seem, since in this way space was made in which new images could be created. And that is necessary, since theological insights constantly need to be adapted to changing circumstances. Theology is done in a particular context. There are no objective truths, nor have there ever been. It is regrettable that people still think that there are. (122)

Given these assumptions, it comes as no surprise that den Heyer produces a very minimalist Christology, reflecting his own very modest and idiosyncratic theological claims.

Of course, given his assumptions and methods, it would probably be more accurate to label it his "Jesusology." To term it Christology would be to legitimate what he views as the homogenizing process of dogmatization, a move that he repudiates. Den Heyer's approach, by contrast, considers the different witnesses of the New Testament precisely in their variety. This includes a reconstruction of Jesus' "own" view of his ministry and its significance, and then a consideration in turn of the views of Paul, the Pauline school, the Synoptics, John and the Johannine letters, Hebrews, the non-Johannine "Catholic Epistles," and Revelation. In taking this approach, den Heyer does not seek to find a common theological thread, but to highlight the differences among these diverse biblical sources. He clearly means to reinforce the point that there is no one proper way to interpret Jesus and his significance, and certainly no one New Testament understanding of the atonement. Stated as a simple observation, it is a conclusion with which I would concur, as would most contemporary scholars and theologians. Yet he further suggests that an urge toward dogma sought to stifle and homogenize this original diversity, even as it built an ever more elaborate superstructure upon the New Testament witnesses. When he mentions the "tradition," he does not consider the ways that this might have represented some broad early consensus, which could serve to counter his emphasis on variety. Nor does he consider that dogma might be less an imposition *upon* the New Testament than an attempt to clarify and explain what is implicit *in* the New Testament.

Having proposed this diversity of views, to what use does den Heyer then put it? A primarily pragmatic and utilitarian one. Having put aside any sense that, for all their variety, writings of the New Testament still point to one "essence" or "objective truth," he has thereby eliminated the means by which that diversity might be evaluated and adjudicated on the basis of how accurately, coherently, and faithfully its views represent this external essence or truth. Instead, he indicates we should accept a pluralism of beliefs: whatever brings persons meaning and comfort ought to be allowed. Of course, by such a "standard" one may be generous enough to indulge even the orthodox their traditional, albeit unbelievable, claims—just as long as they do not claim for them a dogmatic exclusivity. For not only does den Heyer reject such exclusivity on principle, he has also argued at length that the New Testament offers far less basis for interpreting Jesus' death as a vicarious sacrifice along the lines of the Old Testament cult or scapegoat ritual than is traditionally assumed.

In all this, den Heyer seems to reflect an Enlightenment and post-Kantian mind-set regarding both the limits of our epistemology and changed sensibilities in matters of moral responsibility and autonomy. For example, consider the following words: "The church's confession says that his death and atonement brought about reconciliation. But how am I to imagine that? How can the death of someone in a distant past mean salvation and redemption for me, living centuries later? This notion no longer inspires many people today, but rather provokes opposition. Am I not responsible for the consequences of my own words and actions?" (132). Having staked out this individualistic and autonomous position, it comes as no surprise that den Heyer's final chapter bears the title, "An 'Exemplary' Life," and its logic is outlined with the following subheads: "No Doctrine of the Atonement," "Dogmas," and "Believing without Dogmas." Neither is it surprising when the final sentence of den Heyer's book makes such a limited statement regarding Jesus' significance: "His faith in God is 'exemplary' and inspires people, sometimes hesitantly and sometimes enthusiastically, to take the way of reconciliation" (135). As the reader may readily anticipate, my trinitarian theology of the atonement will take a very different approach and reach a far different and fuller conclusion than that offered by den Heyer. The next chapter will begin laying the theological and historical foundations for that work, while the following chapter will establish its scriptural basis. To those considerations I now turn.

2

Theological Underpinnings

A Brief Summary

The first chapter sketched in broad strokes my conviction that a trinitarian understanding of the atonement is theologically the most appropriate and pastorally the most fruitful way to understand God's reconciling and saving work in Christ. It also surveyed a cross-section of current alternate proposals for understanding the atonement—some with similarities to my own approach, and others diverging sharply from it. Doing these two things helped place and orient my approach on the theological landscape, but they do not fully explain how I intend to go about presenting and supporting my case. Such an explanation will be the task of this chapter. It will describe Scripture as the source and starting point of my reflections, the interpretive method I will use, the theological assumptions employed, and the historical context and tradition that will serve as a catalyst for my constructive work. These labors will establish the foundation for the chapters to follow—and I use the term "foundation" deliberately to draw a comparison with its everyday meaning. Building the foundation of a house requires strenuous digging, careful measuring, and the effort to place things just right. Such work is essential yet frequently unheralded, because most of the work is later obscured by backfill and the house itself. But one cannot do a slapdash job without threatening the integrity of the house built upon it. In the same way, this chapter may prove arduous at times, but the hard going is needed to support the structure of the argument to be placed upon it.

Theological Exegesis

As befits a work consciously undertaken within a Reformed framework, but still intended for an ecumenical audience, I employ Scripture as the primary source and norm for my project. That said, I know that a "Reformed" approach may nevertheless take many forms. For example, Calvin's image of Scripture as a pair of spectacles aiding us to see God truly and clearly, along with his notion of biblical language as a divine "accommodation" to our limited human understanding, does not easily correlate with the emphasis of the "old Princeton school" (e.g., Charles Hodge and B. B. Warfield) on the Bible's absolute infallibility. The Bible can, and has been, interpreted in diverse ways using diverse methods. So some further clarification is in order. Stated most concisely, I will not abstract general principles or deductions from Scripture, nor will I engage in a predominantly historical-critical examination of the biblical texts. Instead, I will offer a theological narrative and patterns of thought that echo and grow out of the biblical narratives and thought patterns. This does not mean I will merely paraphrase the Bible or assume that its sense is self-evident. The Bible requires interpretation, and all interpretations, if they are coherent, operate with certain guiding assumptions. Such assumptions may be brought to the Bible from without or they may arise in some sense from within. This distinction may be represented in part simply by comparing modern critical studies of the Bible (an example of the former approach) with premodern and certain contemporary studies of the Bible that are explicitly theological (an example of the latter approach). I will employ primarily the latter approach, which reflects the long-standing Reformed tradition of letting Scripture interpret Scripture. True, the Reformed tradition itself has never literally met this standard, insofar as the ecumenical creeds and the church's "rule of faith" have served as implicit frameworks for reading Scripture. But as the Reformers did before me, I also assume that the creeds and the rule of faith represent an appropriate synopsis of the Bible's basic story line. Thus, insofar as Scripture is the divine witness to and of the church, I will read it in accord with the broad orthodox practice of the church.

A specific example illustrates this approach, particularly since it has direct bearing on the topic. Theological defenders of the Trinity usually acknowledge that the Bible contains no *doctrine* of the Trinity as such. This does not mean, however, that Scripture contains no passages or patterns that support such a doctrine as a logical interpretation of, and conclusion from, the biblical witnesses. Indeed, numerous passages point to the "triadic" nature of God and the divine activity, as well as proto-trinitarian liturgical formulations, and they invite if not require the emergence of some sort of post-scriptural doctrine of the Trinity. Once this doctrine has coalesced, it may then become an interpretive tool for gleaning even more and deeper meaning from the scriptural text. In a similar manner, the New Testament does not itself explicitly use the framework of prophet, priest, and king to describe Jesus' work. But given the context of the Old Testament and inter-testamental writings and the character of Jesus' designation and activity as "the Christ"—particularly in light of the baptism/temptation narratives—I will argue that that framework is an appropriate interpretation of his status and work, not only compatible with but implicit in the scriptural witness itself. And as such, it, too, may then function heuristically, enabling a deeper and more perceptive reading of Scripture.

I also presuppose that the entirety of Jesus Christ's birth, life, work, passion, resurrection, and ascension is a unique, indeed, pivotal redemptive act of God in history. God's prior creation and providential sustaining of the world and his election of the people of Israel anticipate this redemptive act and his subsequent work through the Holy Spirit applies and broadens that redemption and will eventually bring it to culmination. But the hinge of God's eternal purpose of salvation, and the focus of my project, remains the totality of Christ's life—not just one aspect of it, such as his incarnation or his death on the cross—and what this means for the concrete and particular life of Christian faith. In part, this means one should not construe this redemptive act, by way of contrast, as a timeless and mythological representation of some transcendent principle or the symbolic illustration of some deep-seated human reality. So no program of demythologization that seeks to translate scriptural narratives and patterns into a philosophical or ethical system is needed. Neither should one abstract a Christian "essence" comparable to a presumed essence of other religions. Nor should one use Scripture as merely a resource for historical-critical inquiry, especially in order to offer yet another idiosyncratic reconstruction of some supposed past view. Instead, I assume that Scripture represents a unified witness to the intentions and work of the triune God, as manifested and accomplished preeminently in Jesus Christ. I present the scriptural narrative in such a way that its own integrity, richness, and inner logic may be clarified, with an eye toward better enabling Christians to "live into" its meaning as something relevant to, indeed, constitutive of their own faithful understanding and existence. In other words, I am clearly engaged in a work of exegetical, constructive theology. I will employ historical-critical methods when they serve my purposes, but that usage will be governed by the trajectory and norms of Scripture itself, by the church's traditions and pastoral needs, and by the standards of theology as an ecclesial discipline.

This approach is nothing new. My interpretation of Scripture certainly shows the influence of Karl Barth and my early immersion in the "Yale school" of theology. One could label this approach "postliberal," in keeping with the description offered by William Placher:

> Postliberal theology attends to the biblical narratives as narratives rather than simply as historical sources or as symbolic expressions of truths which could be expressed non-narratively. But unlike some other theologians interested in narrative, postliberals do not let the stories of *our* lives set the primary context for theology. They insist that the *biblical* narratives provide the framework within which Christians understand the world. Christian theology describes how the world looks as seen from that standpoint; it does not claim to argue from some "neutral" or "objective" position and indeed denies the possibility of such a position.[1]

This excerpt helps clarify the positive and constructive role that narrative can play in the lives of Christians, but it also raises a question about the authority that narratives may possess. When a narrative has such authority, it functions as a canon. But a canon does not emerge *ex nihilo*. Rather, a particular community acknowledges it as such, and that community is typically also its source. So it does not suffice simply to say that the biblical narratives provide an interpretive framework for the world, because even interpretive frameworks are discerned by interpreters. But what guides the interpreters? I will indeed take a more narrative approach in interpreting the Bible, but as anyone familiar with the claims of deconstructionism knows, such an approach hardly guarantees one self-evidently "authentic" reading. By this light, a piece of literature containing as much diversity as the Bible in terms of dates of composition, authors, contexts, genres, and usage can lend itself to countless different

---

1. William C. Placher, "Postliberal Theology," in *The Modern Theologians* (ed. David F. Ford; New York: Oxford, 1989), 2:117, as quoted in Mary Kathleen Cunningham, *What Is Theological Exegesis: Interpretation and Use of Scripture in Barth's Doctrine of Election* (Valley Forge, Penn.: Trinity Press International, 1995), 15.

interpretations. However, I will not read the Bible "on its own." Rather, I will read it in accord with the broad interpretive framework supplied by the church's rule of faith and creeds, particularly as that has come down to us through the Reformed tradition. Obviously, the church, even in its Reformed branch, has never spoken with one voice in its reading of the Bible. But at least this standard should make my interpretive task a little more manageable.

Of course, I will appeal to the rule of faith not just because it is useful, but because I believe it is necessary and appropriate. Recall the famous parable that Alasdair MacIntyre proposes in his book *After Virtue*, imagining a catastrophe in which all the scientists are killed and much of the scientific infrastructure reduced to shambles.[2] He posits the eventual reemergence of "science," but argues that it would resemble the former discipline in name only. With no communal memory of how true science is done, with no body of experts to educate the new generation in all the tacit assumptions and skills needed, with only fragments of the infrastructure remaining, it would no longer be a living discipline engaged in new discovery, but only a static and scholastic exercise. A similar parable could be told about the Bible: if it is interpreted on its own, apart from the community out of which it arose and for which it is a living and life-giving Word, understandings that are alien to its original use and purpose will inevitably emerge. They may have their own merits and appeal, but they will also tend to lead nowhere, or at least be only tangential to the Christian life of faith.

Put more positively, an interpretation of Scripture done from within the Christian community, following the general direction of the rule of faith and creeds (and, I pray, the guidance of the Holy Spirit), will in fact produce the most appropriate and faithful reading of Scripture, in light of the Bible's own content and the intentions implicit within it. This approach will not consider the various gospels, narratives, letters, and other writings in isolation from one another, nor will its primary concern be to highlight what may be unique to each individually. Rather, I will emphasize what they have in common and the ways in which their differences serve to complement one another and enrich the scriptural story as a whole, in order to produce a theology of the atonement that is comprehensive, coherent, richly nuanced, and pastorally

---

2. Alasdair MacIntyre, *After Virtue* (2d ed.; South Bend, Ind.: University of Notre Dame Press, 1984), 1–2.

useful. This approach presupposes that the one triune God in his will and work stands as the Subject of the passages I interpret. Thus, while the various texts of Scripture may witness to this reality with different emphases and concerns, I assume they are all seeking to be true to the one divine reality and intention. In stating this position, one may readily recognize the similarity to Barth's emphasis on Jesus Christ as the true *Sache* (or "Subject") of the Bible, as well as Brevard Childs's recapitulation of this focus in his "canonical" approach to Scripture.[3]

Another way in which my approach parallels Barth's lies in the hope that my theological reflections will not be taken as an end in themselves, but as a means to foster a living encounter with Christ, the messianic king, priest, and prophet. I do not advocate belief in particular doctrines, however scriptural and "true"; I advocate a personal and living faith in the triune God.[4] But perhaps such a distinction states matters too starkly. The church's doctrines are a key instrument in helping Christians get to know God, indeed, to participate in the life of God. So it is perhaps more accurate to say that they are not so much ends in themselves as they are a means toward a deeper and more sophisticated piety and sense of Christian mission. For this reason, I will complete each of my central chapters with a treatment of the systematic "location," theological implications, and pastoral applications of my project. These sections will, I hope, complete a useful framework and offer some concrete and fruitful ideas to help renew the church's thinking, teaching, and preaching in our contemporary context.

I will engage in a certain amount of historical investigation of my primary concepts as they appear in Scripture, because such investigation

---

3. See, for example, Brevard S. Childs, *Introduction to the Old Testament as Scripture* (Philadelphia: Fortress Press, 1979), *The New Testament as Canon: An Introduction* (Philadelphia: Fortress Press, 1984), and *Biblical Theology of the Old and New Testaments: Theological Reflections on the Christian Bible* (Minneapolis: Fortress Press, 1992). The last of these in particular offers a succinct statement of the issue and Childs's intended alternative on pp. 80–89.

4. By way of comparison, consider how Barth lifts up Job as an example of true witness and faith while he condemns Eliphaz, Bildad, and Zophar. Everything the latter three say to their friend is "doctrinally" correct in Barth's estimation, but it is based on an abstract and lifeless repetition of religious truisms, while Job's complaints against God, while superficially impious, are nevertheless based on a personal, free, and living relation with God. See his exegetical excurses on the book of Job in §70, subsections 1 and 2, in Karl Barth, *Church Dogmatics* (IV/3, first half; ed. G. W. Bromiley and T. F. Torrance; trans. G. W. Bromiley; Edinburgh: T&T Clark, 1961). For a discussion of this section in Barth, see my article "Reclaiming a Theological Reading of the Bible: Barth's Interpretation of Job as a Case Study," *International Journal of Systematic Theology* 2, no. 2 (2000): 175–88.

can help flesh out one's understanding in fruitful ways. But I will not be preoccupied with such investigation, for the simple reason that it will not finally determine my theological reading. One should avoid the mistake that appears all too frequently in exegetical and theological discourse, both implicitly and explicitly, namely, the assumption that if one knows the history of a term or concept, one knows its meaning. My simple rejoinder: etiology is not destiny. It can at times be helpful, but it is not necessarily definitive. Old ideas can and frequently are employed in new ways. Indeed, they can be employed in ways that intentionally turn their old meaning on its head. Such moves are often what give old ideas new life and transformative power. For example, the concepts of king, priest, and prophet all have a long history in both the Old Testament and the inter-testamental literature. I will consider aspects of that history, but what finally matters most in my exposition are the ways in which Christ has, according to the New Testament witnesses, fulfilled and transformed these old definitions. Moving outward from the sphere of the Christian canon, an occasional consideration of the historical and socio-religious context of Jesus' time and the apostolic age will clarify the landscape for discussing my primary concerns. But I will not use, for example, a "history of religions" approach to explain the meaning of the structure and concepts I expound. That meaning must stem from the canonical witness, which is to say, from how the terms and concepts are actually employed in the biblical narratives and exposition, as that has been interpreted in its basic outlines by the church for nearly two millennia.

Here a contrast offered by David Yeago may be helpful.[5] In his argument that the affirmations of the Nicene Creed are, in their way, saying the same thing about God and Jesus as New Testament texts such as Phil 2:6ff., he distinguishes between "*judgements* and the *conceptual terms* in which those judgements are rendered."[6] One of his points is that we cannot make judgments without employing specific verbal and conceptual resources. Another point is that the same judgment may be made with any number of different words and ideas. This being the case, he then notes that knowledge of "the history of concepts is helpful only if we are attentive to the particular ways in which the concepts

---

5. See David S. Yeago, "The New Testament and the Nicene Dogma: A Contribution to the Recovery of Theological Exegesis," *Pro Ecclesia* 3, no. 2 (Spring 1994): 152–64, especially 159–63.

6. Ibid., 159.

are *employed* in affirmation and denial within a body of discourse."[7] That is, on the face of things, two judgments may appear to differ due to the difference in their approach or idiom, but in fact, in their own contexts, they may be saying the same thing. One can only be sure by paying careful attention to the way the words and concepts employed actually function in that context or discourse. Here his similarity to the position of "narrative" and "postliberal" theology is apparent. He goes on to observe:

> In general, judgements are not instrumental to concepts but concepts [are] to judgements; we cannot infer in any but the most general and open-ended way from the structure of a concept, or the history of its previous employment, the range of possible uses to which it may yet be put in the rendering of judgements. The only way to uncover the judgements made in a text is to pay close attention to what is said and implied, to the specific, contingent ways in which its conceptual resources are deployed: to attend, in short, to the *circumstantia litterae* ["the way the words go"].[8]

Concepts should not be viewed along the lines of Platonic ideas, existing eternally with one and the same meaning regardless of concrete historical context and use. In this regard, Yeago's position regarding the flexibility of judgments should not be construed as an attempt to update Adolf von Harnack's "essence of Christianity" or Rudolf Bultmann's "demythologization" project. These approaches are characterized by the search for the enduring and essential thread traceable from one age to the next, a thread that is effectively abstracted from its context. To be sure, a certain family resemblance may linger in the exposition of concepts from one use to the next, but not necessarily—and in any case, that is not what Yeago seeks. New uses of old concepts may in fact be satirical, ironic, co-opted, subverted, or—to employ the Hegelian term—*aufgehoben*, which is to say, negated and transcended simultaneously. The only sure way to tell their meaning in a particular context is to discern their particular usage, and then translate them all in the most precise and full way possible with careful attention paid to the details of both the old and new contexts.

On this point, I should make it clear that I am not starting from scratch. That is, I will not investigate the particular scriptural usage of

---

7. Ibid.
8. Ibid., 162.

terms, titles, or concepts as if their meaning and context were totally unknown or still to be defined. I am hardly seeking to present yet another historical reconstruction of what the early church did or did not believe. Quite the contrary, it should be clear, given my previous statements, that I assume that such scriptural usage presupposes a basic Christian faith, as that is understood not by historians so much as the church's own tradition. I understand my project as building on that basic understanding, refining, at times correcting, and developing it in ways that are scripturally warranted and pastorally helpful.

The Trinitarian Foundation

Why a *trinitarian* theology of the atonement? One could argue that atonement theology is complex enough already without adding to it the arcane intricacies of trinitarian theology. And one might also argue that atonement theology at least has the virtue of being practical, while trinitarian theology is nothing if not abstract and speculative. Yet the logic that sees no benefit in combining these two doctrines because of a presumed contrast between "arcane abstraction" and "practical relevance" is simply misplaced. For what prompted the doctrine of the Trinity's first emergence—and is prompting its reclamation by so many diverse theologians today—has nothing to do with mere speculation and everything to do *precisely with* the concrete life of faith. As with the emergence of a nuanced "Christology," it was a soteriological and not speculative interest that motivated the concern for clarity in developing the doctrine of the Trinity in the first place. Simply put, it arose from concrete, existential questions such as: Who is this God Jesus taught us to pray to as Father? Who is this God who is saving us, indeed, this Son who died to save us? Who is this God, this Spirit we experience in this new community? In sum, how are we to relate to and understand this God with whom we have found new life and personal communion? These are preeminently personal and pastoral questions, and seeking an answer to them is *not* merely an academic exercise. So how does combining the doctrine of the Trinity with a theory of atonement help us to answer them? How does this combination tell us what we need to know for the life of faith?

There are several ways in which the doctrine of the Trinity has served, and continues to serve, the everyday life of Christian faith. First, and most immediately, the doctrine of the Trinity helps the church understand and express more clearly the character of the God with whom it is dealing: this God is not an abstract, isolated, and static deity but a personal, relational, and dynamic God. Indeed, the doctrine of the Trinity functions in part simply to reiterate the Christian conviction that God has what may be called a "personality"—indeed, the biblical God has an abundance of "personality"!—which is to say, a particular orientation and will, indeed, a kind of personal idiosyncrasy with definite and profound commitments. The biblical God is not generic or bland. Yet one of the characteristics classically ascribed to God is "simplicity." God is not a composite being, a being with a certain essence to which various other attributes are added, as creatures were typically described. Put more pointedly, God does not *have* attributes—as if these could be separated from the divine being, as if God could be conceived without them—God *is* these attributes.

The problem arises when this divine simplicity is taken to mean that God exists as a kind of seamless uniformity, a kind of indescribable (read "nondescript") homogeneity that in fact empties God of any real meaning. The doctrine of the Trinity rightly understood acts as a corrective to any such emptying of God by establishing a certain irreducible character and personality to him. To be sure, much of what I am calling God's personality was known from the old covenant: he is a God of grace and mercy, of righteousness and justice, of long-suffering and steadfast love, of holiness and jealousy. But Christianity claims that in the revelation of God as Father, Son, and Holy Spirit we gain a fuller insight into the very being, character, and purposes of God never before known and never to be surpassed or contradicted. To be sure, this revelation does not tell us *everything* about God; God remains ineffable, surpassing human comprehension. But we have made a personal acquaintance with God, and this knowledge provides us with trustworthy insight into the divine character, even if it does not grant us a full knowledge of God. In Bruce Marshall's distinction, we know enough to be able to *identify* God, even if we do not know all aspects of God's *identity*.[9] Of course, this is analogous to what happens in our everyday personal relations. We certainly never come to know fully the thoughts and feelings, fears and hopes of even our closest friends and family, yet this does not preclude our having a true and reliable sense of their characters and personalities. Divine revelation does indeed make distinctions,

---

9. Bruce D. Marshall, *Trinity and Truth* (Cambridge Studies in Christian Doctrine; Cambridge: Cambridge University Press, 2000), 26ff.

confirming that God is like this, and not that. For example, God's triune revelation assures us that there is not another different and terrifying or terrifyingly indifferent deity "behind" or "beneath" the one revealed, a divinity perhaps simply unreachable—or reachable by means other than God's own self-disclosure in Christ through the power of the Holy Spirit. Instead, we know, through the prayer taught us by the Son, that in actuality we have a heavenly Father upon whom we can rely. In sum, in the revelation of Christ God has, quite literally, "given us his Word," and that promise made vitally present to us through the Spirit is the basis for Christian confidence and hope.[10]

Second, the doctrine clarifies the Christian community's encounter with God in salvation history, particularly as that is recounted and reflected upon in the New Testament. The earliest Christians were, of course, Jews—as was Jesus himself. As such, the foundation of their faith was the belief in the one God who had delivered them from bondage in Egypt. Recall the most basic of Jewish prayers, the Shema: "Hear O Israel, the Lord our God, the Lord is one." Christianity did not forsake this faith. But the encounter with Jesus, especially as the risen Christ, and the experienced presence of the Holy Spirit, especially in the Christian community, compelled early Christians to understand their earlier faith in a more complex and nuanced fashion. It was not just that the one God had descended to Earth (can one imagine that heaven was left vacant?). After all, the Bible recounts that Jesus himself spoke of and to his Father in heaven. It also witnesses to God speaking from heaven at Jesus' baptism and transfiguration. In addition, it was not just that after his death, Jesus "stayed on" in some ghostly form or in the church's collective memory. After all, Jesus' words about the "Counselor" to come, the Bible's common insistence on Jesus' bodily resurrection, and the account of the ascension and the events of

---

10. I should also note that this revelation is the basis for our language naming God as Father, Son, and Holy Spirit, and employing masculine pronouns in reference to him. To be sure, such language is metaphorical. But this does not mean that metaphor is somehow free-floating, or that these metaphors are exchangeable with others inside or outside the Christian canon. They are particular metaphors derived from the narrative of Scripture, especially as that is epitomized in the descriptions of Christ and his practice. This is not to say that another construal of the theological task, its sources, and theological language might promote an alternate understanding and usage. Anyone familiar with contemporary discussions knows that there are many such alternate proposals. However, as I have noted above, I am undertaking this project anchored in Scripture, so I will take its usage as normative.

Pentecost all suggest that the Spirit experienced by the community was not understood as simply equivalent to Jesus' continuing presence. Rather, that Spirit was sensed to be distinct. Yet even with this sense of divine presence in three distinguishable forms, the community remained convinced that it had to do with one divine purpose and work, with one divine plan, in short, with only One God. So the impetus for developing a doctrine of the Trinity becomes apparent: the early Christian community's assumption of the oneness of God combined with its triadic experience of that God's saving work made further reflection and clarification virtually inevitable.

Third, insofar as God's personality "models" what our own nature and life should be, then the personal, relational, and dynamic interdependence of the triune God also tells us something about our own truest nature and end. To be sure, this should not be taken to imply a simple transference or analogy. We should never suppose that our goal is simply "to be like God," that God represents idealized humanity or is simply humanity "writ large," and our job is to imitate him. God remains God and we remain creatures—and our nature and responsibilities are guided by God's purpose and will for us *as creatures*. (The two parts of the Great Commandment and the two-fold division of the Decalogue offer one illustration of this distinction.) Nevertheless, we are *God's* creatures, which means we do properly look to him for our orientation and ultimate end. We are *other* than God, but our fullest being and meaning is constituted *in relation to* God. What Colin Gunton writes regarding God, "otherness," and freedom is relevant to this dialectical claim:

> Freedom is to be found in the space in which persons can be themselves in relation with other persons. That is the lesson of the doctrine of the Trinity. Father, Son and Spirit constitute each other as free persons by virtue of the shape their interrelationship takes in the trinitarian perichoresis. Otherness is an essential feature of the trinitarian freedom, because without otherness the distinctness, particularity, of a person is lost. But, in trinitarian terms, the otherness is not the freedom of the *individual*—a freedom *from* others, as we so often make it in the West— because it is a freedom that is a function of relatedness: it is given and received, because personal being is constituted by relatedness. We should say, then, that the essence *of* the being in relation that is the Trinity is the *personal space* that is received and conferred.[11]

---

11. Colin E. Gunton, *The Promise of Trinitarian Theology* (2d ed.; Edinburgh: T&T Clark, 1997), 128.

In keeping with this understanding, we should also recognize that our knowledge of God is not "objective" and detached, but personal and participatory. The Trinity does not merely present a way of life, a way of relationality that we may choose to imitate in our own discrete sphere. Rather, it stands as the source and ground of our very being as free yet interrelated creatures. Christians may thus claim that our participation in the triune God is what enables our truest and most appropriate relation to our neighbor. Of course, this participation in God is not something we achieve; it is a gracious gift of God the Father, represented in our sharing the Son's baptism, as made effective through the Holy Spirit. In Christ, we are adopted into the triune life of God, and on this basis we are simultaneously free to be ourselves for the very first time and bound to be as God intended us from that point on. That is, through our baptism in Christ and thus into the life of the triune God, we find our own most basic and personal identity, and insofar as we are grounded in the being and relation of the Father, Son, and Spirit, we are enabled truly and properly to relate to others. Of course, the Christian understanding of humanity's "fall" acknowledges that this grounding has been corrupted, so that its fruition no longer occurs naturally or inevitably. A separation exists between humanity and God that requires atonement. But with such atonement, real participation again becomes possible. And, as I will develop more fully in the chapters that follow, this participation in God, which is first enabled by atonement but is also the continuing fruit of atonement, offers great benefits: liberation, the renewing power of forgiveness, and a true sense of meaning, purpose, and commitment.

Fourth, I would assert that the paradoxical nature of the doctrine of the Trinity actually serves the ongoing life of faith by making it all that much more difficult to "pin down" or domesticate God. Ellen Charry makes this point succinctly.[12] She observes that especially in our age and culture, with its tendency to reduce God either to some rational or moral principle or to some sentimental or idiosyncratic experience, the doctrine of the Trinity remains elusive, even alien, and that helps keep us honest. The doctrine resists any final resolution, which means we must keep wrestling with it, and therefore also with God.

Fifth and finally, in a culture with many gods and many idols—some obviously religious, some not—the doctrine of the Trinity identifies the Christian God. This claim is implicit in the first two points made

---

12. See her "Spiritual Formation by the Doctrine of the Trinity," *Theology Today* 54, no. 3 (October 1997): 372f.

above, but it is worth making explicit because *our* age, like the early Christian era, is a highly pluralistic, indeed, fragmented age. We cannot simply assume that when we use the word "God" everyone will think the same thing; we cannot assume that in discussing "God" we all start with the same presuppositions or reach the same conclusions. But when we identify God with the phrase "Father, Son, and Holy Spirit," we are identifying in a very precise and particular way the Being whom Christians worship and proclaim—and without this anchoring phrase, we are implicitly or explicitly speaking of a different God. This is the appellation that ties our language of God to the witness of Scripture and the long history of the Christian tradition. This is the name by which we and all Christians—past, present, and future—are incorporated into the body of Christ through baptism.

Having offered five reasons for the continued relevance and centrality of the Trinity for everyday Christian faith, I want to describe briefly some of the key assumptions, implications, and contested claims lying behind the points just made. One of these is the relation between two concepts customarily used to make trinitarian conversations more precise, as indicated by the two labels distinguishing between the "economic" and "immanent" Trinities. The first of these two terms refers to the Trinity as it acts and is experienced in the "economy" of salvation, which is to say, the particular order or unfolding by which God enacts salvation in history. As suggested above, the doctrine of the Trinity emerged as a way of making sense out of a new divine-human encounter. The activity of God in Israel's previous history was presupposed, but now the activity of first Christ and then the Spirit had to be incorporated into this saving history. This threefold activity is referred to as that of the "economic" Trinity. The second term, the "immanent" Trinity, refers to the triadic interrelation of Father, Son, and Spirit within the Godhead itself, apart from any engagement with the created order. The immanent Trinity points to the inner life of God, and affirms that the divine life is in itself, and not merely in its historical activity or in our experience of it, triadic in nature. Thus, the two "Trinities" are distinguishable, but it is a crucial theological point to recognize that they are not separable. Like many other theologians showing renewed interest in the Trinity, I recognize the "epistemological primacy" of the economic Trinity: we know that God is trinitarian because we have experienced him that way. We can speak of the immanent Trinity only because of the encounter with the economic. Christians do not posit the Trinity *ex nihilo;* they do not deduce it as some general and necessary principle or induce it from observations of the world. Rather, Christians speak of God as Trinity because God himself has revealed this triadic being and character to his people in saving relationship with them. This is the story recounted in the narrative of Scripture. Nevertheless, having said this, I also maintain the "ontological primacy" of the immanent Trinity: we know this about God because that is in fact the way he truly is. The revelation of God as triune stems from the prior fact that God's very being is triune. To summarize in a more concise fashion, we *know* God by what he *does* for us in his saving acts, and what he *does* reveals what he *is*—and his *is* not just "for us" or merely in our experience of him, but as he is *in himself*.

Why is it important to maintain these two complementary notions? Because, on the one hand, tying the immanent to the economic guards against the tendency to abstract speculation; the immanent Trinity is *none other* than that made known in salvation history, preeminently in Christ, and it must remain anchored there or cease being a truly Christian understanding. On the other hand, recognizing the immanent Trinity as the *ground* for the economic assures us that in the revealed Trinity we have to do with *none other* than the Godhead itself and the constancy that implies. Without such a grounding or anchor, we could imagine the revelation of another economy and, by implication, another God "behind" the Trinity. The danger may also be described in another way. As Colin Gunton clarifies, if one does not allow God to remain God in the immanent Trinity, with the economic Trinity referring to divine action in the creaturely sphere, then one of two unfortunate consequences results. Either one reduces the personal triune God to a kind of abstract and impersonal historical principle, like Hegel's dialectic, or one robs creation of its own integrity and independent existence by reducing it to being an emanation or aspect of God.[13] So again, the economic and immanent "Trinities" are not separable, yet they do remain distinct. We may not collapse one into the other, but neither are they arbitrarily juxtaposed. Their relation may be formulated thus: the economic *reveals* the immanent, while the immanent is the *basis* for the economic.

Consider next the issues lying behind one of the other points made above. It has been commonplace in Western Christianity, from its earliest centuries, to stress the simplicity of God. The idea stems from the

---

13. See Gunton, *The Promise of Trinitarian Theology*, 23–26, 83–99, 103–17, 128, 132, 142–43, and 201–4.

influence of neoplatonism, and it runs like a red thread through the thought of some of the West's greatest theologians (such as Augustine, Thomas Aquinas, and Friedrich Schleiermacher). An insistence on God's simplicity was deemed necessary because it seemed required by God's perfection: any change in God could only imply either a movement from a lesser to a greater or a greater to a lesser. Such a thought could not be properly ascribed to God, therefore God must be "simple." Of course, the Christian tradition had always maintained its Jewish inheritance that "the Lord our God, the Lord is one," so this emphasis on the divine unity and simplicity appeared self-evident. But it should be clear that as the idea was expounded in theology, its roots were more in the presuppositions of neoplatonism than of the scriptural witness. The divine "simplicity" was typically explained in terms that evoked images of God's homogenous uniformity and eternal inertia. Such images hardly correspond to the Bible's accounts of a vital and dynamic God, actively concerned and involved with his creation generally and his chosen people in particular. This is not to say that the biblical narratives do not speak to the affirmation of God's simplicity, because they do. But that "simplicity" is portrayed in terms of God's unchanging holiness and righteousness, his single-minded purpose for creation, and the unflagging faithfulness and constancy of his love even when his people are faithless. It is not portrayed in terms that evoke images of unchanging and unchangeable stasis.

In this regard, understanding the triune nature and life of God should not fall prey to these neoplatonic assumptions about the divine "simplicity." I assume that the three persons of the Trinity are equal in divinity and of "one mind and heart" in their intention for creation, but they are differentiated in their relation to one another and in how they carry out their roles toward creation. Theologians employ two concepts to help maintain this dialectical tension. On the one hand, the term "perichoresis" emerged as a way to ensure this understanding of God's dynamic unity of being and purpose within the Godhead. The notion originated in the Eastern church, where it is used to discuss the dynamic nature of the immanent Trinity. It is a wonderfully evocative term that some scholars say is derived from the same root as the word "choreography." It speaks to the mutual interaction or "dance" of the three persons of the Trinity. If you have one, you have the other two, even while you cannot reduce or merge one into any other. Celtic knots are a good visual illustration: their intertwined lines form a harmonious whole, yet those lines also pull the eye along in continuous movement.

When I use the term perichoresis in this work, I expand its meaning beyond its historic locus in discussions of the immanent Trinity to help explain the traditional affirmation that "the external works of the Trinity are undivided" *(opera trinitatis ad extra indivisa sunt)*.

On the other hand, the term "appropriation" is now often employed as presupposing but also balancing the affirmation of perichoresis. That is, the term points to the sense that it is "appropriate" to speak of each trinitarian person doing a particular work. Thus, the act of creation is typically ascribed primarily to the Father, redemption primarily to the Son, and sustaining or sanctification primarily to the Holy Spirit, although the faith affirms that all the persons are involved in each of these external acts. Historically, the concept arose in the West, as a corrective to a doctrine of God that so stressed the divine unity that it could be taken as implying an "interchangeability" among the persons and their works. The concept of appropriation means it would be a mistake to assume that each divine role emerges arbitrarily, as if the Father could have been incarnate as the Christ, or the Son become the "paraclete." When I employ the term, it will signify that the persons and relations of the immanent Trinity are reflected in a corresponding sense with the roles that each plays in the economy of salvation, in particular as that is effected in the work of the Mediator, Jesus Christ. In this sense, when I use the concepts of perichoresis and appropriation in this work, it will extend their original definitions to describe in reference to the atonement the way that the divine persons and works complement and complete each other. For to my mind, the doctrines of the Trinity and the atonement belong necessarily together, if one is to correctly understand either.

Use of the Threefold Office *(Munus Triplex)* in the Reformed Tradition

Jesus acquired the titles prophet, priest, and king because the church confessed him as the *Christ,* the Messiah, the *anointed.* The Old Testament suggests that anointing served as the inaugural sign for three "offices": prophets, priests, and kings (see 1 Kgs 19:16, Exod 28:41, 1 Sam 15:1). Seeing Jesus as the fulfillment of each of the offices respectively is as old as the New Testament accounts themselves. Ascribing these three offices simultaneously to the one figure, Jesus, and developing them together theologically is, however, slightly more recent. Several sources indicate that the development of the notion of a distinct "threefold office" began no later than the *Ecclesiastical History* of Eusebius of Caesarea, published in 324–325.[14] However, Eusebius's main concern was not to develop the internal logic of the threefold office in a christological or soteriological way, but simply to argue that previous priests, kings, and prophets were typological foreshadowings of "the only true Christ of God."[15] John Chrysostom (c. 347–407) also referred to the "threefold dignity" of Christ being king, prophet, and priest, according to Thomas Aquinas's quotation of him in the latter's *Catena Aurea,* a commentary on the four gospels collected out of the works of the early church fathers.[16] Like Eusebius before him, Chrysostom implies a typological connection between Old Testament figures (specifically, Abraham and David) and Christ, and indicates Christ's greater status: Abraham was a prophet and priest, but not a king, while David was a king and prophet, but not a priest. Christ, "the son of both," surpasses his forefathers because he obtains all three dignities. Peter Chrysologus (c. 400–450), bishop of Ravenna, also used this framework to explain why Jesus bears the title Christ: "He was called 'Christ' by anointing, and 'Jesus' by name because He poured Himself forth on those anointed with the full plenitude of the Spirit of divinity which in former times had been gathered together through kings, prophets, and priests, into one person, this king of kings, priest of priests, prophet of prophets."[17] Thomas Aquinas, in addition to citing Chrysostom, mentioned a variation of the triad himself in the *Summa Theologica,* where he observes that among humans, "one is a lawgiver, another is a priest, another is a king; but all these concur in Christ as the fount of all grace."[18] Several centuries later, the Catholic

---

14. Alister McGrath, *Introduction to Christian Theology,* 2nd edition (Cambridge, Mass.: Blackwell Publishers, 1997), 348, and Karin Bornkamm, "Die reformatorische Lehre vom Amt Christi und ihre Umformung durch Karl Barth," *Zeitschrift für Theologie und Kirche,* Beiheft 6 (1986), 2.

15. Eusebius of Caesarea, *Ecclesiastical History* (trans. by Kirsopp Lake; Loeb Classical Library no. 153; Cambridge, Mass.: Harvard University Press, 1926), 35.

16. Thomas Aquinas, *Catena Aurea* (trans. J. H. Parker; London: J. G. F. and J. Rivington, 1842), 11. The sources are not precise in this work. The quotation appears to come from Chrysostom's Homily 2 on Matt 1:1, in his collection of homilies on Matthew. This is how J. F. Jansen understands it in his book *Calvin's Doctrine of the Work of Christ* (London: James Clarke & Co., Ltd., 1956), 30. Yet I can locate no such passage in that or the other homily on Matt 1:1.

17. From Chrysologus's sermon 59, quoted in Jansen, *Calvin's Doctrine,* 30–31. It is not clear from Jansen's excerpt to whom the second "He" refers: the Son or the Father.

18. *Summa theologiae,* III, 22, 2.

humanist Erasmus described Christ as "the prophet of prophets," the "priest who has given himself as victim to purge all the sins of those who believe in him," and the "ruler to whom all power has been given."[19]

Among Protestant theologians, Martin Bucer (1491–1551) and Andreas Osiander (1496/8–1552) were apparently the first to portray Christ in terms of the threefold office. Osiander approached it as Chrystologus had, as a way of explaining the title "Christ" in its historical connection with anointing. But he also added a brief indication of its theological significance for Christians.[20] Geoffrey Wainwright points out that Bucer employed the *triplex munex Christi* in his gospel commentaries as early as the 1520s. Bucer makes the historical association, but also offers a rudimentary explanation of its theological significance for the Christian faithful:

> Just as they used to anoint kings, priests and prophets to institute them in their offices, so now Christ is king of kings *(rex regum)*, highest priest *(summus sacerdos)*, and chief of the prophets *(prophetum caput)*. He does not rule in the manner of an external empire; he does not sacrifice with brute beasts; he does not teach and admonish only with an external voice. Rather, by the Holy Spirit he directs minds and wills in the way of eternal salvation; by the Spirit he offered himself as an expiatory sacrifice for us, so that we too might become an acceptable offering to God; and by the same Spirit he teaches and admonishes, in order that those destined for his kingdom may be made righteous, holy and blessed in all things.[21]

The way that Bucer describes Christ's unique exercise of these offices includes the Spirit's role. Bucer's description points to the way I describe Christ's work as a trinitarian undertaking that fulfills and redefines these

---

19. From his *Commentary on the Second Psalm* (1522), as quoted in Geoffrey Wainwright, *For Our Salvation: Two Approaches to the Work of Christ* (Grand Rapids, Mich.: Eerdmans, 1997), 103.

20. Osiander wrote: "For as Christ means anointed, and only prophets, kings, and priests were anointed, so one sees that all three offices apply to Him: the prophetic office, for He is our teacher and master (Matt 23:8), the kingly authority, for He rules forever in the house of Jacob (Luke 1:32), and the priestly office, for He is a priest forever according to the order of Melchizidec (Ps 110:1). That is now His office, that He may be our wisdom, righteousness, sanctification, and redemption, as Paul testifies (1 Cor 1:30)." From Osiander's "Schirmschrift zum Augsburger Reichstag," 1530, quoted in Gussmann, *Quellen und Forshungen zur Geschichte des Augsburgischer Glaubensbekenntnisses* (I/1; Berlin, 1911), 302, as cited by Jansen, *Calvin's Doctrine*, 37.

21. Wainwright, *For Our Salvation*, 104.

offices. Wainwright also observes that Bucer's example likely inspired the one most influential in employing this framework, namely John Calvin (1509–1564).[22] This seems a reasonable conclusion, given the fact that Calvin spent three years (1538–1541) in Strasbourg at Bucer's invitation and, in certain key respects, under his tutelage.

All of this indicates that the notion of the threefold office was by no means restricted to the theological reflection of Calvin or the Reformed tradition. Nevertheless, it is fair to say that the threefold office became a characteristically Reformed way of unpacking theologically the various works of the one Mediator, Christ, and this is due to Calvin's lead. He employed the concept in his Genevan Catechism (1545) by using it to frame his answers to questions 34 through 36. In the 1559 edition of his *Institutes*, Calvin spends a whole chapter expounding the concept and presenting the scriptural basis and support for it (*Institutes*, book II, chapter 15, which has six sections). I want to consider that treatment in some depth. He starts with a consideration of Christ as prophet, which role he understands as equivalent to a "teacher of doctrine." According to Calvin, this is the role that Old Testament prophets had played, so that God's people were never left "without useful doctrine sufficient for salvation,"[23] and this is the role that Christ played—and brought to fulfillment. Thus, Christ is both like the Old Testament prophets, in that he is anointed by the Holy Spirit to teach the people saving knowledge of God, and unlike those prophets, in that after him the office of prophet is "closed," becoming his in power and perpetuity. Calvin writes that Christ "received anointing, not only for himself that he might carry out the office of teaching, but for his whole body [i.e., the church] that the power of the Spirit might be present in the continuing preaching of the gospel. This, however, remains certain: the perfect doctrine he has brought has made an end to all prophecies" (2.496). Intriguingly, Calvin makes both an exclusive and dynamic claim here. There will be no new revelation that surpasses that of the gospel, but that does not mean the gospel remains rooted in the past. Christ's prophetic anointing by the Spirit is such that by its power the gospel can be made ever new.

---

22. Ibid.

23. John Baillie, John T. McNeill, and Henry P. Van Dusen, eds., *Calvin: Institutes of the Christian Religion* (vol. 20 of *The Library of Christian Classics*; ed. John T. McNeill; trans. Ford Lewis Battles; Philadelphia: Westminster, 1960), 495. Hereafter in this chapter, I will refer to it parenthetically in the text. All subsequent citations are from book 2, chapter 15. Specific citations include section and page numbers.

Calvin next considers Christ's royal office, which he immediately cautions "is spiritual in nature" (3.496ff.). Only with this spiritual character can it have its eternal efficacy for the church as a whole and for each individual member thereof. The alternative, which Calvin rejects, is construing Christ as any sort of temporal or earthly ruler. This option is a dead end, as the decline of the Davidic monarchy and the eventual fall of both Israel and Judah indicate. Instead, to recognize Christ's kingship is to recognize that he is the eternal protector and defender of the church, which assures its everlasting preservation. Even if the devil were to avail himself of all the world's resources, the survival of the church would not be in doubt because it is founded upon Christ's eternal throne. As for the individual Christian, while his or her worldly survival is not necessarily assured, the hope for blessed immortality is. Indeed, Calvin makes it quite clear that

> the happiness promised us in Christ does not consist in outward advantages—such as leading a joyous and peaceful life, having rich possessions, being safe from harm, and abounding in delights such as the flesh commonly longs after. No, our happiness belongs to the heavenly life! . . . Christ enriches his people with all things necessary for the eternal salvation of souls and fortifies them with courage to stand unconquerable against all the assaults of spiritual enemies. From this we infer that he rules—inwardly and outwardly—more for our own sake than his. Hence we are furnished, as far as God knows to be expedient for us, with the gifts of the Spirit, which we lack by nature. By these first fruits we may perceive that we are truly joined to God in perfect blessedness. . . .
>
> Thus it is that we may patiently pass through this life with its misery, hunger, cold, contempt, reproaches, and other troubles—content with this one thing: that our King will never leave us destitute, but will provide for our needs until, our warfare ended, we are called to triumph. (4.498–99)

Calvin recognizes that Christ has redefined the meaning of "kingship," and he just as clearly recognizes the liberating power that faith in this form of kingship brings to the Christian believer. Properly understood and embraced, such faith frees one from the fleshly enticements and temptations of the world, as well as its psychological burdens and spiritual corruptions. For Christ's anointing is not one of oils and unguents, but of "the spirit of wisdom and understanding, the spirit of counsel and might . . . and of the fear of the Lord" (Isa 11:2). Calvin sees this anointing symbolized in the Spirit's dove-like appearance at Jesus' baptism, and he indicates how, on this basis, Christians receive their spiritual gifts through their own baptism into Christ: "Especially with regard to heavenly life, there is no drop of vigor in us save what the Holy Spirit instills. For the Spirit has chosen Christ as his seat, that from him might abundantly flow the heavenly riches of which we are in such need. The believers stand unconquered through the strength of their king, and his spiritual riches abound for them" (5.500). In other words, just as the Spirit's anointing affirms Christ as *Christ* (i.e., *the* anointed), so, too, the Spirit's anointing of Christians with new life (or "vigor") properly makes them *Christians*.

Calvin acknowledges that Christ's kingship is not absolute. Rather, he reigns as the "deputy" of the Father. While all power is indeed granted to the Son, its comes from, and will eventually return to, the Father. On this matter, Calvin once again draws a distinction between the larger picture of the church and the whole course of history and the individual Christian in his or her far briefer span. Regarding the latter, Calvin paints a picture of the Son's nurturing care: "For the short time we wander away from God, Christ stands in our midst, to lead us little by little to a firm union with God" (5.500). Christ's kingly rule over godly individuals is portrayed in pastoral terms, the suggestion being that when these individuals are united with God the Father, this aspect of Christ's work is complete. By contrast, Calvin's description of the larger picture evokes not a sense of Christ's pastoral role, but of his sovereign role as protector of the church and judge of the world. But this role, too, has its culmination and limit: Calvin observes that the Last Judgment "may also be properly considered the last act of his reign" (5.501). Calvin insists that none of these observations are to be taken as denying the eternity of Christ's rule, only that "in that perfect glory the administration of the Kingdom will not be as it is now" (5.500). This response may seem to leave matters dangling, but given Calvin's staunch resistance to theological speculation on matters not revealed, it is not a surprising response.

Calvin then considers how Christ fulfills the office of priest. He asserts that Christ accomplishes his reconciliation of humanity to God by offering himself as a pure and holy sacrifice to appease God's wrath and anger with us. The theology of the Letter to the Hebrews is evident in Calvin's treatment, and in summing up that letter's argument Calvin clearly intends to sum up his own position: "The priestly office belongs to Christ alone because by the sacrifice of his death he blotted out our own guilt and made satisfaction for our sins" (6.502). Interestingly, Calvin insists that "we or our prayers have no access to God unless Christ, as our High Priest, having washed away our sins, sanctifies us and obtains for us that grace from which the uncleanness of our transgressions and vice debars us" (6.502). This appears to indicate that Calvin assigned a certain priority to this office, at least over that of the office of prophet. I discuss my own order of priority in the appropriate sections of chapters 4, 5, and 6. This priestly access is not merely a matter of something accomplished in the past. Calvin describes Christ as "an everlasting intercessor," and points to this continuing work as the basis for Christian trust in prayer and peaceful consciences.

In a manner analogous to his previous description of how Jesus' anointing as Christ becomes the basis for our anointing as Christians, Calvin also describes Christ's priestly office as one opened up to us "in him." That is, all the characteristics that allow Christ to enter into the heavenly sanctuary are imputed to us: "For we, imbued with his holiness in so far as he has consecrated us to the Father with himself, although we would otherwise be loathsome to him, please him as pure and clean—and even as holy" (6.502). Thus, Calvin presents his theological basis for the notion of the "priesthood of all believers." The notion of imputation to all, in addition to the assumption of Christ's unique and final sacrifice, enables Calvin to repudiate the Roman view of the Mass as a repeated sacrifice of Christ. And on this note, he concludes his exposition of Christ's threefold office.

Numerous other Reformed theologians employed the threefold office framework—far more than the limited scope of this chapter can attend to fully. One way to summarize this number is to consider Heinrich Heppe's nineteenth-century textbook compendium, *Reformed Dogmatics*.[24] Some readers will recall that Karl Barth relied heavily on this text as he sought to establish his own theological work more self-consciously on a Reformed foundation, especially as he prepared his 1924 Göttingen lectures on dogmatics.[25] Heppe's approach, to continue the foundation analogy, may be likened to a masonry wall: a vast number of shorter and longer citations taken from historic Reformed theologians serve as the bricks of the wall, while Heppe's own expositional and linking comments serve as the mortar. Obviously, such an approach

---

24. Heinrich Heppe, *Reformed Dogmatics: Set Out and Illustrated from Its Sources* (rev. ed.; ed. Ernst Bizer; trans. G. T. Thomson; London: George Allen & Unwin, Ltd., 1950).
25. Heppe, *Reformed Dogmatics*, v.

presupposes a consistency of Reformed teaching that can gloss over contextual nuances and historical differences, but it nevertheless illustrates certain theological patterns and trajectories that are in fact discernible, as well as ecclesiologically appropriate and useful. One of these patterns is, as one could expect, employing the threefold office to explain the work of Christ. Heppe structures his chapter "The Mediatorial Office of Jesus Christ" using this framework, and cites well over a dozen different Reformed theologians of the sixteenth and seventeenth centuries as sources. Heppe uses the words of one of these figures, seventeenth-century theologian Johannes Henricus Heidegger, to offer an introductory summary. I quote them to give a sample of the reasoning evident throughout this section:

> In olden times men of three classes were wont to be anointed, prophets, priests, and kings. Since, then, the truth of ancient unction is to be sought in Christ, just as prophets, priests, and kings were consecrated to their office by outward unctions, so Christ had to exist anointed by God Himself to be prophet, priest, and king. (2) It is abundantly clear that both Moses the prophet bore the type of Christ the prophet, the Aaronic priests that of Christ the priest and the kings of the people Israel, above all David, that of Christ the King. (3) There was added the native condition and indigence of man corrupted by sin, to remove which Christ became the mediator. By nature and by ignorance of spiritual things man was immersed in darkness and was alienated from God and was plainly incapable of returning to Him. Christ, therefore, who was come *sôsai tó àpololós* Matt 18:12 [see Luke 19:10, Matt text doubtful] opposed a triple cure to sweep away this triple misery. As a prophet he ousted ignorance, Matt 23:10 (neither be ye called masters); as a priest he bore alienation from God and His life, Eph 2:13 (ye that were far off are made nigh in the blood of Christ); and as king he filled up the impotence to return to God, Ps 23:3–4 (restoreth, etc.: yea tho' I walk, etc.), 139:24 (lead me in the way everlasting). Rev 7:17 (the Lamb shall guide them unto fountains of waters of life). (4) Moreover the method of conferring salvation upon us imposed the threefold office on Christ. He was bound both as prophet to instruct us by giving teaching anent salvation, in the fruition of which our felicity consists; and as priest to acquire the same through his blood by satisfying the law; and as king by his Spirit to confer the salvation acquired. (5) In a word, in this way he also executed his office. First as a prophet he taught the will of the Father and sealed his teaching by miracles; he bore himself as a priest by

offering his own blood on earth and by entering therewith into the heavenly holy place and standing there before the Father's face; and at length in heaven as King he was crowned with glory and sat down at the right hand of the Father.[26]

Several points in this excerpt deserve highlighting, especially given the general theological assumptions of our modern era and the purposes of this book. First, notice how Heidegger typologically compares Christ and his threefold office with diverse Old Testament figures and their offices, and indicates that primacy belongs to Christ, in that he establishes the standard of which the *others* are "types." Recalling my discussion above concerning theological exegesis, this reflects the role of Christ as the central *Sache* ("subject matter") and interpretive key of the Bible. Second, note how Heidegger posits a "triple misery" that requires a "triple cure." That is, he refuses to define the human predicament in a simplistic, "one-size-fits-all" manner. Rather, he recognizes that our separation from God results from several interacting conditions. As a corollary, he affirms that therefore salvation will also take a multivalent form. In other words, Heppe's use of Heidegger at this juncture suggests that the threefold office framework enabled both a nuanced and integrated interpretation of the work of Christ, along with the doctrines of sin and salvation. This supposition is borne out as Heppe goes on to consider each of the offices in turn—and in considerably more detail, including an extensive treatment of the "satisfaction" that Christ offers as priest.

The threefold office framework was also employed by key Reformed theologians of the modern era. Some who deserve mention include Friedrich Schleiermacher, Charles Hodge, Emil Brunner, and Karl Barth.[27] Theological analysis of their positions is readily available elsewhere, so rather than consider their work I will shift my focus to another aspect of the Reformed tradition. The *munus triplex* framework

---

26. Ibid., 452–53.

27. Friedrich Schleiermacher, *The Christian Faith* (ed. H. R. Mackintosh and J. S. Stewart; Edinburgh: T&T Clark, 1928), §§102–5 (pp. 438–75); Charles Hodge, *Systematic Theology* (New York: Scribner, 1929), 2:459–609; Emil Brunner, *The Christian Doctrine of Creation and Redemption* (trans. O. Wyon; London: Lutterworth Press, 1952), 271–321. See Karl Barth, *Church Dogmatics* (IV/1; trans. G. Bromiley; Edinburgh: T&T Clark, 1956), §58.4 (pp. 128–54). This subsection of Barth's *Dogmatics* offers a survey of his doctrine of reconciliation, and the role the *munus triplex* will play within it. However, Barth's actual exposition of Christ's threefold office occurs in three different sections: §59 (CD IV/1, Christ as high priest), §64 (CD IV/2, Christ as king), and §69 (CD IV/3, Christ as prophet).

also appears in Reformed catechisms, including Calvin's catechism of 1545, where he used the framework to explain the meaning of "Christ" in a series of three questions-and-answers (questions 34–36). In 1563, the Heidelberg Catechism made the same connection between the title "Christ" and the threefold office, and thus it began its historic influence of embedding this understanding in the consciousness of countless Christians. Question 31 of that document asks, "Why is he called Christ, that is, the anointed one?" The given response:

> Because he is ordained by God the Father and anointed with the Holy Spirit to be *our chief Prophet* and *Teacher,* fully revealing to us the secret purpose and will of God concerning our redemption; to be *our only High Priest,* having redeemed us by the one sacrifice of his body and ever interceding with us with the Father; and to be *our eternal King,* governing us by his Word and Spirit, and defending and sustaining us in the redemption he has won for us.[28]

In very succinct fashion, this answer sounds several themes that have become common in Reformed understanding. First, the office of prophet is understood primarily in terms of "teacher," as the one who instructs us in God's redemptive will. Next, the office of priest is understood primarily in terms of the vicarious self-sacrifice offered once, but with ever renewed benefit through his continuing intercession. And third, the office of king is understood in terms of Christ's world-changing victory and ongoing sovereignty in the church and the world. Moving from the continent across the English Channel, the Westminster Confession (in chapter 8) and the Westminster Shorter and Longer Catechisms (in questions 23–28 and 42–56, respectively) also framed their treatments of Christ's work in terms of the threefold office. One intriguing theological development in these documents consists of their combination of the threefold office with the theme of Christ's humiliation and exaltation.

This threefold framework was not restricted to formal theological expositions or works of instruction. In the hymnody of the Congregationalist Isaac Watts, it also took poetic form (arising perhaps out of a youthful inculcation in the Westminster Catechism?). Consider the following work, from his *Hymns and Spiritual Songs* of 1707:

---

28. Allen O. Miller and M. Eugene Osterhaven, trans., *The Heidelberg Catechism: 400th Anniversary Edition* (Cleveland: United Church Press, 1962), 36.

¹ We bless the prophet of the Lord,
 That comes with truth and grace;
Jesus, thy Spirit and thy word
 Shall lead us in thy ways.
² We reverence our High-Priest above,
 Who offered up his blood;
And lives to carry on his love,
 By pleading with our God.
³ We honour our exalted King;
 How sweet are his commands!
He guards our souls from hell and sin,
 By his almighty hands.
⁴ Hosanna to his glorious name,
 Who saves by different ways;
His mercies lay a sovereign claim
 to our immortal praise.²⁹

A fuller hymnic treatment of the theme appeared a little over a century later and across the Atlantic in the hymnal of the Reformed Dutch Church in North America:

¹ Join all the glorious names
 Of wisdom, love, and power,
 That ever mortals knew,
 That angels ever bore;
All are too mean to speak his worth;
Too mean to set my Saviour forth.
² Great *Prophet* of my God,
 My tongue would bless thy name:
 By thee the joyful news
 Of our salvation came;
The joyful news of sins forgiv'n,
Of hell subdued, and peace with heav'n.
³ Jesus, my great *High Priest*,
 Offer'd his blood, and died;
 My guilty conscience seeks
 No sacrifice beside.

---

29. Samuel Worcester, ed., *The Psalms, Hymns, and Spiritual Songs of the Rev. Isaac Watts* (new ed.; Boston: Croker & Brewster, 1855), hymn 132, p. 452.

His pow'rful blood did once atone;
And now it pleads before the throne.
4 My dear and mighty Lord,
    My conqu'ror, and my *King;*
    Thy sceptre and thy sword,
    Thy reigning grace I sing.
Thine is the pow'r; behold! I sit
In willing bonds beneath thy feet.
5 Now let my soul arise,
    And tread the tempter down:
    My *Saviour* leads me forth
    To conquest and a crown.
A feeble saint shall win the day,
Tho' death and hell obstruct the way.
6 Should all the hosts of hell,
    and pow'rs of death unknown,
    Put their most dreadful forms,
    Of death and mischief, on:
I shall be safe, for Christ displays
Superior pow'r and guardian grace.[30]

While this Dutch Reformed hymnal does not mention the author of this piece, the hymn preceding it is, in fact, the Watts piece cited above. The hymnal placed them together because it was intentionally structured to complement the Heidelberg Catechism, and it used these hymns to explain Christ's offices.

To summarize, the Reformed reading of the Bible understood each and all of these "offices" as serving a mediatorial function between God and the covenant people. The king mediated the sovereignty of God, the priest mediated the holiness and forgiveness of God, and the prophet mediated the truth and commands of God. Understanding these offices as now belonging preeminently to Jesus Christ thus suggests that in matters political and social, in matters religious and sacred, in matters legal, moral, and hermeneutical, Christ stands as the unique mediator of God's will and work, and thus as the church's primary authority in these arenas. This further suggests that a Christian understanding of the offices of

---

30. John H. Livingston, ed., *The Psalms and Hymns, with Catechism, Confession of Faith, and Liturgy, of the Reformed Dutch Church in North America* (Philadelphia: G. W. Mentz & Son, 1840), hymn 12, second part, 295–96.

"king, priest, and prophet" must be determined from Christ's fulfillment of them. That is, we cannot come to a proper definition apart
from the biblical witness. Indeed, and even more pointedly, we cannot
come to a proper understanding of them apart from the New Testament
witness. For while the offices and their meaning originated in the ongoing relation of God with Israel, even a cursory reading of the New
Testament soon makes it clear that Christ actually *redefined* them in
crucial ways. Additionally, part of that redefinition consists of the fact
that he integrated them all in his own person, which means, as I will
argue, that a Christian appropriation of them must display a similar
combination and balance.

Such a recognition has not always been apparent. Various theologians have tended to choose one of the offices as preeminent over the
others. Luther, with a twofold conception, stressed the priestly; Calvin
(in spite of his use of the threefold framework) stressed the kingly; the
Enlightenment emphasized the prophetic "Christus als Lehrer!"
("Christ as teacher!"); Barth, for quite different reasons and in a far different manner, also stressed the prophetic.[31] Nineteenth-century
German theologian Albrecht Ritschl objected to the term "office," but
still held Christ's kingship to be the "chief thing."[32] While I do maintain a functional subordination of the Son and Spirit to the Father (as
the economy of salvation inevitably implies), I do not think this requires
a corresponding and permanent subordination of two of the offices to
the other. Quite the contrary, I maintain that a "christological equilib-
rium" should be recognized among them. But this does not preclude the
possibility, indeed, the likelihood that in the history of salvation, and
thus in the everyday exercise of pastoral ministry, one may take relative
preeminence over the others. Insofar as Christians emphasize any, such
emphasis must be determined—with the help of Scripture and the Holy
Spirit—by the pastoral context. Christ's work in each office overcomes
in its own way a particular aspect of the human alienation or separation
from God, and these aspects are not always present to the same degree
or in the same way in various situations or with various persons. One
cannot predetermine when the proclamation of which divine work will
be most fitting, in order to be heard by particular persons in a specific
time and place. But if one cannot predetermine the most appropriate

31. Bornkamm, "Lehre vom Amt Christi," 2.

32. An observation made by George W. Stroup, "The Relevance of the *Munus Triplex* for Reformed Theology and Ministry," *Austin Seminary Bulletin* 98 (June 1983): 25.

and faithful response to a given situation, are there at least some sign-posts or guidelines that can help one prepare? The answer, of course, is yes, and such preparation is the practical purpose of what I will present in chapters 4, 5, and 6. But before I move to that undertaking, I want first to explain the general scriptural and trinitarian basis for this three-fold approach.

3

Scripture's Threefold Witness
Tracing the Theological Roots

Having presented my thesis, situated my approach in the theological landscape, and described briefly the approach, methods, and assumptions I will use, we now confront the challenge of putting it all to work. The first question therefore has to be: Does the Bible actually warrant this particular understanding of God's atoning activity? That is, in a close reading of Scripture, does a trinitarian construal of salvation emerge on its own? Or is it read into Scripture? And perhaps more pointedly, even if a trinitarian framework is intrinsic to Scripture, does it have a practical payoff? That is, does such a reading help us see more clearly the full breadth and depth of God's saving work, and thus make it more accessible and relevant for the concrete life of Christian faith? To respond to these questions and to lay the groundwork for the chapters that follow, this chapter will have a threefold task. First, it will demonstrate how a trinitarian framework is not a superficial addition to, but a thoroughly embedded feature of, the New Testament accounts of God and his work. Second, it will highlight how Scripture portrays Christians as those who are called, in a very concrete and necessary sense, to "live in" the Trinity as the basis of their faith and life. And third, shifting the focus from the work of the Father, Son, and Spirit together to the more particular work of the Son, the chapter will begin my account of how this trinitarian matrix may also be perceived in the crucial centrality of Christ's atoning work as king, priest, and prophet.

The Scriptural Compass

The preceding chapter claimed that numerous New Testament passages speak to a "triadic" or "proto-trinitarian" understanding of God and his work. How should such a claim be understood? These passages certainly did not present at the time of their composition a formal doctrine of the Trinity per se, but they nevertheless invited the emergence of a post-scriptural doctrine.[1] That is, they present assumptions and patterns—as well as a fair degree of ambiguity—that encouraged (and perhaps even necessitated) the development of such a doctrine as a logical interpretation and clarification of the biblical witnesses. Some of these passages are very well known, such as Jesus' command to his disciples at the close of Matthew's Gospel that they "make disciples of all nations, baptizing them in the name of the Father and of the Son and of the Holy Spirit" (Matt 28:19). Paul's benediction to the church in Corinth presents another example: "The grace of our Lord Jesus Christ and the love of God and the fellowship of the Holy Spirit be with you all" (2 Cor 13:14). Yet another is the passage from Ephesians that speaks of "one Spirit . . . one Lord, one faith, one baptism, one God and Father of us all" (Eph 4:4–6). Our familiarity with these passages stems largely from their place in the church's liturgy, and this place bespeaks their significance for the church's faith in, and understanding of, the living God it worships.

Were these three well-known examples just isolated examples, one might be tempted to downplay their significance. Yet they are not the only such references in the New Testament. Quite a number of such succinct passages exist, often reflecting either cultic formulations or doctrinal summaries of this nascent trinitarianism. Other, more extended passages also exist, passages that are not formulaic but more narrative. Such lengthier passages may not at first glance appear trinitarian, but they still display a kind of triadic inner logic and structure. Indeed, these more narrative passages are of particular interest to me because they point less to the triadic nature of God understood in the

---

1. I will ask the reader to keep this clarification in mind. I recognize that it is anachronistic to describe scriptural passages as "trinitarian," if for no other reason than the fact that the term (the Latin *trinitas*) did not exist until coined by Tertullian in the third century (although Theophilus of Antioch used a Greek equivalent, *triás*, or "triad," in the second century). However, I will frequently use that term in this chapter, in part to avoid the more cumbersome, albeit historically accurate, term "proto-trinitarian" and in part because my purposes are not predominantly historical but theological. I will, however, also occasionally employ the term "triadic," as a reminder of this distinction.

abstract and more to the triadic character of God's agency in effecting our salvation. That is, they do not concern themselves with making what might be construed as metaphysical descriptions and distinctions regarding God's triune being (and certainly not his inner being, at least not the way later generations would), but they do exhibit considerable nuance in portraying God's triune redemptive activity. To be sure, the character of God's inner being emerges in the descriptions of what he does, but these descriptions are concrete and narrative rather than abstract and philosophical.

In other words, God's essentially triune character emerges indirectly and gradually in the New Testament, much as the character of a novel's protagonist only fully emerges in the actions she takes as the plot runs its course. This being the case, those passages that in effect portray three "protagonists" working as one to fulfill the divine purpose warrant particular attention. Thus, in this chapter I will sketch a basic outline of God's triune activity, in an order that runs the reverse of the New Testament's historical chronology, as that is typically understood by critical scholarship. That is, I will consider the way the "protagonists" Father (or "God"), Son, and Spirit are portrayed first in those New Testament passages describing their particular roles in the life of the community, then in the summary explanations of those in selected passages from Luke-Acts and Jesus' "farewell address" in John 13–17, and finally tracing them back to their basis in the commissioning of Jesus at his baptism. Such an approach better unpacks the logic of the church's theological reflection on its encounter with the triune God. Such an approach also enables some preliminary observations regarding the ways the respective and particular roles of Father, Son, and Spirit are also reflected in the Son's exercise of his threefold messianic office.

The Early Church: Living in the Trinity

The epistles of the New Testament offer ample evidence that the early Christian communities were taught and admonished to live their lives "in the Trinity"—even if the term was yet to be coined and the formal doctrine yet to be determined. That is, there are many passages that contain either a formulaic or more narrative reference to the Father (or God), the Son, and the Holy Spirit as the basis and means of Christian faith. Such references do not have the character of abstract theologizing, but make it clear that the Father, Son, and Spirit are the direct source of the church's actual existence as church. These three do not emerge as concepts or poetic imaginings or as labels for a group ethos, but as personal agents enabling, undergirding, and engaged in the community's life, from its worship to its daily interactions to the personal piety of its members. Simply notice the fact that when the biblical narrative mentions any of these three, at least in those sentences displaying some variation on a subject-predicate-object construction, it so often portrays them as the *subject*. Consider, for example, these excerpts (which one could multiply a hundredfold): "As the Father has sent me, even so I send you" (John 20:21b), "While we were yet sinners Christ died for us" (Rom 5:8b), "And the Spirit said to Philip, 'Go up and join this chariot'" (Acts 8:29). To be sure, the definition of these three acting subjects as "persons" *(hypostases)* will not occur for several centuries; nevertheless, the impulse to speak of them in such terms is not alien to the scriptural narrative but clearly grows out of it. Moreover, scrutiny of the many passages referring to the figures of Father, Son, and Spirit—particularly those in which all three are mentioned—reveals that each has a distinctive, indeed, unique role to play even while they work in harmonious concert to fulfill the one divine plan of atonement.

Consider first some of the brief formulaic passages that appear in several of the Catholic Epistles. Scholars typically view these letters as brief summaries of true Christian faith and behavior meant to counter false teachers and temptations to laxity, addressed to a general audience. Thus, for example, it is significant that already in the opening salutation of 1 Peter, we find a triadic reference. The letter is addressed to the "exiles of the Dispersion in Pontus, Galatia, Cappadocia, Asia, and Bithynia," who are immediately described as "chosen and destined by God the Father and sanctified by the Spirit for obedience to Jesus Christ and for sprinkling with his blood." That is, in one respect, the recipients of this letter are identified by their geographical location. But in a much more significant respect, their true identity appears in the theological summary that follows. Who they are is determined in relation to the threefold act of God. In the most fundamental instance, this consists of the Father's prior election of them (notwithstanding what "election" might mean precisely in this instance). In the next and most immediate instance, their identity is actually effected by their sanctification in the Holy Spirit for obedience. Yet these are neither a generic election nor sanctification. The particular person and work of Jesus Christ determine their orientation and content, and we should notice that the phrase "for sprinkling with his blood" points to the sacrificial, covenantal nature of this orientation and content, and hence Christ's priestly role. Described another way, the Father stands as the source and impetus of this new life and identity, Christ is that life's substance and objective mediator, and the Spirit acts as the means by which it becomes actually present for Christian believers. In the language of this description we may hear logical anticipations of the pronouncements made by the later formal doctrine of the Trinity, especially if we keep in mind David Yeago's distinction between conceptual terms and judgments described in the preceding chapter. An explanation of this orientation and content, and their implication that Christians, too, will likely suffer as Christ did, comprises a significant portion of the letter's subject matter. In sum, the author of this epistle addresses its recipients as those whom God calls to identify themselves with, and accept their incorporation into, his salvation history, as manifested in Christ and made available through the Spirit. And in this case, we may appropriately describe the Christians of these communities as summoned to "live in the Trinity" in a very practical and pious sense.

In the even briefer Epistle of Jude, the triadic formula appears not at the outset but as the climactic admonition of the letter. The threat posed by false teachers and their immoral behavior motivated the writing of the letter, and the author presents a litany of historical examples describing how God has dealt with the rebellious and apostate. Jude also reminds his readers that such turmoil has been prophesied for their own age. He then offers—in what clearly serves as the theological heart of the letter—this exhortation in response: "But you, beloved, build yourselves up on your most holy faith: pray in the Holy Spirit; keep yourselves in the love of God; wait for the mercy of our Lord Jesus Christ unto eternal life" (Jude 20–21). After calling upon them to save those they can, the author ends the letter with a doxology. Once again, a trinitarian reference displays its thoroughly practical character. In this instance, a call to stability and perseverance is sounded, as the verbs themselves reflect ("build," "pray," "keep," and "wait"). Yet clearly success will not come from mere human willpower acting on its own; the concrete life of faith depends upon one's being grounded in the triune God. Or to shift images somewhat, Christian faith is like a stool: it must have its three legs of the Holy Spirit, God, and Christ if it is to stand. This passage also suggests that each divine person functions in a different manner in building up Christian faith. The Holy Spirit serves as the immediate access or effective agent, God's love undergirds and enables the whole, and Christ's mercy is the means and basis for Christian hope. On this last point, the reference to Jesus' mercy may allude to the affirmation of him as the final Judge, the one whose sovereign decision opens the door to life everlasting. In sum, the logic of this passage recapitulates and points to the same dynamic described in 1 Peter.

In 1 John, the last of the Catholic Epistles I will consider, the triadic references are less formulaic and more woven into the letter's theological argument. In this case, too, the author seeks to counter false teaching, reaffirming the incarnation of Jesus Christ even as he seeks to prevent the schism that its denial will cause. The issue finally becomes explicit in chapter 4:

> Beloved, do not believe every spirit, but test the spirits to see whether they are of God; for many false prophets have gone out into the world. By this you know the Spirit of God: every spirit which confesses that Jesus Christ has come in the flesh is of God, and every spirit which does not confess Jesus is not of God. . . . By this we know that we abide in him and he in us, because he has given us his own Spirit. And we have seen and testify that the Father has sent his Son as the Savior of the world. Whoever confesses that Jesus is the Son of God, God abides in him, and he in God. (1 John 1:1–3a, 13–15)

This excerpt illustrates clearly the interlocking relation and activity of the three persons, especially as that is described in verse 2. Consider their interrelation: the Spirit is not free-floating, it is *God's* Spirit—and it confirms itself as such by inspiring the confession of Jesus Christ as the Son of God, come in the flesh. Consider their complementary activity: God the Father initiates the world's salvation by sending his Son, God the Son incarnate as Jesus Christ accomplishes this salvation, and God the Spirit makes this accomplishment available to those confessing Christ. The love of God, which motivates this divine activity in the first place, then becomes the basis and benchmark for life in the community of faith, as the author makes clear in continuing his exhortation:

> We love, because he first loved us. If any one says, "I love God," and hates his brother, he is a liar; for he who does not love his brother whom he has seen, cannot love God whom he has not seen. And this commandment we have from him, that he who loves God should love his brother also.
>
> Every one who believes that Jesus is the Christ is a child of God, and every one who loves the parent loves the child. By this we know that we

love the children of God, when we love God and obey his commandments. (1 John 4:19–5:2)

Christian faith involves more than mere belief; it entails a way of life.
Indeed, it is new life, a reclamation of that which God seeks for all
humanity, a reorientation toward that which God intended from the
moment of creation. And the root and sustenance of that life entails
"living in" or "into" the Trinity.

Next, consider some of the trinitarian narratives as they appear in the
Letter to the Hebrews. I will examine this letter more fully in my fifth
chapter, "Christ the Priest: The Son's Sacrificial Offering," but I do
want to speak now to my assumption that even in Christ's fulfillment
of a particular office we are still dealing with the triune God. Reference
to the three persons of God, Son, and Holy Spirit is spread rather
evenly through the letter (in chapters 2, 3, 6, 9, and 10), and this frames,
structures, and confirms what the author says more specifically about
Christ's work as high priest and sacrifice. Moreover, those references
present a rather complex picture of how these three act and complement
one another. In the first instance, they are portrayed in relation to revelation. Recall the opening of the letter: "In many and various ways God
spoke of old to our fathers by the prophets; but in these last days he has
spoken to us by a Son. . . ." After briefly describing this revelation, the
author begins chapter 2 with an admonition not to drift away from
what has been heard, followed almost immediately with another
description of its authority: "It was declared at first by the Lord, and it
was attested to us by those who heard him, while God also bore witness
by signs and wonders and various miracles and by gifts of the Holy
Spirit distributed according to his own will" (Heb 3:3b–4). In other
words, we should believe it because all three persons of the Trinity have
vouched for it, as well as the disciples.

The next passage (Heb 3:7–14) first portrays the Spirit as offering
witness and admonition ("as the Holy Spirit says," quoting Ps 95:7–11),
then it voices a direct warning ("Take care, brethren, lest . . . you fall
away from the living God"), and then it offers an explanation ("For we
share in Christ, if only we hold our first confidence firm to the end").
That is, matters have to do with more than just revelation, for here the
faithful are described in relation to the living God and as sharing in
Christ. Here also is sounded the recurring concern of the letter: that its
recipients not slacken in their faith despite temptations to the contrary.

This focus on the life of faith and perseverance appears in the next passage as well. Indeed, it develops matters by describing how this faith both does and must progress. It is not enough that one remain firmly rooted; one must also grow. Moreover, one cannot expect restoration of those who have fallen away after having once been enlightened, after having had a solid and undeniable experience of the new life. This amounts to "crucifying again the Son of God" and "holding him up to contempt" (Heb 6:6). Still, the passage does not portray this progress as merely the product of one's own willpower and efforts. By clear implication, the faithful consist of those who "have tasted the heavenly gift, and have shared in the Holy Spirit, and have tasted the goodness of the word of God and the powers of the age to come" (Heb 6:4–5). The reference to "tasting" in this passage may be a literal reference to the elements of the Lord's Supper, but it also figuratively expresses the fact that the faithful are no longer on the fringe. Hence, they must no longer equivocate. They have not only seen God's goodness and power from a distance, they have imbibed it and incorporated it into their personal being.[2] The faithful have what they need to grow and endure to the end—including a participation in the Spirit and eschatological powers—because God has given it to them.

Intriguingly, this assertion of Christians sharing in the Spirit is preceded and paralleled in Christ's sharing in it, according to the next triadic passage, Heb 9:14. Acknowledging the purifying power of earlier sacrifices, the author emphasizes "how much more shall the blood of Christ, who through the eternal Spirit, offered himself to God, purify our conscience from dead works to worship the living God!" Not only does this triadic activity establish the conditions under which the faithful may approach God, it enables that approach: the Spirit in effect brings the faithful into the circle of divine activity itself. The final trinitarian reference in the letter, Heb 10:11–18, offers a summation of God's achievement. Christ has accomplished the once-and-for-all sacrifice, perfecting those who are sanctified and taking his place at the right hand of God. The Holy Spirit had testified to this work in Jer 31:31–34, which speaks of the new covenant, of the law being written on hearts and minds and sins being remembered no more. In light of what had been written earlier in the letter, we may recognize that the

---

2. See Gerhard Kittel and Gerhard Friedrich, ed., *Theological Dictionary of the New Testament* (trans. Geoffrey W. Bromiley; Grand Rapids, Mich.: Eerdmans, 1985), s.v. "*geúomai.*"

Spirit makes the promised new covenant available to the faithful now. In sum, these passages paint a picture of the Spirit as a messenger or teacher, as well as the power enabling the faithful to share in the Son and his benefits—indeed, in some sense enabling the Son himself. These benefits derive in part from the Son's sacrifice, but this sacrifice does not fully define the Son. He is also portrayed as one who reveals God's purpose and will, as well as God's regent, sitting at his right hand. Finally, God is the living God, the source and goal of the Son and Spirit's work and thereby also our source and goal and the proper object of our human devotion.

We turn next to a consideration of the Pauline corpus. The triadic references in these epistles are too numerous for me to consider individually, but even a cursory examination will reveal that they display the same basic characteristics seen in the passages already studied. And like those passages, these references tend to run the gamut from briefer, formulaic pieces to longer, narrative ones. Some of the formulaic pericopes are quite succinct, such as that found in Rom 15:30: "I appeal to you brothers by our Lord Jesus Christ and by the love of the Spirit, to join me in earnest prayer to God on my behalf." Another appears in 2 Cor 1:21–22: "But it is God who establishes us with you in Christ, and has commissioned us; he has put his seal upon us and given us his Spirit in our hearts as a guarantee." And there is the benediction found in 2 Cor 13:14, which I have already mentioned on page 78. Two additional passages urge what could be called a proper faithfulness. The first admonishes: "Rejoice always, pray without ceasing, give thanks in all circumstances; for this is the will of God in Christ Jesus for you. Do not quench the Spirit" (1 Thess 5:16–19). The second repeats this refrain, at somewhat greater length: "Be filled with the Spirit, as you sing psalms and hymns and spiritual songs among yourselves, singing and making melody to the Lord in your hearts, giving thanks to God the Father at all times and for everything in the name of our Lord Jesus Christ" (Eph 5:18b–20). In sum, these passages display a certain "stand-alone" quality—especially the last—although they remain embedded in their respective letters. And again, each succinctly portrays the work of God as a triune activity and Christian existence as irrevocably and richly bound up "in the Trinity," which is to say that the dynamic interrelations of Father, Son, and Spirit become the source, matrix, and sustenance for the Christian's new and ongoing life.

Many others passages are far less succinct. Indeed, they often display a run-on quality or awkward syntax, an indication presumably that theological integrity and completeness trumped stylistic polish in these cases. The passages are not formal or discrete summaries of God's saving work, and they do not display the stand-alone character of those just considered. But they do serve a summarizing or focusing function when they appear in Paul's various arguments and admonitions. Paul apparently felt compelled to include reference to all three persons and a suggestion of their particular contribution to accurately describe God's work or the Christian's response. Consider, for example, the following two excerpts: "God sent his Son . . . so that we might receive adoption as children. And because you are children, God has sent the Spirit of his Son into our hearts, crying, 'Abba! Father!' So you are no longer a slave but a child, and if a child then also an heir, through God" (Gal 4:4b–7). And "For all who are led by the Spirit of God are children of God. For you did not receive a spirit of slavery to fall back into fear, but you have received a spirit of adoption. When we cry, 'Abba! Father!' it is that very Spirit bearing witness with our spirit that we are children of God, and if children, then heirs, heirs of God and joint heirs with Christ" (Rom 8:14–17). These two passages occur in broader segments of Paul's discussion of the law and the Christian's redemption from it, yet they contain within them a virtual synopsis of the entire gospel. What has God done? Sent his Son, sent his (Christ's) Spirit. To what end? That we might receive adoption. Why is this important? It means we share by grace the benefits he receives by right. How is this accomplished? By the Spirit, we are made joint heirs with Christ. How do we know this? The Spirit enables us to call upon the Father just as his Son did. What are we to do? Simply and wholeheartedly embrace that which God in Christ through the Spirit has given us. In other words, here again a passage presents us with a thoroughly embedded "trinitarian" framework: Christian faith comes from and grows out of the Trinity. God the Father is portrayed as the source and initiator, the Son accomplishes what needs to be done, thus comprising the "content" of God's work, and the Spirit makes Christ's accomplishment available and living in the faithful, that their orientation to God might be enabled and made fruitful.

This same character and orientation appears in several Pauline passages that employ an image of the Spirit (or Christ, or Christ's Spirit) "indwelling" believers. The most clearly triadic is a passage from Rom 8:

> But you are not in the flesh; you are in the Spirit, since the Spirit of God dwells in you. Anyone who does not have the Spirit of Christ does not belong to him. But if Christ is in you, though the body is dead because

of sin, the Spirit is life because of righteousness. If the Spirit of him who raised Jesus from the dead dwells in you, he who raised Christ from the dead will give life to your mortal bodies also through his Spirit that dwells in you. (Rom 8:9–11)

This passage illustrates why the church later insisted that "the external works of the trinity are undivided," for clearly all three persons are involved in effecting this salvation. Far less clear is where the work of one begins and that of another leaves off. The dynamic and intertwined description of divine agency blurs the lines. Indeed, it may be improper even to think there are lines to blur—although the pattern of the Father's initiative, the Son's objective accomplishment, and the Spirit's work in making it subjectively available to believers does seem to hold here as it has in previous passages. Other excerpts from the Pauline corpus that employ this image of indwelling include 1 Cor 6:19–20 (especially when it is read keeping 1 Cor 3:16 in mind), Eph 2:18–22, and Eph 3:16–19.

With these last examples, I have perhaps crossed the line from formulaic to more narrative excerpts. I have no stake in maintaining the purity of these categories, only in stressing the pervasiveness of this triadic undercurrent in Pauline thought. For not only does this undercurrent appear in brief and discrete instances (which some might seek to downplay, by arguing that they are imported from elsewhere), it also pervades Paul's more developed positions. Space does not allow a full exposition of these longer narratives, but several of them do deserve summary mention. A brief one is 1 Thess 4:2–8, a passage of ethical instruction (or paraenesis) in which the various particular exhortations are presented within triadic "brackets." Paul opens by stating that the instructions have been given "through the Lord Jesus," to serve "the will of God" concerning their sanctification. The particulars follow. Then Paul closes with the warning, "Whoever rejects this rejects not human authority but God, who also gives his Holy Spirit to you." The triadic foundation of this paraenesis is further established when one recalls the thanksgiving Paul offered to begin this letter. Recognizing that he frequently summarizes the content of his correspondence in these prayers, notice that a trinitarian framework appears there as well:

We always give thanks to God for all of you and mention you in our prayers, constantly remembering before our God and Father your work of faith and labor of love and steadfastness of hope in our Lord Jesus

Christ. For we know, brethren beloved by God, that he has chosen you, because our message of the gospel came to you not in word only, but also in power and in the Holy Spirit and with full conviction. (1 Thess 1:2–5)

To cast matters in modern terms, Paul's ethics always grow out of his theology. In the case of 1 Thess 4:2–8, the trinitarian basis of that ethics is doubly reinforced.

The next narrative excerpt to consider is 1 Cor 12. Paul interweaves references to the activity of God forming this congregation into the one body of Christ through the agency of the Spirit throughout this well-known chapter on spiritual gifts. The chapter addresses very concrete problems in the Corinthian church with very concrete imagery, and it all relies on a trinitarian foundation and framework. In the face of the partisan acrimony threatening the church, Paul acknowledges that there may be differences, but that they may only finally be practical and not fundamental. Fundamentally speaking, we are all one, because "by one Spirit we were all baptized into one body" (v. 13). That is, God incorporates us into the church—the body of Christ—by means of the Holy Spirit. The Spirit enables us to acknowledge that "Jesus is Lord" (v. 3), an affirmation that describes our irreducible orientation and allegiance. Based on that one allegiance, and only on that basis, may we then consider our practical differences. Yet even these must be tested, to see that they originate in God's purpose for the church and not our diverse party interests. They must serve the common good (v. 7), and if they do, that indicates that they come from God. To be sure, mere utility to the common good is not a sufficient test—an orientation to the Lord and serving his purposes is more basic—but it does constitute one variation on judging a tree by its fruit. All of this lies behind Paul's statement, "Now there are varieties of gifts, but the same Spirit; and there are varieties of services, but the same Lord; and there are varieties of activities, but it is the same God who activates all of them in everyone" (vv. 4–6). One could with justification say that the whole chapter is an exegesis and practical application of this particular statement, one more example of how Scripture portrays the Christian life as one lived "in the Trinity."

Next I want to return to Rom 8 for a fuller examination of its trinitarian implications. This theologically rich and evocative chapter functions as both a culmination of Paul's preceding argument and a transition to his consideration of Israel. Nevertheless, I do not propose to offer a thorough exegesis of the chapter or its place in the letter but only to highlight how Paul refers to God (Father), Christ (Christ Jesus,

Son), and Spirit (Spirit of Christ, Spirit of God) and describes their inter-working. To begin, one should simply note how often Paul employs these appellations in this chapter. In its thirty-nine verses, he refers to the Spirit nineteen times, to God nineteen times (plus one more reference to "Abba! Father!"), and to Christ or Son twelve times. This frequency in and of itself suggests that these three persons pervade his theological reasoning here. How does he characterize their activity and relations more specifically? The starting point for Paul's logic is that God has done what the law could not: he sends his Son to condemn sin, that the law's requirement be fulfilled in us (vv. 3–4). The Son's deeds apply to the faithful because of an implied exchange: he has taken on human flesh (v. 3) and believers are "in Christ Jesus" (vv. 1–2, or he is "in" them, v. 10). Paul then suggests that this implicit exchange or sharing of natures is the work of the Spirit, for those who are in Christ "walk" or "live according to the Spirit" (vv. 4–5); they set their mind on the Spirit, not the flesh (vv. 5–8). Put another way, they are "in the Spirit" or the Spirit "dwells" in them (vv. 9 and 11).[3] Paul most often mentions "the Spirit" without further description, but he also refers to it more particularly as the "Spirit of God" (vv. 9 and 14, as well as "the Spirit of him who raised Jesus," v. 11) and the "Spirit of Christ" (v. 10). Interestingly, this ambiguity in verses 9–11 regarding who—or whose—the Spirit is functions to remind readers that the whole undertaking depends upon God's initiative (cf. v. 11 and v. 3) and to reinforce the sense that all three persons are working to a common purpose. Put another way, it also implies that were any of the three left out, the purpose would remain unaccomplished.

Up to this point, I would say that Paul seeks to establish *that* (and to an extent, *how*) the triune God constitutes Christians in a new life and orientation. From verse 12, he describes *why* this matters and *what* benefits Christians may expect if they embrace this new life and orientation "in the Trinity." Those led by the Spirit become thereby "sons" (v. 14) or "children" (vv. 16–17) of God, receiving a "spirit of sonship," which, accompanied by the Holy Spirit, rescues Christians from a spirit of slavery and its fear, while enabling the faithful to say, "Abba! Father!" In addition to this internal, affective transformation, Christians also become heirs with Christ (v. 17), which means they may anticipate an external and glorious inheritance: bodily redemption in a new creation

---

3. Already considered more fully in pp. 86–87.

(vv. 18–23). Paul then connects sharing in Christ's glory with sharing in his suffering. This could be taken to imply that Christian suffering is a precondition of earning the benefit, that Christ provides an example that Christians are to imitate. However, given Paul's theology of grace generally and his description here of the believer's adoption as children of God, it seems more likely that he sees suffering as simply an inevitable accompaniment to being Christian. Given the Spirit's work, Christians really are "in Christ," although the full benefits of that status must await in hope the final new creation. In the meantime, Paul observes, as he suffered, so, too, will Christians generally.[4] Still, it is not that Christ presents a pattern that Christians reproduce on their own. Rather, it is that Christ presents the pattern into which Christians are incorporated by the power of the Spirit. This means that the faithful are not left merely to their own devices: we "have the first fruits of the Spirit" (v. 23) and "the Spirit helps us in our weakness" (v. 26), "because the Spirit intercedes for the saints according to the will of God" (v. 27).

In light of my trinitarian examination, this reference to God at the close of verse 27 serves several functions in what follows it. First, it reminds readers to keep the whole description of the Christian's new life firmly planted in the will and purpose of God. With this as a starting point, Paul can then describe the logical progression that follows: Christians are those whom, according to his purpose, God foreknew, predestined to conformity with his Son, called, justified, and glorified (vv. 28–30). Second, it serves as a transition. In the verses immediately preceding it, God's primary actor has been the Spirit; the verses that follow focus on God's activity through Christ. In a sense, verses 28ff. portray the christological basis and substance of the Spirit's work described in the preceding verses. Without this background or foundation, the Spirit's work would have no content. Thus, third, the end of verse 27 functions as a bridge, connecting references to the work of the Spirit and the work of the Son to the one overarching purpose of God. This purpose derives from God's gracious love for us. While its glorious culmination remains an object of hope in some future time, nevertheless God's love for us in Christ is still, and ever, present. The closing verses of Rom 8 fairly pulse with the dynamic energy of God and his

---

4. L. Ann Jervis, "Accepting Affliction: Paul's Preaching on Suffering" offers a helpful discussion of Paul's thought on this theme. See William P. Brown, ed., *The Character of Scripture: Moral Formation, Community, and Biblical Interpretation* (Grand Rapids, Mich.: Eerdmans, 2002).

Son, Christ Jesus, such that the agency of each appears both distinguishable and indistinguishable. In one respect, God comes across as the active one, with Jesus as his (relatively passive) instrument: God gave up his Son (v. 32), God justifies (v. 33), and God raised Jesus from the dead (v. 34, as the passive verb structure implies). In another respect, however, Jesus also comes across as active: seated at the right hand of God, he "intercedes for us" (v. 34; compare this with v. 27, which describes the Spirit as the intercessor). Additionally, Paul portrays Jesus' love for us as vital, empowering, and fiercely protective (see vv. 35 and 37). Yet finally, whose love is it? God's or Christ's? Paul concludes that no power or circumstance in all creation "will be able to separate us from the love of God in Christ Jesus our Lord" (v. 39). The question appears misplaced: it is one love, made available to the faithful through the combined work of God and Christ (and by implication the Spirit also, who kindles this love in human hearts). In sum, the theological coherence of Rom 8 would collapse if any of the three persons or their work were removed from the logic of Paul's argument. It depends utterly on its presupposition of this one triadic and "tri-active" God.

Some Nascent Trinitarian Reflection

In the passages I have examined so far, the trinitarian element has, for the most part, been taken for granted, not so much explained as assumed. It forms the implicit basis or framework for the theological teaching and ethical exhortation considered, but it has not itself been an object of direct consideration or reflection. This circumstance changes somewhat with the selections I will examine next. To a lesser extent in parts of Luke-Acts and to a greater extent in John's account of Jesus' "Farewell Address," the relations of the three persons and their respective work becomes an actual focus of consideration. To be sure, it does not take on an abstract form in the manner of later trinitarian speculation. But it does become explicit in its own fashion.

I begin my theological investigation of Luke-Acts by taking advantage of what Luke's literary structure offers us. As students of Scripture quickly learn, Luke presents his full account of God's salvific work in a way unique to the Bible: he has a gospel, but he also offers the Acts of the Apostles. These two "volumes" stand together as a narrative whole, and yet they also represent two distinguishable stages in that narrative. As such, they each have their own beginning, middle, and end, and Luke's recounting of them reflects this. Able author that he is, he also offers a smooth transition between his "first" and "second" volume, although the Bible's placement of the Gospel of John between them can obscure this to latter-day readers. It is this transition I want to consider first, because the concluding chapter of Luke and the initial two chapters of Acts offer, both directly and indirectly, summary reflections on the work and relations of the Father, Son, and Spirit. That is, these passages display a self-consciously reflective quality that the epistles considered above do not. This only makes sense. Letters as a genre represent one person addressing another (or several others); they can and often do leave much unspoken, for various reasons. Narratives, by contrast, are a step removed from personal address and have a more "global" character. They do not presuppose a shared set of assumptions so much as they seek to establish such assumptions. They require that certain details be made explicit, albeit in ways appropriate to a narrative genre, in order to develop characters or clarify the plot or move along the story line. Such details typically can serve a dual purpose. For example, words put in the mouth of a character speak not only to the others in the narrative, but to the hearer of the story as well. Moreover, the narrator may interject certain details in order to set the stage or signal a transition or clear up certain misunderstandings. As I hope to show with regard to his proto-trinitarian reflections, Luke employs all of these methods in presenting his gospel and the Acts of the Apostles.

Let me begin with Luke's introduction to Acts, 1:1–5. This passage is both retrospective and prospective. Luke reminds Theophilus what he presented in the "first book," namely, "all that Jesus did and taught from the beginning until the day when he was taken up to heaven, after giving instructions through the Holy Spirit to the apostles whom he had chosen. After his suffering he presented himself alive to them by many convincing proofs, appearing to them during forty days and speaking about the kingdom of God." Luke then indicates what is in store, namely, an account of how the apostles will receive "the promise of the Father," which is baptism with the Holy Spirit. Once again we have reference to three persons (Jesus, the Holy Spirit, and the Father), but more intriguing are the clues regarding their respective roles and relations. On the one hand, Jesus is clearly an active agent: he is a "doer" and a teacher. His teaching is authoritative (in this passage, "instructions" may also be translated "commandment"), it is done "through the Holy Spirit," it includes proper scriptural interpretation,[5] and it is about

---

5. I suggest that "convincing proofs" alludes to Luke 24: 27, 44–45.

the kingdom of God (and in all this, elements of his prophetic role emerge). What Jesus "did" Luke does not specify fully in this brief introduction, but note that he does refer as well to Jesus' suffering and resurrection, which I will later relate to his priestly and royal roles. On the other hand, the momentum of the passage points to the Father's promised baptism with the Holy Spirit, recapitulating in some sense Jesus' own baptism with the Spirit. This suggests that perhaps the time has come for another active agent to appear on the scene. The particular work and teaching that Jesus was to accomplish he has accomplished, so now the Father will employ another instrument to continue the divine purposes. The plan for salvation has entered its next stage.

This sense is reinforced by what Luke presents next. He recounts Jesus' last words to his disciples and describes his ascension in a version with an intriguingly different orientation from the account with which he ended his gospel (cf. Acts 1:6–11 with Luke 24:44–53). In the gospel account, Jesus emphasizes how "everything written about me in the law of Moses and the prophets and the psalms" had to be, and has been, fulfilled (Luke 24:44). As with the first part of Luke's introduction to Acts, the emphasis is retrospective: what Scripture foretold, Jesus has now accomplished. This stage of God's plan is complete. In the Acts account of Jesus' last words, the orientation is prospective. The disciples ask, "Lord, will you at this time restore the kingdom of Israel?" Jesus seems to rebuff their inquiry, but in fact recasts their question even while he answers it: "It is not for you to know the times or periods that the Father has set by his own authority. But you will receive power when the Holy Spirit has come upon you; and you will be my witnesses in Jerusalem, in all Judea and Samaria, and to the ends of the earth" (Acts 1:6–8). That is, the next stage of the Father's plan will commence with the sending of the Spirit. This stage remains open-ended, although it appears to attain a certain accomplishment, insofar as Luke concludes Acts with Paul preaching in Rome, the center of the world in his day, if not "the ends of the earth." While the distinction should not be pressed too far, with some justification one may describe the gospel as the book of the Son and the Acts of the Apostles as the book of the Holy Spirit. What keeps them together is the one purpose and unfolding plan of the Father.

Luke offers a succinct description of this divine plan, as well as an explanation of the particular roles of Father, Son, and Spirit, in his accounts of the apostolic preaching. These sermons tend to display the same elements regardless of who delivers them. This is commonly explained as an indication of Luke's editorial hand, and within the assumptions of redaction criticism, this interpretation is plausible enough. As Nils Dahl observes, "The speeches, with their kerygmatic summaries and scriptural quotations, give Luke the opportunity to emphasize and to comment upon the significance of the story told in the first volume."[6] Be this as it may, I believe using a narrative approach allows more theological sensitivity. That is, keeping within the structure created by the narrative itself, it is more appropriate to view the "editorial hand" as that of the risen Christ. For the sermons in Acts serve to recapitulate the actual *content* of what Jesus is only described as presenting to the apostles at the end of the gospel. Recall the crucial passage from chapter 24:

> Then he said to them, "These are my words that I spoke to you while I was still with you—that everything written about me in the law of Moses, the prophets, and the psalms must be fulfilled." Then he opened their minds to understand the Scriptures, and he said to them, "Thus it is written, that the Messiah is to suffer and to rise from the dead on the third day, and that repentance and forgiveness of sins is to be proclaimed in his name to all nations, beginning from Jerusalem. You are witnesses of these things. And see, I am sending upon you what my Father promised; so stay here in the city until you have been clothed with power from on high." (Luke 24:44–49)

The narrative connections between the risen Christ and the apostolic preaching in Acts suggest several conclusions: this preaching actually contains the quotations from or allusions to the books of Moses, the prophets, and the psalms to which Jesus refers.[7] This preaching has the particular content that it does—a crucified Messiah raised from the dead enabling forgiveness of sins for all nations—because the risen Christ opened the apostles' minds to it. This preaching takes place when and where it does because Jesus sends "what my Father promised," namely the Holy Spirit, the "power from on high." In other words, the risen Christ becomes both the teacher and the "lesson"; he becomes the "hermeneutical principle" for understanding the Father's plan of salvation and the actual pivot point that enables it; and in accomplishing his task, he becomes the catalyst initiating the work of the Holy Spirit.

---

6. Nils A. Dahl, *Jesus in the Memory of the Early Church* (Minneapolis: Augsburg Press, 1976), 93.

7. Consider, for example, Peter's sermons in Acts 2 and 3, Stephen's sermon in Acts 7, and Paul's sermon in Acts 13.

Yet one need not read the apostolic preaching in Acts through a christocentric lens alone. The trinitarian interrelations of Father, Son, and Spirit suggest one could also read it through a pneumatological or theological lens (the latter in this case being narrowly understood as referring to the first person). Consider Peter's sermon at Pentecost (Acts 2) as primarily an exposition of what God has done, acting through the instrumentality of the Spirit and Jesus, whom he makes the Christ. Peter begins with a quote from the prophet Joel, recalling God's declaration to pour out his Spirit in the last days (v. 17). He reminds his listeners of "Jesus of Nazareth, a man attested to you by God with deeds of power, wonders, and signs that God did through him among you" (v. 22). He immediately continues that it was this Jesus, "handed over to you according to the definite plan and foreknowledge of God," whom you had crucified (v. 23). Nevertheless, "God raised him up, having freed him from the pangs of death" (v. 24), as was prophesied by David (in Ps 16:8–11). David was able to make this prophecy because "God had sworn an oath to him that he would put one of his descendents on his throne" (v. 30). Peter then repeats his main point: "This Jesus God raised up" (v. 32). Following the resurrection, God exalted Jesus to his right hand (as Ps 110:1 prophesies: "The LORD said to my Lord, 'Sit at my right hand, until I make your enemies your footstool'"). Peter then recounts that at this juncture, "having received from the Father the promise of the Holy Spirit," Jesus initiates the amazing events of Pentecost (v. 33). All of this serves to confirm "that God has made him both Lord and Christ, this Jesus whom you crucified" (v. 36). This sermon cuts Peter's listeners to the quick, and they ask what they should do. Peter replies, "Repent, and be baptized every one of you in the name of Jesus Christ so that your sins may be forgiven; and you will receive the gift of the Holy Spirit. For the promise is for you, for your children, and for all who are far away, everyone whom the Lord our God calls to him" (vv. 38–39). Three thousand are converted and baptized (v. 41).

Summarizing Peter's Pentecost sermon in this way highlights how one may plausibly view God as the primary actor in the plan of salvation, using Jesus and the Spirit as his instruments. This emphasis on God's activity, in contrast to that of Jesus or the Spirit, appears in the preaching of Stephen and Paul as well.[8] One can see what fostered

---

8. See Acts 7, 13, and 17. By way of contrast, consider Paul's speech to the elders in Ephesus (Acts 20:17–35), which so describes God, the Lord Jesus, and the Holy Spirit as to indicate that activity is roughly balanced between them.

Irenaeus's famous description of the Son and Spirit as "the two hands of the Father." Yet note, too, that Peter's call to repentance at Pentecost offers another triadic formulation indicating an agency somehow shared among Christ, the Spirit, and God. Baptism in the name of Christ is linked with the forgiveness of sins. The gift of the Holy Spirit follows subsequently, and if verse 42 may be used as an indication of what follows the baptism described in verse 41, then this gift is connected with devotion to apostolic teaching and fellowship, to the breaking of bread and prayer.[9] Finally, all of this has to do with God's far-reaching promise and call to many generations and nations. In light of this distinction and juxtaposition, one can again understand why the early church eventually affirmed that "the external works of the Trinity are undivided" and produced the doctrines of perichoresis and appropriation. Viewed one way according to the scriptural witness, salvation is clearly the common work of all three persons. Viewed another way, however, it can be appropriate to focus attention on the role of one of the persons.

The basis for such shifting emphases appears to derive from the practical needs of evangelization and preaching rather than some abstract or theoretical norm. I could perhaps induce the general rule that the Father initiates, the Son accomplishes, and the Spirit applies, a pattern discernible in some of the previous passages we have considered. John Thompson offers another formulation for this same dynamic in his discussion of God's mission:

> The *ultimate basis* of mission is the triune God—the Father who created the world and sent his Son by the Holy Spirit to be our salvation. The *proximate basis* of mission is the redemption of the Son by his life, death, and resurrection, and the *immediate power* of mission is the Holy Spirit. It is, in trinitarian terms, a *missio Dei*. Thus mission is based on the will, movement, and action of the grace and love of God—Father, Son, and Holy Spirit.[10]

Whatever labels one employs to summarize God's saving activity, some such combination of distinguishable role and common work among the persons must be made if that summary is to be faithful to the scriptural witness.

---

9. This reading appears compatible with Paul's discussion of the gifts of the Spirit in 1 Cor 12.

10. John Thompson, *Modern Trinitarian Perspectives* (New York: Oxford University Press, 1994), 72.

Certainly one can readily observe this juxtaposition between distinguishable role and common work in the broad outlines of Luke-Acts. In one sense the gospel focuses on the role of the Son and Acts focuses on the role of the Spirit. Yet one must be careful not to draw from this distinction the superficial conclusion that the juxtaposition is merely a matter of chronological order. Such an assumption could lead too easily to modalism, the ancient heresy that understood the labels Father, Son, and Spirit as referring to our sequential experience of the one God, but not to any essential threefold dynamism within God himself. To be sure, the economy of salvation recounted in Scripture as a whole, and in Luke-Acts more particularly, does describe the roles of Father, Son, and Spirit in such a way that they fall into a certain temporal order. But these roles may also be understood as having what could be called a "spiritual simultaneity." That is, the economy of salvation refers not just to the broad, momentous strokes of divine activity in history, but also to God's ongoing activity in the daily faith of communities and individuals. Even in the personal and ordinary events of everyday life, the faithful live in and from the triune God. Were this not so, then, for example, one might assume, in light of the belief that Jesus now sits at the right hand of the Father, that latter-day Christians only have to do with the Spirit. But the biblical witness makes clear that this is not the case. Using the terms I suggested above, we may ask, Why not just the Spirit? Because the Spirit is neither generic nor the only divine person accessible to us since Christ's ascension. To the contrary, the Spirit's role is to effect relationship with something other than itself. What is it the Spirit effects? Incorporation into Christ and his accomplishment. What has Christ accomplished? The reconciliation of the world to God, as initiated by the Father. The Father becomes our Father through our adoption in Christ as children and heirs through the power of the Spirit. In other words, when you have one, you always have the other two—even as it is also appropriate to acknowledge that one's relation with the Father and Son is always first effected by the Spirit.

These conclusions seem more than warranted by the texts considered so far. I will examine next a key section from the Gospel of John, namely, Jesus' so-called "Farewell Address" (John 13–17) to determine how it reinforces and refines these conclusions. The setting and content of this "address" are theologically rich and evocative, presenting far more than I can deal with adequately here. I am concerned, of course, with only one aspect of the material presented in these chapters, namely, whatever may speak to a trinitarian understanding of God and his actions. This segment of John's Gospel represents a kind of self-conscious theological synopsis of Jesus' ministry and how it fits into the larger divine plan. It accomplishes this summary not just by its presentation of Jesus' words, but in its description of Jesus' action and the context in which these both occur. For the segment also functions as a bridge in the narrative flow of the gospel in that it takes place following the conclusion of Jesus' public ministry and just prior to his arrest, trial, and crucifixion. In addition to being such a narrative bridge, it also points to how Jesus should be viewed as a link of another sort. His speech to the disciples describes how he has the cardinal role, understood in its etymological sense of "hinge," between the Father's original intention and its culmination in the coming of the Counselor or Paraclete, the Holy Spirit. His is also a cardinal role in the way he reveals the character and will of the Father and describes how he will be the content of the Holy Spirit's message, or, put another way, how the Spirit will confirm his message and work.

The immediate setting of this discourse is the day before Passover, which in and of itself points to one of the theological claims made by John: Jesus' crucifixion the following day makes him the new paschal lamb. The day became known in the Christian tradition as Maundy Thursday, based on Christ's "mandate" *(mandatum)*, given by word and example, that his disciples be servants to others: "Very truly, I tell you, servants are not greater than their master, nor are messengers greater than the one who sent them" (John 13:16, but consider 3:3–16 for the context). I suggest that these chapters of John's Gospel offer five distinguishable points clarifying the triadic nature and relations of Father, Son, and Spirit. The first has to do with the character of their work and their respective roles in accomplishing that work. John does witness to a certain subordination of the Son to the Father and the Spirit to the Son in regard to their different roles.[11] John portrays the subordination of the Son to the Father in several ways: by what could be called "narrative implication," by Jesus' direct statement, and by figure of speech. For example, the opening verses of this segment set the stage with descriptions such as "Jesus knew that his hour had come to depart from this world and go to the Father" (13:1) and "Jesus, knowing that the Father had given all things into his hands, and that he had come from

---

11. At least in this regard, the *filioque* clause inserted by Western Christendom in the Nicene Creed claiming that the Spirit proceeds from the Father "and the Son" *(filioque)* is warranted, even if such unilateral action in altering an ecumenical norm may be criticized.

God and was going to God" (13:3). The former excerpt displays a certain ambiguity, but the latter verse serves to clarify it. The Father is the "giver" and Jesus the recipient, which is paralleled by Jesus' coming from and going to God. Several statements made by Jesus in chapter 14 reinforce such a reading of these opening verses: "The words that I say to you I do not speak on my own; but the Father who dwells in me does his works" (v. 10), "the word that you hear is not mine, but is from the Father who sent me" (v. 24), "the Father is greater than I" (v. 28), and "I do as the Father has commanded me" (v. 31). These verses come close to suggesting the Father indwells Jesus and works through him in an almost instrumental manner. In addition, Jesus offers a now-famous image that complements such direct statements. In chapter 15, he describes the Father as the vinedresser and himself as the true vine. This image portrays the Father as the active one, working on and through "the true vine" to bring to fruition the divine purposes. To be sure, Jesus is not portrayed as simply inert in this image, for he acts as the source providing sustenance to the branches. Still, the force of the whole analogy points to the vinedresser as the truly active subject, with the vine as the object of his work. A parallel of this relationship appears to exist as well between the Son and the Spirit. Jesus' statement, "I will ask the Father, and he will give you another Advocate" (14:16), implies that the Spirit comes from the Father and initiates its work only at the Son's behest. Another statement, "The Advocate, the Holy Spirit, whom the Father will send in my name, will teach you everything, and remind you of all that I have said to you" (14:26), reinforces this understanding of the Spirit's orientation toward the Son. It also suggests that the Spirit's role will be not just confirming of, but conformed to, the Son's lessons. Indeed, the relative subordination of the Spirit to the Son and the Son to the Father seems one inevitable conclusion of John 16:13–15: "When the Spirit of truth comes, he will guide you into all the truth; for he will not speak on his own, but will speak whatever he hears, and he will declare to you the things that are to come. He will glorify me, because he will take what is mine and declare it to you. All that the Father has is mine. For this reason I said that he will take what is mine and declare it to you." The Spirit does not speak on its own authority, just as the Son does not on his; the Son derives his authority from the Father. Yet the Spirit's authority appears dependent upon the Son's prior work (speaking only "whatever he hears" and "he will take what is mine and declare it"). This further suggests that at least in part the Spirit's relation to the Father is mediated through the Son. The Son has "all" from the Father, apparently directly; the Spirit also participates in this "all," but apparently indirectly, through the Son. To be sure, one can't push this schema too far. For example, 14:13 implies that Jesus is the active one, glorifying the Father, which places the Father in the recipient, "passive" mode. And the one explicit statement regarding the Spirit's "procession" (*ekporeúetai*, John 15:26) connects it only with the Father, and not the Son. Nevertheless, these chapters echo and expand a relation we have seen described in other New Testament passages: the Father initiates, the Son is the "content," and the Spirit applies. With a certain justification, one could say the Son works on behalf of the Father, and the Spirit works on behalf of the Son. Or one could say the Father "commissions" the Son and the Son "commissions" the Spirit.

The second key proto-trinitarian point made by these chapters in John is the claim that Jesus reveals the Father and is the only way to the Father. Jesus states this directly, but his revelation of the Father also stems from the deeds narratively framing his words. Thus, in John 14:6–7, Jesus announces "I am the way, and the truth, and the life. No one comes to the Father except through me. If you know me, you will know my Father also. From now on you do know him and have seen him." In 14:9, he states, "Whoever has seen me has seen the Father." With these assertions in mind, the earlier portrayal of "the Lord and Teacher" washing his disciples' feet (John 13:4–17) takes on an added significance, for it can now be taken as indicating something of the character of the Father as well as the Son. Jesus interjects another element in his claim of being the revelation of, and path to, the Father when he speaks of the world's ignorance of, indeed, its hostility toward the Father. Revelation is not just a matter of knowledge, but of fundamental orientation and allegiance. Jesus acknowledges that "the world does not know" the Father (17:25), even while he indicates that this is not merely a matter of circumstance or indifference. Rather, it is the result of active opposition. Notice, for example, the way that John 15:23 presents a kind of negative corollary to 14:9: "Whoever hates me hates my Father also." Jesus' revelation of the Father and his role in doing the Father's work do not elicit a neutral or merely intellectual response, but either hate or love.[12] Yet if it is the latter, then this opens the

---

12. Contrast John 15:24 ("If I had not done among them the works that no one else did, they would not have sin. But now they have seen and hated both me and my Father") with John 17:25–26 ("Righteous Father, the world does not know you, but I know you; and these know that you have sent me. I made your name known to them, and I will make it known, so that the love with which you have loved me may be in them, and I in them").

door to further obligations and even greater possibilities. In John 14:23, Jesus states that anyone "who loves me will keep my word, and my Father will love him, and we will come to him and make our home with him," while in 14:16–17 he says, "I will ask the Father, and he will give you another Counselor, to be with you forever. This is the Spirit of truth, which the world cannot receive, because it neither sees it nor knows it." Thus, Jesus becomes not only the revelation of, and way to the Father, but the catalyst for and way to the Spirit. Here again, we encounter a pattern seen in other writings of the New Testament: communion with Jesus becomes communion with the Father and Spirit, a call for Christians to live in the Trinity.

In the third place, Jesus' "Farewell Address" presents the Son playing a kind of "bridge" role in the economy of salvation. This complements but differs from the preceding point: the earlier image presents Jesus in an interpersonal or existential role, while this one portrays him in a historical role. Put another way, the former portrays Jesus operating "vertically," acting as the mediator between the mundane and heavenly realms, while the latter portrays Jesus operating "horizontally," acting as the catalyst who enables the in-breaking of a new age. The famous ambiguity of John 3:3, which records Jesus saying one must be "born *ánothen*" ("from above" or "anew") to see the kingdom of God, illustrates their complementarity. This birth is both "vertical" and "horizontal," it manifests the irruption of both the heavenly into the world and the new age into the old. Thus, it would be an oversimplification to claim that the "realized eschatology" often ascribed to John's Gospel means that there is no historical element or sense of unfolding events present in his witness. Intriguingly, even though the "Farewell Address" of chapters 13 through 17 comes across as rather static, it nevertheless recalls and places in context the narrative of the gospel as a whole. Consider the implications of the descriptive interjection of John 13:3: "Jesus, knowing that the Father had given all things into his hands, and that he had come from God and was going to God. . . ." On its own, this sentence fragment may not seem all that significant. Yet the preceding verse describes the devil having put it in Judas's heart to betray Jesus, while the following verse describes Jesus rising from the table to begin washing the disciples' feet. In other words, a verse that on its own could be understood rather generically instead serves a very concrete function by indicating how these surrounding verses should be framed. Events are coming to a head—and on a human level, they might appear to be spinning out of control. But Jesus makes the point several times that they are unfolding according to God's plan, and that his mediatorial role in the drama is reaching its culmination. Consider, for example, Jesus' statement that he is going to prepare a place for the disciples in the Father's house, and that he will then return to retrieve them (14:2–3). A similar description of events needing to unfold according to plan appears in Jesus' various statements about going to the Father so that the Advocate may then be sent (in Christ's name) to be with the disciples in the next stage of God's salvific plan (14:25–26; 16:7). Finally, the words of Jesus in John 17:6–11 petition the Father to protect the disciples in this next stage, even as they speak of a "mission accomplished" by Jesus in the stage now ending.

If the conclusions I have drawn thus far tend to emphasize the distinction between the Father, Son, and Holy Spirit, the fourth point tends in the opposite direction, especially as that is relevant to the Christian community. That is, these chapters also emphasize that the Father, Son, and Holy Spirit are all "in" one another, that the Son and Spirit will be "in" the disciples, and therefore, the Father, too, will be "in" the disciples. The various statements to this effect reinforce my earlier conclusions about the community "living in the Trinity," but they also give a suggestion of the character of that life. The unity that has existed between the Father and the Son will become available to the community (17:11, 22–23). The glory that has existed between the Father and the Son will become available to the community (17:22). And the love that has existed between the Father and the Son will become available to the community (17:26). All of these benefits will be assured by the Holy Spirit, who will act as the pledge and guarantor of all that the Son has done on behalf of the Father (14:26; 16:13–15).

Fifth, this being "in" the Son (and hence the Father and Spirit) involves not just benefit but responsibility. This "Farewell Address" contains more than just a teacher's parting thoughts; it includes a commissioning: "As you have sent me into the world, so I have sent them into the world" (17:18). Established in the unity, glory, and love of the triune God, the disciples are called to a life of faithfulness previously unavailable, indeed, unimaginable to them. John 14:12–14 states this in the strongest terms: "Very truly, I tell you, the one who believes in me will also do the works that I do and, in fact, will do greater works than these, because I am going to the Father. I will do whatever you ask in my name, so that the Father may be glorified in the Son. If in my name you ask me for anything, I will do it." Of course, Jesus also balances this promise with another: just as he has been persecuted, so, too, will they be (15:20). The emphasis overall has nothing to do with claims to personal status, power, and prestige, but with remaining rooted in Christ and abiding in him. Indeed, the famous image of the vine clarifies matters succinctly:

> I am the true vine, and my Father is the vinegrower. He removes every branch in me that bears no fruit. Every branch that bears fruit he prunes to make it bear more fruit. You have already been cleansed by the word that I have spoken to you. Abide in me as I abide in you. Just as the branch cannot bear fruit by itself unless it abides in the vine, neither can you unless you abide in me. I am the vine, you are the branches. Those who abide in me and I in them bear much fruit, because apart from me you can do nothing. (15:1–5)

The closing words, "apart from me you can do nothing," act as an explanation of the previous promise regarding the "greater works" that the disciples will do in Christ's name. It is not their power that will accomplish it, but God's. After all, they continue "in" the Son and hence the Father, by means of the Spirit. Similarly, I contend that the disciple's keeping of Christ's commandments is not the precondition of receiving the Father's love; rather, their love of Christ, and hence their abiding in the love of the Father by means of the Spirit, is what enables them to keep the commandments (see John 14:21, 23; cf. John 15:9–10).[13]

At this juncture, let me begin to make the substantial shift in focus that will become explicit in chapters 4, 5, and 6. Up to this point, I have been highlighting the way that Scripture portrays the three persons of the Trinity acting in concert in any given example to bring about God's salvific purposes. In the examples considered thus far, Father, Son, and Spirit have each had a unique role to play, but the focus has been on the complementary unity of their work in the diverse passages examined. Without forgetting this understanding of the unified activity of the triune God, from this point on I will focus more on the way one of the triune persons (namely, Christ) serves as the "instrument" of the other two, even as he fulfills his own "proper" role as the incarnate Son. In particular, I want to keep in mind the five points just made regarding the triadic nature and relations of Father, Son, and Spirit, while considering as well what these chapters of John also offer us regarding the

---

13. I interpret v. 9 as describing the condition that enables the imperative of v. 10.

character of Christ's threefold office as king, priest, and prophet. True, I could undertake this consideration, with its more specifically christological starting point, in the appropriate parts of chapters 4, 5, and 6. But I believe it worthwhile to do it here, while my analysis from a more specifically trinitarian starting point is still fresh in the reader's mind. More generally then, I want the reader to recognize how a fuller perspective on the redemptive activity of the triune God can start from either of these two vantage points: from the three working as one, or the work of one as always triadic. For if "the external works of the Trinity are undivided," then whether one starts with one or the three, the other perspective is always its implicit and necessary complement.

To start then, John's portrayal of Jesus' "Farewell Address" offers more than just food for trinitarian reflection, as addressed under the five points outlined above. It also offers food for thought regarding Christ's kingly role. Perhaps the most striking evidence appears in the opening episode, in which Christ displays his servant lordship by washing his disciples' feet. Note the connection between his knowledge ("knowing that the Father had given all things into his hands") and his act ("he began to wash the disciples' feet") (13:3–5). It seems clear that his act is based on, and meant to illustrate, the character of his lordship, and this reading is reinforced by Peter's reaction to this apparently servile gesture and Jesus' insistence that he must do it if Peter is to have any part "in" him (13:6–8). Keep in mind that John's Gospel last portrayed a conversation between Peter and Jesus at a time when some followers had become disillusioned and were falling away. Jesus asked: "Do you also wish to go away?" Peter replied: "Lord, to whom can we go? You have the words of eternal life. We have come to believe and know that you are the Holy One of God" (6:66–69). In other words, Peter had recognized Jesus as the Messiah, but he was yet to learn how Jesus' fulfillment of this role would overturn all his expectations. Jesus' taking the role of a servant washing his feet represents one aspect of Peter's "reeducation." The things Jesus says in his "Farewell Address" continue the lessons. He speaks of the authority with which the Father has spoken his words and done his works through Jesus (14:10–11). Recognizing where events are leading, he tells his disciples that "the ruler of this world is coming," but that "he has no power over me," for he (Jesus) does as the Father commands (14:30–31), serving in that way as the Father's sovereign instrument. This anticipation of the coming conflict recalls the temptation accounts reported in Matthew and Luke, and speaks to Christ's battle with Satan in crucifixion and his victory over Satan in the resurrection. Moreover, in light of this anticipated conflict and triumph, Jesus can also tell his disciples that "in me you may have peace. In the world you have tribulation; but be of good cheer, I have overcome the world" (16:33). In Christ, God's sovereignty reigns.

These chapters in John also offer clues about the character of Jesus' priestly office and the sacrifice he makes in that role. Perhaps the most telling point is one made implicitly by the narrative's chronology. That is, this climactic section relates these last events of Jesus' life to the celebration of Passover in such a way that his death is presented as a new paschal sacrifice. Scholars have long noted that John's chronology varies from that of the Synoptics, and concluded that this difference stems from his desire to highlight precisely this theological point. John 13:1 sets the "Farewell" episode prior to the feast of Passover, and John 19:31–33 establishes that Jesus' death occurred on the day of preparation for the Passover. Even more telling is the reference to Jesus in verse 36: "For these things took place that the Scripture might be fulfilled, 'Not a bone of him shall be broken,'" an allusion to Exod 12:46, a passage describing the Passover lamb. The association is further reinforced when one recalls that John, alone among the gospel writers, had depicted John the Baptist calling Jesus "the Lamb of God who takes away the sin of the world" (1:29).[14] This narrative framework portraying Jesus as a sacrificial lamb may then be understood as the context for his famous words, "No one has greater love than this, to lay down one's life for one's friends" (15:13), even while the words give further clarity to the context. That is, his death should be understood as a sacrifice, but the key point is to understand that it is a sacrifice motivated by love. Why emphasize this motivation? While the Johannine context to this point suggests his sacrifice be understood as a parallel to that of the paschal lamb, I would suggest that it need not be restricted to just this one association. Simply put, John's language is too evocative to suppose it intends to work at only one level. Thus, for instance, given the many references in this address to the Son and Father being one in love, and its

---

14. Reference to "the Lamb" reappears in another work of the Johannine school, that is, Revelation, where it functions as a title and not just a description or simile. The apostle Paul picks up the association as well ("For our paschal lamb, Christ, has been sacrificed") in 1 Cor 5:7, while 1 Pet 1:19 compares the blood of Christ to that of "a lamb without defect or blemish," although he makes no explicit connection with the Passover.

setting as a meal fellowship, one might also understand Christ's sacrifice along the lines of a "gift offering." The old covenant had its sacrificial rites to share communion with God; Jesus offers a new means and form by which his followers will establish and abide in communion with God. There are other ways in which Christ's sacrifice may be understood, but I will wait until chapter 5 to discuss these.

Finally, these chapters in John offer clues about Jesus' fulfillment of the prophetic office, both in the manner he summarizes his teachings and commandments and speaks of the coming "Counselor" or "Advocate" *(paracletos)*. To begin with, consider the simple fact that he confirms what the disciples have called him: "Teacher" (as well as "Lord," 13:13). In a very straightforward sense, this "Farewell Address" serves as the culmination of Jesus' teaching. Like the prophets of old, he has revealed through speech and deed the word and will of God. Yet unlike those prophets—and in this respect far surpassing them—Jesus actually embodies that revelation, as the incarnate Word of God. Because he is one with the Father, Jesus does not simply convey the will and commands of God, he is able to speak them in the first person: "A new commandment I give to you . . ." (13:34). And this is not the only manner in which he surpasses the prophets of old. Not only can he speak with direct authority, but also his disciples are able to hear with new ability, for Jesus will extend the Spirit to them. Having been anointed by the Holy Spirit at his baptism (and in that sense becoming an instrument of the Spirit like the prophets), Jesus now promises to send the Spirit to consolidate his community and continue his work (in that sense having the Spirit serve as his instrument). "I have said these things to you while I am still with you. But the Advocate, the Holy Spirit, whom the Father will send in my name, will teach you every-thing, and remind you of all that I have said to you" (14:25–26). And again: "When the Advocate comes, whom I will send to you from the Father, the Spirit of truth who comes from the Father, he will testify on my behalf" (15:26). All of this is simply another way of considering how the Father and Son are "in" one another, and the disciples "in" him (and hence the Father), and how the community's life and calling must be shaped by that vital union. One could say that Christ extends his prophetic commission to his disciples, for abiding in him, they, too, will become instruments of Spirit.

Having traced the scriptural basis for my project back through sev-eral layers of theological reflection, I now turn to the event that inaugu-rated Jesus' acceptance of his threefold office.

The Baptism/Temptation Narratives

JESUS' BAPTISM: A TRINITARIAN EVENT

All that I have considered up to this point may be understood as growing out of what I will examine next. For the real scriptural commencement of my trinitarian theology of atonement begins at the point of Jesus' baptism, along with its immediate counterpoint in his temptation.[15] I begin by drawing attention to the fact that all three synoptic gospel accounts of Jesus' anointing lend themselves to a trinitarian reading of his "appointment" as the Christ. All three gospels indicate—as does the Gospel of John, in its particular account of Jesus' public "authorization"—the involvement of three characters, namely, the Spirit descending as a dove, the divine voice pronouncing Jesus' sonship, and Jesus, the anointed. Second, not only do these narratives imply that Jesus' baptismal anointing may be understood as a trinitarian event, the baptism itself implies what he is anointed to *be*. Scriptural tradition long associated three "offices" with anointing: prophets, priests, and kings.[16] Consider the following contextual background.

The broad sweep of the Old Testament suggests that, ideally understood, each of these offices were meant to complement the others in serving a mediatorial function between God and the covenant people. God's transcendent majesty and righteousness and glory precluded a direct encounter with him (as Exod 33:20 states, no one can see God's face and live); a mediator was needed. Thus, Israel's kings mediated the sovereignty and power of God, the priests mediated the holiness and forgiveness of God, and the prophets mediated the truth and commands of God. One portrayal of all three offices working harmoniously together appears in the Old Testament account of King Josiah's reforms in seventh-century B.C. Judah. Hilkiah, the high priest, finds the book of the law in the Temple and has it read to King Josiah. King Josiah is distraught that its commands have not been obeyed, and so he inquires

---

15. I should point out that I do not intend to imply an adoptionist Christology by starting with Jesus' baptism, only that this event inaugurates his public status as God's anointed.

16. Cf. 1 Kgs 19:16 (the Lord commands Elijah to anoint Elisha as his successor); Exod 28:41, 29:7–9; Lev 8 (the Lord commands Moses to anoint Aaron and his sons as priests); and 1 Sam 9:15–17, 9:27–10:1 (the Lord instructs Samuel to anoint Saul, "to save them [the people of Israel] from their enemies"). Cf. God's later instruction to Samuel to anoint David to replace Saul as King (16:1, 11–13).

of Huldah the prophetess to learn what the consequences will be. She says the Lord will indeed bring judgment upon Judah, but because Josiah has been penitent and faithful, that judgment will be delayed until after his death. Josiah then institutes his reforms, holding a Passover, reestablishing obedience to the law, and abolishing all abominations in the land of Israel (see 2 Kgs 22 and 2 Chr 34). Another such portrayal appears in accounts of the prophets Haggai and Zechariah and their relationships to Joshua, who was the high priest, and Zerubbabel, the descendent of King David who was appointed governor of restored Judah by the Persians. According to the biblical accounts, it was the admonitions of Haggai and Zechariah that motivated Zerubbabel and Joshua to undertake the rebuilding of the temple and reestablishing of purified cultic practices (Hag 1:1–15; Zech 4:6–10a, 6:9–15). A third example appears in 1 Kgs 1:5–53, in the account of how Solomon succeeded to the throne of his father. This passage portrays the relationship between the offices in far less idealized terms than the ones just considered, revealing among other things the clear alignment of the prophetic and priestly offices toward the interests of the kingly office. Specifically, King David enlists the help of the priest Zadok and the prophet Nathan, along with David's court guard and several others, to insure that his son Solomon rather than his son Adonijah would succeed him. Of course, the text also makes it clear that Zadok and Nathan had maneuvered David into this course of action, so the question of who is using whom becomes rather ambiguous. Be that as it may, the passage still describes the three offices as complementing one another.

Of course, the Old Testament witness also indicates that often the offices complemented one another only after the fashion of checks and balances, and frequently only with a great deal of friction. At times, this implied all the intrigue, if not downright hostility, typically associated with court politics. Recall, for example, that Jeremiah ended up in the cistern of Malciah (Jer 38:1–13), and that Elijah and Ahab remained in open conflict until the latter finally repented (1 Kgs 17–21). To be sure, "speaking truth to power" could have a more immediate and sanguine outcome. Recall Nathan's parable to King David over his adultery with Bathsheba, and David's response of sorrow and repentance (2 Sam 12). Sometimes the checks and balances of one office toward another could exhibit a certain self-criticism as well, as was the case in Micah's rebuke of other prophets and not just corrupt political leaders and priests (Mic 3:9–12). Recall as well Jeremiah's condemnation of the kings, priests, and prophets who—in precisely the wrong sort of cooperation—have forsaken the God of Israel and led the people to worship Ba'al or idols (Jer 2:4–8, 26–28).

In any event, over the years, hopes for the final fulfillment of that three-part mediation came to be vested in the anticipated Messiah, the one who would combine these offices. Hence, with the confession of Jesus as the Christ, it was virtually inevitable that the titles of prophet, priest, and king should be applied to him. But how should they be understood? In my consideration of the temptation narratives, I will begin to show how Jesus will fulfill, but also redefine, those offices in his words and work. Of course, this fulfillment and redefinition constitutes the primary focus of this book, so how the temptation accounts anticipate this concern will be of particular interest.

My first observation is that, interestingly, in this inaugural event Jesus appears as the most passive of the characters involved. Other commentators have noted his relative subordination in the baptismal accounts. The historical claim that this reflects Jesus' initial discipleship to John the Baptist is well known, as are observations regarding the editorial modifications made by Matthew, Luke, and John over against Mark's account. However, I propose a theological interpretation, emphasizing not Jesus' "subservience" to John, but to the other two divine characters active in the narrative. On the one hand, Jesus' posture accords with the "self-emptying" described in Phil 2; it is also in keeping with gospel descriptions of Jesus' submission to the Father's will (e.g., in the garden of Gethsemane, Matt 26:29 and Mark 14:36). On the other hand, it indicates that Christ acts not alone, but in concert with the Father and the Holy Spirit. Now this is not to suggest that the Son will be merely an instrument in the hands of the Father and the Spirit. I am not trying to counter portrayals of Christ's work that seem to focus on him to the exclusion of the other two persons by offering a portrayal that is simply its negative image. Rather, in keeping with what my exegesis revealed throughout the first parts of this chapter, I am suggesting a work in concert. To be sure, it is appropriate to highlight the place of each person as I consider in turn the offices of king, priest, and prophet in the following chapters. But in each instance, I will also emphasize how Christ's work in each office is also a work of the whole Trinity. This dual emphasis is, of course, the central and recurring emphasis of this whole book—an emphasis that I see initiated in Christ's baptism. Thus, the narratives of this inaugural event are not about the emergence of a forceful personality or spiritual genius or an individual's charisma (understood in a psychological or political sense), nor is the event the inauguration of a "lone ranger" deity. Rather, these narratives focus on the Father who anoints his Son through the Holy Spirit—the same Spirit who then immediately led (or "drove," Mark 1:12) him into the wilderness, as I will address more fully below. My point is that the scriptural witness to Jesus' baptism and temptation points to a *trinitarian* event, not just the spiritual journey or "vision quest" of an individual nor the emergence of a new and different god.

This relative passivity on Jesus' part is not something that has gone unnoticed in Christian history. As indicated in my examination of Calvin's treatment of the "threefold office," that Reformer clearly speaks of the Father and the Spirit as the active agents in the anointing of the Son.[17] It is particularly interesting that Calvin writes, "For the Spirit has chosen Christ as his seat, that from him might abundantly flow the heavenly riches of which we are in such need," because the emphasis appears to be so much more on what the Spirit requires for its ongoing and present work than upon the now past event of Christ's anointing.

CHRIST'S THREE-PART TEMPTATION TO ABUSE HIS MESSIANIC ANOINTING

Following his baptism, the Holy Spirit drives Jesus into the wilderness (Matt 4:1 // Mark 1:12–13 // Luke 4:1–2), the place recognized by tradition as the abode of the prince of demons,[18] where he does indeed confront a direct and immediate challenge to his baptism. Now, to view the temptation narratives as describing a general testing of Jesus as the Son of God in his messianic role is not particularly controversial. While A. W. Argyle perhaps states it most succinctly, ("It was the divine will that Jesus should experience the testing of his vocation to be Messiah"[19]), other commentators make the same basic point in a variety of ways.[20]

---

17. See pp. 66–69.

18. See Lev 16:8–10, with its description of the Day of Atonement's scapegoat "sent away into the wilderness to Azazel," and the pseudepigraphical book Enoch 9:6, 10:4–8. The "Azazel" of tradition becomes, of course, the devil or Satan in the synoptic accounts.

19. A. W. Argyle, *The Gospel According to Matthew* (The Cambridge Bible Commentary, eds. P. R. Ackroyd, A. R. C. Leaney, and J. W. Packer; Cambridge: Cambridge University Press, 1963), 39.

20. C. F. Evans observes that biblical temptations serve "to test the godly for his fidelity to God," and suggests that Jesus' temptation is to be compared with Israel's in the wilderness, especially as that is described in Deut 6–9. He goes on to state: "On this background Jesus would be presented as the true Son of God, in whom the destiny of Israel was recapitulated and the divine purpose accomplished in that he renders to God the obedience

Interestingly, Morna Hooker makes the further claim that Jesus' temptation "amounts to the suggestion that it is God himself who needs to be tested."[21] Such a contention serves to raise the stakes regarding this episode, because it clarifies the fact that the temptation represents not merely some personal struggle on Jesus' part but the opening skirmish in this stage of the cosmic confrontation between God and Satan. Be all this as it may, I contend that Jesus' messianic testing should also be understood more particularly, that is, that the three temptations be viewed as specific tests of his anointing to the threefold office of prophet, priest, and king. This approach is not a common view. Only a few contemporary biblical commentators interpret the three temptations as corresponding to the prophetic, priestly, and royal dimensions of Jesus' messiahship.[22] Nevertheless, I hope my analysis will prove persuasive.

---

and trust that Israel had failed to give." C. F. Evans, *Saint Luke* (TPI New Testament Commentaries; Philadelphia: Trinity Press International, 1990), 255–56. Donald Senior makes a similar point when he states: "Standing as this scene does on the brink of Jesus' public ministry, its parallel to Israel's moment of test before the entry into the land ties Jesus once again to paradigmatic moments in Israel's sacred history. Demonstrating Jesus' fidelity to God's word (in contrast to the failure of Israel) also presents Jesus as fulfilling the biblical promise." Donald Senior, *Matthew* (Abingdon New Testament Commentaries, ed. Victor Paul Furnish; Nashville: Abingdon Press, 1998), 58.

21. Morna D. Hooker, *The Signs of a Prophet: The Prophetic Actions of Jesus* (Harrisburg, Penn.: Trinity Press International, 1997), 32.

22. Ulrich Luz mentions three who do: G. Friedrich, "Beobachtungen zur messianischen Hohepriestererwartung in der Synoptiken," *Zeitschift für Theologie und Kirche* 53 (1956): 300ff., G. Baumbach, *Das Verständnis des Bösen in den synoptischen Evangelien* (Theologische Arbeiten 19; Berlin: Evangelische Verlagsanstalt, 1963), 108–10; and H. Mahnke, *Die Werschungsgeschichte im Rahmen der synoptischen Evangelien* (BBET 9; Bern: Lang, 1978), 122–24. See Ulrich Luz, *Matthew 1–7: A Commentary* (trans. Wilhelm C. Linss; Minneapolis: Augsburg Fortress, 1989), 185n.14. Luz himself argues for the more general messianic interpretation. He states that the "Achilles' heel of [a more particular] interpretation is the second temptation," which is, to his mind, not explicit enough in pointing to a *priestly* messiah. He implies that comparable messianic passages in 2 Esd 13:35–38, Rev 11:3–13, and a Jewish midrash (*Pesikta Rabbati* 36.2) lend support to his more generalist reading. I do not find his position entirely persuasive, and this is not simply because I am concerned primarily with theological interpretation and pastoral application rather than historical-critical reconstruction. His reference to the midrash is especially interesting. In part, it is a question of who might have influenced whom: the earliest suggested date for the compilation of the *Pesikta Rabbati* is 355 A.D., with a seventh-century date more likely. (See William G. Braude, trans., *Pesikta Rabbati* [Yale Judaica Series, ed. Leon Nemoy, vol. 18; New Haven, Conn.: Yale University Press, 1968], 20–26, for a discussion of dating.) Yet let us suppose this particular midrash does represent a much earlier tradition. If it did influence the gospel accounts of the temptation, then a "priestly" reading of the second temptation might well be precluded by the words to which Luz refers: "Our Masters taught: When the king Messiah appears, he will

In addition, these particular temptations also indicate that Jesus will not simply accept the common expectations accompanying these offices, which means neither should Christian theology. I have already suggested how John's account of Jesus' "Farewell Address" offers similar hints regarding the ways Jesus redefines—given the expectations of his day—his messianic office. The larger point is that we cannot determine the theologically proper understanding of these offices apart from the biblical, indeed, New Testament witness. As such, the passages describing Jesus' temptation, and the ones I will consider in the following chapters, serve as a corrective to those who make the common theological misstep of describing—or critiquing—Christ's status based on generic notions of prophecy, priesthood, or kingship isolated from the work of the triune God.

The Prophetic Office

The devil tempts the hungry Jesus, saying "If you are the Son of God, command these stones to become loaves of bread" (Matt 4:3). As Moses had been the prophetic "go-between" for the Israelites' manna (Exod 16:1–36) and as Elijah had provided food miraculously for the widow of Zarephath and her son (1 Kgs 17:8–16), so, too, Jesus—if he is a true

---

come stand on the roof of the Temple and will make a proclamation to Israel, saying: Meek ones, the day of your redemption is come" (page 682 in the Braude edition). It does not mention anything priestly, indeed, it speaks of "*king* Messiah." Yet what are we then to make of a passage that appears earlier in the same midrash (36.1, 678–79)? That passage states:

> [At the time of the Messiah's creation], the Holy One, blessed be He, will tell him in detail what will befall him: There are souls that have been put away with thee under My throne, and it is their sins which will bend thee down under a yoke of iron and make thee like a calf whose eyes grow dim with suffering, and will choke thy spirit as with a yoke; because of the sins of these souls thy tongue will cleave to the roof of thy mouth. Art thou willing to endure such things? . . . The Messiah will say: Master of the universe, with joy in my soul and gladness in my heart I take this suffering upon myself, provided that not one person in Israel perish; that not only those who are alive be saved in my days, but that also those who are dead, who died from the days of Adam up to the time of redemption; and that not only these be saved in my days, but also those who died as abortions; and that not only these be saved in my days, but all those whom Thou thoughtest to create but were not created. Such are the things I desire, and for these I am ready to take upon myself [whatever Thou decreest].

If such a passage does not evoke a priestly understanding of the Messiah similar to the one Christians came to affirm about Jesus' self-sacrifice, I do not know what words could.

prophet—should be able to provide food for himself.[23] Jesus refuses, trusting his care to God with the response: "Man shall not live by bread alone, but by every word that proceeds from the mouth of God."

This quote is taken from Deut 8:3, the broader context of which is Moses' address to the Israelites on their covenant responsibilities as they are about to enter the promised land. They must follow carefully and with humility all that God commands them to do, and avoid thinking they are self-sufficient and autonomous. Jesus demonstrates his allegiance to this command here, in various ways during his ministry, and ultimately with his death, an event that enacts the commitment voiced in his Gethsemane prayer: "Father, if thou art willing, remove this cup from me; nevertheless, not my will, but thine, be done" (Luke 22:42).

Furthermore, if one recognizes that the role of a prophet is that of a "teacher," that is, the servant who conveys the truth of God and how we are to live, then Jesus' response here takes on a greater clarity. Even as the prophet who now surpasses Moses,[24] Jesus will not employ his power to supply sustenance "in case God forgets." Just as God caused the manna to feed the Israelites, so Jesus trusts God to provide. He trusts in God's word. Indeed, Jesus is not only the conveyor of God's word, his is God's Word—the Word whose own body and blood will be conveyed in preaching and through bread and wine to bring life to humanity.

In that sense, his life and death also reveal the hermeneutic by which the church interprets properly God's "other" words. The temptation accounts may be likened to a contest of "dueling prooftexts" between Satan and Jesus. Each time Satan tempts Jesus with a self-serving reference from Scripture, Jesus counters with one more appropriate to his anointed mission—his tripartite mission. In this sense, he is being true not only to himself, but to the Father and Spirit.

The Priestly Office

The devil next sets Jesus "on the pinnacle of the temple." This image indicates Jesus' place at the pinnacle of the priestly hierarchy: above the Levites, above the Aaronic priests, even above the high priest.[25] Satan tempts Jesus saying that if he is the Son of God, he should throw himself

---

23. As an indication of this common view, note also the crowd's response in John 6:14 to Jesus' feeding of them.

24. Cf. the promise in Deut 18:15ff. and the summary description in Deut 34:10–12.

25. This image is reinforced when read in a canonical context with the Letter to the Hebrews.

down so that the angels will scurry to save him. Satan's implied message: as priestly messiah, you need not come to harm. Banish all
thoughts that this office might require any self-sacrificial act. Quite the
contrary, this office comes with an angelic bodyguard: "On their hands
they will bear you up, lest you strike your foot against a stone" (Ps
91:11–12). As God's priestly messiah, you of all persons are set apart
and warrant special protection.

Jesus replies with a countering quote from Torah: "Do not put the
Lord your God to the test" (Deut 6:16). Anyone familiar with the passage could fill in the concluding words: "as you tested him at Massah."
At that time, the people of Israel complained that they had been
brought out into the desert to be killed, and questioned whether the
Lord was among them or not (Exod 17:2–7). Jesus, in contrast, refuses
to engage in such complaint and questioning, just as he has refused to
take advantage of the "perks" of the office by summoning angelic assis-
tants to serve him. (Interestingly, Matthew's subsequent account of
Jesus' arrest in the garden of Gethsemane reinforces Jesus' refusal to use
such prerogatives and derail his mission: "Put your sword back in its
place. . . . Do you think that I cannot appeal to my Father, and he will
at once send me more than twelve legions of angels? But how then
should the Scriptures be fulfilled, that it must be so?" [Matt 26:52–54].)
Jesus trusts God's purpose for him without second-guessing. Jesus does
not exploit his position at the top of the priestly hierarchy or worry
about striking his foot against a stone. To the contrary, he will lay himself down not just as priest, but as sacrifice—and will himself become
the "stumbling stone" to those whose preconceptions blind them to
God's chosen ways.

The Kingly Office

Finally, the devil tempts Jesus with complete earthly sovereignty and
glory if Jesus will but shift spiritual allegiance from God to him.
Interestingly enough, both Luke and Matthew suggest that the kingdoms of the world are, in some sense, Satan's to give. This echoes Pauline
notions of the world's current bondage to oppressive powers and principalities and *Christus victor* notions of Christ's work. Jesus responds,
"Begone, Satan!," citing the fundamental command that one worship
and serve the Lord God alone (Deut 6:13). Jesus will indeed receive
authority over the world as Lord, but he will do so by turning on their
heads all earthly conceptions of sovereignty and by refusing all earthly

accoutrements of a king. One author who recognizes the significance of this refusal is Colin Gunton, who observes regarding Christ's kingship and ultimate victory that "the temptation narratives are of crucial importance, for they depict the choice of one approach to the exercise of power rather than another. The first place where we shall therefore find the meaning of the metaphor of victory is the refusal of Jesus to exercise power demonically."[26]

26. Colin E. Gunton, *The Actuality of Atonement: A Study of Metaphor, Rationality, and the Christian Tradition* (Edinburgh: T&T Clark, 1988), 75.

4

Christ the King
Achieving the Father's Victory

The stage has been set for a detailed consideration of the way in which Christ's threefold office and work may be understood as having a trinitarian character. The next three chapters will describe how that atoning activity should be construed as not only his particular messianic work but also the common work of the Father and the Spirit. The previous chapter has argued from "proto-trinitarian" exegetical evidence that the different persons of the Trinity never act in isolation or separation from one another. The following chapters unpack what that means when the focus shifts to one of those persons, namely, the Son incarnate as the Mediator, Jesus Christ. Recall the basic question arising from Chapter 1: If "God is one" and "the external works of the Trinity are undivided," how may we describe Christ's historical and particular work as "trinitarian"? The general answer was outlined in that same first chapter: by considering Christ's trinitarian work through his anointing to the threefold office of king, priest, and prophet. (For reasons that will emerge during the course of my exposition, I will consider these in the reverse order of the customary phrase "prophet, priest, and king.") More specifically, while recognizing Christ's threefold work to be both fully his own and fully trinitarian, it is also appropriate to understand his royal work as done on behalf of the Father, his priestly work be understood as his own proper work as

Son,[1] and his prophetic work as done on behalf of the Spirit. I believe such an understanding is more true to the dynamic, nuanced, and diverse narrative of Scripture, is a faithful elaboration of Christian (especially Reformed) tradition, and will prove more helpful pastorally than most current or traditional understandings.

The New Testament Witness

"Jesus is Lord!"[2] This confession stands as an early, if not the earliest, Christian claim.[3] It rings forth from Scripture in the earliest preaching, hymns, New Testament exegesis of the Old Testament, confession, as a standard for spiritual unity and discernment, and even as a statement of political defiance.[4] But what does the title "Lord" mean? Why is it ascribed to Jesus? What is its theological significance? Stated succinctly, the title attests that God the Father has bestowed royal authority upon the incarnate Son, Jesus, who becomes Christ the King, to accomplish in the power of the Spirit the proclamation and reestablishment of divine sovereignty in a world enslaved by falsehood, disordered power, corruption, evil, and death. Stated even more concisely, the Son *is* king, but he is such *as* the Father's regent, and the power he wields *is* that of the Holy Spirit.[5] As a

---

1. I say "proper" because as the Son he alone of the triune persons was to be the incarnate one (a prerequisite for his priestly, sacrificial work), and not because this office and work has primacy over the other two.

2. Cf. Acts 10:36; Rom 10:9; 1 Cor 8:6, 12:3; Phil 2:11.

3. Consider the representative words of W. A. Visser 't Hooft in *The Kingship of Christ* (New York: Harper & Brothers, 1948), p. 67: "What then is the rock bottom of the faith of the primitive Church? It is expressed in two words: *Jesous Kurios,* 'Jesus is Lord.' As we dig down deeper and deeper into the strata of the tradition we come finally to that simple affirmation." Cf. Hans Conzelmann, *An Outline of the Theology of the New Testament* (New York: Harper & Row, 1969), 83, who writes that the acclamation "is the real essential characteristic of Christianity. The Christians are named simply 'those who call upon the name of the Lord' (1 Cor 1:2; Rom 10:13)."

4. For examples of early preaching, see Acts 2:36 and 10:36; for hymns see Phil 2:11. For New Testament exegesis of the Old Testament, see Ps 110, as interpreted by Matt 22:44, Mark 16:19, Acts 2:34, 1 Cor 15:25, Eph 1:20, 3:22, and Heb 1:3, 13. For confession, see John 20:28, Rom 10:9, and 1 Cor 8:6. For unity and discernment, see Eph 4:4–5 and 1 Cor 12:3. For political defiance, see Eph 1:21 and, evidently, 1 Cor 12:3. Cf. the attitude regarding the true Lord and false lords pervading the whole book of Revelation.

5. See Ps. 110:1, "The LORD said to my lord: 'Sit at my right hand. . . .'" This became a crucial prooftext to the early church in understanding Jesus' status as Lord and King, as indicated by its frequent appearance—in either direct quotation or allusive reference—in

corollary, to then say "Jesus is Lord" (itself a title granted by the Father and an affirmation possible only at the prompting of the Holy Spirit [1 Cor 12:3]) is to recognize that no one or nothing else can be sovereign, that any pretenders to this title have been unmasked and deposed.[6]

The clearest and most powerful manifestation of this sovereignty is, of course, Christ's victory over death in the resurrection. Easter establishes the turning point of all that is to follow: the long sway of death's usurping dominion has been broken because God the Father has raised his Christ from the dead and seated him at his right hand as his regent. The resurrection means the tide of eschatological conflict has turned decisively and the foes of God's kingdom are in retreat. In this light, we may also recognize that Christ's victory over death is not restricted to the one event of the resurrection—as if Easter were an isolated episode, appearing out of nowhere and with no broader ramifications for God's larger purposes. Prospectively, it is the basis for the corollary events of Christ's ascension and Pentecost. But retrospectively, in light of Easter one may also discern that Christ's decisive victory was foreshadowed in the raising of Lazarus, Jairus's daughter, and the widow's son at Nain (John 11; Mark 5:22ff. // Luke 8:41ff.; Luke 7:11ff.).[7] Additionally, in light of the resurrection victory, one can now also recognize the reassertion of divine sovereignty and power in events with no obvious similarity to Easter. For example, Christ's royal authority and victory show in his triumph over all powers that would enslave humanity (e.g., Heb 2:14–15). His exorcisms and his healing of bodily infirmities (e.g., Mark 1:23–27, 3:20–27 [// Matt 12:22–29 // Luke 11:14–22], and 5:1–19 [// Matt 8:28–34 // Luke 8:26–39]), as well as his regal indifference to

---

different writings of the New Testament. As already noted above, see Matt 22:44, Mark 16:19, Acts 2:34, 1 Cor 15:25, Eph 1:20 and 3:22, and Heb 1:3, 13.

The connection between, indeed, at times the virtual identification of, the Holy Spirit and "power" *(dynamis)* is evident in some crucial New Testament verses. "As God's essence is power, endowment with power is linked to the gift of the Spirit, and this gift confers on Christ his authority *(exousía)*—an authority which he has the power *(dynamis)* to exercise in expelling demons or healing the sick." Gerhard Kittel and Gerhard Friedrich, ed., *Theological Dictionary of the New Testament* (trans. Geoffrey W. Bromiley; Grand Rapids, Mich.: Eerdmans, 1985), s.v. *"dynamis."* Consider Luke 1:35, 4:14, 24:49; Acts 1:8 (which makes explicit the meaning of Luke 24:49), 10:38; Rom 1:4, 15:13, 19; 1 Cor 2:4–5; Eph 3:16; and 1 Thess 1:5.

6. Regarding the title "Jesus is Lord," cf. the various passages interpreting Ps 110:1 and Phil 2:9–11.

7. While these are portrayed as "resuscitations" rather than transformative resurrections, they nevertheless function as signs pointing toward what is to come.

"worldly" powers (e.g., Luke 13:31–33, Matt 12:34–37, and John 19:8–11) all point to an assumption of authority directly counter to powers working against God's purposes. Christ's kingly authority and victory also manifest themselves in the accounts of his power over nature (e.g., Matt 8:23–27 // Mark 4:35–41 // Luke 8:22–25). Moreover, these messianic acts are placed in an explicit interpretive context by Jesus' messianic proclamation of the coming kingdom of God (or "kingdom of heaven.") Finally, the scriptural narrative makes clear that this victory is not merely Christ's private triumph, nor does it simply sway the hearts of believers. Rather, its impact extends beyond the subjective to the public realm. Christ's resurrection ushers in a new reality, and God intends its benefits to be shared. Christians do not witness this victory merely as spectators, but as participants, as they themselves are moved by the power of the Spirit. Paul recognizes this when he writes, "If, because of the one man's trespass, death exercised dominion through that one, much more surely will those who receive the abundance of grace and the free gift of righteousness exercise dominion in life through the one man, Jesus Christ" (Rom 5:17). Baptized into Christ, believers receive as a gift of the Spirit a new way of being and relating in the world. They receive a new identity, a new understanding of the world, a new orientation and allegiance, and a new hope.

This is a rich lot of claims regarding Christ's kingly office and its implications. How does the narrative of Scripture warrant them, what do they mean more precisely, and how do they interrelate? I will address each of these claims more fully by examining a variety of the biblical texts from which they are derived. Such detailed investigation is necessary to establish the variety of (often unexpected) ways the New Testament portrays Christ's kingly role. I should point out that in this preliminary examination, I will not always explicitly connect the Father and Spirit to the Son's royal work; in some instances, the link will be obvious, in others it will not. However, I can offer a kind of general interpretive shorthand: when Scripture speaks of Christ's authority, one may also think of that as the authority granted by the Father and when Scripture speaks of Christ's power, one may also think of that as the power granted by the Holy Spirit. Moreover, based on what the previous chapter presented, the trinitarian connections should be assumed until I address them more directly.

To begin, then, consider the manner in which the Bible understands the events of Easter as the final revelation of Christ's own true royal status and authority. Each of the gospels' post-resurrection accounts assumes this status and authority, either explicitly or implicitly. Matthew recounts Jesus saying to the eleven remaining disciples, "All authority in heaven and earth has been given to me," and as the disciples fulfill their commission, they are to teach all nations to obey what Jesus has commanded (Matt 28:18, 20). Mark's longer ending describes a similar commissioning of the disciples "to preach the gospel to the whole creation" and portrays Jesus endowing them with abilities that reflect his own earlier sovereign acts. Both descriptions presuppose Jesus has the authority and power to initiate such matters, a presupposition confirmed when Mark concludes by describing his ascension to sit at the right hand of God (Mark 16:15, 17–19). A full summary of Luke's account must consider passages from the final chapter of his gospel and the first two chapters of Acts. In them, he likewise describes the disciples' commission by the risen Christ, their "clothing with power from on high" (Luke 24:47–51; i.e., with the Holy Spirit, which is Jesus' response to the disciples' question, "Lord, is this the time when you will restore the kingdom of Israel?" [Acts 1:6–8]), and Christ's ascension to sit at the right hand of the Father (Acts 2:34–36). Finally, the Gospel of John also mentions Jesus ascending to the Father, and describes how he commissions the disciples with power and authority, in essence incorporating them into his own trinitarian work: "Jesus said to them again, 'Peace be with you. As the Father has sent me, so I send you.' When he had said this, he breathed on them and said to them, 'Receive the Holy Spirit. If you forgive the sins of any, they are forgiven them; if you retain the sins of any, they are retained'" (John 20:17, 21–23).

All of these narrative segments present the risen Christ as the regent of the triune God, acting as the mediator of divine authority on Earth. That is, Christ the Son exercises his sovereignty *on behalf of the Father,* and enacts it through the continuing presence and *power of the Spirit* (which is, in the words of Luke, "what my Father promised"). The words of one commentator regarding the closing verses of Matthew may apply more generally: "Jesus is not significant on his own, and in no way displaces the one God. Rather, the one to whom all authority is given, is given it in his capacity as Son to God the Father in a relationship mediated by the Spirit."[8] In other words, even as these accounts have the risen Lord as their narrative focal point, they still point to the trinitarian pattern and "division of labor" I described in the previous

---

8. R. W. L. Moberly, *The Bible, Theology, and Faith: A Study of Abraham and Jesus* (Cambridge Studies in Christian Doctrine; Cambridge: Cambridge University Press, 2000), 197.

chapter. For as they speak to Christ's sovereign victory over the grave, so, too, do they suggest that the Son's kingly work is ultimately grounded in, derived from, and oriented to the authority and purposes of the Father through his power, the Spirit.

Various non-narrative parts of the New Testament reinforce this post-Easter understanding of Christ's royal status and sovereignty exercised on behalf of the Father. Consider the well-known "christological hymn" of Phil 2, especially verses 9–11 and the phrases to which my italics draw attention: "Therefore *God* also highly *exalted him* and *gave him the name* that is above every name, so that at the name of Jesus every knee should bend, in heaven and on earth and under the earth, and every tongue should confess that Jesus Christ is Lord, *to the glory of God the Father.*" A similar dynamic appears in Eph 1:20–22, which describes God putting his "power to work in Christ when he raised him from the dead and seated him at his right hand in the heavenly places." Additionally, God puts "all things under [Christ's] feet and has made him the head over all things for the church." The focus is on Christ's royal status and authority, yet it is the Father who grants it. Next, consider Heb 1:3, which describes the Son as "the reflection of God's glory and the exact imprint of God's very being," who "sustains all things by his powerful word" and who "sat down at the right hand of the Majesty on high." Certainly one may easily discern the Son as the primary focus of this description, but can one as easily discern the primary agent? The Son acts, and his acting is crucial, but it also seems proper to say that he acts on the basis and initiative of God the Father. Finally, and most significantly, consider the following passage from 1 Cor 15:23–28:

> But each in his own order: Christ the first fruits, then at his coming those who belong to Christ. Then comes the end, when he hands over the kingdom to God the Father, after he has destroyed every ruler and every authority and power. For he must reign until he has put all his enemies under his feet. The last enemy to be destroyed is death. For "God has put all things in subjection under his feet." But when it says, "All things are put in subjection," it is plain that this does not include the one who put all things in subjection under him. When all things are subjected to him, then the Son himself will also be subjected to the one who put all things in subjection under him, so that God may be all in all.

The Son truly is the king, but his royal office and work are exercised on behalf of the one who has granted this status and authority to him. All things are subject to his rule, both within God's kingdom and without it, including all alien or enemy rulers and authorities. All things are subject to him, until the Son has completed the task given him, and returns sovereignty to the Father. More than any other, this passage from Corinthians summarizes and ties together the point discernible in all the preceding passages: in his victorious and trinitarian work as king, God the Son acts on behalf of God the Father, the original and ultimate sovereign.

In light of all the preceding—which is to say, Christ's victorious resurrection and all that it represents—may one then discern other ways that Scripture affirms and fleshes out Christ's status as king? That is, does Easter offer us a lens through which other passages become more theologically significant, even if the narrative locates them before Easter? The answer, of course, is yes. To begin, all four gospels portray Jesus' entry into Jerusalem (i.e., on Palm Sunday), as having royal implications. Matthew, Luke, and John present the most explicit witness to Christ's kingship by their quotation of prophecies thought to concern the messianic king (specifically, Isa 62:11 and/or Zech 9:9 and/or Ps 118:26) but even Mark implies the rank by allusion to one of these prophecies. The observations of Morna Hooker speak to this point:

> The insistence of Mark and Luke that the animal had never been ridden before suggests that it was therefore fit to be ridden by a king or for some sacred purpose. In Matthew and Mark, the entry follows immediately after an incident in which Jesus has been hailed as 'Son of David' as he leaves Jericho *en route* for Jerusalem, and we are reminded of the incident in 1 Kgs 1:32–40 when David, on his deathbed, commanded the priest Zadok and the prophet Nathan to mount Solomon on David's own mule, escort him to Gihon, anoint him king and bring him back to Jerusalem to the acclamation of the people. The evangelists certainly saw the messianic implications of their story: Mark simply hints at this by saying that the crowd hailed 'the coming kingdom of our father David,' but in Matthew, Jesus is hailed as Son of David, and in Luke and John he is welcomed as king; Matthew and John refer specifically to Zech 9:9; the Synoptic evangelists all describe how people spread greenery or garments on the road.[9]

To be sure, Christ will fulfill his kingly role in ways quite contrary to the desires and expectations of the cheering crowds. In this respect, knowing

---

9. Morna D. Hooker, *The Signs of a Prophet: The Prophetic Actions of Jesus* (Harrisburg, Penn.: Trinity Press International, 1997), 43.

the outcome of the story, as the Christian community did in light of Easter, increases the dramatic power of the Palm Sunday narrative, because it can be understood as operating at two levels. Auditors of the story know that the crowds are correct to welcome Christ as their messianic king, even as they also know the crowds are mistaken about, indeed, cannot imagine what that kingship will ultimately entail. I will discuss the theological implications of Christ's redefinition of the office more fully below; at this point, I want only to establish the narrative details.

All four gospels also associate the title "King of the Jews" with Jesus' trial before Pilate, his mocking by the soldiers and crowds, and the inscription placed above his head on the cross. As with the account of Jesus' entry into Jerusalem, the narrative of his trial and passion also operates at several levels simultaneously, mixing elements of historical memory, religious polemic, and theological affirmation. At one level, "King of the Jews" simply summarized the charge brought against Jesus by the authorities and the reason for his execution by the Romans (Matt 27:37 // Mark 15:26 // Luke 23:38; cf. John 19:19–20). As such, it obviously functioned as a warning, rather than as an acknowledgment of how the imperial authorities perceived his actual status. It indicated that he was crucified because he represented the threat of political insurrection— even while the evidence for this accusation remained ambiguous. At another level, the Gospels leave open the possibility that the title is either inappropriate or applied only sarcastically. Consider Jesus' reply to Pilate's question, "Are you the King of the Jews?" He responds in the Synoptic Gospels with the ambiguous words "You say so" (Matt 27:11 // Mark 15:2 // Luke 23:3), and then lapses into silence (Matt 27:14 // Mark 15:5). Even the Gospel of John, in which Jesus speaks explicitly of his "kingship" (John 18:36) ends on an ambiguous note, with Pilate asking, "So you are a king?" and Jesus replying in an echo of the synoptic account, "You say that I am a king" (John 18:37). Then note how the soldiers taunt Jesus with the title (Matt 27:29 // Mark 15:18; cf. Luke 23:36–37 and John 19:2–3), while the crowd mockingly repudiates Jesus' claim to it, knowing it conflicts with submission to Caesar (Luke 23:2 and John 19:15; possibly implicit in Matt 27:11–14; cf. John 19:21). Even Pilate apparently doubts the title's applicability, although he continues to employ it (Mark 15:9, 12; cf. John 18:39; 19:14–15, 21–22). Again, these various references to Jesus' "kingship" likely reflect a certain amount of historical memory. But they also serve to set the stage for the passion narrative's later reversal and transformation by the resurrection. For at the most important level—that is, in the church's understanding of faith—all ambiguous and sarcastic ascriptions of "kingship" to Christ display a double irony. Christian hearers of the gospel narrative know that the title "king" truly is properly ascribed to Jesus, albeit in a way entirely unanticipated by the soldiers, the crowds, or Pilate. In the synoptic accounts of the passion, only the words of the repentant thief crucified alongside Jesus point to this new understanding (Luke 23:42), while John's Gospel says a bit more, albeit allusively (18:36–37). That is, understood through the lens of Easter and the affirmation that God has seated him at his right hand, Jesus may now be recognized as transcending previous understandings of "king," and giving the office a wholly new status and definition.

Several other passages from Matthew's Gospel likewise point to Christ's kingly role. For instance, Matthew anticipates and reinforces the narratives of Jesus' entry into Jerusalem and passion in several ways: by means of his genealogy, with the story of the magi from the East, and with Jesus' prophecy regarding the last judgment. As many commentators have observed, Matthew's genealogy emphasizes Jesus' royal descent in a way that Luke's does not. The key difference is that Matthew's genealogy traces Jesus' lineage back through the kings of Judah.[10] Matthew's account of Jesus' birth further emphasizes his status (and foreshadows the passion narrative) when it recounts the magi's question to King Herod, "Where is the child who has been born king of the Jews? For we observed his star at its rising, and have come to pay him homage" (Matt 2:2). Indeed, New Testament scholar Deirdre Good argues that Matthew's account of King Herod serves in part to offer a negative counterpart to the true king, Jesus.[11] Finally, Matt 25:31–46 presents a scene of the Last Judgment, shaped by a general apocalyptic sensibility and, it would seem, the more particular influence of Ps 110:1. The Son of Man, who has come in his glory and is seated upon his glorious throne, will judge the nations, placing "the sheep" at his right hand and the "goats" at his left. "Then the king will say to those at his right hand, 'Come, you that are blessed by my Father, inherit the kingdom prepared for you from the foundation of the world . . .'" (Matt 25:34).[12]

---

10. For example, B. H. Throckmorton Jr., "Genealogy (Christ)," in *Interpreter's Dictionary of the Bible* (New York: Abingdon Press, 1962), 2:365.

11. Deirdre J. Good, *Jesus the Meek King* (Harrisburg, Penn.: Trinity Press International, 1999), 85ff. I will discuss this more fully below.

12. Note that the passage repeats the title "king" again in v. 40, and that it connects it with the title "Lord" used by the king's interlocutors.

The identification of Jesus with the Son of Man, the shepherd king exercising judgment on behalf of the Father, is obvious.

Other New Testament writings also identify Jesus as the messianic king, either explicitly or implicitly. Like that of Matthew, the Gospel of John places a reference to Jesus as king early in his narrative, when in Jesus' first encounter with Nathanael, John portrays the latter as exclaiming, "Rabbi, you are the Son of God! You are the King of Israel!" (John 1:49). The Acts of the Apostles presents two episodes associating Jesus with a kingly status. The first implies the connection by portraying Jesus as God's messianic choice to fulfill the royal role he first gave to Saul, and then to David and his posterity (Acts 13:21ff.). The other episode echoes the complaint made in Luke 23, in which a crowd protests to the authorities that Jesus is usurping Caesar's status. Specifically, Paul, Silas, and the local Christians are accused of "all acting contrary to the decrees of the emperor, saying that there is another king named Jesus" (Acts 17:5–7). The Letter to the Hebrews also implies his royal status through its connection of Christ to the obscure Old Testament figure Melchizedek. While Hebrews employs this figure primarily in order to describe Jesus as a priest "after the order of Melchizedek," it also points out that the latter's name means both "king of righteousness" and "king of peace" (Heb 7:2). Finally, the Revelation of John intertwines a number of titles, speaking of Jesus as "the Lamb" who conquers and "the Word of God" who will strike down and rule the nations—and as this victorious Lamb and sovereign Word, he is also called "Lord of lords" and "King of kings" (Rev 17:14 and 19:13–16). Each of these passages adds a particular emphasis or detail to the picture of Christ as king, even as they mutually reinforce one another in affirming his status as such.

The New Testament speaks to Christ's status as king not just in those passages that explicitly connect the title to him, but also in those passages that describe his sovereign and triumphant activity. That is, he signals his rank by what he does, and he does a number of things with sovereign authority and power. To begin, the various portrayals of Christ's victorious strength in exorcism speak directly to this authority, for the gospel accounts present these acts as nothing less than apocalyptic confrontations between God and the demonic powers. For example, the very first chapter of Mark contains an episode in which Jesus exorcises a man with an unclean spirit (Mark 1:21–28). This episode is significant because it represents Mark's first detailed description of one of Jesus' public acts. The events that precede it serve primarily to set the stage: Jesus' "commissioning" in his baptism and testing in the wilderness (1:9–13),[13] a brief and general statement of Jesus preaching the gospel (vv. 14–15), and a description of Jesus gathering his disciples (vv. 16–20). But then Mark presents this exorcism, which begins the narrative action of his entire gospel. It establishes the sense that someone greater than a mere teacher has come, that a conflict is brewing, and that the stakes will be wagered on a cosmic scale. To be sure, Jesus does teach, and does so as "one with authority" (v. 22). But he will also match his words with powerful deeds, as the exorcism demonstrates. Mark reinforces this picture of Jesus' sovereign authority by following this episode with a brief account of Jesus healing Simon's mother-in-law of her fever (vv. 29–31) and a summary description of how "all who were sick or possessed with demons" were brought to him for healing and exorcism (vv. 32–34). Additionally, Mark implies that this first detailed episode represents the pattern of Jesus' ministry when he writes: "And he went throughout Galilee, proclaiming the message in their synagogues and casting out demons" (v. 39).

This opening exorcism is also noteworthy because the unclean spirit recognizes immediately who Jesus is ("the Holy One of God"), rhetorically asking what he has come to do ("have you come to destroy us?"). More typically in Mark's Gospel, characters do not recognize Jesus' status and role as God's Messiah, or misunderstand it according to their own preconceptions and desires. Indeed, Mark is famous as the gospel writer most apt to portray Jesus as maintaining the "messianic secret," in part as a way to avoid such misconceptions. (Of the exorcisms mentioned in vv. 32–34, Mark writes: "and he would not permit the demons to speak, because they knew him.") Once again, we have a narrative that functions at two levels: the story line says one thing, because its (human) characters miss the truth, yet the gospel's Christian hearers know the truth and so understand the reason behind Jesus' acts and commands. The words of this first unclean spirit effectively anticipate the fate of all ungodly spiritual powers, for he knows that Jesus' appearance represents the beginning of an eschatological conflict that must end in the subjection and destruction of all like him.

The same point is reinforced in another, even more detailed and dramatic exorcism account in Mark 5:1–20 (cf. the parallels in Matt 8:28–34 and Luke 8:26–39), which describes Jesus' encounter with the

---

13. Recall my trinitarian interpretation of this twofold event in chapter 3.

Gerasene demoniac. Here the sense of spiritual tyranny and oppression stands out starkly, for Mark portrays the possessed man as living in a graveyard, tormented by an uncontrollable power, wracked by loud cries day and night, and "bruising himself with stones." The sense that this episode represents not just the misfortune of an isolated individual, but a crucial engagement in a larger spiritual warfare is confirmed by the unclean spirit's name, "Legion." This indicates not just that the man is possessed by a large number of demons; it also indicates their character, for the term refers, of course, to a unit in the Roman army roughly equivalent to a modern division. In other words, the man is not merely "possessed," he is himself a battlefield engaged in mortal conflict with an invading army. Not surprisingly, then, his surroundings are filled with corpses and his symptoms echo the clash and clangor one would expect on the front lines. Neither is it surprising that the battle should end with frightful carnage: Jesus drives the unclean spirits into a herd of (unclean) swine, which then rushes down the bank to drown in the sea. In other words, Jesus has utterly routed the forces that sought to enslave and corrupt this man, and in so doing, indicates once more his sovereign power and authority in reclaiming creation for God.[14] Indeed, the certainty with which he exercises that power and authority shows Jesus to be unintimidated by the powers of this world, whether human or demonic. One notes this attitude especially in his response to Herod's scheming (Luke 13:31–32), his cleansing of the Temple (Matt 21:12–13 // Mark 11:15–19 // Luke 19:45–48; cf. John 2:13–17), his shrewd response on the matter of paying tribute to Caesar (Matt 22:15–22 // Mark 12:13–17 // Luke 20:20–26), his indictment of the "ruler of this world" (John 12:28–31), and his conversation with Pilate (John 18:33–38). He is secure in his sovereignty.

The New Testament frequently renders accounts of Jesus' healings in a manner that echoes and reinforces its accounts of his exorcisms. They, too, are messianic actions undertaken with sovereign power and authority. Indeed, Mark follows this initial exorcism story with brief accounts

---

14. This combination of Jesus' preaching and liberating persons from (demonic?) captivity may also stand behind the obscure references found in the first epistle of Peter. First Peter 3:18–20 and 4:6 describe Christ preaching "to the spirits in prison" and to "the dead." These passages became the grounds for belief in Jesus' "harrowing of hell," a notion that gained popularity in medieval English mystery plays. Whatever the original meaning of these texts or the biblical warrant for the "harrowing" notion, they do seem to suggest that even death does not take persons beyond the reach of Christ's sovereign authority and power.

of several healings and more exorcisms, such that both types of action appear to have the same eschatological significance (cf. Mark 3:9–11). Consider as well the story of the woman healed of her bleeding. The accounts of both Mark and Luke pointedly note that "power had gone forth" from Jesus, healing the woman immediately at her mere touch of his garment (Mark 5:25–33 and Luke 8:42b–48; cf. Luke 6:19). Matthew offers a more abbreviated version, which presents the cure as the direct result of Jesus' pronouncement rather than the woman's touch. Still, in all three renditions, the sense of Jesus' regal authority and power remains, a sense heightened further by the fact that he is portrayed as exercising it in such an off-hand manner. After all, this story is presented as nothing more than an aside to the main narrative trajectory, which describes Jesus going to heal Jairus's daughter, only to raise her finally from the dead. This main event is, of course, an even more telling indication of his sovereign power and authority. And it is repeated, and thus the character of Christ's royal status and role reinforced, in the accounts of his raising of the widow's son at Nain (Luke 7:11–17) and Lazarus (John 11:1–44).

Accounts of Jesus' various "nature miracles" also have implications for his sovereign status and power. Consider first the stories describing Jesus' stilling the chaotic waters of the storm (Matt 8:23–27 // Mark 4:35–41 // Luke 8:22–25), and note especially the amazed response of the disciples: "Who then is this, that he commands even wind and water, and they obey him?" (Luke 8:25).[15] The gospel accounts leave the question dangling, but faithful hearers of the story know the answer: control over the waves is a prerogative of the divine sovereign, as numerous Old Testament passages indicate.[16] Moreover, it is a prerogative with eschatological implications (cf. Luke 21:25 and 2 Esd 16:12). That stilling the waters has specifically "kingly" associations is also suggested by contrasting Jesus' success with the failure of the earlier pretender, Antiochus Epiphanes (see 2 Macc 9:8). In a similar manner, the gospel accounts of Jesus' feeding miracles also evoke a sense of his sovereignty and power over creation.[17] The multiplication of the loaves and fishes would on its own recall the creative power of God, yet the various

---

15. The same basic question is asked in the two parallels (Matt 8:27 // Mark 4:41).

16. See Exod 14:15–16, 21–22, 26–27; Pss 65:5–7, 77:16–20, 89:8–9, and 107:28–9; Jer 31:35; and Isa 43:15–16 and 51:15.

17. Matt 14:13–21 // Mark 6:30–44 // Luke 9:10–17; Matt 15:32–39 // Mark 8:1–10; John 6:1–15, 22–59.

accounts add other details that strengthen the sense that Jesus is acting as a messianic king. All of the Synoptics locate these feedings in "the desert" *(erēmía)*, a word which elicits associations with the place where the Lord God, through his leader Moses, provided manna for the Israelites (see Exod 16:1–35, and especially its prophetic reading in Acts 7:35–38). Four accounts speak of Jesus having compassion for the crowd,[18] a disposition frequently associated with God's sovereign and merciful power toward Israel in the Psalms and prophets.[19] One of Mark's accounts adds that Jesus was compassionate "because they were like a sheep without a shepherd," a predicament that the Old Testament uses to describe the people without a leader or king.[20] Finally, John's account makes the connection between this miracle and sovereignty explicit when he describes the crowd's reaction and Jesus' response: "When the people saw the sign that he had done, they began to say, 'This is indeed the prophet who is to come into the world.' When Jesus realized that they were about to come and take him by force to make him king, he withdrew again to the mountain by himself" (John 6:14–15). Jesus' withdrawal is, of course, not due to the fact that he refuses to be king, but because his "kingdom is not of this world" (John 18:36–37).

Consider more fully a point made earlier, namely, that one must also recognize how these sovereign acts occur within the explicit interpretive context provided by Jesus' messianic proclamation of the coming kingdom of God (or "kingdom of heaven"). Jesus serves not just as the messenger of this "kingdom" or "reign" *(basileía)*, but as its authoritative embodiment and enactor.[21] Conversely, everything he enacts and embodies gains its explicit and final meaning from its reference back to the message of God's in-breaking reign. The present work is not the place to undertake an extensive examination of Jesus' preaching and enacting of the kingdom; other books have already done that, at greater

---

18. Matt 14:14 // Mark 6:34; Matt 15:32 // Mark 8:2.

19. Cf. Pss 77:8–9, 79:8–9, 90:13, 102:13, 103:13–14, 106:45, 135:14, 145:9; Isa 14:1, 49:13–15, 54:7–8, 10; Jer 30:18; Lam 3:32–33; Mic 7:18–19; and Zech 1:16, 10:6, 12:10.

20. See Num 27:15–20, 1 Kgs 22:13–23, Ezek 34:1–16, and Zech 10:2. Cf. Jer 23:1–4. Interestingly, Matt 9:36 also employs the simile, and while the context there is Jesus' "proclaiming the good news of the kingdom, and curing every disease and sickness" (9:35) rather than a feeding miracle, I believe the implications regarding Jesus' sovereignty remain the same.

21. Cf. Morna Hooker's observation: "Jesus refuses to perform authenticating miracles. The miracles he *is* said to perform are not intended as mere 'proofs' of his authority to do what he is doing, but are themselves significant actions which effect God's saving purpose." Hooker, *The Signs of a Prophet*, 35.

and lesser length.[22] I simply want to highlight the obvious and therefore perhaps easily overlooked point that Jesus' proclamation of God's reign has something to say about his own sovereign authority and power. Christ the King and his preaching of the kingdom must not be separated. Sometimes this proclamation occurs in spoken form (consider his parables or his similes: "The kingdom is like . . ."). At other times, Jesus describes God's reign by enacting its various characteristics (consider how he forgives sinners and his graciousness in eating with the "immoral," unclean, or outcast). Whatever the form of proclamation, Jesus' words and deeds further define the sovereign acts and titles discussed thus far, even as those acts and titles further clarify his proclamation. The one substantive observation I will make here is this: Jesus' proclamation of God's reign serves primarily to counter all worldly understandings or expectations of what a "kingdom" might mean or achieve. This is an observation I will discuss more fully below, in the section entitled "Christ's Redefinition of Kingship and Victory."

On the relation between Jesus' acts and his proclamation of the kingdom, I offer a further observation. At one level, many of Jesus' mighty deeds may be understood as "enacted examples" of the in-breaking reign of God. But at another level, these deeds serve to enact and authorize Jesus' role in that reign. In other words, his acts may indeed be construed as illustrations of his descriptions of the kingdom of God. It is certainly appropriate to say that Jesus' feeding of the multitudes illustrates God's care and compassion for his people. His table fellowship with sinners exemplifies how inclusion in the kingdom occurs not because of merit or status or wealth or power, but according to God's graciousness. But in another, more crucial sense, Jesus' acts do not so much illustrate the character of the kingdom as they establish his authority and power within it. Even more pointedly, these acts serve to establish his authority to turn on their heads all prior assumptions about the heavenly kingdom, what a "king" is, and what it means to live under the reign of God. To cite but one example, consider Jesus' healing of the paralytic (Matt 9:1–8 // Mark 2:1–12 // Luke 5:17–26). On the one hand, the story certainly illustrates God's openness to sinners and the divine willingness to forgive—a general lesson one could abstract from a large number of Jesus' teachings about the reign of God. On the other

---

22. See, among others, Hooker's *The Signs of a Prophet*, and N. T. Wright, *Jesus and the Victory of God* (vol. 2 of *Christian Origins and the Question of God*; Minneapolis: Fortress Press, 1996).

hand, the primary point of this episode is to establish Jesus' authority to forgive sins, in the face of those who accuse him of blasphemy in claiming a divine prerogative. Jesus cures the paralytic as a way of answering his own rhetorical question, "Which is easier, to say to the paralytic, 'Your sins are forgiven,' or to say, 'Rise, take up your pallet, and walk'?" In other words, the healing is not just a sign of God's salvation, it is also a means of demonstrating Jesus' divine authority.

Where, then, does all of the preceding lead us? To flesh out my presentation of Christ as victorious king, I have considered many different parts and types of the scriptural narrative. I have unpacked the implications of Easter, examined titles and actions with royal associations, considered Jesus' exorcisms, healings, and "nature miracles," and pointed out how his proclamation of the kingdom of God relates to his own sovereign authority and role. But I also began this whole consideration under the presupposition that as the victorious king, Christ nevertheless acts on behalf of the Father. More precisely, I stated that to affirm Christ as victorious king is to say that God the Father has bestowed royal authority upon the incarnate Son to accomplish in the power of the Spirit the proclamation and reestablishment of divine sovereignty in a world enslaved by alien and illegitimate powers. Before concluding this section, let me return briefly to this theme that Jesus, the incarnate Son, is sovereign on behalf and under the authority of the Father.

The theme arises in various scriptural locations, both directly and indirectly. To begin, the opening verses of John 17 make the point quite explicitly. It is the Father who gives the Son authority over all people, who gives him his work to do, and who gives him a community to whom he may give knowledge of God and eternal life (see John 17:1ff.). Then consider the episode discussed above, that is, Jesus' forgiveness and healing of the paralytic. Matthew's account concludes with these words: "When the crowds saw it, they were filled with awe, and they glorified God, who had given such authority to human beings" (Matt 9:8). The Apocalypse of John reveals that the Son of God will give authority to the faithful, "even as I also received authority from my Father" (Rev 2:26–28). For a more indirect example, consider first the challenge of the chief priests and elders to Jesus, "By what authority are you doing these things?" (Matt 21:23–27 // Mark 11:27–33 // Luke 20:1–8). Jesus answers their question with his own question, and never gives a direct answer. But the unspoken conclusion is that his authority comes from heaven. Recall as well the implication of the centurion's words: "Lord, . . . only say the word, and my servant will be healed. For

I am a man under authority, with soldiers under me; and I say to one 'Go,' and he goes . . ." (Matt 8:8–9).[23] He acknowledges Jesus' authority, even while his comparison suggests that Jesus, too, is "under authority."

Given all that I have considered in the preceding pages, what conclusions may we draw regarding Christ in his office as king, especially in light of this book's trinitarian concern? First, it is apparent that in all these different aspects of his role, Christ never exercises his office of king in isolation from the other two persons of the Trinity. "The external works of the Trinity are undivided." He does not act as a "lone ranger." Rather, he exercises this office in the Spirit (cf. Matt 12:28 // Luke 11:20) on behalf of the proper sovereign, God the Father. But in that sense, then, one may, secondly, understand the victory of Christ in his royal office as the "perichoretical" work of the Father. Recall the diverse exegetical evidence I have gathered. Christ has been anointed the Father's regent to reveal and enact the kingdom of God. Therefore he can proclaim: "All authority on heaven and earth has been given to me" (Matt 28:18; cf. Luke 10:22). Yet at the same time, that authority is neither originally nor finally his own. We recognize this in Scripture's witness, on the one hand, to the Son's testimony that "I do nothing on my own authority, but on that of the Father" (see John 5:30, 8:28, and 14:10). On the other hand, Scripture also affirms of Jesus that "when all things are subjected to him, then the Son himself will also be subjected to the one who put all things in subjection under him, so that God may be all in all" (1 Cor 15:28). In this victory over the principalities, powers, and death, the Son reclaims creation for the Father. The project that the Father, "maker of heaven and earth," initiated in the beginning has been returned to its original course, so that it may ultimately attain its fulfillment.

The Old Testament Witness

In its encounter with the risen Christ, the Christian church was born and given a new way of understanding God's atoning work in the world. Of course, the church was not born ex nihilo; it arose from a Jewish milieu, shaped by the stories of Jewish Scripture. So, a more precise way of putting it is to say that in Christ the earliest believers gained a new way of interpreting the scriptural narratives that had first formed

---

23. This example is cited by Good, *Jesus the Meek King*, 18, to illustrate a point slightly different than the one I am making here.

them. The risen Christ provided his disciples with a new hermeneutical key, as Luke's account of his Emmaus road conversation indicates: "And beginning with Moses and all the prophets, he interpreted to them the things about himself in all the Scriptures" (Luke 24:27). In light of the risen Christ, members of the nascent Christian community knew they could no longer read Scripture as they had before. Indeed, in light of the risen Christ, the Christian community was compelled to read Scripture in a new way. Yet the community had faith that its old Scriptures would also help explain more fully the meaning of this new reality, its risen Savior and Lord. So the stage was set. The Jewish Scriptures remained the Scriptures of the church, but they also became the resource for a new interpretation of God's work, an interpretation which, of course, transformed this resource into the "Old" Testament and became itself the "New."

With these thoughts in mind, this section will outline and summarize the basic Old Testament story and themes available to the church's theological reflection to help explain the new reality of the royal or kingly Christ. Specifically, this section will sketch what the Old Testament says regarding Israel's various kings and its understanding of the royal office, in order to provide the context for my subsequent discussion of how Christ both fulfills and redefines the biblical notion of "king." The biblical story of Israel's monarchy is well known, and need only be outlined here. I will devote more space to a discussion of the Old Testament's theological understanding of the status, role, and responsibilities of the king. But in both undertakings, the goal will not be to offer a reconstruction of the monarchy's "actual" history or the various attitudes and understandings related to the monarchy contemporaneous with that history. Rather, I present this synopsis as a way of outlining the basic stories available to the church, as it sought—and still seeks—to clarify and ground in biblical tradition its affirmation of Christ as king. The early church did not approach its Scriptures with a modern historian's mind-set, seeking to get "behind" the text in order to offer a critical understanding of what happened "back then." It approached Scripture as believers, seeking to find what the inspired text might reveal to them about the new reality confronting them in their own age. I want to offer some suggestion of the theological resources they may have found that remain available in our own day.

The first king of Israel was, of course, Saul, who, it should be recalled, ascended to the office sometime around 1020 B.C. through charismatic anointing rather than heredity. That is, according to the scriptural narrative, Saul was chosen by Yahweh through the prophet Samuel to serve as king, in much the same manner as Yahweh had previously chosen the "Judges" (1 Sam 9:15ff. and 10:1ff.). God transferred the kingship to David following the same procedure, by guiding Samuel to find and anoint him to replace Saul (1 Sam 16:1–13). Of course, Saul and his allies did not acknowledge this transfer of power, so it took some time before David could consolidate his rule. But this he finally accomplished, and after capturing Jerusalem from the Jebusites, he brought the ark of the covenant to it and established it as his capital over all Israel (2 Sam 5:1–10). Jerusalem thus became both the religious and political heart of the nation.[24] Only with David did the practice of hereditary monarchy emerge, with the anointing of Solomon, his young son by Bathsheba, as king. (It is worth noting that this succession occurred only after some palace intrigue by the backers of Solomon, over against the backers of David's older son, Adonijah, and that there is no mention of God prompting the anointing carried out by Zadok the priest and Nathan the prophet [1 Kgs 1].) The shift to a dynastic monarchy was understood as initiated by God, however, and also secured by his promise that it be established in perpetuity (2 Sam 7:8–17, and alluded to in 1 Kgs 2:4; cf. Ps 89:19–37 and 132:11–12). Solomon is famous for being the king who built the Temple (1 Kgs 5–8), but he was also known as a king who laid a heavy burden on his people and engaged in idolatry (1 Kgs 9:15–22 and 11:1–43). Following his forty-year reign, the nation was divided.

The scriptural account attributes this division to Solomon's son Rehoboam, who rejected the plea made by Jeroboam, a former lieutenant and then adversary of Solomon, to lighten the burden placed on the people by Solomon. Rehoboam instead increased that burden, and thereby fomented secession by the ten northern tribes, which created Judah in the south and Israel in the north (1 Kgs 12). Thus began the separate histories of the two kingdoms, evaluated by the Deuteronomic

---

24. Consider the continuing ramifications of this move, as described by Keith W. Whitelam: "The temple, among other things, represented heaven upon earth (Ps 1:4). As the dwelling place of the deity upon earth, situated next to the king's palace and part of the same complex, it symbolized the king's special relationship with the divine world and the political and religious center of the state. In Judah, this was expressed in the royal Davidic ideology of a double election of Jerusalem as the dwelling place of Yahweh and the promise to David of a dynasty in perpetuity (2 Sam 7:1–17; Ps 89:1–37)." Keith W. Whitelam, "King and Kingship," *Anchor Bible Dictionary* (New York: Doubleday, 1992), 4:47.

editor of the biblical account according to the faithlessness or faithfulness of their respective succession of kings. The story of Elijah's prophetic denunciations of, and conflict with, King Ahab of Israel and his wife Jezebel for their idolatry and apostasy stands as the best-known example of the former (1 Kgs 16:29–22:40; 2 Kgs 9:30–37). The favorable accounts of King Hezekiah and especially King Josiah stand as the best-known examples of the latter (2 Kgs 18–20 and 22–23:30). Of course, each kingdom eventually collapsed, when Israel fell to the Assyrians in 721 B.C. and Judah fell to the Babylonians in 587 B.C.

Thus ended the classic "monarchic period" of Israel's history, an era that had spanned over four hundred years. The nation's concept of, and aspirations for, the royal office became more complicated and diverse in the centuries that followed. In Judah, the Persian-sponsored return of the people and reconstruction of the temple raised hopes of a restored Davidic line as well, because the governor appointed by Darius was Zerubbabel, a descendent of David through his great-grandfather King Josiah (see Hag 2:20–23 and Zech 3:8 and 6:12, as well as 4:5–10, 13–14). Moreover, given the catastrophic impact of the Babylonian captivity, such hopes for a restoration were not couched merely in terms of the *status quo ante,* but had begun to take on more expansive messianic overtones and longings. Such hopes were not to be realized by Zerubbabel, however, and thus they were left to grow. Persian dominance was eventually replaced by Hellenistic dominance, as the conquests of Alexander the Great brought Judah into his empire. The machinations of Alexander's successors need not concern us here, except to note that Judah came under the sway of the Seleucids. After the second-century-B.C. Seleucid king Antiochus IV Epiphanes desecrated the temple and proscribed adherence to Torah, the priestly family of Mattathias began what became known as the Maccabean Revolt (after his son, Judas Maccabeus, who succeeded him). The revolt gained Judea a certain independence to practice its faith, which continued even after the loss of political autonomy under the Romans. The revolt also established the Hasmonean dynasty, but this was a priestly lineage, not a royal one, even though from Alexander Janneus on rulers in the family assumed the title of king (including, eventually, Herod the Great). Thus, any hopes for a political, and more specifically Davidic, messiah were still unrealized at the time of Jesus' birth.

In light of this narrative, what was the basic theological understanding of the place and role of the King as presented by Scripture? And how did this understanding evolve over the years to the period of Jesus' life, death, and resurrection? To begin, one must recognize that even with a human king, the true king of Israel (the larger entity encompassing both the southern kingdom of Judah and the northern kingdom of Israel) was still conceived to be God. References and allusions to Yahweh's reign or Yahweh as "king" are widespread, and may be found in all three divisions of the Hebrew Scriptures. For example, and significantly, the following verse concludes, and in a true sense summarizes, the "Song of Moses," the poem of victory celebrating God's defeat of Pharaoh at the Red Sea: "The LORD will reign forever and ever" (Exod 15:18). One of the oracles of Balaam reiterates this point: "The Lord their God is with them, acclaimed as a king among them" (Num 23:21). And later, during the time of the judges, Gideon refuses being made king with the words "I will not rule over you, and my son will not rule over you; the LORD will rule over you" (Judg 8:23).[25] In the "Writings," the commonly labeled "Enthronement Psalms"[26] variously describe Yahweh's accession to his throne as king (with the recurring phrase *yhwh mālak*) and the exercise of his royal power and judgment in the heavenly realm, over creation (and the forces of chaos), and over Israel and her adversaries. Taken together, this exercise prompts the following conclusion: "The guarantee of order, *mišpāt*, peace, security and well-being, is fundamental to Yahweh's kingship."[27] Finally, the themes of the Enthronement Psalms regarding God's kingship are reiterated and reinforced in the prophetic literature as well. Isaiah makes it clear that God is king (41:21, 44:6–7, and 52:7), and portrays his sovereignty over the host of heaven and the kings of the earth and over the events of history (24:21–23 and 44:7–8). Jeremiah proclaims: "But the Lord is the true God; he is the living God and the everlasting King. At his wrath the earth quakes, and the nations cannot endure his indignation" (Jer 10:10). Zephaniah stresses the care, the protection from enemies, and the restoration that God the King exercises on the behalf of Israel (Zeph 3:14–20), while Zechariah envisions the final eschatological victory to be won on the day of the Lord, when all the nations will recognize God as king (Zech 14:1–16).

If God was so widely affirmed as the true king of Israel, what did that imply for her many human kings? A minority view still evident in

---

25. For other passages from Torah, or the historical writings, see Deut 33:5, 1 Sam 8:7, 10:19, and 12:12.

26. Included among these psalms are, at a minimum, Pss 47, 93, 95–99. The following observations summarize and paraphrase the analysis of Whitelam, "King and Kingship," 4:43.

27. Whitelam, "King and Kingship," 4:43.

Scripture considered the inauguration of a human king a usurpation of divine prerogatives, indeed a form of apostasy.[28] But more typically, the human king was viewed as a kind of regent or vassal acting on behalf of the divine king. As such, he was understood as having a unique relationship to God, sometimes indicated by the description that he was God's "son," which was "an expression of the sacral importance and functions of the king rather than the expression of a belief in the divine nature of the king."[29] The human regent was also called "the anointed of Yahweh" (or "the Lord's anointed," *māšiah yhwh*), particularly in accounts of the first king, Saul.[30] But the designation was also applied to Saul's successor David,[31] to the later king Zedekiah (Lam 4:20), and perhaps the post-exilic governor of Judah, Zerubbabel (Dan 9:25–26, although the original referent is not certain). And insofar as the term found its way into a number of Psalms (e.g., Pss 2:2, 18:50, 20:6, 45:6–7, 132:10), it could presumably have been applied to any of Israel's kings. Finally, in a startling use of the term that highlights even more God's universal sovereignty, Isaiah even applied it to the Persian ruler Cyrus as one who serves God's purposes (Isa 45:1).

In any case, as the regent of Yahweh, the king was called to serve and be obedient to him, "walking in his ways and keeping his statutes, his commandments, his ordinances, and his testimonies, as it is written in the law of Moses, so that you may prosper in all that you do and wherever you turn" (1 Kgs 2:3). More specifically, this entailed several concrete responsibilities. Preeminent among them was the king's duty to serve as the guardian of true and faithful worship. Examples of the application of this responsibility occur in the scriptural evaluations of various kings. Some are described in highly favorable terms, such as King Josiah, whose reforms in repairing the temple, reinstituting conformity to the newly rediscovered law, including a renewal of Passover, and abolition of pagan cults earned him the highest praise (2 Kgs 22:1–23:25).[32] Others received mixed reviews, such as King Solomon. First Kings 8:65–66 concludes the account of Solomon's building of the

---

28. Most evident in the perspectives of the so-called "Late Source" in 1 Sam 8:1–22, 10:19, and 12:12. Cf. Hos 8:4. For a succinct analysis, see Stephen Szikszai, "King, Kingship," in *Interpreter's Dictionary of the Bible* (New York: Abingdon Press, 1962), 3:14.

29. Ps 2:7 and Whitelam, "King and Kingship," 4:45.

30. 1 Sam 16:16; 24:6, 10; 26:9, 11, 16, 23; 2 Sam 1:14, 16.

31. 2 Sam 19:21–22, and in slight variation perhaps also Pss 2:2, 20:6, and 89:20.

32. Cf. the similar evaluations of Kings Jehoash (2 Kgs 12:1–8) and Hezekiah (2 Kgs 18:1–6).

temple, and it ends on an approving note. But 1 Kgs 11:1–12 announces God's condemnation of Solomon because he "turned his heart away after other gods," and "did not keep what the Lord commanded." Finally, others are roundly condemned for their apostasy and idolatry, the most notorious example being King Ahab:

> Ahab son of Omri did evil in the sight of the LORD more than all who were before him. And as if it had been a light thing for him to walk in the sins of Jeroboam son of Nebat, he took as his wife Jezebel daughter of King Ethbaal of the Sidonians, and went and served Baal, and worshiped him. He erected an altar for Baal in the house of Baal, which he built in Samaria. Ahab also made a sacred pole. Ahab did more to provoke the anger of the LORD, the God of Israel, than had all the kings of Israel who were before him. In his days Hiel of Bethel built Jericho; he laid its foundation at the cost of Abiram his firstborn, and set up its gates at the cost of his youngest son Segub, according to the word of the LORD, which he spoke by Joshua son of Nun. (1 Kgs 16:30–34)[33]

Clearly, the scriptural narrative intends Ahab, along with his wife Jezebel, and similar apostate rulers, to serve as egregious examples of how Israel's kings were *not* to carry out their religious duties—and the dire consequences facing them if they did so in this manner.

Another aspect of the king's responsibility as "the Lord's anointed" was to serve as a guardian of Israel's common good and the social requirements of the law. That is, the king acted as the defender against external threats and as the defender of the covenant's "social contract" within Israel. Regarding the former, the scriptural narrative actually exhibits a somewhat ambiguous attitude. On the one hand, the king was certainly called to be the military leader of Israel, and prowess in battle was lauded. Indeed, the emergence of the monarchy under Saul and then David clearly followed the pattern established earlier during the time of the judges, in which God chose a champion to lead Israel to victory over her foes.[34] Subsequent kings of both Judah and Israel were likewise called to be military leaders. On the other hand, the scriptural narrative also sought to avoid giving the impression that a king's military prowess alone could secure the nation from external enemies. A

---

33. The reference is to Josh 6:26, which condemned the pagan practice of burying the body of a child under the foundation to insure good fortune for the building project.

34. See 1 Sam 9:15–17 and 17:32–54, and compare them with Judg 3:9–11 and 3:15.

more fundamental basis of victory, so Scripture asserted, was the king's trust in and obedience to God. It is God who truly wins the battle and preserves the nation for his faithful kings and people. (And, conversely, faithless and disobedient kings and people will bring God's wrath and reap defeat in battle.[35]) This view is certainly the message of David's "hymn of praise" (see 2 Sam 22:1–51), it is the oft-repeated perspective of the Deuteronomic editors,[36] and it is the conviction of both the psalmist and the prophets.[37]

The king also was to serve as the guardian of justice: the defender of the widows and orphans (e.g., 2 Sam 14:4–11), the corrector of injustice (see 2 Sam 12:1–6),[38] and the adjudicator of hard cases (the most famous being Solomon's, as recounted in 1 Kgs 3:16–28). More generally, the king was to serve and foster the well-being of the people as a whole. The story of King Rehoboam offers a telling negative example: the king had the opportunity to be a servant to the people of Israel, but forsook it to lay an even heavier burden upon them. This response became the immediate cause of God's removing from him five-sixths of his kingdom, as 1 Kgs 12:1–20 certainly indicates. In a more direct way, the prophetic writings also speak to the king's responsibilities toward the people, primarily through their words of reproach when he neglects this duty (e.g., Isa 3:13–15; Jer 23:1–4, 33:14–17; and Ezek 34:1–16, 23–31). Ezekiel 34 offers a particularly vivid contrast between how the "shepherds" (i.e., kings) of Israel have in fact acted and how they should act. It is a lengthy passage, even with some abbreviation, but it bears hearing in its own voice:

> The word of the LORD came to me: [2] Mortal, prophesy against the shepherds of Israel: prophesy, and say to them—to the shepherds: Thus says the Lord GOD: Ah, you shepherds of Israel who have been feeding yourselves!

---

35. Having said this, I should also note that the Bible draws no simplistic correlation between faithfulness and success or faithlessness and failure. For example, King Manasseh is portrayed as very evil, even while the scriptural author also records that he reigned for fifty-five years! See 2 Kgs 21:1–18.

36. See, for example, 1 Kgs 2:1–4, 9:1–9, 22:1–38; 2 Kgs 17:1–18, 18:1–8, and 19:14–37.

37. For example, Pss 20–21, 46, 60, 74, 79–80, 83, 108, 110, 118, and 124. See also Isa 10:5–27, 13:1–22, 30:15–17, 31:1–5, 36–37; Jer 17:5, 21:3–14, 25:1–16; Ezek 30:20–26; Hos 13:4–11; Amos 2:13–16; Hag 2:20–23; and Zech 12:1–5.

38. This case is, of course, extraordinary because David himself emerges as the guilty party, but it nevertheless illustrates the king's role in such cases. See also the reference in 2 Sam 15:2.

Should not shepherds feed the sheep? ³ You eat the fat, you clothe your-selves with the wool, you slaughter the fatlings; but you do not feed the sheep. ⁴ You have not strengthened the weak, you have not healed the sick, you have not bound up the injured, you have not brought back the strayed, you have not sought the lost, but with force and harshness you have ruled them. ⁵ So they were scattered, because there was no shep-herd; and scattered, they became food for all the wild animals. . . .

⁹ . . . therefore, you shepherds, hear the word of the LORD: ¹⁰ Thus says the Lord GOD, I am against the shepherds; and I will demand my sheep at their hand, and put a stop to their feeding the sheep; no longer shall the shepherds feed themselves. I will rescue my sheep from their mouths, so that they may not be food for them.

¹¹ For thus says the Lord GOD: I myself will search for my sheep, and will seek them out. . . .

¹⁶ I will seek the lost, and I will bring back the strayed, and I will bind up the injured, and I will strengthen the weak, but the fat and the strong I will destroy. I will feed them with justice. . . .

²³ I will set up over them one shepherd, my servant David, and he shall feed them: he shall feed them and be their shepherd. ²⁴ And I, the LORD, will be their God, and my servant David shall be prince among them; I, the LORD, have spoken.

²⁵ I will make with them a covenant of peace and banish wild animals from the land, so that they may live in the wild and sleep in the woods securely. . . .

²⁷ The trees of the field shall yield their fruit, and the earth shall yield its increase. They shall be secure on their soil; and they shall know that I am the LORD, when I break the bars of their yoke, and save them from the hands of those who enslaved them. . . .

³⁰ They shall know that I, the LORD their God, am with them, and that they, the house of Israel, are my people, says the Lord GOD. ³¹ You are my sheep, the sheep of my pasture and I am your God, says the Lord GOD.

The indictment rings clear. The kings have abused their position for their own gain and neglected the needs of the people in the process. And far from being just uncaring neglect that has not protected the weak, healed the sick, or directed the wayward, it has been an actively harsh and oppressive exploitation. Indeed, the covenantal obligations that should bind the people together have been severed, and the people "scattered." So, Ezekiel announces, God will reclaim sovereignty for himself, and grant it to "my servant David" (i.e., someone of Davidic lineage), who will be a good shepherd to the people and more directly and responsibly represent the ultimate reign of God. In sum, Ezekiel prophesied a king whose attributes would correspond to the central elements of Yahweh's own kingship, the ideal that had existed for some time, but which had been unrealized among the nation's many kings up to that point.[39]

This leads rather naturally to my final consideration, namely, the emergence of belief in a perpetual Davidic dynasty and the messianic expectations that frequently came to be associated with it. Historically speaking, this double topic is a large and complex one that I cannot begin to discuss fully.[40] But it does have a scriptural basis. So after locating its origins, I want to speak to some of its theological implications. The divine promise of a dynasty in perpetuity may be found in the words that the prophet Nathan spoke to King David: "When your days are fulfilled and you lie down with your ancestors, I will raise up your offspring after you, who shall come forth from your body, and I will establish his kingdom. He shall build a house for my name, and I will establish the throne of his kingdom forever" (2 Sam 7:8–17).[41] From this promise a number of theological threads must be traced. First, there was no one universally obvious understanding of "the Davidic messiah," and so, naturally enough, diverse conceptions emerged.[42] The pre-exilic prophets presented one variety of images,[43] the prophets at the end of the exile produced another set,[44] and Second Temple Judaism produced yet another variety,[45] including those of the Zealots and Essenes. And, it must be recognized, not all understandings of the messiah were focused exclusively on or even connected with David (cf. Sir 45 and 1 Macc 14:25–48). For instance, some portrayals stressed a priestly connection more than a royal one, while others described both a priestly and royal messiah.[46] Second, while

---

39. See Whitelam, "King and Kingship," 4:44.

40. Indeed, some scholars debate whether a "messianic expectation" even existed historically in the way it is so often used theologically.

41. The words quoted are vv. 12–13. The promise is again alluded to in 1 Kgs 2:4; Ps 89:19–37 and 132:11–12.

42. In what follows, I am dependent upon Marinus de Jonge, "Messiah," in *Anchor Bible Dictionary* (New York: Doubleday, 1992), 4:781–82.

43. See Isa 9:6–7, 11:1–9; Jer 23:1–6; Ezek 17:1–24, chapter 34, quoted above, 37:24–28; and Mic 5:2–4.

44. See Hag 2:20–23 and Zech 3:8, 6:12, and 9:9–10.

45. For example, the *Psalms of Solomon*.

46. See *Jubilees*, the *Testaments of the Twelve Patriarchs*, and the Qumran scrolls, as described in de Jonge, "Messiah," 4:781–82.

long-standing desires conceived in terms of a rather straightforward national and political restoration continued, other understandings began to express hopes in cosmic, and not merely mundane, terms. An eschatological outlook, which could include apocalyptic elements, such as the figure of the Son of Man, began to influence messianic expectations. The words of Isaiah evoke an image of paradise restored by the Davidic messiah (Isa 11:6–9), while Zechariah presents images of the victorious king as well as the terrible final warfare of "day of the Lord" (Zech 9:9–10 and 12:1–14:21). The book of 2 Esdras places the Davidic messiah in the middle of the apocalyptic action (2 Esd 12:31–35). In sum, there was no single, commonly held "messianic expectation," Davidic or otherwise, at the dawn of the Christian era, but only diverse strands. Several of these strands were, however, soon to be braided together in a new and unique way and fulfilled by Jesus, the Father's incarnate Son and messianic king.

Christ's Redefinition of Kingship and Victory

In the opening section of this chapter, I showed how the New Testament portrays Jesus as the messianic king and described the diverse ways in which it presents this claim. Then I briefly considered the narratives and themes offered by the Old Testament regarding Israel's understanding of "kingship," and suggested some of the ways it supplied the context for Christ's mission. I will now consider the ways that Jesus accomplished the royal messianic role assigned by the Father and implemented in the Spirit. Key aspects of this role were, of course, addressed in the opening section of this chapter. At this juncture, I will address more specifically the manner in which Christ both fulfilled and redefined earlier understandings of the king's status, authority, role, and power, and how he also offered a new understanding of the divine realm over which he exercises sovereignty.

In such a consideration, Jesus' parables and descriptions of the kingdom or reign *(basileía)* of God, as well as his deeds illustrating or enacting it, offer unique insight into the ways he transformed common understandings and expectations regarding Israel's king and life under God's sovereignty. Students of Scripture know well that Christ's preaching of the kingdom or reign of God forms a substantial portion of the gospel narratives. Just as importantly, the Acts of the Apostles and New Testament epistles reveal how the early Christian community understood itself as living under a new sovereignty—and struggling with the defeated but still dangerous "principalities and powers" that Christ had vanquished in his death and resurrection. In the discussion that follows, one should keep in mind all that I have already discerned from the scriptural narratives regarding Christ's royal status.[47] For what he said and did regarding the reign of God both complements these earlier observations and further clarifies their significance.

Perhaps the single most telling point one may make about the kingdom that Christ proclaims and inaugurates is that it displays none of the characteristics typically associated with worldly kingdoms. Indeed, it turns such characteristics upside down. The reign that Christ announces belongs not to the powerful or influential, but to the "poor" (Matt 5:3), the "poor in spirit" (Luke 6:20), and those "persecuted for righteousness' sake" (Matt 5:10). Its attainment requires neither ambition nor accomplishment, but a "letting go" and a radical reorientation: it can only be received "like a child" (Matt 18:3 // Mark 10:15 // Luke 18:17), indeed, one must be "born again" to even recognize it (John 3:3). While wealth in the world typically opens doors of opportunity and privilege that are closed to the impoverished, in the kingdom of God wealth will function in just the opposite way, acting as a barrier rather than an aid to admittance (Matt 19:23–24 // Mark 10:23–25 // Luke 18:24–26). Indeed, the kingdom of heaven radically undermines the world's typical understandings of merit, fairness, and just compensation (Matt 20:1–16), and reorders the world's typical priorities (Matt 6:31–33 // Luke 12:29–31). And in a similar vein, this kingdom will not emerge through the usual and obvious means, through force of arms or the political scheming of the powerful or family connections. Rather, it will spring from the humblest of beginnings, like a mustard seed (Matt 13:31–32 // Mark 4:30–32 // Luke 13:18–19), and work with a hidden, even mysterious power, like leaven (Matt 13:33 // Luke 13:20). Indeed, one must finally acknowledge that the kingdom Christ inaugurates "is not of this world" (John 18:36).

In other words, throughout his parables and sayings, Christ the King relativizes and redefines all nondivine assumptions about power and

---

47. As a reminder, my key points referred to the significance of Easter, the implications of his final entrance into Jerusalem and crucifixion as "King of the Jews," the meaning of his power to exorcise demons and heal the sick, the import of his power over creation in stilling storms and miraculous feedings, and the inseparability of the "proclaimer" (Jesus) from his proclamation (the reign of God).

authority,[48] about how the world was to be ruled, and who was to be construed as the most worthy subjects. Jesus rejected being made "king" according to the popular view (see John 6:15), and he refused to take the armed option (see Matt 26:51–54). In addition, he offered entrance into the divine realm based not on one's worldly status or power or condition, but solely upon one's acknowledgement of the transforming power and grace of God. It was precisely in this unanticipated fulfillment of his kingly office and proclamation of a radically new kind of kingdom that the Son accomplished the Father's purposes. Of course, this does not mean that Christ merely "spiritualized" the secular and political aspirations of his day, in effect removing himself and his announced kingdom from the worldly fray. N. T. Wright argues convincingly that both Jesus' parables and parabolic acts were indeed "politicized," yet in a way that precluded a simple identification with any particular party of that— or any—day.[49] Instead, it is more appropriate to recognize that Christ as king returned "kingship" to God: in effect, he made it clear that believers do not finally have a human king "like the other nations," and the "kingdom of God" is not like any human dominion. In this regard, Christ represents the "closing bracket" to Samuel's anointing of Saul to please the people (cf. 1 Sam 8). Christ's kingship repudiates that of Saul, as it redefines what the world should expect and need in its sovereign.

Several scriptural comparisons help illustrate this point, in both positive and negative ways. For an example of the former, consider how the ancient judge Gideon offers a certain positive foreshadowing of Christ's kingship. Barry Harvey describes the events following Gideon's defeat of the Midianites in this way:

> Whereas Gideon attributed his success to the activity of the LORD, tribal elders, impressed with his courage and ingenuity, saw him as someone who could provide stability and security to a loose-knit collection of tribes struggling to survive in a harsh and unforgiving land. And so, in keeping with the practice of the nations and peoples around them,

---

48. Thus, Pannenberg's objection that the "kingly office" is not rightfully ascribed to Jesus does not finally wash. In a nutshell, Pannenberg seems to confuse the popular expectation regarding the awaited messianic king with Jesus' redefinition of such kingship. See a summary of Pannenberg's position in George W. Stroup, "The Relevance of the *Munus Triplex* for Reformed Theology and Ministry," *Austin Seminary Bulletin* 98 (June 1983): 26–27.

49. Wright, *Jesus and the Victory of God,* especially 96–98, but also 168–82, 191ff., 226ff., 461–67, 472–74, 529–39, 544–52, 609–10, and 652–53.

the "men of Israel" offered him the opportunity to establish a dynastic monarchy for himself and his sons. But Gideon vigorously declined their invitation, declaring instead that neither he nor his sons, but only the LORD, would rule over Israel (Judg 6:11–8:23).[50]

A negative foreshadowing may be discerned in the example of Rehoboam (1 Kgs 12). Immediately after he is made king in succession of his father Solomon, Jeroboam and "all the assembly of Israel" come to petition him with the following words: "Your father made our yoke heavy. Now therefore lighten the hard service of your father and his heavy yoke upon us, and we will serve you." Rehoboam consults first with "the old men," who offer the advice that if he will act as a servant to the people, the people will in turn serve him forever. Rehoboam then consults with "the young men" of his own generation, who counsel him to respond to the people's request in part with the words: "Whereas my father laid upon you a heavy yoke, I will add to your yoke . . ." (1 Kgs 12:11). Anyone familiar with the Gospel of Matthew cannot help but hear the very different response of Jesus, who on the authority granted by the Father has become the one true king:

> All things have been delivered to me by my Father; and no one knows the Son except the Father, and no one knows the Father except the Son and anyone to whom the Son chooses to reveal him. Come to me, all you who labor and are heavy laden, and I will give you rest. Take my yoke upon you, and learn from me; for I am gentle and lowly in heart, and you will find rest for your souls. For my yoke is easy, and my burden is light. (Matt 11:27–30)[51]

On this whole topic of Christ's redefinition of the meaning of king-ship, the work of Deirdre J. Good is especially helpful and pertinent.[52] Her slim volume seeks to reclaim the word "meek" in Bible translations

---

50. Barry A. Harvey, *Another City: An Ecclesiological Primer for a Post-Christian World* (Christian Mission and Modern Culture Series; eds. Alan Neely, H. Wayne Pipkin, and Wilbert Shenk; Harrisburg, Penn.: Trinity Press International, 1999), 36.

51. This passage from Matthew also has relevance to understanding Christ as prophet, insofar as scriptural tradition conceives of Jesus as the personification of wisdom. See Craig A. Evans' discussion in "Jesus' Self-Designation: 'The Son of Man' and the Recognition of His Divinity," in *The Trinity* (eds. Stephen T. Davis, Daniel Kendall, SJ, and Gerald O'Collins, SJ; Oxford: Oxford University Press, 1999), 40–42.

52. Good, *Jesus the Meek King*.

of the Greek word *praus,* especially as it is used to describe Jesus as "the meek King." The term has been common in English translations since William Tyndale's work, but it has fallen out of favor recently because of its presumed negative connotations of passive and servile submissiveness. Yet Good argues on the basis of primarily Hellenistic sources that *praus* should in fact be understood as having far different connotations. While she describes many different associated nuances, she defines the word most specifically as "disciplined calmness."[53] To be sure, she acknowledges that in its earlier forms it described a quality that was expected of persons in subordinate positions, especially women, in contrast to the more active virtues expected of men. But she also argues that over time the quiet qualities associated with *praus* came to be associated with good kingly rule. That is, a *praus* king was a benevolent king, displaying compassionate forbearance for subjects rather than despotism or anger. She goes on to associate this further with the positive moral qualities of being good, kind, just, holy, perfect, humble, gentle, blessed, and merciful.[54] Good then compares these Hellenistic understandings with passages in both the inter-testamental literature of Judaism and the New Testament, and argues that these *praus* qualities are clearly ascribed to persons such as Moses and Jesus. Indeed, in the Gospel of Matthew, she argues that the distinction between Jesus' kingship and Herod the Great is that the former epitomizes the *praus* king while Herod represents its antithesis. She concludes by stating that the word "meek" should be reclaimed, because it is the one English term that comes closest to representing the various nuances of the Greek word *praus.*

> One can encourage kings and rulers to be beneficent and compassionate, knowing that of course despots and tyrants exist. Matthew does not present kings either as ideal rulers or as tyrants. Instead he subverts the office of leadership. Jesus teaches in Matthew's Gospel that those who wish to be first must be servants of all. This aspect of Matthew's presentation is in accord with the way Jesus' teaching is presented in the other Gospels. At the same time, and to a degree not found in the other Gospels, Matthew emphasizes the office of king as slave, and he places Jesus in both roles. The strategies by which Matthew casts Jesus as king include the genealogy (in which Jesus is placed within the messianic lineage of David); the identity of Jesus as "king of the Jews"; and the

---

53. Ibid., 7.
54. Ibid., 15.

fulfillment of messianic passages from the Hebrew Scriptures (particularly Zech 9:9, cited in fulfillment of Jesus' entry into Jerusalem as a royal king). A further means by which the Hellenistic ideology of kings is subverted is to situate Jesus as a king over a realm that has permeable boundaries and that is inaugurated but not complete. Auxiliary strategies depict Jesus as a leader to whom other leaders like the ruler (9:18) and the Roman centurion defer.[55]

Now one could argue that the other Synoptics contain many of these same emphases. True, Matthew makes explicit points that are only implicit in the others: only Matthew's genealogy makes a point of assigning David the descriptive title of "the king" and only Matthew explicitly quotes the Zech 9:9 passage regarding the animal(s) the Messiah will triumphantly ride in to Jerusalem. Nevertheless, the larger issue of Jesus' redefinition of kingship appears not only in the other synoptics, but in other segments of the New Testament as well.

Another observation helps reinforce Good's claim that Jesus subverted Israel's very understanding of kingship. One key aspect of the understanding of the king as "Yahweh's anointed" (especially as that term was employed in the royal narratives of 1 and 2 Samuel) included the fundamental assertion that the king's person was sacrosanct. Regicide was virtually unthinkable, not only a human scandal but also an affront to God. Yet precisely in the face of these old assumptions, Jesus Christ, God's anointed, the "king of the Jews," was killed, indeed, publicly and shamefully executed as a criminal. The unthinkable had apparently happened, but was it to be understood finally under the old assumptions? The Romans had disposed of Jesus as casually as they would have a common slave, and this would seem to undermine the plausibility of Jesus' royal status. Yet Good had noted that Matthew stressed the notion of king as slave, and understood Jesus as both. This suggests that the old assumptions no longer explain matters adequately. And while death typically brings matters to an abrupt and definitive end, Jesus is a king "over a realm that has permeable boundaries," which I would argue means, in this case, over a realm in which even death is not an insurmountable boundary. The meaning of Jesus' death cannot be fully understood apart from the victory of his resurrection, which also means his status as God's anointed king cannot be fully understood unless it is interpreted anew in light of both Good Friday and Easter.

---

55. Ibid., 18.

The death and resurrection of Jesus, the Son of God, reveals a new divine king and ushers in a new age and new dominion.

This new understanding of the messianic king and kingdom clearly has implications for the Christian understanding of the divine life. That is, insofar as the crucifixion and resurrection of the incarnate Son stands as one aspect of the activity of the economic trinity, we learn something about the character of the immanent trinity. Consider what David Jenkins says regarding Jesus' redefinition of our typical understanding of the Father's royal might: "We are to be very careful about the way we understand (or misunderstand) the *power* of God. Are we to see 'the Father' as some sort of divine emperor of the universe who rules with an instantly effective power, when 'the Son,' who for us Christians is Christ our Lord, has done his work through the life and passion of a crucified slave?"[56] The answer to his rhetorical question should be obvious. Colin Gunton speaks more directly to the same point when he discusses the implications of the "glory" ascribed to "the only Son of the Father" in John 1:14:

> The glory is the glory of one who washes the feet of his disciples, is lifted up on the cross, and only through the trial of death is elevated to the glory that is reigning with the Father. It is important to realise this if we are to understand what kind of Father is revealed by the incarnate Son. If it is indeed true that those who have seen him have seen the Father, then it is the Father who is revealed in the incarnate humanity of this man glorified through humbling. There is thus a relation of likeness between Jesus and the one whom he reveals of the kind to rule out what has come to be called patriarchy.[57]

It is nothing new for worldly power to use whatever it can to its own advantage. It is part of the sinful human condition that even the good can be abused. Certainly the church knows this from its own history, insofar as it has let others use—or, more damning, has itself abused—its gospel inheritance for self-serving ends. Rightly understood, Christ's kingship stands as a repudiation of all oppressive and coercive forms of rule. It undermines the presumptions of the powerful by revealing and

---

56. David E. Jenkins, "Holy Trinity and Promise: What Is Good News in Today's World?" *Sewanee Theological Review* 35 (Pentecost 1992): 230.
57. Colin E. Gunton, *A Brief Theology of Revelation* (Edinburgh: T&T Clark, 1995), 121.

enacting God's holy and righteous concern for "the least of these," the poor and the powerless.

This all points to the fact that Christ's redefinition of kingship and his particular descriptions of the kingdom of God have profound implications for the Christian life. To begin, simply consider more fully a passage cited above: each of the Synoptic Gospels recounts a version of Jesus' admonition to the disciples that they must become like children if they are to enter the kingdom of heaven. The details vary, but Mark and Luke both indicate that the cause of Jesus' statement was the disciples' prior argument among themselves about who was the greatest. In all three accounts, Jesus uses a child to make the point that the greatest is the one who shows humility, who welcomes those without worldly status, who acts as a servant and becomes "the least" (Matt 18:1–5, Mark 9:33–37, and Luke 9:46–48). Morna Hooker recalls the observation made by another scholar:

> Matthew Black long ago suggested that what we have here is an acted parable, playing on the double meaning of the Aramaic word *tayla*, which means both "child" and "servant." The child set in the midst of the disciples is thus the dramatic representation of the servant whom the disciple is required to become. Although the evangelists have used different traditions of this story, all of them see the child as a symbol of true discipleship.[58]

Mark and Matthew recount another episode that makes a similar point about the humility expected of the true disciple (Mark 10:35–45 and Matt 20:20–28). James and John, the sons of Zebedee, ask Jesus to grant that they be seated at his side, one at his right hand and the other at his left, when he comes into his glory. (In Matthew's version, their mother makes this request, fitting the stereotype of the ambitious stage-mother.) Jesus responds by saying "You do not know what you are asking," and then asking if they will be able to "drink the cup that I drink?"—an allusion to his upcoming passion. Clearly, these disciples (or their mother) are still thinking in terms of the status and power that association with Jesus the "king" will confer. Theirs is the desire of courtesans in every age and place: to bask in the glow and privilege of the sovereign. When the other disciples learn of the request, they become

---

58. Hooker, *The Signs of a Prophet*, 42. Her reference is to Matthew Black, *An Aramaic Approach to the Gospels and Acts* (Oxford: Oxford University Press, 1967), 218–23.

angry with the two brothers—and the anger seems to be due less to the impropriety of their request than to their thinking to ask before the other disciples did. In any event, Jesus again responds that "whoever wishes to be great among you must be your servant, and whoever wishes to be first among you must be slave of all" (Mark 10:44–45). This, of course, is in strict keeping with Jesus' own status: "For the Son of Man came not to be served but to serve, and to give his life a ransom for many" (Mark 10:46).[59]

Of course, an ancient squabble among the disciples regarding their relative rank would hardly concern us now, were their Lord simply another victim of oppression commemorated as a noble and altruistic martyr. But this one who came to serve and give his life for others is also the one whom God raised from the dead—and that event changed everything. For the scriptural narrative makes clear that this resurrection victory was not merely Christ's private vindication, nor simply a parochial triumph for his small band of disciples. Neither is it noteworthy merely for the way it may influence the hearts of latter-day believers. Rather, its impact extends beyond the merely subjective (whether individual or collective) to transform the very roots of reality. Christ's resurrection ushers in a new world, and God intends its benefits to be shared. Moreover, Christians do not witness this victory merely as spectators, but as participants, as they themselves are moved by the power of the Spirit to be both beneficiaries and missionaries of the risen Lord's reign over this new reality. Those who offer allegiance to Christ the King are, through the power of the Spirit, grafted into his death and resurrection. In this union, they receive a share of Christ's own victory and, in the face of whatever the world may conspire to do, the knowledge of their own truest purpose and end. Paul speaks eloquently to this last point: "No, in all these things we are more than conquerors through him who loved us. For I am convinced that neither death, nor life, nor angels, nor rulers, nor things present, nor things to come, nor powers, nor height, nor depth, nor anything else in all creation, will be able to separate us from the love of God in Christ Jesus our Lord" (Rom 8:37–39).

---

59. This reading stands in contrast to that of C. J. den Heyer, who sidesteps the christological implications of this episode and instead focuses on the fact that "a christological statement is made to serve ethics." See C. J. den Heyer, *Jesus and the Doctrine of the Atonement: Biblical Notes on a Controversial Topic* (trans. John Bowden; Harrisburg, Penn.: Trinity Press International, 1998), 16.

Still, as this passage from Paul also implies, Christ's victory, for all its objective reality, does not automatically or coercively transform the world. Creation's goal has been revealed, and the means to that goal made available, but the end has not yet come. History still remains history, with its own inertia, its own intractable elements, its own hostile resisters. In keeping with a God whose power is made perfect in weakness, who in the first creation left room for his creatures freely to reject his good intentions for them, the resurrection victory of Christ the King establishes a new realm but does not force the allegiance of its subjects. In a manner recapitulating and broadening the divine challenge to the Israelites (Deut 30:15–20), Christ's reign sets before the whole world the ways of life or death, blessings or curses. He, too, implores all people to "choose life," and through the power of his Spirit offers them the means to make and abide by that choice (see Eph 6:10ff).[60] But he will not coerce people to make that choice. And as both Scripture and the world's continuing history make clear, some inexplicably choose otherwise.[61] So while the ultimate outcome has been assured (see, e.g., Rom 8:18–21, 1 Cor 15:51–57, and Rev 21:1ff.), in the kingdom that Christ initiates, the struggle between life and death, good and evil, continues.

On Not Reducing Christ's Victorious Reign to Ethics or Politics

What does the claim of Christ's kingship and the reality of this continuing struggle between good and evil imply for concrete Christian practice? If Christians are both the beneficiaries and missionaries of God's reign, how is this to be worked out precisely in the church's ongoing life? How should Christianity understand its own place and role in the Son's exercise of the sovereignty granted by the Father? The church and her theologians have promoted many different answers to these questions over the centuries. From the emergence of "Christendom" and the Christian state to notions of the separation of church and state, from "just war" theologies to Christian pacifism, from Amish separatism to

---

60. Regarding v. 10, recall my point in chapter 3 that references to the "power" of God or the Lord function as virtual synonyms to references to the Holy Spirit.

61. Some scriptural passages imply that such recalcitrance stems from within the human will itself (see, e.g., Mark 6:1–6a, John 5:39–40 and 9:13–41, perhaps 2 Tim 2:12, and also Titus 1:15–16). Others speak of external influences or powers outside the human (see, e.g., 2 Cor 4:4, Gal 4:8–11, Col 2:8, 2 Pet 2:1–3, and Rev 19:20).

"culture Protestantism," from private morality to the "social Gospel" and liberation theology, how the church and individual Christians are to understand, seek, and exercise power in the world is a perennial and much debated issue. Simply put, it is an enormous topic, one far larger than I can deal with in this brief section. That being the case, I propose a far more modest, two-part agenda. On the one hand, I will raise some open-ended questions regarding the use of worldly power by Christians, based on the portrait of Christ the King that has emerged from my analysis of the scriptural narratives. Numerous theologians are raising such questions nowadays, and the issue is far from being resolved. But the issue can be clarified, which is beneficial in a more limited manner to the ongoing discussion. On the other hand, I will argue against a tendency that has emerged in the modern era, which is to say, a way of interpreting the Christian life that downplays or omits its constitutive theological and eschatological elements, reducing it, in effect, to either ethics or political action.

So, to the first item. As the exegetical analysis in the preceding section indicates, Christ's sovereignty and his exercise of it differ from the way sovereignty is typically exercised in the world—indeed, even in Israel's own royal history. Christ the King does not wield or even glorify earthly power. He is the "meek" king. He is the king who comes not to be served, but to serve; he is gentle, and his yoke is light. He does not raise an army, or wield the power of the sword. Indeed, he apparently does nothing to resist the Roman power that will finally execute him as "king of the Jews." He proclaims a kingdom that is for the poor, a kingdom that must be received as if one were a child, a kingdom that is "not of this world." Yet the reign that Christ inaugurates is not merely an "other-worldly" one, nor does it advocate a merely private morality. It challenges the world's established powers and authorities, and is social in scope and not just individual.

In some aspects of its history, the church has recognized that Christ's royal office speaks against embracing or glorifying earthly power. Recall the early Christian martyrs, the fundamental impulse motivating the monastic movement, the pacifistic ethos of the Friends (commonly known as Quakers), or the nonviolent resistance promoted by the Reverend Martin Luther King, Jr., of the American Civil Rights movement. Nevertheless, the church also has a long history of honoring the repudiation of earthly power in theory only and not in actual practice. From the machinations and power politics of the medieval and Renaissance papacy, to the Crusades, to the legal strictures of Calvin's

Geneva, to the Puritan revolution of Oliver Cromwell, to name just some examples, the church has often wielded power (whether directly or indirectly) in a manner indistinguishable from secular entities. In response, a number of theologians now consider that the Constantinian "establishment" of Christianity and the notion of a "Christian" monarch represented a perverse application of Christ's kingly rule. Yet the implications of this recognition have not always been fully acknowledged or worked out, although the issue is hotly discussed.[62] To offer one example (given the Reformed theological orientation of this book), what might this new recognition imply for the Reformed tradition's heritage in the "magisterial Reformation," in which the church and state were understood as partners in the ordering and correction of society? To put the question more pointedly, can a Christian, in good faith, seek to transform the world by employing not only the powers of persuasion, personal or corporate example, or nonviolent resistance, but also by enlisting the coercive powers of the state? Might the Anabaptist tradition in fact be more faithful to the example and implications of Christ's redefinition of kingship than the Reformed tradition? For Christ the King offers us an eschatological vision that not only subverts the workings of politics as usual, but also subverts the world's notion of politics as such. Recall how Paul records Christ's words to him in prayer: "My grace is sufficient for you, for my power is made perfect in weakness" (2 Cor 12:9). Could a governmental body or state that has power—even a democracy—ever be described as exercising it in this way? If so, is the church then justified in "joining forces" with it? And if not, does that mean the church has compromised, perhaps even betrayed, the practice and commissioning of her sovereign Lord?

I turn now to my second consideration. However contemporary Christians finally answer the above questions in their efforts to be faithful to Christ the King, one tendency appears to me to be one that should not be taken, namely, equating Christ's reign with nothing more than either ethics or politics. This tendency can be the fruit of assumptions and approaches that emerged in the modern era, assumptions and

---

62. The many recent works of Stanley Hauerwas and William Willimon come immediately to mind (and behind them, the work of John Howard Yoder). Also, several volumes in the Christian Mission and Modern Culture Series published by Trinity Press International address this issue. One is the work of Barry A. Harvey, *Another City,* cited above, while another is Douglas John Hall's *The End of Christendom and the Future of Christianity* (1995).

approaches that are theological/philosophical on the one hand and political/social on the other. I especially want to contrast these with what I have argued regarding Christ's redefinition of "kingship," and summarize my basic position in the following way. Christ's victorious reign will necessarily have ethical and sociopolitical ramifications, and of a distinctly Christian character, but these ramifications do not comprise the whole of that reign. Christ's kingship and the theological exposition of it are not equivalent or reducible to any particular ethical or sociopolitical agenda, nor is their sole or even primary purpose to authorize or motivate such agendas. Christ's reign may be understood as motivating and even authorizing certain behaviors and social structures, but only insofar as they are placed within a larger, indeed, transcendent and eschatological framework. Put more simply, without a faithful theological understanding of who Christ is as the Father's messianic king and a vision of the eschatological end he opens for us, the practical implications of his reign will inevitably be distorted.

The roots of this particular tendency may be traced back to the work of the German philosopher Immanuel Kant (1724–1804). In his groundbreaking *Critique of Pure Reason* (1781), Kant argued that many of the claims typically promoted by philosophers and metaphysicians were actually beyond the competence of human reason to make. In particular, he claimed that the various argued "proofs" of God's existence were fallacious and could not be rationally justified. In a similar manner, his *Critique* undermined speculative theology's claims to knowledge regarding God's attributes and actions. Simply put, Kant argued that there are intractable limits to the things the human reason can know. Knowledge derives from our mind's structuring of sense experience, from our empirical interaction with objects or "phenomena." If we claim to "know" certain things about God, such claims exceed that of which pure reason is capable. All this is not to say, however, that Kant viewed himself as an atheist or that he discounted the demands that faith in God typically placed upon believers. While Kant rejected the notion that there could be a rational proof of God's existence, he did argue for a moral proof. As one scholar describes it, such a proof

> begins neither from a concept nor from a fact about the world, but from an immediately experienced moral situation. The moral agent feels called upon to achieve certain results, in particular to bring about a state of affairs in which happiness is proportioned to virtue, and knows that

he cannot do it by his own unaided efforts; insofar as he commits himself to action he shows his belief in a moral author of the universe.[63]

In other words, from an overwhelming sense of moral obligation, one becomes convinced of the need for the existence of God—because otherwise, one could not meet that obligation and virtue would not triumph (an unthinkable prospect!). In any case, as the scholar cited above also notes, such a moral proof of God's existence does not constitute "objective knowledge, but a species of personal conviction, embodying not logical but moral certainty."[64]

But all this means that the traditional connection between the true and the good, between knowing and doing, in which the knowledge of God and his intentions for humanity and creation serves as the source for right human action, had been severed. Or, to put it another way, the former had been collapsed into the latter, so that theology becomes, for all practical purposes, ethics. Such an interpretation is borne out by the character of Kant's later work *Religion Within the Limits of Reason Alone* (1793).[65] A summary exposition of this volume is more than can be offered here, but one may discern the tenor of his approach from the titles of the four books that comprise this work: "Concerning the Indwelling of the Evil Principle with the Good, or, On the Radical Evil in Human Nature"; "Concerning the Conflict of the Good with the Evil Principle for Sovereignty over Man"; "The Victory of the Good over the Evil Principle, and the Founding of the Kingdom of God on Earth"; and "Concerning Service and Pseudo-Service under the Sovereignty of the Good Principle, or, Concerning Religion and Clericalism."[66] In these titles, one can clearly hear echoes of certain traditional Christian doctrines, such as original sin and the coming of the kingdom of God. Nevertheless, one may also detect a decided shift away from a clearly biblical and narrative context to a philosophical and abstract one, from the more traditionally theological or spiritual to the moralistic. Indeed, his

---

63. W. H. Walsh, "Kant, Immanuel," in *The Encyclopedia of Philosophy*, Vol. 3, Paul Edwards, Editor-in-Chief (New York: Macmillan Publishing Co., Inc., and The Free Press, 1967. Reprint ed. 1972), 317.

64. Ibid.

65. Immanuel Kant, *Religion Within the Limits of Reason Alone* (trans. Theodore M. Greene and Hoyt H. Hudson; Chicago: The Open Court Publishing Company, 1934; New York: Harper Torchbooks, 1960).

66. Ibid., iii–iv.

last book takes pains to critique much that is typically—some would say, constitutively—associated with the church and the Christian's life of faith. For example, "revealed doctrines" may be commended only insofar as they may serve as a means of confirming "universal human reason as the supremely commanding principle in a natural religion."[67] More than that, such doctrines must not be viewed as actually describing anything about the deity in itself.[68] Indeed, if the rational basis and moral usefulness of any dogma or revealed statute cannot be discerned, it is to be rejected as arbitrary and illusory.[69]

Although it greatly oversimplifies a complex development, one may still say that Kant's philosophy was a key reason for nineteenth-century Liberal Protestantism's tendency to avoid making the transcendent truth claims that Christianity had traditionally made. In any event, Liberal Protestant theology, both willingly and under a certain rationalist compulsion, came to understand Christian claims as descriptions of human feeling or human values, and it frequently channeled the import of such revised claims into ethical or social agendas. But once the Christian faith lost its mooring to the transcendent particularity of the Bible's triune God and became instead a set of human feelings and values, it left itself open to the ideological critiques of opponents such as Ludwig Feuerbach, Karl Marx, and Friedrich Nietzsche. These thinkers viewed the claims of Christianity as nothing more than the self-interest of certain social groups projected onto the screen of the eternal. More pointedly, they asked why these to-their-mind bourgeois projections should have any greater claim to acceptance than the views of other groups, such as the proletariat or humanity's natural aristocrats, the *Übermensch*. The predominant Protestant theology of the day was hard-pressed to counter such charges, precisely because it had already abandoned its claims to be founded on a transcendent reality. Still, it continued its sway through a combination of still-rigorous scholarly theology and cultural inertia—at least until the horrors of World War I devastated many of the old verities and residual assumptions. The implicit identification of Western civilization's values (whether bourgeois or Socialist) with those of the kingdom of God became difficult, if not impossible, to sustain. Into the vacuum stepped the totalitarian ideologies of the twentieth century (Communism, Fascism, and

---

67. Ibid., 152.
68. See, for example, Kant's treatment of the Trinity. Ibid., 132–33, 136–38.
69. For example, see his treatment of the practice of penance. Ibid., 156ff.

Nazism) as well as the seemingly nonsectarian but tradition-eroding expansion of global capitalism.

For Christianity, the root problem consists of the severing of human *acting* from a more fundamental and God-given understanding of human *being,* an understanding that offers a clear vision of humanity's origin and end and thus supplies a framework for guiding its ongoing life. In the biblical narrative, God presents Christian theology with a sacred and unique insight into the nature and purpose of human life. If theology lays aside this gift—whether from a Kantian reticence to make transcendent truth-claims or from a certain embarrassment in the face of those who acknowledge only natural, scientific explanations—to pursue a (seemingly) more modest and (supposedly) more generally acceptable ethical or political agenda, then one of two outcomes is likely. Either that agenda will be co-opted by a more powerful "partner" or it will be abandoned in favor of a more comprehensible and comprehensive worldview. In either case, the usual outcome is for the ethical or political purpose to determine the theology, rather than growing from it. And in this case, theology no longer serves God's sovereign purposes in Christ. Instead, it has become a merely human ideology, seeking to cloak and justify itself with a divine sanction.

Systematic Location and Theological Implications

The preceding sections have presented a rather detailed argument about how Christ's royal office should and should not be understood. Now it is appropriate to move beyond those details to consider the broader issues of context and ramifications. That is, where does this understanding of Christ's work fit in a larger understanding of God's atoning work, and what is its practical upshot? Recall my goal to offer a dynamic and multifaceted understanding of the atonement, in which this aspect of Christ's work is balanced and completed by the other aspects I will discuss in chapters 5 and 6. Immersion in this chapter, or either of the following, should not make one lose sight of the material in the other two. I intend the various claims made in these three chapters to be interconnected. More than that, I see their interconnection as following a certain internal theological coherence, even if their pastoral application at times follows the more haphazard dictates of particular circumstances.

Why should it matter that one be aware of this distinction between theological coherence and pastoral application? It relates to the differing functions of systematic versus practical theology. Systematic theology may inform, guide, and correct, but cannot replace practical, pastoral theology. The former remains abstract and reflective, and thus, in a sense, one step removed from the immediate life and language of Christian faith. The latter (practical theology) is immersed in the immediacy of Christian faith, and must be responsive to the moment, discerning which word to speak, when, and how. Yet without a broader view and a sense of where one should be speaking from, the moment can too easily disorient and lead astray. For example, a minister's pastoral discernment may lead her to preach a series of sermons on Christ's sacrifice because that is what her congregation needs to hear. But she might have to balance this series with a different emphasis later, so as to avoid leaving the impression that Christ's crucifixion is the only significant aspect of his atoning work. Or, recall an example from my introduction, which I will address further in chapter 6: one may indeed properly think of Jesus as a prophet, or even as a "Spirit person," but only if one's understanding of those labels is not reductive. They must be anchored in a broader sense of his divine work and person, an anchoring that the reflective nature of systematic theology helps supply. Having a clear sense of theological coherence helps guide one through the idiosyncrasies and often conflicting pressures of the everyday life of faith.

With this in mind, I want to suggest that the royal understanding of Christ's work should be recognized as having primacy, viewed from the perspective of systematic theology. This is so for three reasons: first, because of the primacy of the Father, the first person of the Trinity, the "unoriginate" and eternal source of the other two persons, the one from whom the Son exercises his sovereignty. Second, because in this royal work the Son reestablishes the Father's original intentions for creation. And third, because of the circumstances of our present human condition. Let me begin with this last point. To illustrate it in biblical terms, we are not Adam and Eve, but their descendents, which is another way of saying that our historical and sociological context comes to us neither empty nor untainted. The reality of our situation as social, historical beings means we cannot start with a "clean slate"; much is already determined before we are born. In this sense, human history and culture necessarily precede any given collective or individual situation. Certainly a key point of the Adam and Eve story is this: *they* may have had the opportunity to encounter God in a strictly "natural" setting, which is to say, one uninfluenced by an inherited human culture. But that context is no longer available to *us*. We are their descendents, which means that our context is inevitably cultural rather than solely natural. As Aidan Nichols notes:

> Vis-à-vis nature, we can describe culture as a *new kind of replication*. Human animals, in grouping together to form cultures, manage to overturn that primary law of genetic science which states that no acquired characteristic can be inherited. By means of culture, those born from nature succeed in passing on acquired characteristics in a cumulative way, communicating learned information and acquired habits from one generation to another.[70]

One point of the Adam and Eve story is that any who hear it belong to a latter generation, a generation that will have received a whole host of "acquired characteristics in a cumulative way."

Of course, this point needs to be sharpened. The Adam and Eve story does not try to explain any and all habits and characteristics that have been passed down through human culture. Its point, rather, is to focus on one particular aspect of that "learned information and acquired habit," namely, human sinfulness. Premodern accounts of original sin seem to promote an almost biological understanding of that sin's communication, as if it were a genetic defect passed from one generation to the next. Such an understanding strikes the scientific mind as implausible and primitive. Yet we should not use this as an excuse to dismiss the theological insights of these accounts. For have we not learned enough about the insidious power of vindictive historical memory, the corrupting obstinacy of certain social ills, and the multigenerational impact of given family dysfunctions to acknowledge that the doctrine of original sin might actually speak to our human condition? The battle against sin is never just an individual matter, an isolated person wrestling with his or her own failings, his or her own immorality, his or her own guilt. And even when in particular cases it might be primarily an individual matter, it is never this in the *first* instance. As historical, cultural beings, our context exists before we are born and will exist after our death. In sum, our context can exist without us, but we can never exist without our context.

Thus, I suggest that our context must be redeemed from the powers that hold it in thrall before the next two models of atonement would

---

70. Aidan Nichols OP, *Christendom Awake* (Grand Rapids, Mich.: Eerdmans, 1999), 9.

"work" or even make sense. Christ's victory as king over the principalities and powers reclaims creation, which is to say, the "natural," and
those born from a now fallen nature, for God the Father's original purposes. It thereby establishes the conditions needed for the reclaiming
and reconciliation of human culture in his work as priest and prophet.
Christ the King must come first because it signifies the in-breaking
kingdom of God: no King, no kingdom. If there is no kingdom, which
is to say, the reign of God creating a new and redeemed "culture," then
one's understanding of Christ's work is diminished to an individual
piety. This is a common enough assumption—if not explicitly, then
practically—yet it is not true to Christ's proclamation or Scripture's
larger witness. Christ's victory does not seek merely to save individuals
or an aggregate of individuals, it seeks to establish a new people, to
establish a new history and a new creation (see Rev 21:1ff.). Christ's
victory both reveals and inaugurates this reign, making clear the world's
reorientation to its original end.

What, then, are the theological implications of this understanding of
Christ's work? For one, Christ's victory gives us back our identity and
restores our meaning. Put in more philosophic terms, Christ's victory
reestablishes our true human ontology and *telos*. We do not know who
we are and do not know where we should be going, because we have
been captivated by a false understanding of ourselves and the purpose
of human life. As the Adam and Eve narrative tells it, we have been
seduced into believing we can "be like God, knowing good and evil"
(Gen 3:5)—indeed that we may rule ourselves and determine for ourselves the good and the evil, quite apart from God's intention for us as
his creatures. But this is to fall captive to a lie that contradicts the very
essence of our God-given being and purpose, a fall that opens us help-
lessly to the powers of falsehood and evil. This model of Christ's atoning work assumes that humans are separated from God because we
are held in bondage to "powers and principalities" opposed to God.
Christ the victorious king defeats these powers, frees us from their
propaganda, and enables us once again to embrace our true humanity and God-given purpose.

But does this mean the war with evil is over? Neither Scripture nor
our own Christian experience will allow us to make this claim. For
example, New Testament scholars typically describe the Gospels' witness to God's reign with the dialectical phrase "already/not yet." Paul
speaks to both the internal "civil war" that typifies the Christian's ongoing struggles with his or her own passions and the external struggles in,

and with, the world (Rom 7:23, 2 Cor 10:1–6, and Eph 6:10–18). To cite an analogy used by a professor of the World War II generation, Christ's victory represents the irreversible beginning of the end of the war, just as the Battle of Leyte Gulf did in the south Pacific. As a result of this victory, the final outcome of the war was no longer in doubt, but mopping up battles of varying intensity remained to be fought. The same can be said of the Christian's spiritual warfare (cf. Rev 17:12–14), and this understanding of Christ's work helps arm Christians for the struggle (again, see Eph 6:10–18). It does so most fundamentally by revealing that human identity is determined not by these illegitimate powers, but solely by God. "You shall know the truth, and the truth shall set you free" (John 8:32). Knowing this truth and embracing this freedom can, in the Spirit's strength, empower the faithful to oppose the powers that continue to challenge the Father's end for humanity (cf. Eph 1:17–22 and 1 John 5:4–5).

This understanding of Christ's royal work helps arm Christians for the struggle in another way as well, for Christians are called to active participation in that work ourselves. This becomes possible not just as an effect of our new knowledge, but as an effect of our new being. Christ, acting as the Father's regent, liberates humanity from the powers that had enslaved and corrupted it. But once liberated, humans are not then simply left to fend for themselves. Christ does not just reclaim creation, he initiates a new creation. Christ's death and resurrection—foreshadowed in his acts of power during his ministry—reveal and effect the salvific breaking of humanity's slavery and its re-creation, the benefits of which are made available through the power of the Spirit. On the basis of this new creation and power, Christians are then called to serve Christ's continuing work ourselves, carefully following the example he set—and never presuming that this new being and power are ours by right, to do with as we please. It is ours by grace, to be used in service to others and to glorify God.[71] Given Christ's redefinition of kingship, the exercise of the power he bestows can only follow his example. That is, it must demonstrate the same humility, compassion, forbearance, benevolence, and service toward others that Christ himself showed. If it does not, then it cannot truly be an exercise of Christ's divine power, nor may it legitimately claim to be Christian. Indeed, if it

---

71. As Jesus makes clear in Matt 5:16, 20:28; Mark 10:44–45; John 13:13–17 and 21:15–19.

fails to reflect Christ's lead, it thereby demonstrates its source in another, worldly power, and perhaps even allegiance to a sinister lord.

Christ's royal work and victory, his reclaiming of creation for the Father's originally intended purposes, also give one indication of why we are called to be the church. As Miroslav Volf notes: "No church without the reign of God . . . no reign of God without the church."[72] Christians are not called as isolated individuals in order to escape the world. Rather, we are called together, to become a new community, embodying God's reign in our own lives, acting as a counter to the powers that seek to control the present age, and serving as a pointer to that end that God intends for all creation.

Pastoral Applications

Much of the preceding section was couched in rather abstract language. How might it be translated into more practical terms and employed pastorally? A first step is to recognize that the bondage Christ the King defeats takes myriad forms. Earlier eras often conceived such bondage in images of devils and demons—images that a modern age might find naïve or even quaint. But this should not blind us to the fact that the twentieth century has certainly embraced the demonic in its own particular ways. In our age, the demonic has often taken an ideological shape. Sometimes it manifests itself in a totalitarian state, as in Hitler's Germany, Stalin's Soviet Union, or Pol Pot's Kampuchea. It is no coincidence that each of these modern embodiments of evil offered a comprehensive vision of humanity and its end, of the good and the evil, which repudiated and replaced a faithful Christian view. None of these episodes of our recent history were simply unthinking or irrational barbarism. Rather, they were all ideologically driven, whether by a vision of the Aryan master race ruling over "lesser" races, of the new "Socialist man," or the noble agrarian proletariat rejecting decadent urban life. Each had its definition of humanity, its understanding of the "good" life, and the proper end and purpose of both individuals and the collective. Each sought to establish a comprehensive culture that would make humanity over in its own ideological image, even if that entailed the use of war, concentration camps or gulags or "reeducation centers," and genocide.

---

72. Miroslav Volf, *After Our Likeness: The Church in the Image of the Trinity* (Sacra Doctrina: Christian Theology for a Postmodern Age Series; ed Alan G. Padgett; Grand Rapids, Mich.: Eerdmans, 1998), x.

But our courtship with the demonic has also taken—and continues to take—much more insidious (but equally ideological) forms. Such forms need not be obviously evil; indeed, they may dress themselves in the seemingly innocuous or even the good. For example, in contemporary North America, some say we are enthralled by entertainment[73] and ceaseless consumption. And we are indeed held in thrall. We are captivated by the new and different, so much so that we frequently obtain the new not for its content but simply because it is new. We have interiorized the values and judgments of the marketplace, and often fail to recognize it for what it is. Consider these observations of Rabbi Jonathan Sacks:

> Socialism is not the only enemy of the market economy. Another enemy, all the more powerful for its recent global triumph, is the market economy itself. When everything that matters can be bought and sold, when commitments can be broken because they are no longer to our advantage, when shopping becomes salvation and advertising slogans become our litany, when our worth is measured by how much we earn and spend, then the market is destroying the very virtues on which it in the long run depends. That, not the return of socialism, is the danger that advanced economies now face. And in these times, when markets seem to hold out the promise of uninterrupted growth in our satisfaction of desires, the voice of our great religious traditions needs to be heard, warning us of the gods that devour their own children, and of the temples that stand today as relics of civilizations that once seemed invincible.
>
> The Market, in my view, has already gone too far: not indeed as an economic system, but as a cast of thought governing relationships and the image we have of ourselves. A great rabbi once taught this lesson to a successful but unhappy businessman. He took him to the window and asked him, What do you see? The man replied, I see the world. He then took him to a mirror and asked, What do you see? He replied, I see myself. That, said the rabbi, is what happens when silver covers glass. Instead of seeing the world you see only yourself. The idea that human happiness can be exhaustively accounted for in terms of things we can buy, exchange, and replace is one of the great corrosive acids that eat away the foundations on which society rests; and by the time we have discovered this, it is already too late.[74]

---

73. See Neil Postman, *Amusing Ourselves to Death: Public Discourse in the Age of Show Business* (New York: Penguin Books, 1985).

74. Jonathan Sacks, "Markets and Morals," *First Things,* no. 105 (August/September 2000): 28.

In this sort of setting, what then is it that Christ's victory achieves, what is it that his sovereign rule makes available to us? Nothing less than our true identity. In Jer 2:5, the Lord asks, "What fault did your forefathers find in me, that they wandered far from me, pursuing empty phantoms and themselves becoming empty. . . ?"[75] The formula still holds true in our day: you become what you pursue. If you pursue that which is ephemeral, then you should not be surprised if your life becomes ephemeral. If you are fixated on the new and different, then you shouldn't be surprised if your life has no stability or continuity. If in a consumer culture we live by the ever increasing stimulation of desire, then we will soon become nothing more than the sum of those desires—desires that can never be fully satisfied. As Augustine learned centuries ago, "O God, our hearts are restless until they rest in thee."

Additionally, we in North American culture are also held in thrall to our principles of autonomous individualism, of being a "law unto our-selves,"[76] of being free to determine our own destinies. How is freedom typically conceived in a North American context? Usually as freedom of choice, of having a variety of options to select from, and having those options always open. Usually, a practical timelessness is presupposed: previous choices can always be canceled out with subsequent choices. It is always possible, and highly desirable, to be able to start over, to be able to "reinvent" oneself. This is supposed to be true freedom. Moreover, a person's freedom understood in this sense is typically con-strued as a zero-sum game when viewed in relationship with God. That is, if we are to consider ourselves free, we must be free from any divine

---

75. Quote taken from NEB; the RSV and NRSV translate "phantoms" instead as "worth-lessness" and "worthless."

76. Consider this claim from Alan Wolfe's book, *Moral Freedom: The Search for Virtue in a World of Choice* (New York: W. W. Norton, 2001), 2:

> One thing can be said with some certainty about the way we live now: to find out whether our public and private lives are in accord, we survey opinion. For those who insist on the moral superiority of the good old days, this is proof enough of how low we have stooped, for how can ordinary people presume to know what is best either for their society or themselves? Yet compared to a time when the rules were set by a few and expected to be obeyed by the many, we have become more democratic, and if the voice of the people counts in determining who will fill public offices, it also provides the only acceptable account of how we understand ourselves. With social science methodology, the consumer sovereignty that dominates our economy comes to influence our morality. Instead of reading novelists and philosophers to tell us what we ought to think, we tell them instead what we actually do think.

constraints. The more freedom and agency we ascribe to God, the less we may ascribe to ourselves.

Yet is this really freedom? Is a person merely the product of the ability to choose arbitrarily first this and then that, free from constraint (whether human or divine), following whatever impulse moves her or him to act? While it presumes an active and liberated subject, is there in fact a "self" there? If what causes a person to act is some external object or goal, then there can be no continuity or integrity established in the person. Indeed, one could easily conclude that there is no "person" *acting* at all, but only a "receptor of stimuli" *reacting* to whatever comes along. Of course, the advertising industry would like its audience to accept such a definition, because it plays right into its desire to sell us ever more products. And it is not reluctant to suggest that we deserve or even need these things: "Costs more, but I'm worth it"; "You deserve a break today"; "Must see TV"; "Gotta have it." Yet if we *have* to have whatever it is selling, then that necessarily means we are not free to be without it. But this means we are not its master, but its slave. We have become enthralled, in both senses of that word.

By contrast, a truly free person, one liberated by sharing in Christ's victory, displays the ability to discern ideals, establish priorities, make commitments, direct actions accordingly, weather challenges, and maintain an integrity of purpose over time. Indeed, because of Christ's kingship, we recognize, and may truly know for the first time, that we have a future, as well as a past. We learn where we have come from and where we are headed, and with the revelation of this true identity we may actually become ourselves for the very first time. Christ the King opens up for us a new identity because he himself remained always true to his own identity, a share of which he offers to us. In the light of his revelation, we, too, stand revealed. In our current condition, of course, this remains an unsettling, even frightening thought. We do not want to be exposed. We are embarrassed or ashamed in myriad ways. Yet Scripture suggests that when such light does actually break into our lives, the sense of embarrassment will be momentary and the sense of astonishment and joy the predominant sensation.

Consider the story of Jesus' encounter with the Samaritan woman at the well (John 4:4–30, 39–42). When Jesus reveals that he knows she has had seven husbands, her reaction is one of discomfort over her past but also awe at the prospect of an entirely new way of life. Her past story seems so familiar to us, at least in modern American culture: seven husbands, seven failed attempts at creating her own life. Seeking repeatedly to reinvent herself, one can easily imagine that she has actually lost herself irretrievably. Where is her "self"? Has there been any continuity in her life, any common thread that would anchor her true self to something enduring? But now Jesus reveals that he knows her, and in this being known, a door of possibility opens to her that she never knew existed. As Paul writes, "For now we see in a mirror, dimly, but then we will see face to face. Now I know only in part; then I will know fully, even as I have been fully known" (1 Cor 13:12). In our current condition, being known by God is as frightening to us as it was to Adam and Eve when they hid in the garden. But in Christ's victory, fear and shame are banished, to be replaced by profound joy that we are no longer strangers to God and to one another, that we are no longer so utterly isolated and alone. Liberation from the bondage of our past and yearning for a fulfilled future—represented so tellingly and poignantly by the woman at the well—find their realization in Christ's reclaiming of creation.

Christ's victorious sovereignty, in reclaiming us as beings created "good" and "in the image of God," also has the definitive word with regard to our self-worth as human beings. In a highly competitive and image-driven culture, many persons are more than familiar with the sense that they just do not measure up. Indeed, many may feel—perhaps adolescents most particularly, but even adult women and men—overwhelming sensations of inadequacy in the face of our culture's media-hyped standards, whether they be of beauty or strength or intelligence or success. Alternately, under the bombardments of a media society, many fall prey to the self-serving enticements, the oppressive or, perhaps more often, vacuous role models, and nihilistic mores of an ultimately impersonal mass culture. Christ's victory over the powers of sin and emptiness and death, however, challenges us to recognize that such feelings, standards, and responses do not measure our true reality in the eyes of our loving Creator. Paul Fiddes speaks with passion and clarity to these feelings, their source, and how we should respond to them:

> In our own experience there is a voice within us that makes us face our weaknesses and failings, not to cope with them but in order to break us; it harps upon our flaws in order to persuade us that we are worthless. It uses the yardstick of the law to beat us into despair. It is in this aspect of the Satan that Jesus comments, when he calls him "the father of lies," for

nothing can in fact separate us from the divine love which accepts us and values us as we are.[77]

Finally, proclaiming Christ as king is important for another reason: our sovereign is a person, and not an abstract concept or impersonal force. Why should this be considered a good thing? After all, human history is full of examples of arbitrary despots and tyrants, held accountable to no higher law or authority than themselves. It is one of the advances of the modern era that legal and political systems have been codified and standardized to serve the end of "equal justice under law." Fair enough. But the twentieth century in particular knew the horrors that "standardized" ideological systems can also inflict. The evil produced by the totalitarianism of the Communist left and Fascist right was magnified—if not actually made possible!—by the fact that they were "systematized." Organized bureaucratically to be impersonal and efficient, both became juggernauts of death and destruction. In the face of such structures, such "principalities and powers," human beings cease to be human beings and instead become cogs in the machine—or expendable fuel to keep it running. They cease having names and become instead numbers. The writings of Franz Kafka early in the last century describe well such life lived at the whim of impersonal regulations and faceless bureaucrats, yet even his insight could not anticipate the horrors to come later in the century as the wheels of these systems inexorably turned.

Nevertheless, knowing "whose you are," knowing that you belong "body and soul, in life and in death" to Jesus Christ,[78] can make all the difference. As Dietrich Bonhoeffer exemplified in his struggle against the Nazis, such a faith can truly free one to serve the Lord and resist evil. As African-American faith has long known in the face of slavery and institutional racism, if Jesus is Lord, then no one else can be. As Archbishop Romero of San Salvador and the many Christians of numerous base communities demonstrated, this liberating recognition can inspire even the powerless to work for justice and righteousness in the face of systemic oppression. Sometimes the challenge confronts us with more beguiling or insidious forms, yet knowing "whose you are"

---

77. Paul S. Fiddes, *Past Event and Present Salvation: The Christian Idea of Atonement* (Louisville, Ky.: Westminster/John Knox Press, 1989), 120.

78. See the answer to the opening question of the Heidelberg Catechism of 1563.

can still be life-saving. A young person nurtured in the reality that she or he truly belongs to Christ is far better equipped to resist the twin temptations of prideful narcissism or damning self-denigration. While antithetical in one respect, in another sense these temptations both display an excessive preoccupation with oneself. Of course, that is one classic understanding of sin: being "curved in upon oneself." In sum, Christian allegiance to the lordship of Christ offers us the way to resist the faceless principalities that would force us or the mass market powers that would lure us from the true and fulfilling communion with God and one another that God intended with our very creation.

Moreover, Christian allegiance to the personal lordship of Christ is not something that happens on an individual or abstract basis. Rather, we are incorporated into a body of believers, into a group of other persons likewise called by Christ to mutually support and upbuild one another, that our common service to Christ and the world might be stronger and more secure. In baptism, Christians are baptized into the death and resurrection of Christ, but we are also baptized into an eschatological community. We are joined to Christ, but we are also joined to Christ's body, the church. In the Lord's Supper, we participate in the eschatological banquet with our risen Lord, but we also participate in it with our Christian brothers and sisters.

5

Christ the Priest

The Son's Sacrificial Offering

In the considerations of this chapter, I again remind my readers of my presupposition that Christ's threefold work is both fully his own and fully trinitarian. He is indeed the Messiah and mediator of God, yet at the same time "the external works of the Trinity are undivided." So having argued in the previous chapter that his royal work should be understood as being done on behalf of the Father, I now address how his priestly work should be understood as his own proper work as the incarnate Son.[1] When this task is accomplished, I will consider in the next chapter how his prophetic work may be understood as done on behalf of the Spirit.

The New Testament Witness

"For it was fitting that we should have such a high priest, holy, blameless, undefiled, separated from sinners, and exalted above the heavens. Unlike the other high priests, he has no need to offer sacrifices day after day, first for his own sins, and then for those of the people; this he did once for all when he offered himself" (Heb 7:26–37). The Letter to the

---

1. As first stated on page 22, I say "proper" because he alone of the triune persons was to be the incarnate one (a prerequisite for his priestly, sacrificial work), and not because this office and work has primacy over the other two.

Hebrews stands as the prime New Testament locus for an explanation of Christ as priest and sacrifice. But it is not the sole locus for this complex of images associated in some way with Israel's cultic practices. Passages representing Christ as some variety of sacrifice or a new temple (or its cornerstone) or functioning as a priest or referring to his blood appear in a variety of New Testament texts. He is "the Lamb of God who takes away the sin of the world!" (John 1:29). All "are now justified by his grace as a gift, through the redemption that is in Christ Jesus, whom God put forward as a sacrifice of atonement by his blood, effective through faith" (Rom 3:24–45). "Then he took a cup, and after giving thanks he gave it to them, saying, 'Drink from it, all of you; for this is my blood of the covenant, which is poured out for many for the forgiveness of sins'" (Matt 26:27–28). "Christ loved us and gave himself up for us, a fragrant offering and sacrifice to God" (Eph 5:2). "In this is love, not that we loved God but that he loved us and sent his Son to be the atoning sacrifice for our sins" (1 John 4:10). "Jesus answered them, 'Destroy this temple, and in three days I will raise it up.' . . . He was speaking of the temple of his body" (John 2:19, 21). Taken together, these passages express the general claim that in the priestly intercession and sacrificial death of Jesus Christ, the incarnate Son, the triune God provides what humanity needs to be reconciled to God and reestablished as his covenant people. In a world corrupted by human sin, the eternal Son himself became human and, representing humanity, took upon himself its guilt and bore the punishment that was its due, even as he provides the means for overcoming this corruption. In other words, in his priestly representative role, as atoning sacrifice, as paschal lamb and a sacrifice of "first fruits," Christ shields humanity from its deserved punishment and death and offers it access to new life. As a corollary, to say that Jesus Christ is high priest and perfect sacrifice—a status and accomplishment enabled and accepted by the Father and that the Holy Spirit enables us to affirm—is to recognize that no other person need, or even may, stand in this intercessory position and that no other sacrifice need, or even may, be made in order to reconcile us to God and grant us access to him.

The whole thrust of the New Testament narrative points to Christ's death on the cross as the clearest manifestation of this priestly role and sacrifice. Yet the Son's crucifixion does not merely manifest, it accomplishes God's reconciliation of the world to himself. Christ's sacrifice simultaneously offers satisfaction for the debt incurred by humanity's guilt, protects it from the punishment of death, and establishes the basis for a new way of human being and relating. That is, in his passion and death, Christ breaks the tyrannous cycle of the world's justice, of wrong and retribution, by freely offering himself to the demands of that justice while also establishing an alternative means of forgiveness and reconciliation. In addition, with his passion and death, Christ also enacts a new covenant, a new way for persons to relate to God and therefore to one another (Matt 26:26–29 // Mark 14:22–25 // Luke 22:15–20). This priestly role was fulfilled in Christ's passion and death, but it was also anticipated in his words and deeds prior to his crucifixion. For example, consider his proclamation of God's grace and mercy (e.g., Matt 18:23–35), his admonition to "turn the other cheek" (e.g., Luke 6:27–30), his pronouncement of forgiveness of sinners and insistence that persons do the same (e.g., Mark 2:1–12, Luke 17:3–4, and, of course, the Lord's Prayer [Matt 6:9–13 // Luke 11:2–4; cf. Matt 6:14–15 and Mark 11:25–26]), and his association with outcasts and sinners (e.g., Luke 5:29–32). Finally, to serve this new life, Christ continues to act as a priestly intercessor on humanity's behalf (Luke 23:24, Rom 8:34, and Heb 7:24–25).

Yet what does this complex of labels and metaphors derived primarily from the cultic sphere mean, more precisely? What does it signify to apply these images to Jesus in describing this facet of his atoning work? To begin, I propose that these various labels or images may be understood as complementing and enriching one another theologically, even though their original historical settings do differ. For example, most sacrifices were typically associated with the temple cult, but the Passover lamb was sacrificed in the context of the family household, and it was understood as serving a different purpose than that of temple sacrifices (see Exod 12:1ff). In yet another context, covenants could be sealed with a sacrificial ritual (e.g., Gen 15:7–21, 31:43–54; and Exod 24:3–8). To be sure, some of the same primal assumptions about the power of blood are presumably at work in all these cases, yet the diverse forms of sacrifice were nevertheless understood as serving different functions. But does that mean it is artificial, perhaps even illegitimate to use them all in seeking to interpret Christ's death as "sacrificial"? I would say no, for two reasons. First, Christian theology may associate and develop these diverse meanings, along with the other images I have mentioned, because they are all part of the New Testament narrative describing Christ's death. Their inclusion in the canon itself legitimates their being brought into theological conversation and connection with one another. But this is not merely an arbitrary correlation. I maintain they have a kind of natural affinity for one another because they serve a similar explanatory role within the New Testament narrative. My second reason undergirds the first by recalling the claim made in chapter 2 that "etiology is not destiny." Theological reflection may associate these otherwise diverse concepts because its task is not determined by their historical origin. Christ himself is the norm. The New Testament authors employed a diversity of Old Testament concepts to help explain Christ's sacrifice because of the manifold significance of this aspect of his atoning work. But one should not therefore suppose that their received meaning determines or limits the meaning that may be found in them when ascribed to Christ's work. Quite the contrary, his priestly sacrifice determines and in some cases transforms the inherited, historical meanings of this diverse usage.

So consider first the extensive complex of images associated with Christ's priestly function as the one who offers himself as the final and sufficient sacrifice.[2] One needs only a quick survey to recognize that the New Testament portrays Christ's death with a variety of sacrificial images. The Letter to the Hebrews offers the most self-conscious and developed description of Jesus as both priest and sacrifice, based on an understanding of the atoning rituals performed by the priests in the temple. But other parts of the New Testament offer different, albeit far less developed, ways of speaking about Christ's death as sacrifice. This was due in part to the multiple kinds, and hence meanings, of Old Testament sacrifices. While Christ's death had indeed accomplished a new thing, it was only natural that the New Testament authors searched for whatever explanatory intimations they could find in the Jewish Scriptures. These intimations produced different ways of describing Christ's sacrificial work, but these differences did not preclude their being used by the same author or "school." For example, the apostle Paul can refer to Christ as the "paschal lamb" in one passage, and speak of his redemptive work as "a sacrifice of atonement by his blood, effective through faith" in another (1 Cor 5:7 and Rom 3:25, respectively). Similarly, the Johannine school described Christ as the sacrificial lamb,[3]

---

2. Addressing what this means and what it implies will be the primary task of this chapter. My explanation of Christ as priest and sacrifice will proceed on the presuppositions of christological and trinitarian orthodoxy. Undertaking it on any other ground can only lead to misunderstanding and problems, as I will discuss in my section below, "Why Enlightenment and Feminist Critiques Are Useful but Finally Misplaced."

3. As noted briefly in chapter 3.

but in some places this alludes to the paschal lamb, in others it evokes the lamb of the temple cult, in yet others the association is not specified. In other words, the New Testament sees no problem in interpreting Christ's sacrifice in multiple ways. The implication is that these different types are not exclusive, but complementary of one another. To insure that this variety and complementarity be recognized, I will consider them thematically but seek to make connections between them as I proceed.

The temple and its cult of atoning sacrifices still serves as the key source for the assumptions and imagery behind the New Testament's understanding of Christ's sacrificial death. One can see these associations in several Pauline letters,[4] as well as 1 John 2:2 and 4:19 and Heb 2:16–17. Human sinfulness and thus estrangement from God is presupposed, yet God does not leave humanity without a remedy. Christ's giving of himself in death, and especially the shedding of his blood, serves as an atoning sacrifice.[5] Here it is worth keeping in mind a crucial observation made by Paul Fiddes: "Sacrifice, according to the Israelite and earliest Christian conceptions, is not something human beings do for God (propitiation), but something God does for humankind (expiation)."[6] That is, in the biblical view, sacrifice is not a human attempt to "buy off" a bullying god or assuage an angry god; rather, it is a divine gift enabling that which humans cannot bring about on their own. Thus, what Christ's sacrifice accomplishes these letters describe variously as redemption, reconciliation, and the forgiveness of sins, which are further explained as a breaking down of the dividing wall or hostility that humanity has built between itself and God, and the establishing of peace. Scripture presents God as acting out of gracious righteousness and love, and also out of divine forbearance. The benefits that Christ's sacrifice makes available accrue to persons as sheer gift, appropriated by means of faith in this Son of God. Clearly, the initiative is God's, and it is God who makes the sacrifice effective. Moreover, the character of the act is objective: God's "attitude" or "posture" is described (righteousness, love, forbearance), as is the human response (faithfulness, with gratitude implied), but the focus remains on the real

---

4. Rom 3:23–26, 5:8–10; Gal 2:19–21; Eph 1:7–8, 2:13–14, 5:1–2; Col 1:20.

5. I will discuss the "logic" of atoning sacrifice more fully below, in the section entitled "The Old Testament Witness and the Cultic Context."

6. Paul S. Fiddes, *Past Event and Present Salvation: The Christian Idea of Atonement* (Louisville, Ky.: Westminster/John Knox Press, 1989), 71.

change effected by the shedding of Christ's blood. And this "real change" does not refer to some change within God, but to the transformation of the actual circumstances of humanity's relation to God.

The multilayered significance of Christ's sacrifice is reflected in the seemingly disparate variety of scriptural references it spawned. For example, in a passage from Romans considered for the summary above, Paul speaks of "the redemption that is in Christ Jesus, whom God put forward as a sacrifice of atonement by his blood, effective through faith" (Rom 3:23–26). However, later in that same letter, Paul suggests yet another definition of sacrifice when he encourages believers "to present your bodies as a living sacrifice, holy and acceptable to God, which is your spiritual worship" (Rom 12:1). Is this simply an inconsistency on Paul's part, or is something else going on? Clearly, because of what Christ has accomplished, the meaning of sacrifice for believers has been radically transformed. Now this transformation occurred not because a formerly meaningful literal practice had become implausible, yet gained a new lease on life through a new figurative or symbolic interpretation. Rather, Christ was seen as fulfilling once and for all everything that sacrifice was meant to accomplish. The meaning of his sacrifice remains rooted in the assumptions informing the cult, even while his act of sacrifice rendered the actual practice of that cult forever unnecessary. Christ's sacrifice was understood as real; the sacrifices Christians are to continue to make are likewise understood as real. But if the old forms are obsolete, then these continued sacrifices will need a new form, which is precisely what they acquire. Consider Peter's reference to "spiritual sacrifices" (1 Pet 2:5), the Pauline reference to "living sacrifice"[7] just cited, as well as Paul's use of sacrificial imagery in describing his own efforts on behalf of the Philippians or their gifts to him (Phil 2:17 and 4:18, respectively). These all suggest that the sacrifice now required of Christians refers to their joyous, thankful, and generous self-giving toward God and others in everyday life. The inner reality of sacrifice continues, but without its former cultic dress and procedures.

One may better understand this notion of living sacrifice as "real, but not cultic" by connecting it with those Pauline passages that describe Christians as a "(holy) temple" of the Holy Spirit or of God. This image also derives from a concrete aspect of Jewish worship, and its interpretation depends in part upon the associations brought with it from that

---

7. This is a contradiction in terms if understood within the context of the temple cult, since the offering of a sacrificial animal necessarily entailed its death.

sphere. But its meaning also obtains from the new thing done by Christ. Thus, in one respect, to call Christians God's "temple" is clearly a figurative and derivative use of that term. In another respect, however, it must be understood in a very real, and in fact now primary, sense as referring to believers as the temples in whom the Spirit now dwells (1 Cor 6:19). Christ had said he would raise up a new temple (John 2:19, but see also Matt 26:61 and 27:40; cf. Acts 6:14). Certainly one interpretation connects this statement with Jesus' resurrection (John 2:19 and Rev 21:22), but it is also fruitful to hear it as referring to Christians themselves. The association of these two images produces an obvious conclusion: If Christ is the true and final sacrifice, what better place to "locate" that work than where it actually accomplishes its purpose, namely, within believers, through the efficacious power of the Holy Spirit? (cf. 1 Cor 3:16–17, 6:19; 2 Cor 6:16b; Eph 2:19–22). Christians truly become temples of God, because God is truly present within them through the indwelling Spirit, which incorporates them into Christ's body and the benefits of his sacrifice. While the metaphors overlap (and to our sensibilities may seem to be hopelessly mixed), these personal temples of God also serve as loci of "living sacrifice" when they open themselves up to be used by the Spirit as instruments of God's ongoing work of reconciliation.

Up to this point, I have considered Christ's sacrifice according to scriptural descriptions of its atoning function. This is certainly one of its crucial purposes, understood in the specific sense of expiating, which is to say, "purging" or "covering over" the believer's sin in the eyes of God. In this respect, Christ's sacrifice overcomes the *problem* created by the person's sin that prevents right relation with God. But the biblical witness also presents his sacrifice in a more positive sense as an act actually *establishing* such communion. The most obvious locus of such a construal may be found in those passages describing Jesus' Last Supper with his disciples (Matt 26:26–29 // Mark 14:22–25 // Luke 22:14–20; and 1 Cor 11:23–26; cf. 1 Cor 10:14–18). True, Matthew's account associates the pouring out of Jesus' blood with the forgiveness of sins, but that interpretive approach does not predominate in his version or those of Mark, Luke, and Paul. Instead, the focus centers on two overlapping and complementary themes: the establishment of a new covenant between God and humanity and the anticipation of its final consummation in the eschatological kingdom of God. The former is expressed in some variation of the words, "This is my blood of the new covenant" (Matt 26:28 // Mark 14:24 // Luke 22:20; 1 Cor 11:25). The latter finds expression in some variation of the words, "I will never again drink of the fruit of the vine until that day when I drink it new in the kingdom of God" (Matt 26:29 // Mark 14:25 // Luke 22:16, 18; cf. 1 Cor 11:26). Additionally, the first of these themes also includes the notion that a new communion has been made possible among believers themselves.[8] The second theme points to the peculiar circumstance that believers exist in a unique place between past and future, between remembering Christ's death (Luke 22:19 and 1 Cor 11:25–26) and anticipating reunion with him at the messianic banquet (Matt 26:29 // Mark 14:25 // Luke 22:16, 18)—even while participation in the Supper mysteriously joins them to him in the present moment. Partaking of the bread and wine, of Christ's sacrificial body and blood, believers become, through the power of the Spirit, communicants with him and therefore also with God the Father.

The fact that all three Synoptic Gospels portray Jesus' Last Supper as a Passover meal points to yet another understanding of Christ's sacrifice: he is associated with, or actually portrayed as, the new "paschal lamb." In other words, in addition to the context of the temple cult, with its atonement and communion sacrifices, the New Testament draws upon another aspect of Israel's history to help describe the meaning of Jesus' sacrifice, namely, the festival of Passover. To be sure, the New Testament offers only one explicit parallel between Christ's death and Passover, but this one is significant, as are the various implicit associations, because of the way they all creatively connect or evoke other scriptural images and themes. The one explicit parallel comes from the apostle Paul, who refers to Christ as the "paschal lamb" in 1 Cor 5:7, although at first glance the label may seem more a rhetorical flourish than anything theologically crucial. Paul does not appear to develop it (on which more in a moment). The most significant implicit association comes from the Gospel of John. Recall that the Fourth Gospel presents a passion chronology that differs from that of the Synoptic Gospels. The latter indicate that Jesus celebrated the Passover meal with his disciples (see Matt 26:17ff. // Mark 14:12ff. // Luke 22:7ff) and that his crucifixion followed it. John's Gospel describes this Last Supper as occurring before the feast of Passover (John 13:1–2) and then presents its account of Christ's passion with the repeated narrative comment that his death occurred on the "day of Preparation" for the Passover (John

---

8. This is explicit in 1 Cor 10:16–17, but implicit in the other passages cited.

18:28, 39; 19:14, 31, 42). In other words, John implies that Jesus' death occurs on the same day that the Passover lambs are traditionally slain.[9]

Why is this timing significant? The answer should be obvious: John clearly intends to conflate Christ's death with that of the paschal lamb. In his crucifixion, Christ becomes the new paschal lamb, whose blood saves God's people from death (cf. Matt 27:62 and Luke 23:54 with Mark 15:42). Is this why John's Gospel had so early labeled Jesus, through the words of John the Baptist, "the Lamb of God" (John 1:29, 35)? The appellation is ambiguous, because in the first instance John further specifies that as this lamb Jesus "takes away the sin of the world." This seems to allude more obviously to a lamb of the regular temple cult than to the Passover lamb. Yet because the usage is already figurative, and in light of the fact that John offers no direct clarification, I conclude that he actually wants to evoke and conflate multiple associations. Such a conflation can be coherent precisely because these multiple associations cohere in the one person, Christ. In him and his perfect sacrifice, all sacrifices come together and achieve their final meaning. This claim recapitulates in one specific way an assumption I have used before in other contexts: the New Testament narrative portrays Christ bringing (theological) unity, in both his person and work, to what was once (historically) separate and diverse.

With this in mind, one may now recognize that Paul's brief reference to Christ as the "paschal lamb" is much more significant than one might have first concluded. Consider the passage in its context:

> Your boasting is not a good thing. Do you not know that a little yeast leavens the whole batch of dough? Clean out the old yeast so that you may be a new batch, as you really are unleavened. For our paschal lamb, Christ, has been sacrificed. Therefore, let us celebrate the festival, not with the old yeast, the yeast of malice and evil, but with the unleavened bread of sincerity and truth. (1 Cor 5:6–8)

The context is Paul's rebuke of the Corinthian Christians over their tolerance on boasting of certain sexual immorality and their rationalization of that tolerance on the grounds of Christian freedom. He is concerned

---

9. It should be recognized that while the Synoptic Gospels do not portray Jesus as the Passover sacrifice in the way that the Gospel of John does, the accounts of the Last Supper nevertheless make use of sacrificial images that should not be ignored.

that the behavior of one individual, and the acceptance of that behavior by the community, actually threatens to corrupt the whole community.

With these particulars in mind, consider the theological assumptions and associations that are implicit in the seemingly jumbled imagery of his admonition. Paul conjures up the Passover, that event when God acted to liberate his people from the bondage of their old life and opened for them the way to a new life. As it was then, so it is now: the paschal lamb serves to protect the people from the divine wrath that inflicts such a deadly toll on the old order enslaving them. But such benefit comes only if one follows the divine prescription. At this point, Paul invokes another element of the Passover, the unleavened bread, used in contrast to bread that is leavened. He speaks of the latter to illustrate the danger of one person corrupting the whole. This is the "old" way, which has been cleaned out; the new (unleavened) bread represents the new life the community may now, and should now, pursue. Here Paul faces the limitations of his own imagery. It seems likely that he would have pushed his yeast analogy in a positive direction as well, to illustrate how one person can also rectify the whole, had not the metaphor of unleavened bread obviously precluded it. Be that as it may, is this "unleavened bread" meant to represent Christ and evoke an association with one element of the Lord's Supper? Both of these seem likely.

The logic implicit in the yeast metaphor (i.e., that one small part can transform the whole) may serve as a natural segue to yet another understanding of Christ's death, namely, as a sacrifice of "first fruits." Indeed, Paul himself connects the two in a passage where the tangle of metaphors actually reinforces the theological point: "If the part of the dough offered as first fruits is holy, then the whole batch is holy; and if the root is holy, then the branches also are holy" (Rom 11:16). What is the sacrifice of first fruits? I will detail its Old Testament background more fully below, but for now it may be defined as the offering of thanksgiving and tribute made in recognition of God's gracious bestowal of life. At its most basic level, the sacrifice consisted of the first part of the harvest, which was understood as having a special status and role. Apart from the virtually universal status that attaches to anything that is first, the first fruits also possess the special practical importance of being that which represents renewal and continuing life: a new harvest represents one more season of survival. It means that one is no longer dependent simply on one's prior resources. It signals, symbolically and sometimes in actuality, that one may "break the fast" because a new crop has arrived. Thus, it is of particular significance when the first fruits of this new harvest are not immediately consumed, but ritually offered to God, the source of all good gifts. Yet in being so dedicated to God, the true and final source of all life, it was also understood as serving to protect the rest of the crop.[10]

Given this definition, one may anticipate some of the ways in which Scripture understands Christ's death as being a sacrifice of first fruits offered to God on behalf of believers. Christ the sacrifice of first fruits represents a new season of not mere survival, but thriving. His sacrifice means Christians no longer live from the old harvest, from the fruits of the old humanity, but from a new way of being, from the risen Christ. "But in fact Christ has been raised from the dead, the first fruits of those who have died. For since death came through a human being, the resurrection of the dead has also come through a human being; for as all die in Adam, so all will be made alive in Christ. But each in his own order: Christ the first fruits, then at his coming those who belong to Christ" (1 Cor 15:20–23). Being incorporated into Christ's death through baptism and the Lord's Supper, Christians are also incorporated into Christ's resurrection. Its benefits include not just new life at the End, but a new *way* of life here and now, namely, life in the Spirit that is continually dedicated to God the Father (e.g., 2 Thess 2:13–14, 16–17). And in this new way of life, Christians may also serve as a kind of "first fruits" for others, indicating the future that God intends for the whole of creation (see, e.g., Rom 8:22–23 and Jas 1:17–18; cf. Rom 11:16 with Matt 13:33 // Luke 13:21).

In other words, Christ's sacrifice is indeed a vicarious sacrifice, a sacrifice made "in our stead." But as such, it is not just a sin or guilt offering. It is also the sacrifice of the new paschal lamb. And it is an offering of "first fruits." Not only does he suffer punishment "on our behalf," he also shields us from the deadly consequences that stem from our attachment to our old way of life. And finally, he becomes the new creation and, on our behalf, establishes access to it and full enjoyment of it. He has indeed placed himself in our stead to bear the condemnation we deserve, but he also places himself in our stead to enable our

---

10. The same logic applied to the first-born male of livestock, as well as human offspring, the latter being "redeemed" with a substitute offering of two turtledoves or pigeons. This is what lies behind the statement in Luke 2:22–24, which describes Mary and Joseph bringing their first-born son Jesus "up to Jerusalem to present him to the Lord" and offer the appropriate sacrifice. See also Exod 13:1–2, 11–16, 23:16–19 (// 34:22–26); Lev 2:14, 23:9–14, 17–20; and Num 28:26.

safe passage from old bondage to new life, and then in our stead bears fruit for our re-creation and fulfillment. The Christian tradition has not been wrong to promote Christ's death as a sacrificial offering for our sin. But it has been one-sided in not also promoting Christ's death as a liberating paschal sacrifice and a sacrificial sowing that enables a new harvest of unity with God and one another. Christ serves as the "old humanity" and in his death that old humanity is confronted by divine judgment and abolished. But Christ is also the new human, the first person of a new harvest—and in his sacrifice, through the power of the Holy Spirit, we, too, are made new. In all these aspects of Christ's sacrifice, he accomplishes for us what we could not accomplish ourselves, enabling us to escape the self-imposed bondage and guilt of our own sin and reclaim the concord and communion that God intends for our lives.

These diverse and mutually reinforcing understandings of Christ's sacrifice also make apparent the significance of another aspect of his priestly role. The Bible presents Christ as priest in part because he continually intercedes on our behalf before God: "He holds his priesthood permanently, because he continues forever. Consequently he is able for all time to save those who approach God through him, since he always lives to make intercession for them" (Heb 7:24–25). Paul evokes the image of the risen Jesus sitting at God's right hand, speaking on our behalf (Rom 8:34). Christ is the mediator, the representative, and the advocate through whom, in the power of the Spirit, we approach God the Father and God the Father comes to us. This function is most commonly enacted in the church's continuing practice of praying "in Jesus' name," but it is also indicated by the fact that Jesus teaches his disciples—of whatever era—how to pray, with the words "Our Father . . ." (Matt 6:9–13 // Luke 11:2–4). Commentators have also interpreted the rending of the temple curtain at Jesus' death (Matt 27:51 // Mark 15:38 // Luke 23:45) as a sign that his priestly mediation has opened access to God. No longer is it just the high priest who, only on the Day of Atonement, may enter the holy of holies, and thus into the divine presence. In Christ, the new high priest, all may now approach God, and do so on any day of the year, whenever they invoke the name of Jesus in prayer.

That Christ's priestly intercession has this triune character can be gleaned from the juxtaposition of various Scripture passages, but it appears most obviously in Paul's comments in Rom 8. In verses 26–27, he describes the Spirit helping us to pray by interceding for us "according to the will of God." Yet only a few verses later, he writes: "Who is to condemn? It is Christ Jesus who died, yes, who was raised, who is at the right hand of God, who indeed intercedes for us" (Rom 8:34). Now one could say that Paul's reference to the Spirit's intercession involves our prayer while his reference to Christ's intercession involves our coming before the judgment seat of God. But I contend such a reading would be artificial, making a clear-cut distinction where the biblical text employs a useful ambiguity. If one recalls the observations made in chapter 3 regarding the ways Scripture describes God's triadic activity, one may recognize in the unfolding of these verses a similar character. Paul presents God the Father as both the instigator and recipient of our desire to approach him, while the Spirit and Son are presented as effecting this approach. The implication may seem to be that the Spirit's efficacy works in us, while the Son's efficacy works in the Father. But such a reading should not be pushed too far. On the one hand, it can imply too great a separation between the Spirit and Son, an implication excluded by Paul's many references to the work of both Spirit and Son in us (Rom 8:2, 10; 1 Cor 6:11; 2 Cor 3:3; cf. Titus 3:6), and even more by his occasional reference to the Spirit as *Christ's* Spirit (Rom 8:9; Phil 1:19). On the other hand, it can imply too great a separation between the Son and the Father—as if the Son had to change the Father's mind, when it is the Father who initiates the whole dynamic in the first place! Scriptural accounts of the work of the triune God describe the activity of the three persons in a tightly interwoven manner that resists any simple unraveling. That being the case, whether our "approach" to God refers to the daily petition of prayer or coming into his presence at the eschatological judgment, we are justified in claiming that in all times and places Christ acts, in the power of the Spirit, as our priestly intercessor.

The Old Testament Witness and the Cultic Context

I have already suggested a number of the ways that the Old Testament was used to explain Christ's crucifixion as a "sacrifice." But I have presented the connections in a rather allusive way, and have considered them more in terms of their New Testament appropriation than their Old Testament roots. So my central questions in this section should be clear: What are the basic Old Testament stories and themes available to the church to help explain the new reality of Christ in his office and function as the messianic priest? And how does the risen Christ become the hermeneutical key for the church's understanding of its received Scriptures? I will focus on the Old Testament witness, offering a brief sketch of what those Scriptures present regarding Israel's understanding of the priestly office and its work of sacrifice. This examination will then provide the context for my further discussion of how Christ both fulfills and redefines the biblical notion of "priest" and "sacrifice."

Two sets of questions arise for us here: First, according to the scriptural narratives of the Old Testament, what is the role of the priest and why is it necessary? And second, what is the meaning of sacrifice? That is, what motivated it and what was it understood as accomplishing? Regarding the first, in the Old Testament context, the priest was the mediator of right order between the holy God and the covenant people. As God is holy, so, too, should the covenant people be holy: Israel is to be a kingdom of priests and a holy nation, which is to say, "set apart" and "devoted" to God. The terms of this special status are given in the law *(torah)*, so that holiness is determined by one's obedience to and fulfillment of the law's diverse requirements. Yet life under the law was not merely "legalistic," as we might imagine. That is, one's status under the law was not determined merely by one's faultless obedience to its requirements such that any failure in adherence resulted in penalty without appeal or remedy. To the contrary, a prominent aspect of the law was its provision for the reconciliation and restoration of persons who had for whatever reason fallen short of the holiness required of them. In concrete terms, this provision was the sacrificial system, delegated by God to the priests, the purpose of which was to maintain— which is to say, regularly restore through the rituals of the cult—the people's proper relation to God. Otherwise, the chasm between the people as creatures and God as their Creator, between the people as unclean and sinful and God as holy and righteous would be simply too great.

This "proper relation" between God and Israel was not understood in a merely psychological or subjective sense, but as an objective reality. The Old Testament understood a law of God much as we moderns understand a "law of nature": it is just how things are, so a purely subjective response would not suffice to set things right. If such laws are broached, restoration must take the form of some practical and concrete action. While the comparison is not perfect, consider the following. Feeling remorse that you "defied" the law of gravity by using a ladder carelessly and falling off is beside the point to gravity and thus of no objective value to you; putting your broken leg in a cast and securing the ladder next time are the appropriate responses. On this analogy, priests may be seen as the persons commissioned to serve as the "doctors" and "safety consultants," with cultic sacrifices being the practical means for reestablishing the proper objective order. The one factor not included in this analogy is, of course, the subjective element of repentance, because God is not merely an impersonal force but a being with whom one is in personal relation. One might feel sorry or stupid for having defied gravity, but gravity does not concern itself with our "repentance." God, however, does.

These observations have already begun to address the second set of questions, namely, how were Old Testament sacrifices understood? What was their meaning, and what were they viewed as actually accomplishing? Giving a succinct summary is difficult. Old Testament sacrifices took several forms, and in these diverse forms, they could simultaneously "mean" a number of different things and have various motivations, which often interacted in complementary or simply overlapping ways. Three general categories are evident. Sacrifices could function as gifts or tributes to God, as an offering of daily "sustenance" intended as a means "of forging or reaffirming ties of kinship or alliance," or as expiation.[11] Consider first the meaning of sacrifice understood as thanksgiving or tribute, especially in its scriptural form as the sacrifice of "firstfruits." The "logic" of sacrificing the first fruits (or, in the case of a human firstborn, offering an alternate sacrifice to dedicate the child) was to recognize ritually the distinction between Creator and creature, and the fact that life itself is a gift dependent upon God's vivifying act. In addition, "new things" such as first fruits and the firstborn were understood as having a special "virtue," which required their being reserved for God, while it was also "commonly believed that the surrender of the prime part will protect the rest from hurt and blight."[12]

Second, consider the meaning of sacrifice understood as a communal meal, especially as that is understood as forging or reaffirming an alliance or covenant. In one common respect, such sacrifices simply represented the worshipper's care for God, offering a special portion as "sustenance" to the Lord (see Lev 3:14–17 and Num 28). But such a relation does not just happen, it must be established—typically, at God's gracious initiative. So a certain priority belongs to those sacrifices that

---

11. See T. H. Gaster, "Sacrifices and Offerings, OT," in *Interpreter's Dictionary of the Bible* (New York: Abingdon Press, 1962), 4:148–53. Roland de Vaux, in his *Religious Institutions* (vol. 2 of *Ancient Israel*; New York: McGraw-Hill Book Co., 1965), 451–54, offers a very similar list: sacrifice as gift, as means of union with God, and as expiation for sin.

12. Gaster, "Sacrifices and Offerings," 4:149. Some scriptural references to this kind of sacrifice include Exod 13:1–2, 11–14, 34:19–20; Lev 27:26; Num 18:15–17; and Deut 15:19.

establish or commemorate God's "taking the first step." The ritual sacrifice and meal of Passover certainly speak to such an understanding, but there are references to similar meals following Yahweh's giving of the law and the promised land (see Exod 13:3–8, 18:10–12, and 24:9–11; and Deut 12:10–14). At other times, the covenantal element had less to do with a meal and more with a ritual application of blood. This may be seen in the blood smeared on doorposts and lintels to distinguish the Israelites from the Egyptians at Passover (Exod 11:4–7 and 12:5–13) and in Moses' sprinkling sacrificial blood on the people to ratify the covenant and the book of the law (Exod 24:3–8).

Finally, consider the significance of sacrifice understood as "expiation." To begin, one should recognize that expiation is a broad term. Its meaning may be fleshed out by considering that it was effected by means of three complementary rituals, namely, "purgation" sacrifices (NRSV: "sin offerings"), "reparation" sacrifices (NRSV: "guilt offerings"),[13] and the scapegoat ritual of the Day of Atonement. The purgation or purification sacrifice was understood as removing the taint or contagion of sin. From *what* that contagion was removed is a matter of some scholarly dispute: the sacrifice at least removed the taint from God's violated "sanctum," but it may have cleansed the violator as well.[14] In either case, an objective rectification or "regeneration" occurs. That which had been contaminated, even "attacked"[15] by the sin—whether deliberately or not—has been restored to its original, proper state. The "reparation" sacrifice, by contrast, "was not an indemnification, but simply a mulct. Indeed, it had to be paid over and above the actual restitution of the damage (Lev 5:14–16). Its purpose was punitive, not compensatory. . . ."[16] Here the emphasis is not so much on the objective as it is on the subjective, not so much on a restoration of the previous condition as on the guilt, repentance, and forgiveness of the sinner. If the goal is the reconciliation of a personal bond, then this aspect of sacrifice ritually addresses the relational reality that some breaches cannot be put right simply by restoring the *status quo ante* and pretending nothing ever

---

13. John H. Hayes, following the lead of Jacob Milgrom, argues that the labels "purgation" and "reparation" sacrifices are more accurate and therefore more helpful translations of the Hebrew terms than those given in the NRSV (and RSV). See John H. Hayes, "Atonement in the Book of Leviticus," *Interpretation* 52 (January 1998): 8 and 10.

14. Cf. Gaster, "Sacrifices and Offerings," 4:151–52 with the Hayes article just cited.

15. The word is Hayes's. See Hayes, "Atonement," 8.

16. Gaster, "Sacrifices and Offerings," 4:152.

happened. Something more must be done, something more must be offered. Especially in the face of infinite holiness, one cannot help but know infinite shame and guilt. In such light, one would give anything for forgiveness—even one's life. But God's gracious gift of the sacrificial system obviates the need for a self-annihilating sacrifice. The "reparation" sacrifice accomplished this "something more": atonement can be effected in the ritual shedding of blood because "the life of the flesh is in the blood" (see Lev 17:11; cf. Heb 9:22). In sum, while the purification and reparation sacrifices are distinct, they complement one another in ways that cover the variety of human shortcomings in relation to the Holy One and other persons. From the relatively minor infraction to the sin that racks the conscience, these expiatory sacrifices were intended to offer a means of restoration and absolution.

These sacrifices were offered on an individual basis. The preeminent example of communal expiation took place on the Day of Atonement. The rituals of that day included several sacrifices, and the unique rite involving the scapegoat. T. H. Gaster makes some helpful observations about the latter:

> The expulsion of the scapegoat was, among the Hebrews as elsewhere, essentially a public ceremony. . . . Its primary purpose, therefore, was to rid society as a whole of any latent miasma, *responsibility for which could not, for one reason or another, be assigned precisely to particular individuals.* In such circumstances the only possible means of riddance was by pronouncing a collective, blanket confession of sins and then saddling the collective taint upon some one deputed being. In other words . . . the real and sole purpose of the institution was *to do that which had to be done for the public benefit but which could not be done by individuals.*[17]

These comments describe Israel's recognition that they were theologically and morally responsible before God, but even as individuals they were not in any absolute or final sense theologically and morally discrete. No one is morally autonomous. No one remains untainted. Yet no one is clearly or solely to blame for the human condition. Culpability and innocence mingle indecipherably. Yet if this is so, then humanity's collective position would be untenable, were it not that God graciously provides the means by which we can reconcile what we are with what

---

17. Gaster, "Sacrifices and Offerings," 4:153. Emphasis mine.

we should be in the presence of God. In the Old Testament, this means was the sacrificial system, and in this case more particularly, the rituals prescribed for the Day of Atonement.

While the New Testament retains the same conceptual framework, it also obviously witnesses to a new means: "For Christ . . . entered into heaven itself, now to appear in the presence of God on our behalf. . . . [H]e has appeared once for all at the end of the age to remove sin by the sacrifice of himself" (Heb 9:23–26). God the Son becomes Christ the priest and sacrifice by combining and fulfilling these various expiatory rituals in his own life and death: he takes human flesh upon himself and restores it to its original condition. He offers up his own lifeblood, and so makes possible forgiveness and the personal reconciliation of humanity to God. And he takes human guilt upon himself and "carries it away" that we may begin anew. These comments anticipate and help clarify the Christian tradition's connection between Christ's expiatory sacrifice and its doctrine of original sin. Indeed, the notion of vicarious sacrifice cannot make sense unless there is some corresponding concept of humanity's corporate culpability. Both notions presuppose the irreducibly social character of human life, even while they also build upon a transformed understanding of the means that God graciously provides to reconcile what we are with what we should be in the divine presence. Of course, with these observations, the focus has clearly shifted from the assumptions of the old covenant to those of the new.

Christ's Transformation and Fulfillment of the Priestly Role

With this examination of Old Testament practice and assumptions in mind, think about the ways Christ as priest and sacrifice fulfills yet also redefines these three fundamental meanings of sacrifice. Consider first the way in which Christ as priest fulfills and transforms sacrifice understood as tribute, specifically the sacrifice of "first fruits." It begins in the customary fashion, with his dedication as the firstborn (Luke 2:22–24). Given the meanings assigned to first fruits and the firstborn, one can readily anticipate how these meanings will be especially true in the case of Jesus, as the only-begotten Son of God's self-sacrifice on the cross assumes but also transforms these customary understandings. To begin, the ritual recognition of life's giftedness is subsumed with another gift: God himself provides the sacrificial offering. "The one who, according to the old dispensation, received the sacrifice, now becomes the giver."[18] To be sure, this transformation is foreshadowed in the Old Testament (cf. the binding of Isaac, and Abraham's faith that "the LORD will provide," Gen 22:1–14), but now the provision that God makes is God himself. Moreover, the benefit redounding to the rest from the dedication of this firstborn comes to surpass all previous expectation. As the firstborn who sacrifices himself on the cross, Christ expands access to the assembly of God (Rom 8:29; Heb 12:23), as the firstborn from the dead he offers new life to others (1 Cor 15:20–22; Col 1:18; Rev 1:5; 2 Thess 2:13–14; cf. Acts 26:22–23), and as the firstborn of creation he becomes the means of its re-creation (Col 1:15; cf. Rom 8:19–23). Consider Paul's comparison of Adam and Christ in Rom 5 and 1 Cor 15. Recall that the original Hebrew name, *'Adham*, is actually a generic term for "human."[19] Paul's point in these chapters is that in Christ's "free gift" we have access to a new life, a new way of being human. Christ does indeed release us from the burden and guilt of our collective sin and our individual sins. But Christ's sacrifice does not merely open a door and offer a possibility, it also leads us across the threshold and creates something actual in us. He initiates in us a new way of being, a new humanity: "Just as we have borne the image of the man of dust, we will also bear the image of the man of heaven" (1 Cor 15:49). Grace abounds and the free gift of righteousness reigns, for the "last Adam" is an active, life-giving spirit (1 Cor 15:45; see also Phil 3:20–21).

Consider next the manner in which Christ as priest fulfills and transforms the sacrifice understood as a communal meal shared with God for the purpose of forging or maintaining a covenant. Any vestigial assumption that the worshipper must supply the food for God (cf. Lev 21:6 and Num 28:2–3) is now clearly reversed: it is the priest himself who supplies the food and drink, in the form of his own sacrificial blood and body (1 Cor 11:23–26; Mark 14:22–24; Matt 26:26–28; Luke 22:14–20). The initiative is God's, and the emphasis no longer

---

18. Colin Gunton, "The Sacrifice and the Sacrifices: From Metaphor to Transcendental," in *Trinity, Incarnation, and Atonement: Philosophical and Theological Essays* (eds. Ronald J. Feenstra and Cornelius Plantinga Jr.; vol. 1 of *Library of Religious Philosophy*, gen. ed. Thomas V. Morris; Notre Dame, Ind.: University of Notre Dame Press, 1989), 217.

19. Recall as well that Adam's creation from the "dust of the ground," or *'adhamah*, involves a Hebrew play on words perhaps best captured in English when translated as "human" because made from the "humus." See Gen 2:7.

focuses on the duties of the worshipper but on the graciousness of the divine act. Just as we have become a new being in Christ, so, too, in Christ shall we have a new relationship with God and with one another. Indeed, in a biblical context, the transformation of the individual would be pointless without a corresponding, and prior, transformation of the whole community. The most obvious narrative locus of this transformed communion is Jesus' Last Supper with his disciples. But indications of the new relationship are also foreshadowed in Jesus' earlier table fellowship with sinners and tax collectors and in his feast parables. In such meal fellowship, God not only reveals a new relationship between himself and all people, he also offers a foretaste of the benefits to come when that relationship is brought to fulfillment at the end of the age. In this sense, Christ's sacrifice offers and enables a new basis for communion, one not based on ethnic lineage, social status, or natural condition (Gal 3:28), but based on divine promise, grace, and hospitality. The liturgical meal of the Lord's Supper is a sign of this new communion, a reality that is meant to inform the whole life of the community.[20] Christ's offers his body, that we might become members of it (1 Cor 6:15, 17; 10:16; 12:12–27), and in becoming members of Christ find new communion with others and God (Rom 8:14–17, 12:5; 1 Cor 6:19–20, 10:17; Gal 4:4–7; Eph 2:11–22, 3:6, 4:6).

Finally, consider the manner in which Christ as priest fulfills and transforms sacrifice understood as expiation.[21] Here the separation between God and humanity stands at its starkest, because of the great contrast between the holiness of God and the sinfulness of humanity. In this understanding, humanity is its own "victimizer." In its sin, humanity falls short of, indeed works actively against, the purposes of God and its own divinely intended *telos*. This is in one sense an offense against the holiness and intentions of God. Yet it is also an offense of humanity against the divinely created "order and beauty of the universe." The phrase is Anselm of Canterbury's, and it raises an often overlooked insight of his work, *Cur Deus Homo?* That insight is his

---

20. It is no theological coincidence that Paul offers instructions on how to celebrate the Lord's Supper properly after rebuking the Corinthians for their scandalous and embarrassing communal gatherings. See 1 Cor 11:17–34.

21. I will treat this transformation more extensively than the other two, because notions of Christ's expiatory sacrifice are so often critiqued nowadays (and also, in my view, so often misunderstood, by both its supporters and opponents).

recognition of the objective disruption caused in the broader fabric of creation by human sin.[22]

Anselm's position is often dismissed as portraying a self-important God overly preoccupied with affronts to the divine honor. One summary of his various points claims that they "all portray God as a status-paranoid power-monger who deliberately humiliates and infantalizes human beings under the guise of justice."[23] This caricature is wrong on two counts; in fact, his position is actually much more nuanced. First, Anselm clearly states that God is not preoccupied with his honor, because

> As far as God himself is concerned, nothing can be added to his honor or subtracted from it. . . . But when the particular creature, either by nature or reason, keeps the order that belongs to it and is, as it were, assigned to it, it is said to obey God and to honor him. . . . But when it does not will what it ought, it dishonors God, as far as it is concerned, since it does not readily submit itself to his direction, but disturbs the order and beauty of the universe, as far as lies in it, although of course it cannot injure or stain the power and dignity of God.[24]

In other words, references to "honor" and "dishonor" describe in the first and proper sense the character of human actions, and only derivatively and figuratively any divine state, attitude, or "feeling." Anselm's assumptions and logic are not unique to this topic, for he employs the same scholastic distinction in discussing how God may be described as both compassionate and impassible: "You are compassionate in terms of our experience, and not in terms of your own being. . . . For when you see us in our misery, we experience the effect of compassion; you, however, do not experience this feeling."[25] In other words, suggestions that Anselm portrays a vain and petulant God are not just a little off the mark, they are completely off the mark, because the conditions necessary to make them accurate simply do not exist, due to God's impassability.

---

22. See Anselm of Canterbury, *Why God Became Man*, in *A Scholastic Miscellany: Anselm to Ockham* (ed. and trans. Eugene R. Fairweather; Library of Christian Classics, vol. 10; Louisville, Ky.: Westminster/John Knox Press, 1956), 123–24.

23. Darby Kathleen Ray, *Deceiving the Devil: Atonement, Abuse, and Ransom* (Cleveland: Pilgrim Press, 1998), 51.

24. Anselm, *Why God Became Man*, 123–24.

25. From Anselm's *Proslogion*, ch. 8, quoted in Alister E. McGrath, ed., *The Christian Theology Reader* (Cambridge, Mass.: Blackwell Publishers, Inc., 1995), 110.

Second, these stereotypical representations of Anselm's position neglect to consider where the impact of human sinfulness is actually felt, namely, in the created realm. Sin may be said to dishonor God, but, as Anselm makes clear, that does not mean it affects him. Rather, the affect or impact of sin is manifested in the way it "disturbs the order and beauty of the universe." In an observation that is grounded in an analysis similar to the one I have just made, Colin Gunton draws much the same conclusion:

> It is sometimes dismissively observed that Anselm takes his view of legality from the mediaeval feudal order, and the suggestion is that this is to liken the deity to an arbitrary or oppressive ruler. The fact is, however, that the opposite is the case, and Anselm will not be understood unless this is appreciated. It was the duty of the feudal ruler to maintain the order of rights and obligations without which society would collapse. Anselm's God is understood to operate *analogously* for the universe as a whole: as the upholder of universal justice.[26]

Here we might compare Anselm's concern for order and beauty, shaped as it is by his feudal context, with our modern insights into the interdependence exhibited in ecosystems or described by "chaos theory": a minor disturbance one place can escalate to disrupt parts elsewhere, or even the whole. Such a disturbance God cannot simply accept or forgive. God could, if it affected only him, but it does not. Humanity's sin threatens creation itself and God's purposes for that creation; as such, this collective sin cannot be simply ignored or arbitrarily excused.

In this respect, then, it does not suffice to cite the parable of the Prodigal Son (Luke 15:11–32) as prescribing unconditional forgiveness in such a situation, as some theologians do.[27] The father of the parable can forgive and embrace this son without "satisfaction" or penalty if he so chooses, because the father truly is the only aggrieved person (in spite of the older brother's offended sensibilities). Were the offense actually against someone else, however, or against a group, it would hardly be

---

26. Colin E. Gunton, *The Actuality of Atonement: A Study of Metaphor, Rationality, and the Christian Tradition* (Edinburgh: T&T Clark, 1988), 89.

27. Both Michael Winter and Paul Fiddes refer to this parable as evidence against any claim that God requires some satisfaction or prerequisite for forgiveness. See Winter, *The Atonement* (Collegeville, Minn.: The Liturgical Press, 1995), 89 and Fiddes, *Past Event and Present Salvation*, 101.

the father's prerogative to excuse or ignore it. Indeed, in such a circumstance, it would be egregiously unjust for the father to grant forgiveness, if the actual injured party had not first done so or actually refused to. The parable of the Prodigal Son may offer a model of forgiveness for individual Christians to emulate. But the parable cannot be turned into a prescriptive universal principle because it simply does not function on a general or collective level.

Returning to Anselm's phrase, then, for God to ignore or excuse a sin against "the order and beauty of the universe" would amount to a denial of the reality and scope of evil, its collective impact and the fundamental value and purposes God intends for later generations and for creation apart from humans. Something other than mere forgiveness is clearly required:

> If the divine wisdom did not add these requirements wherever wrongdoing tries to disturb right order, there would arise a certain ugliness, derived from the violation of the beauty of order, in the very universe which God ought to regulate, and God would seem to fail in his direction of the world. Now, since both of these things are unseemly, and therefore impossible, every sin is necessarily followed either by satisfaction or by punishment.[28]

The dilemma facing Anselm, and us, in this instance is the recognition that humanity is burdened by a guilt for which it is now indeed collectively responsible, but which cannot be responsibly apportioned to the individuals or nations or generations who have not simply inherited this sin, but willingly acted upon it. Thus, Anselm's initial dilemma remains: humanity owes a debt that it *must* but *cannot* pay.

To respond to this dilemma, I suggest that Anselm's reference to the "order and beauty" of the universe lead us to think of Christ's atoning sacrifice not in terms of a rigid "legal" justice but rather in terms of a "poetic" justice. That is, humanity's initial sinful estrangement from and subsequent reconciliation with God has less the character of a legal interaction and more the character of an unfolding narrative drama. The resolutions of such dramas are never perfect, because they never simply return one to the *status quo ante;* rather, they resolve themselves somewhere later "along the line." Christ's vicarious sacrifice simply

---

28. Anselm, *Why God Became Man*, 124.

cannot be understood correctly if it is explained in static rather than dynamic terms, as something taking place in a timeless mythical realm rather than on a historical continuum. As Robert Jenson suggests, following Aristotle, in describing the dramatic coherence of the biblical narrative, "a good story is one in which events occur 'unexpectedly but on account of each other,' so that before each decisive event we cannot predict it, but afterwards see it was just what had to happen."[29] *This* kind of necessity, this "having to happen," only makes sense in retrospect; it is not something one could determine as necessary in prospect. Anselm was offering an *a posteriori* explanation, based upon the givenness of Christ's incarnation, death, and resurrection; he was not proposing a rigid *a priori* argument that God was required to act in this way, and this way alone.

In this regard, Anselm's argument represented a form of reasoning known to the medieval scholastics as *ex convenientia:* it was not itself a necessary belief, a dogmatic given. Neither was it a logically necessary inference from one of the dogmas of the church. Rather, it was a soteriological proposal that cohered with church dogma on the incarnation in a theologically appropriate and culturally intelligible way, even as it implicitly recognized that God in his freedom could have acted in a different manner.[30] Anselm's proposal truly was "faith seeking understanding," and not without a certain aesthetic sensibility. This character, I suggest, is the reason for Anselm's recurring phrase that it was "fitting" the God-man should die in humanity's stead.

Allow me to illustrate from the biblical narrative one way in which Anselm's view on Christ's vicarious sacrifice may be understood as a fitting and "poetically just" way to counterbalance the violation of creation's order and beauty. Consider Christ's sacrifice in relation to an event described in the opening chapters of that narrative, namely, Cain's murder of his brother Abel (Gen 4:1–16). While a brief story, it is hardly a simple one. Historically, it apparently reflects tensions between nomadic herders and settled farmers, but gives no obvious indication that this is theologically significant. Some details seem inconsistent: Does Cain become a "fugitive and wanderer on the earth," or the founder of the first city? (Gen 4:12, 17). It leaves unanswered the serious and

---

29. Robert W. Jenson, *Systematic Theology* (New York: Oxford University Press, 1997), 1:64.

30. Derived from a discussion in Bruce D. Marshall, *Trinity and Truth* (Cambridge Series in Christian Doctrine; Cambridge: Cambridge University Press, 2000), 121–22.

inevitable question, "Why did God regard Abel and his offering, but not Cain's?" Laying these matters aside, I draw attention to this narrative sequence: Cain kills Abel, Abel's blood cries out from the ground, Cain is "cursed from the ground" and driven from it, but—the divine word is clearly uttered—in spite of what Cain has done, God will not permit his death. How will this fit in the biblical story? Consider first the way in which this story of fratricide represents the long dormant yet final culmination and consequence of Adam and Eve's first disobedience. Having fallen prey to the temptation of sin themselves, imagine the heartbreak and self-recrimination they would feel when their first-born child becomes a murderer, the murderer of their second-born child! Then notice that the victim's blood cries from the ground for vindication, and one senses that the earth itself, the very order of creation, reels in revulsion at the crime. The ground had been cursed once before for the father (Gen 3:17), but now that curse is redoubled for the son. And yet for all that, God does not wish to take Cain's life, but in fact seeks to preserve it. God marks him, but then the story seems to be left dangling. Cain simply wanders off, to dwell "in the land of Nod, east of Eden," to become a father himself and found a city. What happened to the story? Does it really end in such anticlimax? I suggest that in a Christian reading, this story arrives at its true climax and resolution in the narrative of Christ's death and resurrection. That later story, too, has to do with a firstborn, but a firstborn who brings life, not death (Rom 8:29; Col 1:15–20; Rev 1:5). In that story, too, there is a spilling of a shepherd's blood, but it is a pouring out that brings healing, not condemnation (Heb 12:24). In that story, too, the external order of creation itself is implicated, but now the crying and groaning bespeaks the in-breaking fulfillment of creation, not its cursing (Rom 8:19–21; cf. Jesus' words in Luke 19:37–40). In other words, one could not have predicted the full consequence of Cain's story until the unexpected story of Christ brings it full circle to a divinely appointed resolution. An "Anselmian" reading of Cain's story in light of Christ's sacrificial death enables the faithful to "see it was just what had to happen."

Consider this summary of my various conclusions. In Christ's priestly sacrifice, God remedies humanity's untenable situation: in his mercy, he provides a way to stop the spread of humanity's collective sin and indeed "carry it off" as the scapegoat carried off Israel's collective sin on the Day of Atonement. In that sense, Christ's priestly sacrifice expiates our sin and returns us in effect to an "original" state, equivalent to our first parents. Yet Christ's sacrifice does not return us to this "original" state and then simply leave us to our own devices. In addition to being an expiatory sacrifice for sin, Christ's death and subsequent resurrection also constitute a sacrifice of "first fruits." In him, death is transformed from being merely the "wages of sin" to the means of new life. His resurrection offers the sign and the surety that God will complete his purposes for humanity, and not let humanity be deterred or destroyed by death. Indeed, Christ's sacrificial offering of his body and blood establishes a new basis for human communion and human fellowship with God. In sum, a full and biblically based understanding of Christ's sacrifice will not construe it only in a negative way as a vicarious expiation or punishment for sin, but also in a positive way as the God-given means for humanity's personal transformation and restored relation.

Why Enlightenment and Feminist Critiques Are Useful but Finally Misplaced

Much of the preceding may seem utterly alien to a modern way of thinking. At best, the term "priest" is understood as a rather generic title for religious leaders, and "sacrifice" is understood largely as a synonym for any act of self-denial, whether explicitly religious or not, however trivial or substantial. Terms that once had quite precise definitions grounded in a very specific context are now understood in figurative ways in a variety of situations. Few people likely consider the original ritual connection between the two terms, and if they do, it is likely associated with ancient or still "primitive" cultures. Moreover, ever since certain critiques first arose during the Enlightenment (and reiterated in various forms up to the present), to some people the assumptions underlying the whole practice of priestly sacrifice have become implausible, if not actually suspect. The notion that blood has some special and sacred power capable of appeasing an angry deity seems weird and superstitious at best, and the notion that one person could die in order to remove the guilt of another seems hideously misguided, indeed, unjust and evil. Modern conceptions of individual freedom, autonomy, and moral responsibility as well as understandings of the natural realm that have arisen since the late seventeenth century appear to make traditional notions of a vicarious sacrifice offered by a "priest" simply unconvincing and reprehensible.

Students of history know that one motivation behind Enlightenment critiques of classical Christian positions lay in the desire to leave behind the religious warfare and persecutions of the sixteenth and seventeenth centuries. Many critics framed the issue in terms of church officials abusing the faith to pursue their own self-interests. Others, however, also believed that the root cause of such battles lay in the very nature of dogmatic claims. No means of adjudicating between competing religious claims seemed available, which meant religious conflict was inevitable. But if one could undercut dogmatic claims altogether and reconstitute the nature of the religious life, the reasons for conflict would be eliminated. As this approach suggested, if Christians would be more modest in their claims to truth and concentrate instead upon the moral consensus that is more easily reached, then everyone would be better off.

Such critiques and alternative approaches were appealing then and have become commonplace among many now, so they merit a careful response. But I will say at the outset that I believe the best, and perhaps only sufficient, response must be made on the presuppositions of christological and trinitarian orthodoxy, and a nuanced understanding of the doctrine of original sin. Apart from the fact that I affirm these traditions as true, I also believe that they offer us a more useful way of employing a theory of atonement in approaching and acting in our modern and "postmodern" world. The modernist approach may have solved some problems, but I believe it has also fostered some unintended consequences that a more traditional theology is better able to address. Specifically, I insist that the humanity of Jesus must not be isolated from the divinity of the Son, the divine-human Christ must not be isolated from the other two persons of the Trinity, and the solidarity of Christ with humanity—of the "last Adam" with the "first Adam"—must be affirmed and understood. Should a separation be supposed in any of these connections, then one could readily construe the Son's priestly sacrifice as somehow forced upon him by the Father and of no possible connection or benefit to humanity. Were this the orthodox position, then it would be open to the theological and moral censure of the modernist perspective. But in fact, the orthodox position specifically rejects any such bifurcation in Christ, and states that there is *no* appropriate way in which the work of Christ the priest can be understood in isolation or as imposed upon either the humanity or divinity of the incarnate Son. The Son shares the being of God, his will is freely one with the Father's, he lays down his life for his flock of his own accord, and in sharing our humanity he is able to redeem it (John 1:1–2, 14, 16; 10:15, 18; Phil 2:5–8; 1 Cor 15:21–23; 1 Tim 2:5–6; Heb 2:14–18).

Furthermore, one must recognize that while the Christian understanding of Jesus Christ as *the* sacrifice draws upon the concrete history of Israel's temple cult, it is not simply a literal extension of that cult, its practices, and underlying assumptions. As Colin Gunton so ably points out, the ascription of "sacrifice" language to Christ is itself metaphorical, employed to help explain a new reality.[31] Christ does not simply continue the priestly sacrificial tradition unchanged; he transforms and fulfills it. And in this fulfillment, he also paradoxically does away with it. To say that Christ is *the* sacrifice means that no other such sacrifice is needed or appropriate. The dilemma for modern Christian theology is not to reinstate a sacrificial system, but to make the mind-set accompanying it sufficiently comprehensible so that contemporary believers may understand fully how and why Christ has made it obsolete. In this regard, Christ's act counters the seemingly perennial human desire to propitiate the gods through explicit ritual sacrifice or the sociological seeking after scapegoats. The sacrifice of Christ is not something a human does to placate an angry God; rather, it is something a gracious God does to subvert human manipulation and self-righteous violence. Thus, Christ's sacrifice does not offer us a mythological model or principle to emulate. Rather, it is a once and for all event that forever alters how we relate to God and understand our own fundamental existence. But those theologies that typically construe theological language as offering us "models"—especially when a model is understood primarily as prescribing human behavior, rather than describing divine activity and transcendent reality—will miss this key distinction.

However, if one recognizes that the Son's sacrifice is an offering of the whole Godhead, for the benefit of humanity collectively, expressed metaphorically to evoke the new reality of grace rather than in the strictly literal language of mundane reality, then one can understand why certain critiques of vicarious sacrifice simply miss the point. In particular, Enlightenment concern that vicarious sacrifice is both implausible because it smacks of superstition and magic and also immoral and because it punishes the innocent can be seen as too one-dimensional. Such concerns derive from presuppositions that are too literal, individualistic, and ahistorical. That is, such presuppositions are insufficiently nuanced regarding the complexity of human existence, especially in the convolutions of its cultural and temporal conditioning. They also tend to rule out any transcendent explanations at the outset. Still, to make my argument cogently, I must first offer some historical background on

---

31. See Gunton, *The Actuality of Atonement*.

the criticisms raised against traditional satisfaction theory by modern thinkers. To begin, let me acknowledge that I am defining these critiques as "modern" in a very broad sense. They derive from a variety of sources—far more than I can hope to consider here.[32] To outline the basic critique, I begin by examining three highly influential Enlightenment thinkers. They include the iconoclastic French *philosophe* Voltaire (1694–1778), the German playwright and critic Gotthold Ephraim Lessing (1729–1781), and the German philosopher Immanuel Kant (1724–1804).

Voltaire makes clear his views on the matter of vicarious sacrifice in his *Philosophical Dictionary* entry "Expiation." This entry does not directly attack the central dogma of Christ's atoning expiation, or the Christian's sacramental reception of it through baptism. Instead, Voltaire takes an oblique approach by describing, and commenting upon, examples of expiation from other religions, as well as the corruption of the Roman Catholic system of penances and indulgences. Nevertheless, his attitude toward the fundamental logic of vicarious expiation is evident in the following excerpt:

> As soon as religions were established, there were expiations; the ceremonies accompanying them were ridiculous: for what connection is there between the water of the Ganges and a murder? How could a man repair a homicide by bathing himself? We have already remarked this excess of aberration and absurdity, of imagining that he who washes his body washes his soul, and wipes away the stains of evil actions.
>
> The water of the Nile had later the same virtue as the water of the Ganges, and to these purifications other ceremonies were added, which were even less to the point. The Egyptians took two goats, and drew lots for which was to be cast down, charged with the sins of the guilty. The name of "Hazazel," the expiator, was given to this goat. What connection, I ask you, is there between a goat and a man's crime?

---

32. Perhaps the earliest "modern" critique appears in the anti-trinitarian Socinian reaction of the Racovian Catechism of 1605. The critique received an updating at the beginning of the twentieth century from the influential "moral examplar" perspectives of Hastings Rashdall, in his book *The Idea of Atonement in Christian Theology* (1919), which I will discuss more fully in the next chapter. As one scholar observes, "It is Rashdall's conviction of the primacy of individual moral responsibility that leads him to reject on moral grounds any substitutionary view of the atonement" (Brian Hebblethwaite, "Rashdall, Hastings," in *The Dictionary of Historical Theology*, gen. ed. Trevor Hart; Grand Rapids, Mich.: Eerdmans, 2000). Many feminist theologians continue the same basic critique in our own day.

> It is true that God later permitted this ceremony to be sanctified
> among the Jews, our fathers, who took over so many Egyptian rites; but
> doubtless it was the repentance, and not the goat, which purified the
> Jewish souls.[33]

Voltaire seeks to "disenchant" the concept of expiation, apparently
because he views it as a distraction from what should be one's real concern: focusing the guilty party's moral accountability toward the per-
son(s) directly wronged and fostering a change in one's moral
disposition and actions. That is, he emphasizes the individual and his or
her own ethical agency. This is admirable, as far as it goes, but notions
of any sort of corporate accountability, whether trans- or intragenera-
tional, whether systemic or a matter of cultural ethos, simply do not
appear. One may recognize in his words Voltaire's rejection of the traditional doctrine of original sin, which doctrine in a Christian context
is, of course, the main presupposition making the concept of Christ's
expiatory sacrifice "necessary."[34] Voltaire implies that understanding
human nature is a straightforward matter and that moral responsibility
can always be readily delineated and assigned, and thus accountability
and correction easily determined. This is an assumption we will see
again in other Enlightenment thinkers—one that, in light of the history
of the twentieth century, seems woefully inadequate and naïve.

Gotthold Ephraim Lessing's understanding of the notion of Christ's
vicarious satisfaction and of the doctrine of original sin displays none of
the dismissive character of Voltaire's; indeed, he seeks to make a certain
constructive use of them. Yet this use must be understood within the
context of his dictum that "accidental truths of history can never
become the proof of necessary truths of reason." That is, the "truths" of
history, including historically based revelation, are too uncertain and too
particular to serve as the basis for any religion that seeks to be rational
and universal. Lessing's response is to abstract from the particular traditional understandings of original sin and Christ's satisfaction a rationalist, evolutionary, and more universal meaning. Such an evolutionary
model of human religious understanding from the more primitive and
narrative to the more sophisticated and idealistic appears in Lessing's
"The Education of the Human Race." In this work, Lessing portrays

---

33. Ben Ray Redman, ed., *The Portable Voltaire* (New York: Viking, 1963), 117.
34. Voltaire, *Philosophical Letters*, (trans. Ernest Dilworth; The Library of Liberal
Arts; Indianapolis: Bobbs-Merrill Educational Publishing, 1961), 119 and 121.

scriptural revelation as a useful primer for inculcating in humanity a moral sense that would otherwise take too long to arrive at by reason alone. To be more precise, Lessing sees the Old Testament and its fundamental lesson regarding the unity of God as the appropriate primer for humanity up to a certain age of its "youth." At this point, however, "A better instructor must come and tear the exhausted primer from the child's hands,"[35] which instructor Lessing proclaims to be Christ, whose fundamental lesson is the immortality of the soul. The disciples gather up Christ's teaching into the New Testament, and it becomes "the second, better primer for human reason."[36] Even though the disciples add several doctrines of their own to Christ's, Lessing only sees this as an additional opportunity for humankind to exercise its skills of rationality and discernment. As a result, the evolution of human reason does not stop here. Indeed, Lessing asks:

> As we can by this time dispense with the Old Testament for the doctrine of the unity of God, and as we are gradually beginning also to be less dependent on the New Testament for the doctrine of the immortality of the soul: might there not be mirrored in this book also other truths of the same kind, which we are to gaze at in awe as revelations, just until reason learns to deduce them from its other demonstrated truths, and to connect them with them?[37]

For Lessing, dogma becomes another way of speaking about ethics, because his fundamental concern lies with moral and practical prescription rather than any theological or existential description. For Lessing, Jesus was at most an exemplary teacher. As such, he performed no unique and miraculous reconciliation between God and humanity. Indeed, even his teaching was not miraculous, and it was only temporarily "unique." That is, in keeping with Lessing's more general understanding of revelation, he asserts that Jesus' particular teachings only consist of universal truths made known "early." Eventually, all persons will be capable of discerning for themselves through the exercise of their own reason and judgment the lessons that Jesus taught. Lessing's

---

35. Gotthold Ephraim Lessing, *Lessing's Theological Writings* (ed. and trans. Henry Chadwick; A Library of Modern Religious Thought; London: Adam & Charles Black, 1956), 91.
36. Ibid., 93.
37. Ibid., 94.

faith is that the rational progress of humanity that will eventually render the traditional notion of divine satisfaction unnecessary.

Lessing was not the only or even most influential Enlightenment figure seeking to explain traditional theological assertions in terms of their value to ethics. The most influential figure to do so was Immanuel Kant. Because I have already considered some of the ways Kant modified traditional Christian doctrines in the preceding chapter, I need not offer a lengthy summary of his work here. Instead, I need only summarize one connected aspect of his thought that indicates why he had no need for any notion of Christ's vicarious sacrifice.

This aspect of his thought regards his "moral individualism." Kant assumed that humans are rational and capable of willing the good, and that as such we are all capable of discerning what is moral. It therefore becomes the duty of the individual to discern rationally on his or her own the right thing to do, and then do it. In other words, Kant assumed we are morally autonomous, and do not need an external authority to tell us the good. Indeed, only those ideals that are self-generated may truly count as moral. Kant goes so far as to say: "Even the Holy One of the gospel must first be compared with our ideal of moral perfection before we recognize him to be such." To be sure, such autonomy does not grant the individual license to do whatever he or she pleases. Being rational means acting only on the basis of decisions that could become "a universal law." For example, it is irrational, and thus immoral, to make a false promise to gain some benefit, because the practice of promise making only works on the presumption that the promise will be kept. If promise breaking became the norm (a universal law), the conditions for its possibility would disappear, because no one would ever accept a promise in the first place.[38] This illustration points to Kant's assumption that each person, when faced with a moral dilemma, could resolve it by asking, could it become a universal law? How we answer this question determines what is moral. We are left to our own rational devices, but they are sufficient for the ethical task to which we are bound.

Kant's construal of ethics and religion diverges in crucial ways from classic Christian orthodoxy. Indeed, using the categories of historic Christian doctrine, Kant's position comes across as a variation of Pelagianism, in which one's own efforts effect salvation. This position construes the Christian life in essentially moral and individual terms.

---

38. Immanuel Kant, *Groundwork of the Metaphysics of Morals* (trans. H. J. Paton; London: Hutchinson & Co., Ltd., 1956; New York: Harper Torchbooks, 1964), 89–90.

One cannot be given the holy life, one must achieve it—indeed, for God to grant such holiness without our effort would be an act of indulgence contrary to divine justice. Furthermore, the language and practices of piety do not point to a new reality actualized through divine grace, but may only serve as a spur and encouragement for one's continuing progress toward perfection. As one may imagine, the practical impact of Kant's views is substantial. On Kantian presuppositions, much of the traditional significance of the church's theology and liturgy is simply eliminated. Long-standing assumptions about Christ's role in human justification and sanctification are undercut and removed. The intercession of Christ on our behalf would constitute an unjust favoritism, and charismatic gifts of the Spirit would be an unfair advantage over those who did not receive them. Similarly, the sacraments would no longer signify a gracious divine activity on our behalf, but at most would only point to a human commitment and encouragement. In other words, just as it was with Voltaire and Lessing before him, the cumulative impact of Kant's views is a further "disenchantment" of the traditional Christian thought-world. The difference in mind-set from that of the biblical narrative should be starkly evident. The web of assumptions and attitudes that enabled the traditional Christian worldview have been exchanged for an alternate web of assumptions and attitudes, so that over time the standards of plausibility and function were themselves transformed.

It is within the context of these earlier reactions and alterations that contemporary feminist appraisals of vicarious sacrifice may be usefully understood. For many of the key concerns voiced by such current critiques are not new, and they rely on many of the assumptions promoted since the seventeenth century. As with the Enlightenment's critique, feminism employs a "hermeneutic of suspicion" that challenges the ways that Christianity has used theology for self-interested and ideological, specifically patriarchal, ends. Like the Enlightenment, this critique is less concerned with distinguishing between the proper use and improper abuse of a given language, and more concerned to reconstitute the very way one thinks about and uses theological language. That is, like the Enlightenment, feminist theology[39] tends to construe theological language

---

39. As students of theology know, it is actually misleading to speak of feminist *theology* rather than of feminist *theologies*, for the movement is hardly monolithic and exhibits much creative diversity. That point recognized, there still exist some general assumptions shared among the various feminist theologies currently being produced. It is these common characteristics that the following remarks will address.

less as a description of a transcendent reality, and more as a means of prescribing certain human attitudes and behaviors.

Still, in certain particulars, feminist challenges do offer a particular new take on earlier critiques, and bring the internal logic of these critiques to a pointed but consistent fruition. Many of these new themes appear in the following quote from the opening essay in Joanne Carlson Brown and Carole R. Bohn's now standard feminist work, *Christianity, Patriarchy, and Abuse: A Feminist Critique:*

> The central image of Christ on the cross as the savior of the world communicates the message that suffering is redemptive. If the best person who ever lived gave his life for others, then, to be of value we should likewise sacrifice ourselves. Any sense that we have to care for our own needs is in conflict with being a faithful follower of Jesus. Our suffering for others will save the world. The message is complicated further by the theology that says Christ suffered in obedience to the Father's will. Divine child abuse is paraded as salvific and the child who suffers "without even raising his voice" is lauded as the hope of the world. Those whose lives have been deeply shaped by the Christian tradition feel that self-sacrifice and obedience are not only virtues but the definition of a faithful identity. The promise of resurrection persuades us to endure pain, humiliation, and violation of our sacred rights to self-determination, wholeness, and freedom. Throughout the Scriptures is the idea that Jesus dies for our sins. Did he? Is there not another way for sins to be forgiven? Why an idea of original sin? Christianity has functioned to perpetuate the Fall, for without it there would be no need for a savior. Mary Daly argues that imitation of this savior is exactly what is desired: "The qualities that Christianity idealizes, especially for women, are also those of a victim: sacrificial love, passive acceptance of suffering, humility, meekness, etc. Since these are the qualities idealized in Jesus 'who died for our sins,' his functioning as a model reinforces the scapegoat syndrome for women."[40]

On its own terms and presuppositions, this is a devastating critique. How can a faith ostensibly committed to love and mercy, compassion and justice become instead the cause of suffering, pain, and denigration?

---

40. Joanne Carlson Brown and Carole R. Bohn, eds., *Christianity, Patriarchy, and Abuse: A Feminist Critique* (New York: Pilgrim Press, 1989), 2–3. The opening essay bears the title "For God so Loved the World?" and is written by Joanne Carlson Brown and Rebecca Parker.

Honorable Christians of whatever tradition or denomination should be outraged that such abuse could be justified in the name of the Prince of Peace. More than that, they should draw on the true heart of the Christian tradition to show how such abuses represent a perversion of the gospel. But of course, the critique does not merely condemn the misuse of an otherwise laudable tradition. Instead, it argues that that tradition at its very heart is inherently abusive, that its central images and theological assumptions cannot help but produce these unconscionable results.

Yet is this bitter conclusion necessarily warranted? Must one inevitably accept its terms and presuppositions? As I hoped to suggest in my analysis of three representative Enlightenment thinkers, the terms and presuppositions of modernity do not necessarily coincide with those of the older Christian tradition. Insofar as "modernity" represents a generally coherent ideology and way of understanding the world, it has a fundamentally different view about the nature of theological language and what it "does." Let me illustrate this point by examining several of the claims made in the above citation. Consider first these two, related assertions: "The central image of Christ on the cross as the savior of the world communicates the message that suffering is redemptive" and "Our suffering for others will save the world." The first statement implies that the church has stressed suffering itself, rather than *Christ's* suffering, as the locus of redemption. The second statement reinforces this misconstrual by implying that we, too, can be saviors of the world, which flies in the face of the ancient Christian axiom that only God can save. Moreover, these two statements also appear to assume that theological descriptions and images do not refer to unique historical events, but rather serve only as universal models that the faithful are to emulate. The particulars of this assumption derive from a modern, rationalist mind-set, not the Christian tradition.

Second, consider the way the above citation frames the crucifixion as a form of divine child abuse, in the way the Father wills the Son's suffering and requires that he do so "without even raising his voice." Once again, if the function of theological language and imagery were only to provide us with examples to emulate, so that the crucifixion were used to justify the abuse of children or women, then this critique would have scathing merit. But what if the crucifixion is not something a tyrannical Father imposes upon a submissive Son, but is instead an undertaking of the one triune God to subvert and destroy the power and corruption of human sin? Would it be preferable to confront that human power and corruption with an even greater divine power? Or is the way of nonviolent resistance more in keeping with the end God intends? What if the crucifixion of the Son, in his divine-human uniqueness, does not function as a "model" to reinforce the "scapegoat syndrome," but instead functions as the one scapegoat event that could subvert and do away with the syndrome forever?

Third, consider the following challenges: "Throughout the Scriptures is the idea that Jesus dies for our sins. Did he? Is there not another way for sins to be forgiven? Why an idea of original sin? Christianity has functioned to perpetuate the Fall, for without it there would be no need for a savior." The tenor of these comments perpetuates a cynicism also evident in Enlightenment critiques of "the priests," namely, the assumption that some doctrines were promulgated for no other reason than to create a need that the church could then address. To be sure, as students of history well know, religious beliefs may be abused quite readily as tools of psychological and political manipulation, but the same may be said of all deeply held and socially pervasive ideas, including the foundational beliefs of the Enlightenment. For instance, did not an ideological emphasis on individual autonomy and responsibility serve as one justification for the laissez-faire policies shaped by the "social Darwinism" of the nineteenth century? The point is, if any such set of fundamental beliefs may be abused, then, assuming adequate safeguards and self-correcting mechanisms, the real issue becomes, "Which addresses most accurately our human predicament?" Consider the example just cited: Does not the now common recognition of "systemic" evil suggest the limitations of a merely individualistic construal of morality and indicate the necessity of something like a doctrine of original, collective sin? And given the carnage and devastation of the twentieth century, is it even plausible to promote a sanguine understanding of human nature, as the Enlightenment generally did? Apart from these general questions stand more specifically Christian ones. One could certainly eliminate the doctrine of original sin, and hence the need for a savior, but then one would be following in the footsteps of Enlightenment philosophers. Would the result still be identifiably Christian? Would it still be true to the gospel? Similarly, one could certainly imagine other ways that sin could be forgiven, but one would still have to deal with the unavoidable fact of Jesus' crucifixion and Scripture's undeniable claim that his death was "for our sins."

Insofar as feminist theology has brought its particular insights to the modern recognition of the ways Christian doctrine may be manipulated

as a tool of abuse, it has done the church and Christian faith a true service. But does this mean that the feminist critique is irresistibly compelling,
that Christian theology must adopt in full its various presuppositions
and conclusions? Stated generally, feminist theological critiques appear
compelling if any or all of the following is assumed: (1) a non-trinitarian
understanding of the relation between the Father and the Son, (2) a
modernist individualism positing the radical autonomy of humans, (3) a
"Feuerbachian" understanding of the character of theological language as
a projection of human values, or (4) that theological language should be
judged on the basis of its "positive" psychological impact. Conversely, if
these assumptions are not held, that critique loses its force.

If one understands the will and work of the Father as distinct from
and in some sense imposed upon the Son, or the merely human Jesus,
then concern for the fundamental injustice of the procedure is clearly
warranted. Such a construal may stem from either a tritheistic or
Ebionitic understanding of the relation between these two persons, but
whatever the case, the work of salvation cannot help but appear the
result of an irresistible and therefore unjust imposition of the Father's
power. Yet part of the point of the doctrine of the Trinity has been to
emphasize the divine equality of being between Father and Son, as well
as their complete harmony of will and purpose. In such an understanding, coercion becomes impossible, because the conditions needed to
enable it simply do not exist.

If one assumes some variation of modern individualism, which posits
the radical autonomy and isolation, moral and otherwise, of humans,
and therefore also the separation between any human being and the
humanity of Jesus, then to speak of a vicarious sacrifice is meaningless.
To continue to insist on its centrality would be at best irrational, at
worst unconscionable. No person may stand as a representative of
another; each stands or falls on his or her own. Yet standing in the
docket, are we ever truly "on our own"? Part of the point of orthodox
Christology has been to emphasize the solidarity of Jesus—and hence
God—with all humanity, and, as a corollary, the many bonds of relation
in our collective existence. Orthodox Christology implicitly recognizes
our social, historical existence, and serves as the redeeming counterpoint to our solidarity with the representative figures of Adam and Eve.
In such an understanding, Christ's vicarious sacrifice means that the
collective momentum of historical and social evil is not allowed the last
word in judging the individual's final merit or demerit amid the accidents of time and place.

If one assumes that the character of theological description is at root the projection of (merely) human ideals and norms, then again, a critique and change may be warranted.[41] That is, if the fundamental claims and stories of the Christian faith are not divinely given and eternally true, but are instead a human product, then their validity is inevitably relativized and implicitly open to change or rejection, according to our best human insights. Each time and place may feel fully justified in determining its own ideals and norms. This attitude is epitomized in the following statement: "Because of the ultimate character of the Divine—because for most people 'God' connotes what is the greatest and best, what one should aspire toward—the influence wielded by models of God is enormous. Such influence demands of theologians and practitioners of religion that we take seriously the implications of our God-talk and that we reconfigure our metaphors and concepts when necessary."[42] But orthodox Christian tradition, even with its sophisticated recognition of the limitations of human language, has never viewed theological claims as incapable of echoing divine revelation or as expressing merely human ideals. In particular, seeing saving significance in Christ's death on the cross has never been understood as a human projection, but as reflecting a transcendent, divinely self-disclosed, and uniquely authoritative act and reality. Christ's redemptive death on the cross is not a metaphor that may be reconfigured to serve a model of God that reflects any human conception of what is greatest and best. It is an ineluctable and necessary given in God's mysteriously gracious dealings with humanity, and therefore an ineluctable and necessary given in Christian reflection.

Finally, if one judges theological language primarily in light of its psychological impact, rather than for its ability to describe and explain some object, then it would be only appropriate to modify that language according to the effect desired. That is, if the purpose of theological language is to elicit certain mental or emotional responses or promote certain behaviors, then the criteria for judging such language adequate

---

41. The nineteenth-century figure Ludwig Feuerbach is commonly cited as initiating such a "projectionist" and reductionistic understanding of theological claims (see his key work, *The Essence of Christianity*, which was published in 1841, and translated with considerable impact into English in 1854 by the novelist George Eliot). But he was hardly alone. The groundwork for this approach was laid by his more famous teacher, G. W. F. Hegel, and its basic assumptions were developed in different ways by later figures such as Marx and Nietzsche.

42. Ray, *Deceiving the Devil*, 52.

become purely pragmatic. Whatever images or metaphors or models foster the desired result will do—while images or metaphors or models that seem contrary to that result may be rejected. As may be recognized, this psychological understanding of theological language bears a resemblance to the preceding "projectionist" understanding, its key difference being that its implementation is most effective when done implicitly, and not openly. That is, the third understanding calls on people to embrace self-consciously certain ideals as their own highest norms and creation. This fourth understanding seeks to effect certain results by working at a mostly subconscious level. To be sure, the Christian tradition knows full well the evocative and conditioning power of its language, especially as it is reinforced in ritual and the liturgy, in sacred music and hymnody, in catechetical repetition and the ever recurring Christian year. The key issue in all this is: To what end? This psychological understanding of theological language typically brings with it an implicit metaphysic, one not necessarily grounded in the Christian tradition. For example, it may be minimally asserted that "God is on the side of life and its fulfillment,"[43] and that theological language must be shaped or changed to serve this general claim. But how are such concepts as "life" and "its fulfillment" defined, and on what basis? Typically, psychologized understandings of theological language want to use it to cultivate behavior promoting specified ethical norms and/or to foster a sense of personal well-being, flourishing, and self-satisfaction. Just as typically, these social norms and this psychic state are defined in terms derived from a secular context, and not the basic claims or inner logic of the Christian story. That is, in this approach, theological language is understood as a means to serve an end determined apart from the fundamental claims of the faith. But this means that language is subservient to a lordship other than Christ's. Christianity is indeed concerned with life and human flourishing, but only as such concepts are themselves derived from the biblical narrative. In this view, the psychological utility or impact of a doctrine should not be judged according to some secular norm or subjective feeling, but according to the

---

43. See, for example, Sallie McFague's defense of her book, *Models of God: Theology for an Ecological, Nuclear Age*, in *Readings in Modern Theology* (ed. Robin Gill; Nashville: Abingdon Press, 1995). The full set of critiques and reviews are found on pp. 67–97, while the phrase cited comes from p. 91. Similarly, Darby Kathleen Ray, considered extensively in chapter 1, states that a "sophisticated, pragmatic, prophetic 'biophilia,' or love of life, is at the heart of feminist theology." Ray, *Deceiving the Devil*, 103.

truth of the gospel and how well it helps foster mature personhood in Christ and allows growth in the fruits of the Spirit.

Such are some of the key objections made by current feminist theologians to the notion of Christ's saving death on the cross. In addition to these philosophical and more academically oriented critiques, other writers are content to make the initially persuasive observation that the whole notion of sacrificial atonement is simply implausible to the modern mind. We have already encountered one such theologian in Michael Winter, whom I considered in chapter 1. Because I have already analyzed his position rather thoroughly in that location, I will only add a brief observation here. His claim of sacrifice's implausibility to the modern mind may be true, if he means those people consciously adopting the assumptions and commitments of modernity as an intellectual movement. This does not acknowledge, however, that many persons in our contemporary world have made no such conscious and exclusive ideological commitment, nor does it speak to the fact that those same people could learn to find it plausible. Indeed, one could argue that in our highly scientific and technologically sophisticated but spiritually pedestrian age, the religious wisdom of the past might have something enriching to teach us.

In a similar vein, Paul Fiddes, in *Past Event and Present Salvation,* also claims that certain metaphors are "dead" (such as "sacrifice") or that the scriptural assumptions giving them plausibility are no longer modern assumptions (such as "the life is in the blood")—and that they are beyond rejuvenation. He therefore argues that we require new metaphors derived from our own sensibilities and plausibility structures. Again, I am not willing to concede that such metaphors are irretrievably dead, nor do I believe that the presuppositions underlying them are necessarily implausible to the modern mind-set. Indeed, I would say that our modern assumptions and attitudes are often the very source of our dilemmas, so that learning a new—which in this case will actually be an old—way of conceiving matters may in fact be enlightening and liberating. Consider the biblical connection of life with blood. Is this connection in fact so alien to us? Some theologians believe not. For example, as Frances Young points out in her study, *Sacrifice and the Death of Christ,* the various associations traditionally made between blood, life, and sacrifice may also be found in works of modern literature. To illustrate, she offers a brief exposition of two novels, John Steinbeck's *To a God Unknown* and William Golding's *Lord of the Flies,* to back up her claim.[44]

---

44. Frances M. Young, *Sacrifice and the Death of Christ* (London: SPCK, 1975), 13–16.

Perhaps more persuasively, does not modern mass culture still use the term in ways that evoke far more than just its physiological definition? Are there not many contemporary uses of, and associations with, the word "blood" that suggest we still understand and employ it metaphorically in many "traditional" ways? Consider the following phrases, and the way they are typically used as figures of speech: "blood is thicker than water," "blood brothers," "blood feud," "blood money," "bloody-minded," "blood oath," "blood sucking," "life's blood" or "lifeblood," "bloodcurdling," "blood red," "blood lust," "blueblood," "red-blooded American," "pureblood," "hot-blooded," "cold-blooded murder," "bloodthirsty," "bleeding heart," "in the blood," "makes one's blood boil," and "bleed" (when used as a figurative term for exploit, or suffer, or grieve). Taken together, these terms and phrases all suggest that metaphorical uses of the word "blood" are far from meaningless and obsolete. On the contrary, they may well reflect something utterly primal and perduring in human experience. Note the way these terms all raise the stakes, as it were, in describing a condition, a relation, or a characteristic of a person or situation. When "blood" is invoked, the matter is not trivial, it is serious, indeed, often a matter of life and death. Perhaps I only need recall the recent advertising slogan used by the American Red Cross in its search for donors: "Give the gift of life—give blood." This admonition speaks not just at a physiological level, but at emotional, moral, and spiritual levels as well—which is to say, at a level and with a power that is not confined to the biblical era, but that speaks as clearly to what we, too, know. The starkest recent illustration of this has to be the overwhelming number of Americans who sought to donate blood in the aftermath of the September 11th attacks on the World Trade Center and the Pentagon. I believe it is naïve to suppose that these persons were motivated merely by an impulse to render "physical" first aid. For even when it soon became devastatingly clear that there were not going to be masses of the wounded, but only the dead or the relatively uninjured (at least in a physical sense), people still kept donating blood. It seems obvious that they continued to do so out of a deep-seated and even unconscious desire to give (quite literally) of themselves, to offer "life," and thereby to offer solace and hope in the face of such mind-numbing evil, destruction, and death.

But if this is the case, if the connotations of blood still have such evocative power and meaning that we continue employing them in common speech (in modern advertising slogans, social and political rhetoric, and popular as well as high culture) and indeed continue acting as if they were true, then surely we need not abandon the scriptural connections of blood with life and sacrificial atonement. Rather, it makes more sense in a theological work on the atonement to enrich our thought-world and life by relearning the many nuances and connections of the biblical heritage regarding sacrifice than to discard them on the basis of rather limiting modern assumptions and outlooks. In this light, it can indeed be deeply meaningful to say that in accord with the loving and righteous will of God the Father, God the Son freely takes on flesh by means of God the Spirit to become Christ the priest and sacrifice, to atone for human sin and restore creation to right relation with God and its own integrity. In this work, one may recognize Christ's priestly work of atonement as the work appropriate to the Son. For it is the Son "who, though he was in the form of God, did not regard equality with God as something to be exploited, but emptied himself, taking the form of a slave, being born in human likeness. And being found in human form, he humbled himself and became obedient to the point of death—even death on a cross" (Phil 2:6–8). God the Son takes to himself this role, he becomes Christ the Priest, in order to reconcile a sinful humanity to God's holiness. He takes on human flesh to serve as humanity's representative and priest, because it is humanity that stands in need of making sacrifice to God.

Systematic Location and Theological Implications

Just as the affirmation of Christ as king means that God the Father reclaims our context from bondage to alien and evil powers, so, too, the affirmation of Christ as priest means that God the Son also reclaims us from our own sinfulness and guilt. Speaking from a soteriological viewpoint, therefore, it is appropriate to consider this aspect of Christ's work second because only here can its placement in the broader context of God's purposes for the whole of creation be clearly affirmed. In this act, the Son accomplishes his own "proper" work as the triune person eternally destined to become incarnate. In that sense, it is mistaken to think of Jesus Christ doing the work of the Son in the same manner as his work on behalf of the Father and the Spirit. Christ does not act on "behalf of" the Son or "in relation to" the Son, because he *is* the Son, come in the flesh. As the incarnate one, he alone is able to enact and subsume past sacrificial practices in a new and transformative way. To be sure, this does not mean he is working alone, accomplishing this task apart from the Father and the Spirit. It is still one undivided act of the triune God, based on the one unified divine will, and made available through the one unified divine action. In this regard, I reject any construal that suggests the Son's will and work somehow counters and finally alters the Father's will and intentions. Christ's sacrifice does not "change the Father's mind," as if the latter would vent his wrath on humanity were it not for the former's intervention. Rather, Christ serves as the Father's instrument, enacting in humanity through the Holy Spirit's power the common mind, will, and purpose of the one God.

Consideration of this priestly office and work belongs in this second location for another reason as well. Christ's vicarious sacrifice has too often been construed in strictly individualistic terms, as if God were concerned only with saving certain persons here and there while writing off the rest of humanity and even creation. Understanding the Son's vicarious sacrifice in the context of the Father's victory in Christ over the principalities and powers gives a more appropriately balanced construal of God's larger concerns. It also properly sets the stage for understanding the Spirit's work in Christ, to which I will turn in the following chapter.

In light of this systematic contextualization of Christ's priestly work, it is appropriate to make explicit an implication of that work that may not yet be obvious. Specifically, it is important to stress the "once and for all" character of Christ's sacrifice. Stated simply, because our reconciliation to God has been effected by Christ's passion and death, it does not demand our own. Faithfully following the risen Lord may result in persecution or even martyrdom, as evidenced by the early church and contemporary Christians in hostile environments today, but does not require it. Thus, it is simply wrong to claim that suffering *as such* is a Christian virtue. Such a mistake arises from a misunderstanding that Christ's accomplishment demands of us an answering accomplishment, which was the mistake made by the ancient Pelagian heresy. And the mistake is compounded through a misconstrual of the character of Christian language and claims, which happens with the intrusion of Idealistic philosophy or its general assumptions into the reading of the biblical narrative. Indeed, the mistake of reading the scriptural narrative through the lens of idealism echoes the error of Pelagianism, insofar as it understands the Bible (and especially Christ) as offering us an archetype to imitate, a "model" to follow, or a general principle to unpack. It reads the biblical stories as if they were simply representing in mythological form the timeless truths that are the ideals of Christian thought and action. In so doing, it ignores at least two of the crucial aspects of narrative: its "historicity" (i.e., the fact that things happen that change conditions and the flow of events) and its diverse characters (i.e., that they are different to begin with and then act and react in different ways). If the story of Christ's sacrifice is read in a mythological or idealistic fashion, as a "model" we are to imitate, then the story cannot help become an illustrative way of saying suffering and sacrifice are basic Christian virtues. Christ and his deeds become a general principle, abstracted from his particular context and his specific act. But if the story of Christ's sacrifice is read in a truly narrative fashion, then it may be understood as an event that actually changes things. It requires some kind of appropriate response, but we should not think it needs to be repeated. If we see ourselves in such a narrative, we should not be too quick to identify ourselves with the character of Christ, seeking to imitate him in some univocal fashion. Rather, we should identify ourselves with the disciples, recognizing how the conditions and obligations of their lives have been changed because of what Christ has accomplished for them, and because of the Spirit's continuing power and guidance.

I can illustrate such sensitivity to the biblical narrative by referring to a source first cited in chapter 2. Consider Heinrich Heppe's summary of the intercessory aspect of Christ's work in his priestly office, as understood by the Reformed tradition:

> After his exaltation Christ exercises the high-priestly office. In continuation of the intercession offered to the Father in his immolation of himself, he appears before the Father as he who has consummated the sacrifice for the guilt of the world; and in virtue of the satisfaction accepted by the Father he mediates and effects the appropriation of his merit by the elect, as a gift of grace to be lavished by the Father, he protects and advances the faithful in the enjoyment of the salvation of grace, and he offers their prayers to the Father: this is why the faithful may call upon the Father only in the name of Christ.[45]

This summary does not dwell on Christ's death on the cross, as if that were the sole significant aspect of his priestly role. And it certainly does not present Christ as a fundamentally timeless or passive model effective only as Christians act upon his example. Quite the contrary, Heppe

---

45. Heinrich Heppe, *Reformed Dogmatics: Set Out and Illustrated from Its Sources,* (rev. and ed. Ernst Bizer; trans. G. T. Thomson; London: George Allen & Unwin, Ltd., 1950), 479–80.

makes clear that as the heavenly high priest, it is Christ's continued activity, now as mediator and intercessor, that is most central. Christians are summoned to respond in accord with this fundamentally reordered circumstance, in living relation with the Father through the auspices of the Son and the enabling of the Spirit. It is not wrong, but indeed necessary to have a clear theological understanding of Christ's sacrificial death on the cross—but not to the exclusion of his other priestly functions. Practically speaking, this may well mean that, in sermons and catechesis, in the liturgy and in hymns, less attention be focused on Christ's priestly sacrifice and more on his role as priestly intercessor.

Pastoral Applications

What are some of the other practical implications of this understanding of Christ's work? The priestly/sacrificial understanding of the atonement assumes primarily that humans are separated from God not because of bondage to "powers and principalities" opposed to God, but because of their own failings and transgressions. They stand tainted in the presence of God's holiness. Yet the Son's table fellowship with sinners, his healing of the ritually impure, and above all his sacrificial death all reveal and effect the Father's initiative in reconciling alienated, sinful humanity in a new covenant made available through the power of the Spirit. Humanity is the victim of its own willful mistakes and sin, its failings in holiness, and Christ—acting as the Father's priest—absolves it of these shortcomings and transgressions. It is not a reconciliation humans individually or together could accomplish themselves. Especially given the tangled lines of responsibility and guilt that characterize our collective historical and social existence, the task is impossible for us. But Christ our priestly sacrifice, like the representative scapegoat on Israel's Day of Atonement, takes our sins upon himself and carries them away. Additionally, like the sacrifice of first fruits, he initiates us into a new season, offering us protection and interceding for us as high priest in the power of the Spirit, as we enter into restored communion with the Father.

One of the first practical implications of Christ's priestly sacrifice is that his death on the cross gives us an alternate approach to thinking about, and enacting, "justice." Especially in the collective sphere, but also in individual relations, far too often justice is conceived as an elaborate exercise in bookkeeping, with "true" justice only achieved when accounts are balanced to the very last penny. And yet real life and real relations are never reducible to such precise figures. In this mind-set, could justice ever truly be satisfied? In the history of nations, one can easily think of examples for which the answer is no. Following the First World War, the allied forces of the Triple Entente (Great Britain, France, and Russia) felt fully justified in imposing the harsh conditions of the Treaty of Versailles, which included staggering reparations, upon the defeated powers of Germany and the Austro-Hungarian Empire. Surely Germany's guilt was obvious, its punishment and required reparations fully justified. Yet anyone familiar with the origins of that conflict, and possessing any degree of objectivity, knows that there was more than enough blame to pass around among all the belligerents. And anyone at all familiar with the decades following the end of that first world conflict also knows that the hardships created in Germany by the Treaty of Versailles fostered the conditions that gave rise to Adolf Hitler, National Socialism, and the even greater carnage of the Second World War. At least some lessons were learned, as demonstrated by the very different behavior of the victors toward the vanquished following this second global conflict.

In an analogous manner, Christ's atoning death on the cross presents us with another way to conceive and respond to sin and injustice than a simplistic "settling of accounts." It enables us to take with utmost seriousness the true evil of evil, the true injustice of injustice; after all, these powers crucified God. But it also enables us to short-circuit the endless cycle of recrimination, retribution, and revenge, due to God's utter transformation of the meaning and reality of that death. Christ's atoning sacrifice offers us a way of acknowledging our own complicity in evil and accepting the divine forgiveness bestowed, and in the process reveals to us the necessity of doing the same toward those whom we would condemn. This understanding of Christ's work offers a fresh start to those burdened by sin and a guilty conscience. The disorder in the objective order has been overcome; the tainting of the relationship has been healed and forgiven. The debt owed to God has been paid. "You shall know the truth, and the truth shall set you free" (John 8:32). Knowing this truth and embracing this freedom can, with the help of the Spirit, enable persons, both individually and collectively, to overcome the repercussions of their misguided attitudes and deeds and strengthen them to reorient their lives to the *telos* that God intends. Certainly expiation and forgiveness enable the restoration of individual relationships. All of us can recount such instances from our own lives or the lives of those we know: friendships reconciled, parent-child relations healed, marital unions restored. But the power of expiation and forgiveness can occur on a larger scale as well, although such occurrences are usually less neat and take more time and multiple individual acts. Consider three examples that are not narrowly ecclesiological: first, the tone set by Abraham Lincoln's phrase "with malice toward none, with charity toward all" in healing the divisions caused by the American Civil War.[46] Second, consider the willingness of most Germans to face the guilt incurred by the nation during the Nazi years (especially when compared to the silence or denial apparently still common in Japan over its atrocities in World War II). And third, recall the efforts by Archbishop Desmond Tutu and the Truth and Reconciliation Commission to overcome the injustices of the apartheid era in South Africa. None of these are perfect examples of reconciliation, but how much worse would these situations have been without openness to such healing?

To be sure, in these historical examples, the degree to which the actors involved were self-consciously influenced by a specifically Christian motivation is open to debate. Nevertheless, these examples may be read through the lens of the biblical narrative and understood in light of a christologically oriented providence. In such an understanding—historical, and not timeless or mythological—Christ's death on the cross "breaks" history: it is a new event, which enables persons to leave behind the past and begin a new future. It ends the tyranny of the endlessly recurring cycles that seem so often to dominate life—or at least our ways of conceiving life—and offers a real alternative and a fresh start. That is, Christ's death on the cross pays the debt that had accrued to humanity. But just as significantly, it presents us with a radically different paradigm and possibility. With accounts once more balanced, Jesus summons us to cease thinking in terms of settling scores, of retribution and revenge, even of "justice" conceived in distributional terms and to begin thinking in terms of forgiveness, of generosity of spirit, of love even for enemies. The cross of Christ is as scandalous today as it was two thousand years ago. True, through its appropriation by Christianity and even its trivialization by modern consumer culture, it

---

46. The full quote is: "With malice toward none, with charity for all, with firmness in the right, as God gives us to see the right, let us strive on to finish the work we are in, to bind up the nation's wounds, to care for him who shall have borne the battle, and for his widow and his orphan, to do all which may achieve and cherish a just and lasting peace among ourselves, and with all nations." It comes from his second inaugural address delivered on March 4, 1865, just weeks before the end of the war and his assassination.

has lost its association with a curse and its offense as a form of execution. But as a call to forsake our right to fairness, as a summons to surrender what is rightfully ours, as an admonition to turn the other cheek, it elicits as much abhorrence, scorn, anger, and rejection as it ever did—perhaps even more, in a culture where self-assertion is typically viewed as a virtue and humility as almost a pathology. But Christ's sacrifice on the cross—especially as it is captured in Jesus' dying words, "Father, forgive them . . ."—offers us a different way.

In this way, the act of divine forgiveness accomplished in Christ's sacrificial death gives us, both collectively and individually, true freedom. This is another of its practical implications. Paradoxically, in "breaking" history, divine forgiveness grants us a true history, rather than just a mechanistic sequence of cause and effect. Forgiveness means we have an authentic and vital present, a present that is truly open to the future, and not merely the accumulation and consequence of the past's events. As such, it becomes the enabling condition of our human freedom. Forgiveness means that we can begin again, change direction, and plot a course toward a new goal, rather than being forever and merely the product of our own past failings and sin. This does not mean that the past is simply discarded and forgotten, as if it had no influence or power over the present and future. Such an ahistorical attitude is a common mistake made by popular American culture, which often insists that one can reinvent oneself at will, through a new diet or exercise or job or place of residence or the purchase of the right new car or makeup or clothing. People who make such assumptions underestimate the power of the past, and are by that very fact more susceptible to its influence and less free to plot their own course. But forgiveness, as an act of transcendent divine grace accomplished in Christ's sacrifice, breaks in from the outside and interrupts the patterns and habits of the past. It does not forget the past—indeed, it takes it with the utmost seriousness. And precisely in its recognition of the past and its power, the greater power of divine forgiveness is able to disrupt the chain of inevitability that would otherwise continue between past events and the future.

To be sure, from a Christian perspective the genuinely free and open present, which this forgiveness enables, is not an end unto itself. It is a present open to a future oriented toward and enabled by the beckoning of the Holy Spirit. However, it may be understood within the framework of Christ the sacrifice of first fruits. Such an understanding of his sacrifice certainly differs from understandings of it as a penal substitution, although it is complementary to the latter. Christ as first fruits represents our being claimed by, and our own fundamental reorientation to, God. In this sense, Christ's sacrifice stands not as a solution to the consequences of our pride and sin, but as a sign of a new and glorious harvest. In being set free from our guilt, we are also set free for new and abundant growth. Christ the Priest accomplishes this sacrifice as a means of opening up a relationship to all who would seek their own truest fulfillment in their God-given future.

Having established this fresh start, Christ's once-for-all sacrifice also serves to redefine "sacrifice" for Christian living. Because our reconciliation to God has been effected by Christ's death, it does not require our own. True, being faithful to Christ may, in certain contexts, bring about physical, sacrificial suffering, even martyrdom. But that does not make suffering or death a prerequisite for true Christian faithfulness. The sacrifice Christians should now make becomes something quite different. As Paul's phrase from Rom 12:1 has it, Christians are called to offer "living sacrifices." Of course, in light of the original definition of sacrifice, a "living sacrifice" is a contradiction in terms. But Christ's act redefines the terms. Thus, the faithful are to offer the sacrifice of "spiritual worship" and the transformation of minds (Rom 12:1–2), "a sacrifice of praise to God" (Heb 13:15), the sacrifice of doing good and sharing with others (Heb 13:16; cf. Phil 4:18), and the sacrifice of banishing vices that hurt the community in order to better incorporate all as a "spiritual house" and a "holy priesthood" (1 Pet 2:1–5). On the basis of Christ's death on the cross, Christians have crucified their sin and "died" to their old selves, while also sharing in Christ's status as a sacrifice of first fruits in a new creation. Moreover, this new creation is not something to be undertaken alone or without aid, for Christ offers continual intercession as heavenly high priest. In this sense, Christ's atoning work as priest is not a matter restricted simply to the past. Rather, it is ongoing and ever present, as his benefits are made effective each moment in the power of the Holy Spirit.

Finally, all the practical implications of Christ's priestly sacrifice described in the preceding pages are reflected in the church's liturgy. The connections are many and interwoven, and that liturgy would be enriched were they more consciously highlighted and clearly known. To offer an initial example, Christ's expiating sacrifice undergirds baptism "for the forgiveness of sins," it enables all prayers of confession and ministerial words assuring God's forgiving grace, it makes possible "the passing of the peace," and its unique, "once and for all," history-changing character is remembered and reaffirmed each time the Lord's Supper is celebrated. Similarly, Christ's death understood as a sacrifice of "first fruits" also informs the sacrament of baptism, insofar as that rite signifies a dying to the old and a rising into a God-given life of new possibilities and relations. As such, it also shapes the essential character and identity of the church itself, as that body of believers joined together in Christ's new way of being. It certainly informs the Lord's Supper, insofar as this sacrament offers the people of God both a present and anticipatory meal of eschatological communion. And third, Christ's continuing role as priestly mediator and intercessor undergirds and enables every Christian prayer. Clearly, he offered one kind of mediation in teaching his disciples of all generations to pray, "Our Father, who art in heaven. . . ." But more immediately, his direct and powerful intercession is invoked with every prayer offered "in Jesus' name." Indeed, one should recognize that that priestly mediation and intercession is what makes Christian worship possible in the first place. Christ is our heavenly high priest, the head of the church, enabling and sustaining all who minister and worship in his name. More intimately, his priestly role means that each and every one who calls upon him, no matter how dire his or her circumstance, will never be abandoned and left alone. Such pastoral applications of this model of the atonement could be multiplied indefinitely. The multifaceted character of Christ's priestly work can be summarized in the words of this evocative benediction: "He goes before us to guide us, above us to bless us, beside us to guard us, beneath us to uphold us, and behind us to forgive us."

6

Christ the Prophet
The Spirit's Living, Life-Giving Word

Lastly, we come to Christ the Prophet, the revealer and enactor of God's truth and will, indeed, the living and life-giving Word of the triune God himself (John 1:1). He is indeed the Mediator, the Messiah of God, yet at the same time "the external works of the Trinity are undivided." Having argued in the preceding chapters that his royal work be understood as done on behalf of the Father and his priestly work be understood as his own appropriate work as the incarnate Son, I now consider how his prophetic work may be understood as done on behalf of the Spirit. To be sure, the manner in which the Son works on behalf of the Spirit in his prophetic office does not simply recapitulate the way he works on behalf of the Father in his royal role. The relation of the Son to the Father is not formally equivalent to his relation with the Spirit. In one sense, the Son and Spirit stand on a more equal footing in relation to one another than either does in relation to the Father, in that both have their origin in, and direction from, the Father. In the famous image of the second-century theologian Irenaeus, the Son and Spirit are "the two hands of the Father." In another sense, as the scriptural narrative suggests, the Spirit is subordinate to the Son, insofar as it "follows" the Son and serves as his instrument in the ongoing life of the church.

Yet in a third sense, focusing on a different but complementary thread of the scriptural narrative, one may also recognize that the Son serves as an instrument of the Spirit. Consider, for example, that the

Holy Spirit acts as the agent of Jesus' conception (Matt 1:18 and Luke 1:35), that the Spirit descends upon him in his baptism (Matt 3:16; Mark 1:10; Luke 3:22; and John 1:32), and subsequently "drives" him into the desert for a time of testing (Matt 4:1; Mark 1:12; and Luke 4:1). Jesus apparently ascribes higher status to the Spirit than to himself in declaring blasphemy against the Holy Spirit, and not the Son of man, the unforgivable sin (Matt 12:31–32 and Luke 12:10; cf. Mark 3:28–9). Finally, recall what Jesus yields up at the moment of his death: the couplet that is usually translated "his spirit" could equally well be translated "the Spirit" *(tò pneuma)* (Matt 27:50 and John 19:30; cf. Luke 23:46).[1] At least in Western Christendom, theologians, historically, have tended to underplay this aspect of the Spirit's relation to the Son. But I will speak to it directly in the following pages, in order to present what I believe is a more balanced, indeed, more scriptural and trinitarian understanding of Christ's atoning work.

The New Testament Witness

The New Testament offers many episodes that portray Jesus fulfilling the role of prophet. In both word and deed, he fits the pattern established by the prophets of the Old Testament. Yet the New Testament also clearly portrays Jesus as more than a prophet: not just a proxy of God, he speaks and acts with his own authority and power. He proclaims the kingdom of God; more than that, he is himself the revelation of God's truth and purposes. Indeed, he not only enlightens, but empowers persons to recognize and claim God's truth as their own true meaning and end, and as such in him prophecy itself is fulfilled. He receives the Spirit and serves as the means and catalyst by which it is communicated to others.

> "The Spirit of the Lord is upon me,
>   because he has anointed me
> to bring good news to the poor.
> He has sent me to proclaim release to the captives
>   and recovery of sight to the blind,
> to let the oppressed go free,
> to proclaim the year of the Lord's favor."

---

1. An indication of this possible translation survives in the old words of the King James (Authorized) version of the Bible, which says that at the moment of his death, Jesus "gave up the ghost" (John 19:30).

And he rolled up the scroll, gave it back to the attendant, and sat down. The eyes of all in the synagogue were fixed on him. Then he began to say to them, "Today this Scripture has been fulfilled in your hearing." (Luke 4:18–21)

The New Testament sketches the multifaceted character of Jesus' prophetic office with the numerous descriptions, titles, and metaphors it employs to broaden and magnify this aspect of his atoning work. He is a rabbi, or teacher (Mark 9:5, 11:21; John 1:38, 49; 3:2; 4:31; 6:25; 8:4; 9:2; 11:8), and clearly an exceptional one: he astonishes his hearers because he teaches with authority (Matt 7:28–29; 13:54; Mark 1:21–22, 27; 11:27–33; Luke 4:32; John 7:14–15), unlike the scribes. His teaching has this authority because it is not (merely) his own, but the truth of God (John 7:16–18), given in the power of the Spirit (Luke 4:14–15). Like the prophets before him, Jesus holds people accountable to God's will, as expressed in the law (Matt 5:17–18), even while he sharpens its demand, displaying authority over it because in a real sense the Spirit makes him autonomous over it (Matt 5:21–22, 27–48; 12:1–32, esp. in light of vv. 18 and 28; John 9:16–17). He proclaims the gospel, the coming of the kingdom of heaven (Matt 4:17; Mark 1:38; Luke 4:43; John 4:24–26). By means of his parables, he fulfills the prophecy of proclaiming what has been hidden from the foundation of the world (Matt 13:35). He reveals the "foolishness" of God, which is greater than the wisdom of the world (1 Cor 1:22–25, 2:14, 3:19). He rejoices in the Spirit because he is the one who reveals the Father to "infants," and is the sole means by which even the wise and intelligent may come to know the Father (Luke 10:21–22). He is the one who brings sight to the blind.[2] He is the light that enlightens all people (John 1:4, 9); indeed, he is "the way, and the truth, and the life" (John 14:6). His anointing grants knowledge and truth, it teaches about all things (1 John 2:20–21, 26–27). Taken together, these characteristics delineate how God the Father, in bestowing the Spirit upon the Son, makes his prophetic work the ultimate revelation and fulfillment of divine truth and wisdom. To recognize Jesus as prophet is to recognize that he is God's living and life-giving Word, the teacher of God's truth

---

2. Blindness is often portrayed in Scripture as not just a physical malady, but a spiritual one. The Gospel of John plays with the double meaning frequently (e.g., the classic interchange in John 9), but other witnesses use it as well to describe the effect—or lack of effect in the stubborn!—of Jesus' prophetic work (cf. Matt 15:10-14, 23:16-26; Luke 6:39-42).

who thus discloses the world's meaning and our own to us. But it is also to recognize that he is such as the Spirit is upon, indeed, within him.[3] He becomes the mediator of the Spirit, the door through which it becomes available to the people. In this sense, the Spirit speaks through the Son, continuing the work it had done through the prophets preceding him, and which it has continued in his name from Pentecost on. In another sense, the Son liberates the Spirit, unleashing its dynamic power such that God's truth and will is written on human hearts. In both senses, the Son may be said to work on behalf of the Spirit, fulfilling yet one more aspect of the triune God's atoning purpose.

Now in one respect, claiming for Jesus the status of "prophet" is presumably the least contestable of the offices one could ascribe to him. The gospel narratives retain ample evidence that this was at least one aspect of his own self-understanding (Luke 13:33). And he was certainly understood as such by many in his own day, because his teaching, demeanor, and actions all fit what could be called the "prophetic profile" known from Israel's history and tradition (Matt 21:10–11, 45–46; Mark 6:14–16; Luke 7:12–16a, 24:18–19; John 4:19, 6:14). How do the gospel narratives respond? On the one hand, they do not deny but actually promote the identification of Jesus with the "prophets of old" (Mark 6:15). On the other hand, however, they promote the conclusion that his status and authority are unique, that he is much more than a prophet. One succinct and dramatic indication that Christ is in line with, but also fulfills and transforms, the prophetic office may be discerned in the synoptic descriptions of Christ's transfiguration (Matt 17:1–8 // Mark 9:2–8 // Luke 9:28–36). Jesus goes up a high mountain, taking Peter, James, and John with him. There, Jesus' face and garments are dazzlingly transformed, and Moses and Elijah appear, to talk with him. A cloud overshadows them, and a voice speaks: "This is my beloved Son; listen to him." That is, the narrative presents Jesus ascending a mountain, evoking an earlier place of theophany, Mount Sinai. It describes his shining face and clothes, evoking a sense of God's presence and glory while anticipating the coming glory of his resurrection. He is joined by the greatest of prophets, Moses, and the prophet whose reappearance was to herald the coming of the Messiah, Elijah (cf. Mal 4:4–5). At the very least, this "collegial conference" signifies his equal

---

3. Recall his anointing with the Spirit described in the accounts of his baptism and his conception by the Spirit in the birth narratives of Matthew and Luke, as well as Matt 12:18, Luke 4:14–15, 18, 10:21.

status with them. But then a voice from the cloud speaks, reiterating the words of Jesus' baptismal commission, but also adding to them a further and final grant of authority, "Listen to him." Jesus is certainly warranted in claiming the prophet's mantle, but in fact, as God's Messiah, he may also claim much more. Peter's confession at Caesarea Philippi, which appeared earlier in the narrative, serves a similar function, which is to say, indicating Jesus' "prophetic pedigree" while also stressing his unique consummation of that office. To Jesus' question, "Who do people say that I am?" the disciples respond with what are presumably the most common opinions: John the Baptist (revived from his recent death), Elijah, or one of the (old) prophets. But Peter makes it explicit with his confession: "You are the Messiah" (Mark 8:27–30 // Matt 16:13–16 // Luke 9:18–20). Again, this confession does not deny or exclude Jesus' prophetic office, but suggests that it has been both absorbed and transcended to become but one aspect of Jesus' larger messianic role.

But what does it mean to say that Jesus' prophetic role has been assimilated into, and become but one aspect of, his messianic role? In what way does Jesus' being a prophet affect his messianic role? And conversely, in what way does Jesus' being this messianic "more than a prophet" affect his prophetic office? Perhaps the most illuminating way to enter this cluster of questions is to recognize how Jesus' prophetic office should also be understood as a "teaching office." That he was recognized as a teacher is beyond dispute. Two of the most common titles ascribed to him are "teacher" *(didáskalos)* and "rabbi" *(rhábbi,* or its alternate form *rhabbouní)*—ascribed by his opponents as well as the more sympathetic among the crowds, and his disciples.[4] Indeed, the very term used to describe Jesus' closest followers, that is, "disciple" *(mathētēs)*, implies a relationship of a "pupil" to a teacher. To be sure, those portrayed as suspicious or opposed to Jesus—the scribes and Pharisees, the Sadducees and lawyers—no doubt had their reservations about his qualifications, and may have used the title merely as a courtesy, or perhaps with a tinge of mockery. Nevertheless, the very fact that they posed questions of him and engaged in disputes over the interpretation of the law itself represented a certain concession that the title was deserved. So, we can say that he was a teacher. But what does it mean to say further

---

4. The gospel narratives recount literally dozens of instances in which this title is used with reference to Jesus. For a representative sample, see Matt 8:19, 9:11, 17:24, 22:23–24; Mark 4:38, 9:17, 12:13–14, 14:14; Luke 9:38, 10:25, 21:7; John 1:38, 3:2, 13:13, 20:16.

that he was a *prophetic* teacher? The first clue may be found by recalling the exclamation of the crowds that he taught "with authority." The gospel narratives give no indication that he gained this authority by the regular means, which is to say, through long years of study under the tutelage of a recognized master.[5] This is how the scribes, for example, earned their status. Instead, the gospels give every indication that Jesus' authority was charismatic, which is to say, a direct bestowal by the Spirit. In this sense, the source and character of his authority appeared to recapitulate that of Israel's classic prophets—no small matter, given the widespread assumption at the time that God had ceased raising up prophets.

So, the authority with which Jesus spoke and acted, and much of what he actually said and did—his calls to repentance, his condemnations of hypocrisy, his summons to true faithfulness, his symbolic acts, as well as his healings and miracles—clearly match many elements of the "prophetic profile." The biblical narrative also portrays him as exceeding that profile, in a number of ways. First, consider his relation to the law. A key function of the Old Testament prophets was to call Israel to account as a covenant people under God's law. Whenever Israel betrayed its obligations to God (through idolatry, apostasy, lax worship, and the like) or neighbor (through neglect of the poor, abuse of the powerless, and the like), the prophets summoned them back to the faithfulness and responsibility God's *torah* required. In this task, the prophets often displayed great fervor and creativity in portraying the people's sinfulness, in describing God's dismay, sorrow, and wrath, and in presenting the inevitable consequences, should they not repent. They were God's agents and were bestowed with charismatic authority; but in a very concrete sense they were also agents of the divine law, and subordinate to it.

By contrast, one of the most striking characteristics of Jesus' prophetic work is his stance of authority over, and in crucial respects, autonomy from the law. This stance shows itself in numerous ways. In the Sermon on the Mount, Jesus' insistence that "not one letter, not one stroke of a letter, will pass from the law until all is accomplished" (Matt 5:18) appears to focus primacy and authority on it. Yet he had prefaced these words with a statement that implicitly shifted primacy and authority to him, the law becoming in effect an instrument over which he had control. The narrative confirms this sense when later in the

---

5. Actually, they let it be known that he was not a "professional" religious scholar. See Mark 6:2–3 and its somewhat modified parallel in Matt 13:54–57. See also John 7:15.

Sermon, he increases the law's stringency, declaring simple anger as liable to judgment as murder and lust equivalent to adultery, and tightening the rules on divorce, oaths, self-defense, and numerous religious practices, among other matters. Intriguingly, he demonstrates his authority over the law not just in tightening it, but in loosening it, as three prophetic acts show. First, his disciples apparently violate the Sabbath by plucking heads of grain to eat as they walked. When challenged by the Pharisees, Jesus legitimates their actions with the principle that the Sabbath was made for humans, and not humans for the Sabbath (Mark 2:23–27). Second, in what his opponents construe as another violation of the Sabbath, Jesus heals a man with a withered hand (Mark 3:1–6; cf. John 9:16). Third, he heals a man by commanding "Stand up, take your mat and walk"—a command that gets the man, and hence Jesus, in trouble with the authorities because it likewise occurred on a Sabbath, when it is unlawful to carry one's mat (John 5:1–18; cf. as well John 9:13–17). His summary words after the first incident can apply to both cases: "The Son of Man is lord even of the sabbath" (Mark 2:28; see parallels in Matt 12:8 and Luke 6:5). Consider as well that he did not separate himself from the outcast or unclean, as many believed the law required, but characteristically associated with "tax collectors and sinners" (Matt 9:9–13 // Mark 2:15–17 // Luke 5:30–32; Matt 11:18–19 // Luke 7:33–35; Matt 21:31b–32; Luke 19:1–10).

In addition to Jesus' unique authority in relation to the law, the biblical narrative also connects his status as the messianic prophet with his proclamation of God's reign. Indeed, the New Testament indicates that he is himself the realization and revelation of God's truth and purposes. In other words, as God's messianic prophet Christ does not simply announce a message, he *initiates* what the message announces; he does not simply deliver a message, he *is* the message. A sense of this may be detected in an early summary statement from Matthew: "Jesus went throughout Galilee, teaching in their synagogues and proclaiming the good news of the kingdom and curing every disease and every sickness among the people" (Matt 4:23; reiterated in Matt 9:35). Mark had offered a similar early account of Jesus teaching, preaching, and healing, although instead of a brief summary stating this, he presents a series of brief narratives illustrating it (Mark 1:14–15, 21–39). Luke follows Mark's example, offering a series of telling anecdotes and descriptions that enact the prophetic words of Isaiah presented just before (Luke 4:31–44; cf. the passage from Luke 4:18–21 cited above). In each case, the narratives function to make the same point: the kingdom is not only proclaimed, but actually begun, exemplified and made available in what Jesus says and does.

This raises another question: What is it, precisely, that Jesus makes available? Several things stand out: liberation from powers that hold people in bondage, expiation and forgiveness of sin, and the basis for a new beginning. In addition, the New Testament also speaks of Jesus making available what may be labeled "enlightenment" or "wisdom." The various New Testament narratives describe it in a variety of ways, but they all make a similar assumption: Jesus presents a new reality ("the kingdom of God") and beckons his hearers to accept it as their own. He teaches a new way of thinking and a new way of being in the world. The Synoptic Gospels present this new way of understanding the world, of relating to neighbor and to God primarily through their inclusion of Jesus' many parables. Jesus' parables do not intend simply to add to the knowledge his hearers already had. Rather, they intend to turn such worldly knowledge on its head. They surprise, they jar, indeed, they often shock, in order to foment an evaluation of one's current assumptions and expectations and a reorientation toward a more fundamental and God-given reality. The parable of the Laborers in the Vineyard (Matt 20:1–16) cannot help but offend everyday notions of fairness and justice. Abandoning ninety-nine to search for a single missing one seems foolish, if not irresponsible (Matt 18:12–14 // Luke 15:3–7). A common-sense hearing of the story of the Prodigal Son (Luke 15:11–32) will conclude that the older brother had legitimate grounds for complaint. Nevertheless, Jesus tells these stories in order to point to a new reality and establish a new norm. The parables reveal God's true, original, and final attitude toward and intentions for creation, including what its relation to its Creator should be, and they beckon their hearers to align themselves with these attitudes and intentions. The Gospel of Matthew goes so far as to state that by means of his parables, Jesus fulfills the prophecy of proclaiming "what has been hidden from the foundation of the world" (Matt 13:34–35).

The Gospel of John does not portray Jesus as one who teaches by means of parables, but it still portrays him as a teacher, frequently describing him as the one who enlightens the world. John employs this imagery in his Gospel's prologue, repeatedly referring to the Word as the "light" (John 1:4–5, 7–8) and fleshing out its significance by connecting it with God's glory and truth as embodied in the incarnation of Jesus Christ. This theme of Jesus as the light of the world then recurs throughout the Gospel (John 3:19–21, 8:12, 9:5, 11:9–10, 12:35–36,

12:46), and is presented as the antithesis of "darkness" and the judgment of worldly wisdom (see especially John 8:12–18). John further reinforces the contrast between the light of Christ and the darkness of the world in the ironic way he contrasts physical blindness with spiritual blindness in chapter 9 of his Gospel. Here he presents an account of a man born blind receiving his sight, and of the controversy that ensues. At one level, the chapter simply describes another of Jesus' physical healings. On another and more important level, it describes the conflict between those willing to be enlightened and those resisting it: a man born blind can now see, accepting, indeed, worshipping Jesus, while those who can see with their eyes nevertheless remain blind spiritually, because they reject Jesus. Complementary to these descriptions of Jesus as the "light" and as the one who "enlightens," John also portrays his status as prophetic teacher in a much more straightforward fashion in the so-called "Farewell Discourse" that Jesus gives his disciples at the Last Supper. Having explicitly identified himself as the disciples' "Lord and Teacher," Jesus offers them an extended lesson in how, on the basis of their relation to him and hence the Father, they should act in the world and toward one another. For finally, he is "the way, and the truth, and the life" (John 14:6). As it was in the Synoptic Gospels, so, too, is it here: Jesus presents his disciples with a new reality, which is to say, a new way of understanding the world and a new way of being in the world, based on God's truth and intentions and not the world's own mistaken self-understanding.

Jesus' distinction echoes as well in Paul's contrast between the wisdom of the world and the "foolishness" of God. To be sure, Paul focuses his attention on the cross as the main lesson "taught" by Christ and does not present anything comparable to the popular teacher of parables found in the Synoptics or the enlightened teacher of John's "Farewell Discourse." Still, Paul does not entirely ignore the teachings of Jesus. For example, one hears reverberations of material found in the gospel in Paul's use of "Abba! Father!" in addressing God (Rom 8:15 and Gal 4:6),[6] in his ethical exhortations in 1 Corinthians,[7] and in his description of the words uttered by Jesus at the Last Supper (1 Cor

---

6. Cf. Mark 14:36 as well the use of "Father" on its own throughout Paul and the Gospels.

7. Cf. 1 Cor 6:2 with Matt 19:28; 1 Cor 6:9–10 seems to be a summary paraphrase of the "Sermon on the Plain" found in Luke 6:20ff.; 1 Cor 9:14 echoes Luke 10:7; 1 Cor 13:2 presupposes Matt 17:20; and 1 Cor 14:37 implies a link to a saying of Jesus, but the source is not clear.

11:23–25).[8] More significantly, the radical reorientation to a new reality that Jesus taught is not so much a discrete element of Paul's writing as it is an all-pervasive presupposition. One need only consider his account of his conversion (Gal 1:11–24 and 1 Cor 15:8–10) and the way he contrasts his past and current life (Phil 3:2–11) to recognize the radical realignment that Paul's own life took. This realignment is itself the starting point of his theology, and on this basis one can appropriately claim that the "Christ crucified" of his letters does indeed function as the "Christ the Teacher" found in the Gospels. That is, in both cases, persons are confronted with a new reality, a new way of understanding themselves, the world, and their relation to God—and invited to make it their own, while forsaking the attitudes, outlook, and norms of the world. Paul could be summarizing Jesus' own approach when he rhetorically asks, "Where is the one who is wise? Where is the scribe? Where is the debater of this age? Has not God made foolish the wisdom of the world?" (1 Cor 1:20). For Paul, Christ crucified reveals the power and wisdom of God, even as it turns on its head all the wisdom, experience, and common sense of the world. Christ must become the Christian's wisdom, righteousness, life, and truth (1 Cor 1:26–31, 2:1–16, 3:18–19; cf. Eph 4:17–24 and Col 2:2–4, 3:2–11). That is, not just Christ's teaching, but Christ himself subverts worldly knowledge and strength and becomes the source of a new way of thinking and being—a new way rooted in, and foreshadowed by, the Old Testament witness.

The Old Testament Witness

What Old Testament stories and themes are available to the church to help explain and ground this new reality of Christ, the messianic prophet? And how does the risen Christ become the hermeneutical key for the church's understanding of its received Scriptures? This section sketches briefly what the Old Testament presents regarding Israel's various prophets and its understanding of the prophetic office, to better clarify Jesus' continuity with the Old Testament prophets and in order to provide the context for my further discussion of his fulfillment and redefinition of Old Testament prophets and prophecy.

Two sets of questions arise for us here: First, according to the scriptural narratives, what is the role of the prophet and why was it necessary?

---

8. Cf. with Matt 26:26–29 // Mark 14:22–25 // Luke 22:14–20.

In the Old Testament, the prophet served as the mouthpiece of God to his people. God had acted in history to create Israel, and its continued existence depended upon its ongoing and proper relation to him. Stated most generally, the prophet functioned as a conduit for the revelation of the divine will and, more often, as the means by which God summoned the people back to his will when they had strayed from its requirements. The preeminent example of the former was Moses, who served the role of prophet because through him came *torah*, the initial and ongoing basis of God's covenant with the people of Israel. Figures such as Isaiah, Jeremiah, Amos, and Hosea stand out as classic examples of the latter, for their prophecy always presupposed *torah*, whether they were denouncing the people's apostasy and injustice or proclaiming a new and better future that God would accomplish. Of course, these well-known charismatic figures were not the only kinds of prophet present in Israel. The Old Testament also applies the term more generically to those acting in the institutionalized role of cult or court prophet. And the "charismatic" and "cultic" could overlap: Elisha appears to have been on collegial terms with the "sons of the prophets" based at Bethel, Jeremiah was of priestly lineage, and Ezekiel was himself a priest.[9] Likewise, the term could carry negative connotations, when referring to the "false" prophets of Baal and Asherah (1 Kgs 18:17ff.) or of the royal court (e.g., 1 Kgs 22:5–12; Jer 23:25–27 and Lam 2:14; Ezek 13:3–16). In some instances it was used in a limited sense simply as a synonym for "seer" (e.g., 2 Sam 9:9, 18–19; 24:11; 2 Kgs 17:13; 1 Chr 9:22; Amos 7:12) conveying at times rather mundane (e.g., 1 Sam 9), and perhaps also negative (e.g., Mic 3:7), connotations. Be all this as it may, for my present purposes, the roles played and precedents set by the classic charismatic prophets are most significant, because it is this lineage that most clearly informs the prophetic office of Christ.

In their role as the mouthpiece of God, the prophets served more particularly as teachers, counselors, and advocates—in a word, as Israel's conscience. They instructed, admonished, rebuked, and encouraged, doing so not on their own authority but on the basis of their divine commissioning and of *torah*. Typically, they reminded the people and/or leaders of Israel of their heritage, that is, of the nation's creation by, its blessings from, and its covenantal obligations to God. The prophets challenged their practice of following the desires and imaginations of

---

9. 2 Kgs 2:1–3; Jer 1:1; Ezek 1:3.

their own hearts, and confronted them with visions of the inevitable and tragic consequences, should they persist. And then they urged them to follow instead the purposes that God intended for them, to return to him and thereby attain their own truest fulfillment, in relation to him and to one another. This dual orientation is why the requirements of the law took two basic forms, as represented by the two tablets of the Decalogue, namely, duties to God and duties to neighbor. The prophet became a teacher and advocate of God's will with regard to true worship and right behavior—and in the process, the people's own truest fulfillment. And yet the people still fell short, so that this teaching and advocacy most often came as prophetic denunciations of idolatry and apostasy and of unrighteousness and injustice toward the poor and disenfranchised. Consider the words of Jeremiah:

> As a thief is shamed when caught, so the house of Israel shall be
>   shamed—
>   they, their kings, their officials, their priests, and their prophets,
> who say to a tree, "You are my father," and to a stone, "You gave me birth."
>   For they have turned their backs to me, and not their faces.
>   But in the time of their trouble they say, "Come and save us!"
> But where are your gods that you made for yourself?
>   Let them come, if they can save you, in your time of trouble;
>   for you have as many gods as you have towns, O Judah. (Jer 2:26–28)

The reference to the tree and the stone allude to the worship of the pagan deities Asherah and Baal, while the impotence of these idols is meant to stand in contrast to the known saving power of God. Then consider the words of the prophet Amos:

> Thus says the LORD:
> For three transgressions of Israel, and for four, I will not revoke the
>   punishment;
> because they sell the righteous for silver, and the needy for a pair of
>   sandals—
>   they who trample the head of the poor into the dust of the earth,
>   and push the afflicted out of the way;
> father and son go in to the same girl, so that my holy name is profaned;
>   they lay themselves down beside every altar on garments taken in pledge;
>   and in the house of their God they drink wine bought with fines they
>   imposed. (Amos 2:6–8)

Passages describing similar social corruption and immorality may be found throughout the prophetic writings.

Of course, as the mouthpiece of God's will, the prophets did more than just pronounce decrees and denunciations. In revealing God's will, they also revealed much about his character—as one who is loving and long-suffering, but also holy and jealous—and also about the covenantal, indeed personal, relationship he seeks with his people. God is gracious toward Israel, but he also requires its exclusive allegiance, a correlation stated most succinctly in the first commandment: "I am the LORD your God, who brought you out of the land of Egypt, out of the house of slavery; you shall have no other gods before me" (Exod 20:2–3). God is the author of Israel's existence as a people, of their origin and their end, and it is for this reason and for this purpose that he has authority over them.

Secondly, in revealing God's will, the prophets revealed much about the character and purposes of creation, human and otherwise. In this sense, they acted as commentators and interpreters of God's activity in the world. They described history and presented its true and final, which is to say, God-determined, meaning. Such interpretation could take a straightforward form, in which the prophet's description of an event simply gave expression to what was most likely the common understanding.[10] But the prophets could also construe events in ways that ran counter to their apparent significance. That is, they might insist that what was "really" going on in certain events, and what their final outcome would be, could not be gleaned from a surface reading of circumstances. God can and does use the ebb and flow of human events to accomplish his own purposes, purposes that might not be obvious from a merely human perspective. Perhaps the most famous example of such a counterintuitive reading of historical events is Jeremiah's purchase of his cousin's field, when Babylonian armies were besieging Jerusalem, and Jeremiah himself was under house arrest in the court of King Zedekiah for having prophesied the latter's defeat and exile (Jer 32:1ff.). Why did Jeremiah undertake this transaction at a time when the fulfillment of his earlier prophecy seemed disastrously imminent? Because the Lord had given Jeremiah to know that defeat at the hands of the Babylonians would not end his dealings with his people, that

---

10. For example, Miriam and Deborah were each identified as a "prophetess" (Exod 15:20 and Judg 4:4), and their respective victory "songs" (Exod 15:21 and Judg 5) presumably voiced the common sentiment regarding the events they celebrated.

"houses and fields and vineyards shall again be bought in this land" (Jer 32:15) that restoration would come.

And of course, the Old Testament does not portray the prophets as being restricted to interpreting current or imminent events; it also presents them as able to offer a longer and more comprehensive, indeed eschatological, view of history. As focused as the prophets were on Israel's (dis)obedience to God in the myriad occasions and situations of its everyday life, they also gave that life a larger context and a particular orientation and *telos*. The book of Isaiah, in its words of comfort to the Babylonian exiles, evokes images of a new exodus, indeed, of a new creation and a restored Eden (see, e.g., Isa 44:18–21, 48:20–21, 51:1–6, 52:11–12, 55:12–13, 60:19–22, and 65:17–25). Certainly such passages derive from, and respond to, a particular historical context, and yet in their scriptural function they also speak to a more general yearning and of a more comprehensive divine promise. Moreover, prophetic visions of eschatological fulfillment include the transformation of persons, and not just creation. The well-known passage from Jeremiah presents the future vision, even as it makes clear that this vision has been the unachieved goal since God first covenanted with the people.

> The days are surely coming, says the LORD, when I will make a new covenant with the house of Israel and the house of Judah. It will not be like the covenant that I made with their ancestors when I took them by the hand to bring them out of the land of Egypt—a covenant that they broke, though I was their husband, says the LORD. But this is the covenant that I will make with the house of Israel after those days, says the LORD: I will put my law within them, and I will write it on their hearts; and I will be their God, and they shall be my people. No longer shall they teach one another, or say to each other, "Know the LORD," for they shall all know me, from the least of them to the greatest, says the LORD; for I will forgive their iniquity, and remember their sin no more. (Jer 31:31–34; cf. Ezek 36:26–29b)

The passage is breathtaking in its historical sweep and summary allusions, as well as in its intimacy. The distant events of the exodus and the Mount Sinai covenant are recalled, the former described as a personal rescue ("I took them by the hand") and the latter as akin to marriage ("I was their husband"). These are juxtaposed with the Lord's intended new work, which will be similarly historic and intimate: writing the law on the heart, as momentous in its own way as the first giving of the law, which will have the effect of granting immediate and personal knowledge of the Lord to all so touched.

Other well-known prophecies enrich the picture of this promised future. For instance, Isaiah and Micah depict the end of warfare and the beginning of a reign of peace and justice (Isa 2:3–4 and Mic 4:1–4). Joel describes the Spirit being poured out on all flesh, in effect making all persons prophets and seers (Joel 2:28–29). Ezekiel foretells hope even for those who have already perished, in his vision of the valley of dry bones, from which the following are the concluding verses:

> Then he said to me, "Mortal, these bones are the whole house of Israel. They say, 'Our bones are dried up, and our hope is lost; we are cut off completely.' Therefore prophesy, and say to them, Thus says the Lord GOD: I am going to open your graves, and bring you up from your graves, O my people; and I will bring you back to the land of Israel. And you shall know that I am the LORD, when I open your graves, and bring you up from your graves, O my people. I will put my spirit within you, and you shall live, and I will place you on your own soil; then you shall know that I, the LORD, have spoken and will act," says the LORD. (Ezek 37:11–14; the entire passage is 34:1–14)

Taken together, these various passages illustrate the "meta-narrative" or hermeneutic with which Israel was to interpret its own ongoing existence. That is, these passages, rather than either the mundane apostasies and duplicities of daily life or the nation's worldly ambitions and occasional catastrophes, disclosed the true trajectory and meaning of Israel's life. And in all of these prophecies and visions, one may also discern an elaboration and the culmination of the promise first made to Abram, that he would become a great nation and through him all the families of the earth would be blessed (Gen 12:1–3; see also Isa 49:6).

Christ's Redefinition and Fulfillment of Prophecy

As the Old Testament background indicates, labeling Christ as a "prophet," indeed *the* prophet of God need not signal a reduction of his status or uniqueness. However, the church affirmed Christ as much more than a prophet, indeed, as redefining and fulfilling what it meant to be a prophet. The New Testament promotes this new understanding both implicitly and explicitly. For an example of the former, consider how the Gospel of Matthew distinguishes the different ways Jesus is

addressed. His disciples and those who approach him in faith call him
"Lord" (Matt 8:2, 6, 25; 9:28; 14:28–32; 15:22–28; 17:14–15; 18:21;
20:30–34) while those who misunderstand or oppose him consistently
call him nothing other than "teacher" or "rabbi" (Matt 8:19, 9:11, 12:38,
19:16, 22:15–18, 23–29, 34–36). This is particularly noteworthy in the
case of Judas (Matt 26:25, 49). This does not mean Matthew denies
Jesus' teaching role; quite the contrary, his is the gospel most concerned
with portraying Jesus as the new Moses, the new prophetic law-giver
and preeminent teacher. But Matthew also portrays Jesus as elevating
this role to a unique and now ultimate status. Consider next the distinction made in the first verse of the Letter to the Hebrews: "Long ago God
spoke to our ancestors in many and various ways by the prophets, but in
these last days he has spoken to us by a Son." This verse recognizes the
continuity of God's speaking over the generations and implies a certain
parallel between the prophets and the Son. But the verse also clearly
indicates the unique and preeminent place of the Son. Christ the
Prophet fulfills but also transcends previous understandings of prophecy.

Jesus stands as the transcendent prophet of God. What does this
mean more specifically? To begin, recall the episode describing Jesus'
reading of the prophet Isaiah in the synagogue, and his pronouncement
that "Today this Scripture has been fulfilled in your hearing" (Luke
4:16–21). Not only do Isaiah's opening words become Jesus' own ("The
Spirit of the Lord is upon me," a point made earlier in his baptism and
reconfirmed in Luke 4:1), but Isaiah's prophecy will itself be realized in
the person and work of Christ. Put another way, Jesus becomes both the
prophet and the prophecy, both the messenger and the message. And
on this basis, he then empowers his disciples and his church, through
the gift of the Spirit, to participate in this fulfilled prophecy.

Let me draw attention to this point for a moment. Jesus' words and
deeds are not separable from his person. Nowhere in the Gospels, or
elsewhere in the New Testament, are Jesus' words and deeds presented
as somehow standing on their own, as offering a truth or blessing that
could have just as well been delivered anonymously or by someone else.
Jesus' proclamation and enactment of God's in-breaking reign are
inseparably bound up with his person, for is he not just an ordinary
prophetic spokesman of God, a merely human conduit for the speaking
of God's Spirit. Rather, he is the messianic embodiment of God's Word,
the one conceived of the Holy Spirit, the one upon whom the Spirit
rests, the one commissioned by the Spirit who in turn commissions the

Spirit to enact his teaching. The truth of God's reign is not an abstract, but a living and personal truth, one that cannot stand on its own, but is revealed by and in Jesus, the messianic prophet—a distinction that has crucial implications for how that truth is to be received. Were God's truth abstract, an impersonal object, then presumably it could be received abstractly and objectively. But God's truth is embodied in a person, and thus must be received personally and subjectively. Indeed, it must be communicated in order to be received, in the form of personal address—and this Christ does, through the instrumentality of the Spirit. Christ is the culmination of the prophets, who throws open the doors of access to the Spirit. In him the hope of the prophets is realized (e.g., Ezek 36:26–27 and Joel 2:28–29), for he is the one who baptizes with the Holy Spirit (Matt 3:11 // Mark 1:8 // Luke 3:16; John 1:32–33; and, of course, see Acts 2:1–42). In other words, and as I suggested at the outset, Christ in his office as prophet not only enlightens but empowers persons to recognize and embrace God's revelation of a new reality as their own true meaning and end.

The New Testament witnesses to this point in a variety of ways. According to the chronology of the biblical narrative, the events of Pentecost stand as the pivotal manifestation of it. Yet the synoptic narratives anticipate the events of Pentecost with their descriptions of Jesus sending out his disciples to preach, exorcise, and heal (Matt 9:35–10:41 // Mark 6:7–13, 30 // Luke 9:1–6, 10).[11] In effect, the disciples become what one might call "deputy prophets" (cf. Matt 10:40–41a). Moreover, their mission is not presented as an isolated event, but as establishing a pattern that recurs on a much broader scale following the more general commissioning event of Pentecost. One sees this in numerous episodes recounted in the Acts of the Apostles, and one can also recognize it as a context evident in several of Paul's letters. So consider first some of the details recounted in the sending of the disciples. All three Synoptic Gospels indicate that the disciples proclaimed the good news of the kingdom, healed the sick, and had authority to cast out demons—which is, of course, a precise recapitulation of Christ's own activity, as Matthew

---

11. Luke also recounts Jesus sending seventy others in a separate episode (Luke 10:1–24). Clearly, Mark presents a much more abbreviated account of the episode(s) than Matthew or Luke, and each of the latter two include material the other does not. Still, taken together the three accounts all create the same impression, with Matthew and Luke especially supplying details that produce an intriguingly rich sketch overall.

especially indicates (Matt 9:35).[12] They are further enacting the reality that Jesus himself had first proclaimed and enacted.

In addition, the details that Matthew recounts make especially clear the connection between the wisdom the disciples receive from Christ their teacher, as well as the fact that Christ serves as the catalyst making the disciples instruments of the entire Trinity:

> See, I am sending you out like sheep into the midst of wolves; so be wise as serpents and innocent as doves. Beware of them, for they will hand you over to councils and flog you in their synagogues; and you will be dragged before governors and kings because of me, as a testimony to them and the Gentiles. When they hand you over, do not worry about how you are to speak or what you are to say; for what you are to say will be given to you at that time; for it is not you who speak, but the Spirit of your Father speaking through you. . . .
>
> A disciple is not above the teacher, nor a slave above the master; it is enough for the disciple to be like the teacher, and the slave like the master. If they have called the master of the house Beelzebul, how much more will they malign those of his household! (Matt 10:16–20, 24–25 // Mark 13:9–11 // Luke 12:11–12)

The disciples become agents of the new reality revealed in Christ only as they are in fact empowered by him. It is not something they accomplish on their own, but only in the name, and hence the power, of Jesus (Luke 10:17–20; cf. Mark 9:38–41 and John 1:12–13). And as the above citation from Matthew and my earlier argument suggest, that power may be identified with the Spirit, the Spirit of the Father.

Consider these matters from another perspective. I have argued that the gospel narratives present Jesus as a prophetic teacher, especially the accounts of Matthew and John. Perhaps the most famous example of his teaching is the Sermon on the Mount, recorded in the former gospel. Many have debated the meaning and intention of this collection of sayings and admonitions. Is Jesus simply presenting a more stringent version of *torah*? Is he offering a rigorous "interim ethic," valid only for the brief time it takes for the reign of God to establish itself fully? Is it intended to drive the faithful to despair, so that they might finally

---

12. Cf. Mark 1:39 and Luke 4:31–44, the latter being not a summary statement of Jesus' preaching, healing, and exorcising, but a narrative sequence describing him doing precisely these three things.

depend solely on the grace of God and not their own abilities? Is it better understood as an ideal, which is to say, as a description of behavior in the eschatological future rather than as a prescription for the still tumultuous and difficult present? I believe that the last two views are closer to the way the Sermon should be understood than the first two views. Jesus did not advocate a new legalism, whether for the long or short term. Rather, he preached the kingdom of God, a new and powerful reality that would upend the old order and transform the faithful. But what does this claim imply for Jesus' prophetic teaching? First, and most obviously, it means that the Sermon on the Mount does not stand on its own, as a distilled list of imperatives. There are many other "lessons" that Jesus conveyed, in both word and deed, embodying the new reality he brings. Second, and more to the point, I want to emphasize that none of these teachings are properly appropriated unless one recognizes the initial and continuing role of the Teacher. Jesus' teaching function was undertaken in his office as prophet, an office which exercises this function at the prompting and with the power of the Holy Spirit. In this function, the Spirit is active still. Simply put, one cannot follow the teachings of Jesus unless the power of the Spirit enables it.

Think about the way the assumptions, particular details, and general orientation of Jesus' Sermon on the Mount find an abbreviated but substantive echo—and also reinforcement—in Paul's contrast between the works of the flesh and the fruit of the Spirit as described in Gal 5:16–26. For example, observe the way both contrast the behaviors to be shunned with those to be enacted. Jesus does it provocatively and at length, with his hyperbole and parables; Paul does it more succinctly, with his two lists. Yet both make it clear that a fundamental choice confronts those who would be faithful. Moreover, at the heart of Jesus' preaching stands the assumption that "false prophets"—and by implication, all persons—are known "by their fruits": that your choice of a fundamental orientation toward or away from God determines what you truly are, and what you are will inevitably become evident in your behavior (Matt 7:15–20). The same assumption underlies Paul's distinction between the works of the flesh and the fruit of the Spirit (Gal 5:19ff.; cf. 5:22ff.). There are also many similarities in the specific dispositions and behaviors called for by each. For instance, each in his own way admonishes his hearers to demonstrate love (Matt 5:43ff. and Gal 5:22, as well as Matt 7:12 and Gal 5:14), generosity and kindness (Matt 5:42 and Gal 5:22, 6:9–10), self-effacement coupled with forbearance toward others (Matt 5:7, 7:1–5 and Gal 5:26–6:5), patience and meekness

(Matt 5:5, 38–41 and Gal 5:22), joy and peace (Matt 6:25–34 and Gal 5:22), while also admonishing them to avoid enmity and strife (Matt 5:23–26 and Gal 5:13–15, 20), anger (Matt 5:22 and Gal 5:20), sexual license (Matt 5:28 and Gal 5:19), and false religion (Matt 6:1–18 and Gal 5:20).[13] One may also detect a similarity in the tone with which these imperatives are pronounced. When Jesus' insists his hearers cut off an offending appendage rather than let it become the cause of sin, one may hear a reverberation of that challenge in Paul's assertion that "those who belong to Christ Jesus have crucified the flesh with its passions and desires" (Matt 5:29–30 and Gal 5:24). Finally, just as Jesus' sermon both presupposes and seeks to evoke a concrete sense of God's in-breaking eschatological reign, so, too, does Paul present his admonitions within a similar context, assuming that those who do the works of the flesh "will not inherit the kingdom of God" (Gal 5:21; cf. Mt. 5:20).

In addition, I suggest that these two passages and others like them should be placed within the context of one from John's Gospel: "I have said these things to you while I am still with you. But the Advocate, the Holy Spirit, whom the Father will send in my name, will teach you everything, and remind you of all that I have said to you" (John 14:25–26). The Spirit continues Jesus' instruction, and just as it enabled Jesus' teaching in the first place and empowered his first disciples, so now it enables Christians to continue learning and living his lessons. Paul speaks to this point in the Galatians passage cited above when he correlates belonging to Christ with living in the Spirit: "And those who belong to Christ Jesus have crucified the flesh with its passions and desires. If we live by the Spirit, let us also be guided by the Spirit" (Gal 5:24–25; cf. 1 Cor 2:12–16 and 12:4–11). In other words, adherence to Jesus' Sermon on the Mount, or any of his teachings, is not a product of human willpower, but a gracious gift of God, delivered by the Spirit. Jesus' imperative to "be perfect, therefore, as your heavenly Father is perfect" would be a counsel of despair were it not for his additional command and promise: "Ask, and it will be given you; search, and you will find; knock, and the door will be opened for you. For everyone who asks receives, and everyone who searches finds, and for everyone who knocks, the door will be opened . . ." (Matt 7:7–8). With a heavenly Father who gives such good things, Christians need no longer be conformed to this world, but may be transformed by the renewal of their

---

13. On this theme, it must be noted that Jesus was more concerned with hypocrisy and Paul with idolatry and apostasy.

minds. The gift of Christ's teaching, made available and active through the Spirit, enables believers to discern the will of God, what is good and acceptable and perfect (Rom 12:2)—and to act upon it.

Thus, to say that persons are "in Christ" is only another way of saying that they are baptized into the Holy Spirit (Acts 11:15–18; 1 Cor 6:11) and gain access to the gifts, indeed, the personal power and activity of the Holy Spirit. Scriptural narratives frequently depict the Christian life in terms of the intrinsic role played by the Spirit. For example, the Spirit acts not just as a kind of "stage manager" for the unfolding events described in the Acts of the Apostles, but also as a kind of "cooperative" agent in the acts of individuals. Recall some telling phrases: "Then Peter, filled with the Holy Spirit, said . . ."; "For it has seemed good to the Holy Spirit and to us . . ."; and "Through the Holy Spirit they told Paul . . ." (Acts 4:8, 15:28, 21:4).[14] Clearly, a certain dual agency is here presupposed. Additionally, Gordon Fee, in his discussion of Paul and the Trinity, lists a variety of ways in which Paul portrays the personal agency of the Spirit acting in the lives of believers:

> The Spirit also *teaches* the content of the gospel to believers (1 Cor 2:13), *dwells* among or within believers (1 Cor 3:16; Rom 8:11; 2 Tim 1:14), *accomplishes* all things (1 Cor 12:11), *gives life* to those who believe (2 Cor 3:6), *cries out* from within our hearts (Gal 4:6), *leads* us in the ways of God (Gal 5:18; Rom 8:14), *bears witness* with our own spirits (Rom 8:16), *has desires* that are in opposition to those of the flesh (Gal 5:17), *works* all things *together* for our ultimate good (Rom 8:28), [and] *strengthens* believers (Eph 3:16).[15]

In other words, a new way of acting follows upon baptism by the Holy Spirit.[16] And behind this new ability lies the more basic fact that through the Spirit's power, access to God has, in Christ, become available in a new way. Those in the Spirit gain new abilities and a new knowledge of, and relation to, their heavenly Father, because in their baptism into Christ's death and resurrection they have become new persons (2 Cor 3:12–18).

---

14. See also Acts 2:4; 4:25, 31; 6:3, 5, 10; 11:24; 13:52; 19:21; 20:22–23.

15. Gordon Fee, "Paul and the Trinity: The Experience of Christ and the Spirit for Paul's Understanding of God," in *The Trinity* (eds. Stephen Davis, Daniel Kendall, and Gerald O'Collins; New York: Oxford University Press, 1999), 69n.32. The emphasis is his.

16. As this quote and the comparison of Matt 5–7 and Gal 5 make clear, but see also 1 Cor 12:4–11 and Acts 4:32.

This point is important for many reasons, some of which I have already discussed in chapters 4 and 5. But let me make explicit one additional implication of the preceding, as it pertains to the discussion in the next section. Christ as prophet taught as "one with authority," displaying as the Messiah of God a certain autonomy from, indeed, over *torah*. The gospel accounts make this clear on numerous occasions, and it is certainly a theme picked up by the Apostle Paul. Yet Christ does not do this merely as a human teacher, and his point is not to suggest that his disciples may claim a similar autonomy, becoming a "law unto themselves." Far from it. Insofar as Christians are called to "imitate Christ," this is never merely the individual's response to a divine or perhaps at most sublimely human archetype or teaching. Life in Christ is always the gift and work of the Holy Spirit, and entails much more than an autonomous human agent simply following a moral example or a list of imperatives. As Paul writes in Rom 7, we have died to the law, but we are now alive in Christ through our dying and rising with him in baptism: "But now, having died to that which held us bound, we are discharged from the law, to serve God in a new way, the way of the Spirit, in contrast to the old way, the way of the written code" (Rom. 7:6; cf. as well the implications of 1 Cor 12:3b). Christ, through the power of the Holy Spirit, becomes the divine agent by which the law no longer remains written on tablets of stone, but on the human heart, fulfilling the prophecy of Jer 31:31–34.

Yet at precisely this point an important further distinction must be made, especially for our age and culture, so influenced as it is still by romantic notions of the primacy of the heart in matters spiritual and moral. In the New Testament view, we are indeed freed from the law, but this means we are freed to live in the Spirit. It does not mean we are free "to follow our own heart." In biblical terms, the human heart is not autonomous, it is not in itself a source or judge but must be oriented to the proper object outside itself if it is to fulfill its purpose. Thus, Scripture often portrays the heart in contrasting terms. On the one hand, the faithful are called to "take to heart that the Lord is God in heaven above and on earth beneath" (Deut 4:39; cf. Deut 32:46) and to love God with all their heart, and to serve only him (Deut 6:5; Josh 22:5; 1 Kgs 2:4; 2 Kgs 23:25; 2 Chr 22:9, 34:31). On the other hand, not setting one's heart on God or—what amounts to the same thing— "following one's own heart" is a recipe for both disaster and divine judgment, for evil and/or idolatry are the inevitable outcome (2 Chr 12:14, 36:11–14). Indeed, it is a standard formula in the Bible that such a turning entails a rejection of God and his will: "You yourselves have done worse than your forefathers; for each of you follows the promptings of his own wicked and stubborn heart instead of obeying me" (Jer 16:12; see also Num 15:39, Job 15:12–13, Ps 10:3–4). Indeed, it often entails turning from God and serving other gods (1 Sam 7:3; 1 Kgs 11:4, 14:8–9). But Christ the prophet enables the Spirit to do its transforming work. He serves as the mediator, for joined with him through baptism in his death and resurrection, we are released to have the law written on our hearts in a new and ongoing life of the Spirit.

The Inadequacy of "Great Teacher" Christologies

The preceding observations have direct implications for the material to be discussed next. Orthodox Christian faith has always affirmed Jesus' prophetic role, but it has never understood him as *merely* a prophet or great teacher, an "exemplar" who offers spiritual wisdom or moral commands for people to accept or reject as they are inclined and able. To be sure, such an underestimation or misunderstanding appears to be a recurrent problem in understanding Christ's prophetic teaching role. It appeared during his own ministry (cf. Matt 21:11, 46; Mark 6:15; Luke 7:16; John 4:19), it reemerged in another guise during the Pelagian controversy of the fourth and fifth centuries, and it has become increasingly familiar in our era, under the influence of the Enlightenment. Particularly in its modern forms, calling Jesus a prophet has become a common device for rejecting traditional claims about his unique place and role in God's work. Voltaire was one Enlightenment figure intent upon revising the definition of "true" Christianity: "Christianity teaches nothing but simplicity, humanity, charity; to wish to reduce it to metaphysics is to make of it a source of errors."[17] In the eighteenth century, Thomas Jefferson's edited Gospels presented a truncated portrayal of Jesus as a great moral teacher—but nothing more.[18] In our own day, Marcus Borg's bestselling *Meeting Jesus Again for the First Time* classifies Jesus as one example of the genus "spirit person." Other examples include Moses and Elijah—and also Honi the Circle Drawer, Hanina ben Dosa, the Apostle Paul, the Native American Black Elk, the

---

17. Voltaire, *Philosophical Letters* (trans. Ernest Dilworth; Library of Liberal Arts; Indianapolis: Bobbs-Merrill Educational Publishing, 1961), 120.

18. See the newly reissued volume, *The Jefferson Bible: The Life and Morals of Jesus of Nazareth* (Boston: Beacon Press, 1989).

Buddha, Francis of Assisi, Muhammad, Lao-Tzu, and by implication numerous others.[19]

What is wrong with such characterizations? In one sense, nothing. They present a portrait of Jesus in keeping with the historical evidence, describing him as a thoroughly admirable figure, one who is able to keep company with a select group of other admirable, historic figures. But in another sense, of course, the Jesus thus described bears no relation to the Jesus of Scripture or traditional Christian proclamation. This historical Jesus is not God's Messiah, the royal Son sitting at the right hand of the Father, the self-sacrificing high priest who died that we might have new life, the living, life-giving Word who bestows the power of the Spirit. Rather, such characterizations present a person whom one may respect, but perhaps also ignore. Such characterizations present a person to whom we may choose to listen, but whose presence and words do not possess the divine charisma and embodied authority that compel us to listen. Such characterizations present a figure whose teachings are separable from his person, which allows us to exercise our own editorial authority over them. To reduce Jesus to one of a type is often promoted as a means to encourage inter-religious dialogue and respect, but one might be forgiven for also suspecting that it allows us to keep him at a comfortable and manageable distance. The Spirit-filled Jesus of Scripture, whose presence commanded attention, whose encounters left people either for him or against him, bears scant resemblance to such a domesticated figure.

Unfortunately, the often unrecognized correlate of keeping Jesus at arm's length, of reducing his teachings to a set of generic admonitions or principles separable from his person, is that we also thereby cut ourselves off from the power he is able to bestow. As my earlier exposition of Scripture indicated, Jesus not only taught but also granted the ability, through the power of the Spirit, to follow those teachings. Indeed, the granting of the power of the Spirit became in a very real way the identifying characteristic and gracious birthright of the church, Christ's community and living body. But in separating Jesus' teaching from his person, we also separate Christian community from its life-giving source and animating power. If his teachings are understood as standing on their own, which we may choose to follow or not, then if we do choose to abide by them, we will have to do so on our own resources.

---

19. See Marcus Borg, *Meeting Jesus Again for the First Time* (New York: HarperCollins, 1995), 31–36 and 44–45n.42.

But that means worship ceases to be an event in which the community encounters the living and life-giving God, and becomes instead an exercise in mundane social support and reinforcement. Prayer ceases to be an act of interpersonal communion from which we gain transcendent sustenance, and becomes instead an exercise in self-reflection and self-motivation. How could it be otherwise, if we transform the living and life-giving Word into a mere ideal? Having reduced Christ's teachings to abstract and inert principles, we should not be surprised that they only now possess power insofar as we are able to animate them through our own efforts.

The Danish philosopher and theologian Søren Kierkegaard addressed this practice of separating Jesus from his message in his 1844 work, *Philosophical Fragments*. In this book, Kierkegaard posed the problem in terms of the difference between the teachers Socrates and Christ.[20] Kierkegaard initiated his discussion with the question, "How far does the Truth admit of being learned?"[21] He then framed the contrasting answers in the following way. For Socrates, the truth is immediately accessible to all. Socrates does not so much "teach" students as "remind" them of what they already know, illustrating the principle that through the exercise of innate reason, the Truth is eternally available to all. Christ, by contrast, does not remind students of a Truth they already implicitly know (to the contrary, if they think they have the Truth, they are in error, indeed in sin). Rather, he offers *revelation* to *disciples*, making Truth available to them for the first time in an interpersonal encounter—an encounter that itself makes the personal reception of Truth a possibility. The scholar Louis Pojman charts Kierkegaard's distinction between the "Socratic Way" and the "Christian Way" of coming to the truth in a succinct and helpful manner:[22]

Socratic Way	Christian Way
1. Truth is within man and man is open to truth.	1. The truth is not within man; rather, man is in error, closed to the truth.

20. This was Kierkegaard's way of addressing what he saw as a personal issue in human existence, as well as the more immediate contrast between philosophical idealism (such as that offered by Lessing and Hegel) and Christianity (rightly understood).

21. Søren Kierkegaard, *Philosophical Fragments* (orig. trans. David Swenson; rev. trans. Howard Hong; Princeton: Princeton University Press, 1962), 11.

22. Louis P. Pojman, *The Logic of Subjectivity: Kierkegaard's Philosophy of Religion* (Tuscaloosa, Ala.: University of Alabama Press, 1984), 39.

Socratic Way *(cont.)*	**Christian Way** *(cont.)*
2. The teacher is incidental to the process of discovering truth.	2. The Teacher is necessary to the process of discovering the truth; he must bring it out from without and create the condition for receiving it in man.
3. The moment of discovery of the truth is accidental. The opportunity is always available; we must merely use our innate ability to recover it.	3. The moment is decisive for discovering the truth. The Eternal must break into time at a definite point (the fullness of time) and the believer must receive the condition in a moment of contemporaneity with the Teacher.

I draw attention to the fact that what enables a latter-day Christian's "contemporaneity" with the Teacher, who otherwise would be a distant figure of the past, is the living power of the Holy Spirit. It is the Spirit, the agent of Christ's conception and the one who conceives him as well in our hearts, who makes such an encounter possible and viable. Without the Holy Spirit, Christ can only be a figure of the past or a historical reconstruction. But with the Holy Spirit, Christ remains the living Lord, able to encounter and empower persons in all ages.

But what does such an encounter look like? Does it have any specific character or content? John Calvin speaks to the basic issue—the believer's continuing relation to, and dependence upon, the living Christ—by clarifying the particulars of its occurrence, namely, through the Holy Spirit's mediation of that relation through the narrative of Scripture. William Placher summarizes the Reformer's position well:

> This aspect of the Spirit's work involves two parts. First, it "enlightens" the mind; it produces "knowledge" and enables us to understand what the Bible means. Second, it "establishes the mind"; it brings our minds (and our hearts) into "a firm and steady conviction" regarding the claims embodied in the text. Amid feelings of humility and gratitude, in a life lived in obedience, Christians find that the stories the Bible tells of Christ as the revelation of God's identity have a compelling force. They sense that that force does not result from their own efforts, and Calvin, again on scriptural grounds, attributed it to the work of the Holy Spirit.

"To sum up, the Holy Spirit is the bond by which Christ effectually unites us to himself."[23]

Return this to Kierkegaard's framework. If one approaches the biblical Jesus and his teaching as nothing more than a compilation of general religious and ethical truths, then this Jesus can at most only "throw light" on the truth, leaving the student to realize and act upon it. But if one approaches the biblical Jesus openly expecting a living encounter, through the Spirit's active intervention, then he will not only enlighten the mind but also establish it in truth. That is, this Teacher will not only present, but also make real what he teaches, in an act of grace enabling the disciple to achieve that which she or he could not on her or his own. Notice as well the described attitude and posture that necessarily accompanies this establishment: a firm conviction of the heart as well as mind, accompanied by humility, gratitude, and obedience. This knowledge can never be received in a detached or impersonal manner. Indeed, because of its living and personal nature, it makes a claim and requires a response.

These various observations should help indicate some of the ways in which seeing Christ as merely a prophet or great teacher misconstrues his true significance and transforming power. To be sure, he truly is a prophet and great teacher, but these must be understood as expansive rather than limiting titles. Similarly, we may address the same underlying issue by also considering what it means to call Christ an "exemplar," especially given the fact that one common understanding of the atonement often bears the label "moral exemplar" theory. How is "exemplar" understood? If Jesus Christ is our "exemplar," does this mean that he is unique in his person and work? Does he establish the pattern to which, by God's justifying and sanctifying grace, we will all be conformed? Students of the Christian tradition know that the "imitation of Christ" has a long and orthodox history. The Apostle Paul, in his preamble to the famous christological hymn of Phil 2, writes: "If then there is any encouragement in Christ, any consolation from love, any sharing in the Spirit. . . .

---

23. William Placher, *The Domestication of Transcendence: How Modern Thinking about God Went Wrong* (Louisville, Ky.: Westminster John Knox Press, 1996), 67. Placher draws on Calvin's *Commentaries on the Epistle of Paul to the Ephesians* (on Eph 1:13) and from *Institutes of the Christian Religion*, vols. 20 and 21 (Library of Christian Classics; ed. John Baillie, John T. McNeill, and Henry P. Van Dusen; trans. Ford Lewis Battles; Philadelphia: The Westminster Press, 1960), 3.1.1.

Let the same mind be in you that you have in Christ Jesus . . ." (Phil 2:1, 5). Similarly, in his Letter to the Romans, Paul describes those whom God "predestined to be conformed to the image of his Son" (Rom 8:29), which establishes the basis for his later admonition, "Do not be conformed to his world, but be transformed by the renewing of your minds . . ." (Rom 12:2). These passages indicate that the imitation of Christ becomes a possibility only as a result of the initial and sustaining activity of God. In this sense, an imitation of Christ is definitely not an act of the individual's will, an autonomous effort of spiritual virtuosity. Quite the contrary, it is the opening up of one's self to the transcendent God and transformative power of the Spirit, that one's old self might be recreated in Christ.

Yet characterizing Christ as "exemplar" can indeed mean something quite different. It has been used to diminish Christ's role and significance, to bring it down to a more mundane level. It may be a way of saying that he only provides an example, and if we are to follow it, we are left to our own abilities and efforts. The imaginative and practical framework has shifted. Instead of focusing on how God's eschatological regeneration of us through Christ enables us to put on all Christ-like graces, the focus concentrates instead on our own self-improvement, albeit following Christ's lead. Or, from a different and more extreme angle, it may be a way of saying that Christ is only one example among others, that he only illustrates an ideal or principle and is in fact dispensable once we grasp the concept "behind" him. This second way of understanding Christ's "example" is actually the more pernicious. While the first makes the mistake of reducing Christ to an ethical exemplar, he at least retains the privileged and practical position of role model. The second way suggests that Christ's example is finally dispensable, once one has grasped the larger point or principle he presents. Christ might be illustrative, but he is not constitutive for the ongoing life of faith.

Given such potential problems, might Christianity be well advised to avoid a "moral exemplar" understanding of Christ's person and work? Is the problem inseparable from the very nature of the model? My response to both questions is no. As indicated above, Scripture itself presents something very much like this "model" as one aspect of Christ's atoning work, which is sufficient warrant for its continued theological consideration and pastoral use. But as I have also indicated, this understanding may be developed in both appropriate and inappropriate ways. To offer a final illustration of these ways, let me present a very brief historical comparison between two advocates of the view. The classic proponent of the "moral exemplar" model of the atonement is typically said to be the medieval scholastic Peter Abelard (1079–1142).[24] He proposed this model as an explicit alternative to Anselm's "substitutionary" view of the atonement, which to his mind raised more theological problems than it solved. He argued for a change of focus, namely, that Christ's death be seen not as effecting a transformation in God (as if the Father could not forgive humanity until the Son's propitiatory act changed his mind!) but as effecting a transformation in human hearts. That is, Christ's crucifixion is better understood as an example, indeed, as the supreme revelation of God's self-giving and forgiving love for humanity than it is as an intra-divine transaction paying off a human debt that could not otherwise be met. To Abelard, the effect of such self-sacrificial love is its power to transform the hearts of those who witness it from a fear of God to love and gratitude toward God.

> By the faith which we hold concerning Christ love is increased in us, by virtue of the conviction that God in Christ has united our human nature to himself and, by suffering in that same nature, has demonstrated to us that perfection of love of which he himself says: "Greater love than this no man hath," etc. So we, through his grace, are joined to him as closely as to our neighbor by an indissoluble bond of affection [*Amor*]. . . . A righteousness, I say, imparted to all the faithful in the higher part of their being—in the soul, where alone love can exist—and not a matter of the display of outward works.[25]

One should recognize that Abelard's position may only be correctly understood when viewed within the broader sacramental and pietistic context of medieval Catholicism. Assumptions about the believer's reception of Christ in the Eucharist and meditative practices focusing on Christ's suffering love lend Abelard's theory a reality and substance that modern interpreters might miss in labeling it a "subjective" theory of the atonement.

Indeed, on this last point some will argue that our current evaluation of Abelard's stance owes more to the interpretation of Hastings

---

24. His argument appears in his *Exposition of the Epistle to the Romans*, which most students of theology know only in abbreviated form, in Eugene R. Fairweather, ed. and trans., *A Scholastic Miscellany: Anselm to Ockham* (Library of Christian Classics, vol. 10; Louisville, Ky.: Westminster/John Knox Press, 1956), 276–87.

25. Fairweather, *A Scholastic Miscellany*, 278.

Rashdall than it does the interpretation of Abelard's own writings.
Rashdall's 1915 Bampton Lectures sought to popularize the medieval
scholastic's theory, but one cannot help sense that in the process he lost
some of Abelard's nuance and complexity.[26] For example, Rashdall does
acknowledge in passing that there are "of course passages in Abelard in
which the death of Christ is treated in the conventional way as a 'sacrifice,' a punishment, etc.," but he claims this should not be surprising,
"since Abelard was professing to explain the doctrine of the New
Testament (including St. Paul) and of the church and not to supersede
it."[27] Now Abelard did indeed have a high opinion of himself and his
abilities, but Rashdall's comment implies that he gave credence to his
own theory alone, and none to the doctrine taught by the New
Testament and the church. More than that, Rashdall summarizes
Abelard's position in a way that the latter would have found mislead-
ingly simplistic, if not simply wrong:

> In Abelard not only the ransom theory but any kind of substitutionary
> or expiatory atonement is explicitly denied. We get rid altogether of the
> notion of a mysterious guilt which, by an abstract necessity of things,
> required to be extinguished by death or suffering, no matter whose, and
> of all pseudo-Platonic hypostasizing of the universal "Humanity." The
> efficacy of Christ's death is now quite definitely and explicitly explained
> by its subjective influence upon the mind of the sinner. The voluntary
> death of the innocent Son of God on man's behalf moves the sinner to
> gratitude and answering love—and so to consciousness of sin, repen-
> tance, amendment.[28]

Abelard did not, in fact, eliminate "all pseudo-Platonic hypostasizing of
the universal 'Humanity'" from his understanding of Christ's relation to
us. To the contrary, Abelard's theory depends upon the assumption of
the (increasing) union between Christ the exemplar and the faithful.
Christ's self-sacrificial love awakens love in the hearts of believers, but
it is anachronistic of Rashdall to imply that this is a purely "subjective
influence" that "moves" the sinner. Rashdall appears to be describing an
individual's emotional response, whereas Abelard is concerned to

---

26. Hastings Rashdall, *The Idea of the Atonement in Christian Theology* (1915 Bampton
Lectures; London: Macmillan and Co., Ltd., 1920).

27. Ibid., 359n.2.

28. Ibid., 358.

describe the effect produced through the imparting of a (by definition, supernatural) grace.

Why does Rashdall present Abelard this way? Apparently in order to buttress his own theological take on the atonement. For what matters most to him is the revelation of self-giving love as the highest moral and religious ideal.[29] He is willing to say that Christ represents "the culminating, supreme, and unique revelation" of God (which is posited on the assumption that "God is to some extent revealed in all men"),[30] but Christ's revelation may be distilled down to one word: love. The love Christ showed in his life, teaching, and death stands as the supreme revelation of God's character, the clearest manifestation of God's love for us, and the one true ideal by which humanity will be saved from sin and attain the highest perfection of which it is capable.[31] Consider the way Rashdall translates into

> more modern language the meaning of the church's early creed, "There is none other ideal given among men by which we may be saved except the moral ideal which Christ taught by His words, and illustrated by His life and death of love: and there is none other help so great in the attainment of that ideal as the belief in God as He has been supremely revealed in Him who so taught and lived and died." So understood, the self-sacrificing life which was consummated by the death upon the Cross has indeed power to take away the sins of the whole world.[32]

For all Rashdall's talk of Christ's unique role, in his thoroughly modern understanding of the atonement, Christ is finally only incidental and not essential. Whenever and wherever humanity has recognized or acted out of self-giving love, it acts upon and displays the divine ideal. In historical and practical terms, Christ has been and may continue to be an effective illustration of the love ideal. But he is not necessary for its realization, and thus he is separable from it.

But why is this finally a problem? Why should an exemplarist model of Christ's atoning work understood in this way be considered inadequate? How could it be wrong for human beings to show self-giving

---

29. This summarizes a theme woven with various strands throughout his final lecture, found on pp. 435–64.
30. Rashdall, *Atonement*, 448.
31. Ibid., 450, 453, and 463.
32. Ibid., 463.

love and altruism in imitation of Jesus—or to show it for whatever reason? In one sense, of course, one should encourage altruism whatever the source of its motivation. But in light of a trinitarian understanding of the atonement, one recognizes that merely exemplarist models portray Christ's revelatory "example" in ultimately passive terms, rather than active ones (cf. Matt 11:25–27 // Luke 10:21–22). They do not recognize that in his prophetic office, he does not merely teach us that character of life for humanity that God the Father intends as our original and final *telos*. Nor does he merely exemplify that life. Rather, as God the Son acting in effect as the perichoretical agent of God the Holy Spirit, he also endows us with the power to realize that end. If we are to be true to the scriptural narrative, we must reaffirm Christ's promise, made to his disciples and to us: "If you love me, you will keep my commandments. And I will ask the Father, and he will give you another Advocate, to be with you forever. This is the Spirit of truth, whom the world cannot receive, because it neither sees him nor knows him. You know him, because he abides with you, and he will be in you" (John 14:15–17; cf. John 16:13–14). Christ the Prophet, the Spirit's living and life-giving Word, does not leave us to our own devices, but quite literally inspires and enthusiastically empowers us to enact what he proclaims.[33]

Systematic Location and Theological Implications

Given the unfolding logic of my project, it may be obvious why I believe this aspect of Christ's atoning work should be considered third: there is a soteriological correspondence to the theological place of the Holy Spirit "after" the Father and the Son. To use a farming metaphor, the ground must be prepared to receive the gift of the Spirit. That is, now that the principalities and powers have been defeated, now that the pollution of human sin and guilt has been washed away, the new creation can take root and grow. This aspect of the Messiah's work is accomplished through the outpouring of the Holy Spirit. Moreover, the Spirit represents and is the effective agent of God's eschatological future. As Christ the King's work served to reclaim creation from its past bondage for the Father's original intentions, as Christ the Priest's work served to reclaim, indeed, establish a free and truly open present, so, too, does

---

33. Of course, given the literal meaning of "enthusiasm" (to be filled or possessed by God), it is somewhat redundant to also speak of "inspiration."

Christ the Prophet's work proclaim and serve the in-breaking power of God's intended future for humanity and all creation.

Such an ordering of Christ the Prophet's work also helps alleviate certain misunderstandings. For one, to consider this aspect of Christ's work apart from the Spirit's empowering agency would run the risk of Pelagianism. For another, to neglect it might suggest the faithful are not to build on the new creation they have become through Christ's royal victory and the restored communion they have been granted through his priestly sacrifice. But in the power of the Spirit, the disciples can truly understand who Jesus was and what he taught; now they truly understand the whole story, and can spread the good news of Christ. Now the new community knows that it may live as children of God, adopted through the Spirit and guided by that Spirit. Recall the conversations of chapter 1, which noted that this aspect of Christ's work also assumes that a particular kind of divide exists between God and humanity, a divide that requires bridging. In this instance, the divide is caused less by bondage to oppressive powers or the guilt of human sinfulness; rather it is due to human weakness or ignorance or finitude, uncertainty about one's meaning or purpose, a misinformed identity or a misplaced fear of God. Given God's victory and sacrifice in Christ, what humans now need are instruction and example and a vision that shows them a better way, that implants in them a sense of meaning and hope and leads them toward their God-given fulfillment. This Christ the Prophet and living Word provides through his teachings, his self-sacrificial death and his gift of the Spirit. By these means, God reveals divine love—and offers an example that, in the power of the Holy Spirit, transforms those who come in contact with it. "You shall know the truth, and the truth shall set you free" (John 8:32). Knowing this truth and embracing this freedom means that new life in the Spirit becomes a reality—and anything but complacent. The faithful will face the future with joy and hope, embracing their accountability toward God and actively engaging in their part of God's plan for creation. Such engagement will be both personal and social, and it may be constructive or it may require resistance, life in the Spirit will still require the discerning of the spirits (cf. Rom 12:2 and 1 John 4:1), but it will never be absent.

In all this, God the Holy Spirit works through the incarnate Son, Jesus, who becomes Christ the Prophet on the basis of what he accomplishes in reestablishing God's truth and will in an ignorant, misguided world. In other words, this aspect of Christ's atoning work also reveals itself as the simultaneous and appropriate trinitarian work of the Holy

Spirit. This should not be surprising, for the prophetic voice has always been that of the Spirit ("The Spirit of the Lord is upon me"; cf. as one example Isa 61:1–2 and Luke 4:18–19), just as the vivifying power of God also comes through the Spirit ("I will put my spirit within you, and you shall live"; Ezek 37:14a; cf. Pss 33:6 and 104:29–30). The Christian faith affirms that the voice of the Spirit finds its fulfillment in the Word of Christ. Recall that it anoints Jesus at his baptism (Matt 3:16 // Mark 1:10 // Luke 3:22; cf. Jn 1:32), that Jesus rejoices in it during his ministry (Luke 10:21), and that it is what Jesus offers up finally in return to God (Matt 27:50; Luke 23:46; John 19:30). One may even say that the Spirit uses Christ as the mediator or conduit for reaching his followers, both the disciples during his earthly ministry and the Christian community following his ascension.[34] In this way, Christ remains a prophet, indeed, the Prophet, the Spirit's living and life-giving Word.

This last point warrants clarification. It is commonly argued nowadays that in the Western theological tradition, the role of the Spirit has often been subservient to or submerged in that of the Son. To correct any such imbalance, it has been appropriate to reconsider and reemphasize the particular agency and role of the Spirit. Thus, for example, I have clarified that Christ is not merely an "exemplar" whom we imitate on the basis of our own resources and efforts; rather, he is an exemplar whom we may faithfully imitate only in the power of the Holy Spirit. In this sense, Christ's place and function in the Christian life cannot be understood appropriately apart from the continuing vivifying role of the Holy Spirit. But having said this, one should also recognize that neither can the continuing role of the Holy Spirit be understood appropriately apart from the continuing particularity of Christ. That is, the needed theological reemphasis on the place and role of the Holy Spirit in the Christian life must not be accomplished at the cost of deemphasizing or even disregarding the place and role of Christ. Christ stands as the specific "content" of God's reconciling will, while the Spirit acts as the agent effecting that content's realization in the world. To recall Irenaeus's image, the Son and Spirit are the Father's two hands—they complement and complete one another, and both are necessary for an adequate understanding of God's atoning work.

---

34. See references to Christ's baptizing with the Spirit (Matt 3:11 // Mark 1:8 // Luke 3:16, John 1:33, Acts 1:5; cf. John 20:21–22) and Jesus' various promises regarding the Spirit being with them (e.g., Matt 10:19–20 // Mark 13:11 and John 14:26; John 15:26, 16:13–15).

But why is this important? What are the theological implications of this general claim? Recall the assertion that Christ the Prophet both revealed the truth and enabled those with whom he came in contact to accept that truth on faith. The repeated references to Jesus as one who taught "with authority" may be unpacked in several ways, but at least one must be that his auditors not only heard his words but were also convinced of their truthfulness. The faithful received his words not as something to consider and debate and perhaps accept, but as something immediately life changing. Using Calvin's later distinction, the words of good news did not merely flit about in the brain but took root in the heart.[35] And this revelatory word and transformative power remain available to the faithful today. Christ the Prophet continues his life-changing proclamation of the truth through the inner testimony of the Holy Spirit. He addresses us personally, and calls us by name. He presents us with a God-given vision of reality, and then offers us the means by which we may embrace, indeed, live into that original and new reality.

This claim is significant for several reasons. In modern theological conversations, it has become a cliché to say that Christ did not reveal "doctrines" but a divine attitude or a relation or an existential way of being. Metaphysical claims of the traditional sort are ruled out. This change in assumption stemmed in part from Kant's *Critique of Pure Reason*, which argued that if a "noumenal" or transcendent realm exists, it is in any event epistemologically inaccessible to us, and thus closed to any meaningful statements describing it. The naturalistic assumptions of scientific methodology, as well as some of the critical and reductionistic philosophies of the emerging modern era,[36] reinforced this assumption. Thus we have the "father of Liberal Protestantism," Friedrich Schleiermacher, adjusting the Christian tradition to say that theological statements do not make any objective claim to "knowing" (and are not reducible to a "doing"), but are derived from a universal, though historically conditioned, human "feeling." This "turn to the subject" typified much of Protestant theology in the nineteenth century. However, the critiques of this approach by the neo-orthodox theologians of the early twentieth century and the postmodern theologians of our own day have reduced its persuasiveness. In this context, I, too, contend that Christ's revelation claims to "know" something—and tell us something—about

---

35. Calvin, *Institutes*, 1.5.9, 61–62.

36. Consider, for example, the works of Hume, David Friedrich Strauss, Marx, and Nietzsche.

God, the world, and ourselves. And this knowledge can transform us, which makes it one aspect of God's grace toward us.

This modern emphasis upon "religious subjectivism" may also take another, unnecessarily limiting, form. In some contemporary circles there appears to be a suspicion of the value of knowledge that is given to us, rather than learned through our own experience or rooted in our own meditation. As a corollary, some will insist that one cannot truly know something until one has experienced it. In one sense this latter point is certainly accurate. But in another sense both claims are misleading, given the manner in which knowledge actually determines one's experience. That is, one must recognize that raw—which is to say, uninterpreted—experience is essentially meaningless. For experience to mean anything at all, it must be fit into some kind of explanatory framework. Indeed, without such a framework, without some prior categories, an "experience" may pass us by unnoticed. Assuming this to be the case, then, taking matters one step further, we may also acknowledge that a new explanatory framework may enable one to perceive new things, to *experience* the world differently. Certainly this is what key scientific theories have done for us. Why else would the label "Copernican Revolution" have emerged, if not to express how a new idea and a new description of things can change our entire outlook, even regarding matters with no direct relation to the new idea? Darwin's theory of evolution through natural selection certainly counts as another such idea, as does Einstein's theory of relativity. In one respect, each thinker only made claims about how the world or cosmos works within the rather narrow confines of his particular discipline. But, of course, in another respect, each of their claims had an earth-shaking impact on humanity's perception of "the way things really are," even though the actual experience of those things presumably did not change. The stars and planets did not actually "look different," even to Copernicus himself, while evolution and relativity are not, strictly speaking, something we "experience" at all. But once a new framework enables us to "see" new things, once we become convinced that a new framework explains reality more accurately and fully, then we do typically see the whole of reality differently. I suggest that this is precisely what the teaching of Christ the Prophet does, this is what his revelation accomplishes: it changes our perception of "the way things really are."

Moreover, if we embrace such a changed perception, then it cannot help but transform our lives. In this sense, we may speak of "living into the revelation of God." But this living transformation is not merely something we effect on our own, for God's revelation includes the promise of the Holy Spirit. That is, once we have entered this new life, we will recognize that our entrance into it was the work of God's own Spirit. The frequently over-used image of a "paradigm shift" is appropriate here: there was nothing in the prior worldview that would necessarily or logically lead to this changed perception, but once the jump has been made, it becomes self-confirming in a number of ways. Let me illustrate this point by connecting it with the traditional Christian doctrine of inspiration. It is a commonplace of that tradition, especially in the Reformed heritage, to assume the divine inspiration of Holy Scripture. It is God's Word, and the agent that makes it such is the Holy Spirit. The Spirit acts as the intermediary between God the Father speaking his gracious Word to the Bible's diverse human authors. Yet another aspect of that Reformed tradition, although often less well known, is the recognition that the Holy Spirit is required not just in the writing or proclaiming of Scripture, but in the hearing of it. For the Bible to be *received* as God's Word requires the inspiration of the Holy Spirit as well.[37] Christ's prophetic office functions in precisely the same manner. This office comprises that aspect of the Son's messianic work displaying the perichoretical imprint of the Spirit. That being the case, I would add that the Spirit acts not only in giving voice to Christ's teachings, but in enabling our continued hearing and following of them. Indeed, the Spirit acts to undergird and enable every moment of the Christian's life.

Such a claim regarding the Spirit's ongoing sustenance of our life in Christ is hardly new to Christian belief, but why make an explicit point of it here? For one thing, in an age when many Christians tend to reduce theology to ethics or "spirituality," it helps the church avoid an excessively moralistic or privatistic understanding of the Christian faith. To use a more traditional Protestant term, it helps avoid "works righteousness." More to the point, it is a particular weakness of the "moral exemplar" theory of atonement, especially in its modern forms, to be construed in an all too natural and individualistic manner. When Christ is portrayed as the good or sublime teacher, his "students" are typically left to fend for themselves in assimilating and applying his lessons. But such a construal makes it much more likely that the scriptural

---

37. Karl Barth in particular makes this point both eloquently and at length, but Calvin and numerous Reformed confessions established it much earlier.

narratives testifying to the Spirit's continued presence in the church, the body of Christ, will likewise be downplayed or ignored. Yet without a recognition and embrace of the Spirit's continued presence and activity in the community as such, any truly collective understanding of the Christian life becomes impossible. But with such a recognition and embrace of the Spirit's ongoing presence and activity, a real transformation in the life of a people becomes possible.

And this should not be taken as describing a merely present reality, or even simple extrapolations from that reality. The Spirit's starting point is not so much where we are, as where God intends us to be. As the Old Testament prophets did before him, Christ tells us the will and purposes of God, what we are to do and what we are to become. But Christ also enables, through the power of the Spirit, the all-encompassing future into which we are moving. It is fashionable in scholarly circles to say that prophecy is not about predicting the future, but about changing one's heart and deeds to comply with God's will. That is, it is not so much a matter of "foretelling," but "forthtelling." Certainly prophecy includes this "forthtelling" aspect. Yet I do not want to lose all sense that prophecy also contains statements about the future. Put simply, Christ the Prophet does indeed reveal to us our true and final end, the goal or *telos* that God intends for us and all creation, as we and it are transformed through the power of the Holy Spirit. Christ the Prophet grants us knowledge of a new reality—new to us, but in fact envisioned by God from before creation—and as the living life-giving Word of the Spirit, he also enables us to realize that reality, both now and as it beckons to us from creation's eschatological consummation. In the power of the Spirit, Christ remains in continued and immediate relation with the faithful. To be sure, God is providentially present throughout creation. But the church is the community of those who know this to be so, and who live and act in the eschatological awareness that this is the "year of the Lord's favor."

Pastoral Applications

Why does such knowledge matter? And what practical difference does it make to insist that this aspect of Christ's work include the ongoing activity of the Holy Spirit? These two questions will guide the remaining reflections as this chapter concludes. Such knowledge matters because it saves us from meaninglessness and aimlessness, while presenting to us the rich and fulfilling communion that is our true end.

Recall the conversation from chapter 1, which discussed the nagging doubts and sense of futility our human finitude can evoke. The lack of meaning or purpose can be enormously dispiriting, while the recognition and embrace of meaning and purpose is just the opposite, that is, vitally inspiring. Indeed, Christians should recognize this "inspiring" as "in-Spiriting," a gift of the Spirit, "the Lord, the giver of life." Christ the Prophet encounters us with a vision and a summons, empowering us for life and creating a bond of unity for a people, thereby offering a sign of hope for all peoples, indeed, for all creation.

Of course, such knowledge, meaning, and purpose, such inspiration, can be too easily understood in merely psychological or sentimental terms, and it should not be. Christ's living, life-giving Word is not a panacea that banishes all of life's challenges and tragedy. But it does offer, in the midst of challenges and tragedies, a larger framework of meaning and a longer view. Humans are capable of bearing untold burdens, if they understand that doing so has some meaning or purpose, while courage and perseverance crumble when faced with suffering that seems simply pointless. In the context of our finitude, true knowledge can be liberating: truly knowing who we are, truly knowing our limitations, truly knowing our end as God's beloved creatures can set us free from the imaginings of our heart, the vain images of our age, and all unrealistic expectations that cloud our vision. For example, human effort and striving can produce magnificent achievements, but one should not expect the magnificent to be the norm. As C. S. Lewis somewhere observed, "The mistake of the Stoics was thinking we can do all of the time what we can do some of the time." Knowing and embracing our human limitations enables us to be more humane toward one another and accepting of each other's gifts and shortcomings. It can also free us from any misplaced sense of our own inadequacy.

In a similar example, the strength and vigor of youth are a glory of human existence, and are rightly celebrated. But in a culture obsessed with youth and its beauty, have they become idols? Does our zeal for health and fitness betray a hidden terror of our mortality? Knowing and embracing both our mortality and our glorious future among the company of heaven can free us to accept with dignity and grace our inevitable aging and death. It can allow us to let go, a truly liberating gift to those obsessed with always "being in control," and offer our lives fully to God. There is a reason the Creed refers to the Holy Spirit as "the Lord the giver of life": not only is the Spirit the agent whose breath animates the living at their creation, but the Spirit also animates creatures in their re-creation. The Spirit does not simply exercise its power in the past, but also reaches out to us from the future, drawing us into the fullness of life that God intends for us from all eternity. And it gives such life as "the Lord," as one with authority and to whom we owe allegiance. All this together establishes the basis of Christian hope, which does not consist of subjective desires or wishful thinking on our part, but stems from the God-given reality and communion that shapes and animates us with ever greater power from an ever diminishing distance.

Christ's prophetic word reveals our true destiny and the assurance that its final realization lies entirely in God's gracious and almighty hands, a conviction enabled by the Spirit, who thereby also liberates us to live more fully and richly in the everyday demands or doldrums of our present life. Knowing the truth of God gives us a context and a goal that transcends the narrow, the ideological, the banal, and the all too often debilitating perspectives contending for attention in our contemporary consumer culture. God's truth enables us to clear our eyes and see the truth about ourselves for the first time: we are not merely the sum of our desires, perpetually stoked to consume an endless string of material goods, sexual partners, "extreme" adventures, or even spiritual experiences in the name of individual self-fulfillment. Nor are we merely the sum of our many and often frenetic activities—whether that consists of sixty-hour work weeks or the busy-ness of a student's schedule filled from morning to night (or the parent who spends countless hours as that student's "servant" and chauffeur). Nor are we merely the sum of our misfortunes—whether that consists of personal or family illness or loss, poverty, discrimination, or simply "bad luck." God's truth enables us to recognize that nothing in this life or this world has the power and right to define who we are, for that truth comes to us exclusively from our Creator, who is also our final end. This is the true reality proclaimed by Christ, which he gives us through the power of the Spirit.

But how do we come to know all this? How are we convinced of it? It is not an abstract principle we discover or deduce, and it is not even a lesson we learn through our own experience. Rather, it is living reality that comes to us through personal encounter and address. This reality is not merely an "interior" or "spiritual" attitude, but must be acknowledged as a new and external reality—a point manifested by the fact that at Pentecost the Spirit empowered not just individuals, but established a new community, one open to all nations and all ages (Acts 2). As the biblical narratives of humanity's creation indicate, we were not meant to be alone (Gen 2:18). We were intended to be in deep and intimate communion with God and one another—even if those same narratives also indicate how such communion has been derailed, if not destroyed, and a sense of our true end lost.[38] But Christ the Prophet summons us to reclaim our birthright of meaning and communion, and grants the power of the Spirit to make it a reality. Such an encounter may occur as an extraordinary event in the life of an individual or a group. But more typically, Christ's prophetic word to us is made a living reality through the power of the Spirit in the life of the church, in particular its ongoing worship. Indeed, this living reality is both the presupposition and the effect of that worship, as it is embodied in corporate liturgy and individual devotions.

Worship serves as the divinely ordained nexus that constitutes the people of God as such. It is the regularly recurring event in which the community is built up, or "edified," through the practices of preaching, sacrament, prayer, praise, hymn singing, and the like. It represents the God-given time when Christ's presence may be assumed as irrevocably given (Matt 18:20). And it also represents the Word that Christ himself taught and embodied, in effect translating the worshipping community, through the power of Christ's Spirit, from its old reality into the presence of God's new and eschatological reality. Christian worship is that event constituted by Christ's new story, and not the world's old story, even as it is an event shaping its participants toward their God-given end.

Consider the implications were Christ's living and life-giving word *not* present for us in prayer and in preaching, and in the sacraments of baptism and the Lord's Supper.[39] Prayer would become impossible, its very meaning and purpose undercut. No longer could it be an interpersonal dialogue, but at most only an exercise in self-reflection or self-motivation. And the problem would not be resolved by having silent, personal prayer become spoken, communal prayer, even though individuals might thereby gain the support of the group. For if Christ's Spirit is not understood to be an independent, empowering participant in the life of the community, then any understanding of that community's

---

38. Consider the Genesis accounts of the fall, Cain's slaying of Abel, the flood, and the Tower of Babel (Gen 3:7ff., 4:3ff., 6:5ff., and 11:1ff.).

39. Recall the *Westminster Shorter Catechism,* question and answer 88: "What are the outward means whereby Christ communicateth to us the benefits of redemption? The outward and ordinary means whereby Christ communicateth to us the benefits of redemption are his ordinances, especially the Word, sacraments and prayer. . . ." *The Constitution of the Presbyterian Church (U.S.A.) Part 1: Book of Confessions* (Louisville, Ky.: The Office of the General Assembly, 1991), sec. 7.088.

interactions can only be mundane. Similarly, preaching would be merely the minister's opinion—or perhaps an expression of the congregation's "collective consciousness"—but not a means by which the Spirit enables Christ's personal address to those in need of the gospel. Baptism might signal an initiation into the group, but not a dying to the old and rising to Christ's in-breaking future. And the Lord's Supper could be a moving experience of communal solidarity and hospitality, but not a participation in the eschatological banquet of God, a sign of the transcendent and eternal communion intended for us all. Such "worship" would cease to be an event in which the people of God encounter God, and become instead merely an exercise in group dynamics and stimulation: perhaps a thought-provoking aesthetic experience, perhaps an energizing "pep rally," but not true worship.

Of course, the Christian faith does not assume the Holy Spirit will be absent. To the contrary, every aspect of worship may be understood as the work of the Holy Spirit realizing that which Christ the Prophet, the living Word, reveals. Christ summons us to our true reality and fulfillment, and worship grants us a foretaste of that destiny. In this, Christ serves as the teacher and moral exemplar building up his people and establishing a new reality. This is why it is important to recall worship's necessarily "edifying" nature:

> From the very beginning Reformed theologians have been fond of speaking of worship as being edifying. Martin Bucer in particular liked to use this word to describe Christian worship. He had in mind that passage where the Apostle Paul tells us that everything in the service of worship should edify the church (1 Cor 14:1–6), that is, should teach or build up the church. Worship which puts first the praise of God's glory, worship which is according to God's Word, worship which serves God and God alone does in fact edify the church. It edifies the church because it is the work of the Holy Spirit in the body of Christ. . . . Worship is the workshop where we are transformed into his [God's] image.[40]

The church's worship can work this transformation precisely because it is there we most commonly, collectively, and recurrently encounter Christ's prophetic vision of God's redemptive plan for the whole of creation. And

---

40. Hughes Oliphant Old, *Worship That Is Reformed According to Scripture* (eds. John H. Leith and John W. Kuykendall; Guides to the Reformed Tradition; Atlanta: John Knox Press, 1984), 8.

it is there that we are most commonly, collectively, and recurrently offered access to Christ's empowering Spirit, that God's "countercultural" vision of a new heaven and a new earth might become a reality.

Finally, as a complement to the preceding comments on the church's communal worship, I would suggest that in understanding Christ as the one revealing our true end (as "prophet" or "teacher," as "guide" or "pastor"), we may also, indeed must, conceive of him in the most personal, particular, and attentive terms. In the parables of the Lost Sheep, the Lost Coin, and the Lost Son (Luke 15:1–32), Jesus makes it clear that God cares for persons in their particularity. The story of Jesus' conversation with the Samaritan woman at the well makes much the same point. He does not offer her a general lesson or platitudes, but speaks to her directly, aware of the intimate details of her past and selecting his words to her accordingly. Individuals matter to God; God knows and cares about them in their individuality. They are not simply faces in a crowd—or even faces in a congregation. Pastorally, this point probably cannot be emphasized enough. But its prior theological basis should also be made clear: God displays this personal care and concern precisely as a reflection of his own personal and particular nature. To put it in a "negative" rule of thumb, one cannot expect particular care from a generic God. This is why Jesus' prophetic teaching must never be reduced to an abstract principle or ideal, however noble or moving. Put more positively, much of Jesus' teaching is about nothing other than the very particular nature and "personality" of God: as the loving Father, as the one more than willing to forgive, as overflowing with gracious care and concern. This is the recurring content of Christ's prophetic message, a message that will take root and grow in our hearts, transforming even our present reality, if we but allow Christ's Spirit to address us personally, and bring us to our God-given end.

7

Some Integrating and Concluding Remarks

Do not answer fools according to their folly,
    or you will be a fool yourself.
Answer fools according to their folly,
    or they will be wise in their own eyes.
    (Prov 26:4-5)

As this book draws to a close, one might be tempted to assume that these words from Proverbs are suggesting two alternative responses to the proposals presented in this book. Of course, I am mindful that humility in the making of theological claims is always appropriate, so I pray that the reflections I have offered are not folly, but may bear useful and faithful fruit. I have sought to present an understanding of the atonement in accord with Scripture and drawing upon classic, especially Reformed, Christian tradition. I have also intended that this proposal display theological integrity and help foster coherent theological reflection. And, perhaps most crucially, I have sought to offer a framework and constructive interpretation that serve the practical pastoral task of proclaiming the good news of God's atoning work, a work accomplished in the intertwining activity of the Father, Son, and Holy Spirit.

That divine work of atonement, of making "at one," inevitably takes diverse forms because human beings, individually and collectively, are separated from God in diverse ways. All persons are in some manner held in captivity to oppressive powers, all are in some manner alienated by their own sin and guilt, and all are in some manner floundering due to their human limitations, ignorance, or weakness. Yet no one is separated in these several ways to the same degree, or at the same time—whether this refers to an individual's own life or that individual compared with others. Thus, the proclamation of the good news of God's atoning work will, indeed must, vary in its emphases according to context, audience, and moment in time. Pastors and teachers—indeed, all Christians ministering in their diverse ways—must discern when, in their witnessing and pastoral care, to speak the redeeming and liberating word of the Father's messianic victory in Christ, or the forgiving and reconciling word of the Son's messianic sacrifice as Christ, or the enlightening and empowering word of the Spirit's messianic instruction and exhortation in Christ. Just as crucially, Christian ministers must also know when *not* to speak a particular word, because a given context may make a *mis*hearing inevitable, transforming the gospel from the word of life into a life-corrupting or killing word. Each of the described aspects of Christ's redemptive work is an intrinsic aspect of the gospel witness. But just as the triune God is gracious and wise, reaching out in Christ to humanity where it is, so, too, should Christ's ministers show an analogously gracious, and wise discernment in their preaching, teaching, and care. I hope that my reflections offer such ordained or lay ministers a framework with which to understand and accomplish that task more fruitfully and faithfully.

These points made, I am mindful of the limitations of this book. Practically speaking, it offers nothing more than a tool: three complementary ways, grounded in the act of the triune God, of framing and presenting the gospel message of atonement. The actual efficacy of this tool will depend finally upon the skill with which the pastor is able to discern the spirits and be open to the prompting of the Holy Spirit in particular settings and circumstances. After all, the gospel message of Scripture does not speak itself, but must be proclaimed. Likewise, if the preceding chapters have any value, that value will not apply itself, but must be applied. The quotation from Proverbs heading up this chapter exemplifies the point I am trying to make. These two verses, linked as they are, illustrate the fact that Scripture functions as Scripture only insofar as one has a living relation to it. Scripture serves as the source and norm for Christian faith, but it does not do so in a mechanical or automatic fashion, as these two verses demonstrate. After all, they each posit the same basic situation, yet offer antithetical advice. It would be naïve to suppose that the compilers of Proverbs did not notice the tension. One can only conclude that they linked these verses in order to teach yet one more lesson, namely, the importance of discernment. Regardless of how similar two situations may appear, one must always exercise careful judgment in how to speak and act, based on the persons, circumstances, and history involved. The book of Proverbs may belong to the "wisdom literature" of the Bible, but wisdom itself can only belong to persons. True wisdom shows itself not in formulas or aphorisms, but in how one lives, speaks, and acts in ways faithfully appropriate to each time and place. The same emphasis on personal discernment appears in the New Testament. Paul admonishes: "Do not be conformed to this world, but be transformed by the renewing of your minds, so that you may discern what is the will of God—what is good and acceptable and perfect" (Rom 12:2). John counsels: "Beloved, do not believe every spirit, but test the spirits to see whether they are from God; for many false prophets have gone out into the world" (1 John 4:1). Of course, the discernment to which Christians are called is not merely a cultivation of human wisdom. It is an ability that stems from one's new life in Christ; indeed it is a gift of the Spirit (1 Cor 2:10–16). Still, one is nevertheless called to employ such gifts, and to employ them responsibly and appropriately.

This last point needs clarification and emphasis because I am aware that my mode of presentation may still lend itself to old habits. A key factor motivating this book has been the desire to counter the all too common tendency of advocating one atonement theory to the exclusion of others. I have advanced three expansive understandings of the atonement and argued for their rootedness in the triune God, their scriptural basis, and their theological complementarity as a concrete way to counter this tendency. Yet I am aware that the last three chapters have focused on each understanding in turn, and perhaps thereby reinforced the common penchant for not only distinguishing but also separating—and not only separating but viewing as mutually exclusive—different "models" of the atonement. Greater descriptive skill on my part and more flexibility in the customs of academic exposition would no doubt have helped, but perhaps some concluding cautionary comments will also help. Recall the words of Reformed theologian W. A. Visser 't Hooft:

> The three offices are so related to one another that Christ is Prophet in a priestly and royal manner; Priest in a prophetic and royal way; King, but King as priest and prophet. The three offices can be distinguished;

they cannot be separated. At every moment Christ acts in all three capacities. . . . It is, therefore, not permissible to emphasize one of the three offices to such an extent that the other two are forgotten.[1]

These words make it clear that Christ controls and determines the offices, the offices do not control and determine him. In the context of the Old Testament narrative, these offices may have been assigned to different persons—indeed, many different persons, through many different ages. But in Christ they are assigned to one person, the eternal and incarnate Son of God, and in the unity of this person, they mutually reinforce one another in ways they never could before. The most fundamental of these ways is the fact that in the unity of Christ they are caught up in the triune being of the one God. Thus, in a partial modification and paraphrase of Visser 't Hooft, I could summarize my point by saying that Christ is prophet, priest, and king only as he is such as the Son with the Father and the Holy Spirit. None of these offices may be taken on its own, forgetting the other two, and Christ's work in them may not be taken on its own, forgetting either his status as the Son or the role of Father and Spirit.

From a different angle, with the recognition that the triune Savior's work in one office is never sealed off from his work in the others, neither should one assume that believers appropriate the effects of one office apart from the effects of the others. The offices and works, and the way they are received, may be distinguishable for the purposes of clarification and instruction, but in actual life they overlap and intertwine in countless ways. The richly woven narratives of Scripture bear witness to this reality with their very form, and not just in their content. Indeed, it is hard to imagine communicating this multifaceted reality adequately in anything other than narrative form. I have sought to imitate but also illuminate the complexity of this pattern in the various parts of my own exposition. One may begin with a particular thread in the presentation, but tugging at one will, I hope, eventually indicate how it is connected with all the others.

Consider the following illustration. Regarding Christ's prophetic role, he teaches us the truth about our world and ourselves by teaching us about God and his purposes in relation to us. In a very fundamental

---

1. W. A. Visser 't Hooft, *The Kingship of Christ* (New York: Harper & Brothers, 1948), 16–17.

sense, we learn who we are as a result of this teaching. Likewise, I spoke in the first chapter about how one's sense of alienation and separation from God might in some particular cases be described most accurately in terms that do not employ moral categories. That is, one's separation is not so much a matter of one's fault as it is a matter of one's finitude. It might be caused by a limited or false perspective or even ignorance; it might be caused by the limits of one's strength or time; it might be caused by the final limits set by our inevitable mortality. Whatever the specific circumstance, whatever the specific cause, such limitations are a given of creaturely existence and thus an unavoidable aspect of how life unfolds. For all of us at some time, but some of us more frequently and starkly, confronting such limitations can be overwhelmingly enervating, sapping life of meaning and purpose. But Christ's prophetic teaching serves to place life within a broader context, embedding it in a matrix of meaning that transcends the possibilities imagined by our finite and obscured perspectives. Christ's prophetic work reveals that the confines or intransigence of the finite do not finally define us. Rather, he proclaims and enables enlightenment to those who grope for meaning, a transcendent purpose to those enervated by the limitations of their lives, and an eternal identity to those lost in despair over their mortality.

Still, our consideration of Christ's accomplishment must not stop there. Coming to a full awareness of our transcendent identity is not simply a matter of overcoming our finitude. Knowing who we are requires more than just acknowledging Christ's prophetic teaching— even if for certain individuals or groups it is the necessary starting point. Learning our true and full identity is also a matter revealed to us through our liberation from enslaving false gods (an outcome of Christ's royal work) and through the expiation of our own sin and guilt and rebirth into new life (an outcome of Christ's priestly work), which may be the necessary starting points for other individuals or groups. And one should not overlook the fact that these aspects of Christ's work may also have direct bearing upon the weakness, false perspectives, or ignorance just mentioned. After all, those who exploit the weakness or ignorance of others, or who foster in them false assumptions and perspectives should be held accountable, and not the victims. Alternately, there is such a thing as "willful ignorance." It is not unheard of for individuals or groups to use the limitations of their finitude as a convenient excuse for sins of commission or omission, for embracing false perspectives and self-serving ways. In other words, there are times when human limitations cannot avoid moral categories; indeed, there are times when they can only be understood properly within a framework that considers culpability. In sum, even when a particular instance of the human predicament seems best explained by a particular understanding of the atonement, one should still recognize that the other understandings of Christ's atoning work will likely have a corrective and broadening word to say.

The layering and mutuality I am striving to promote among these three offices understood in a trinitarian manner may well be more easily realized in practice than in abstract exposition. So perhaps some concrete illustrations will evoke the sense I am seeking to describe. Consider first a very ordinary, even trivial example: think how a piece of music or a particular song can take on ever deeper personal significance over time. Perhaps it is connected with a historic event, a turning point in your life, or the person you married. When you hear it now, it not only calls to mind a memory of that past time, but the past and present connect and intertwine in such a way that they seem to exist simultaneously. Certain smells can create a similar effect: the scent of sage in a desert landscape, of fir in a boreal forest, of the sea and tidal flats; the smell of factory or farm; the aroma from the hot dog stand on the corner; the fragrance of a particular perfume or a father's roses; the odor of wet wool or a wet dog, the aroma of pine burning in a fireplace or a cake baking in a grandmother's kitchen. Most of us have probably had the experience of smelling again a long forgotten fragrance, and being immediately caught up in the memory and sense of an earlier time. In such an experience, past and present once again come together, so that who you were then and who you are now embrace in a single moment of suspended time. In such situations, you know yourself in multilayered ways: youthful obliviousness may now stand side by side with hard-earned wisdom, an earlier desire for unfettered freedom may now be tempered by the satisfaction of a long-lasting marriage, a once unshakable friendship may now be but a bittersweet memory, earnestly sought-after dreams may have finally been realized—or exchanged for more realistic ones. A clear self-detachment and intimate self-knowledge combine in a single moment.

The same layering of memory and present experience can also be illustrated with more specifically religious examples. For instance, imagine how the meaning of the Christmas story deepens and grows as one hears or perhaps recites it as a child, hears it as an adult, hears one's own children tell it, and finally one's grandchildren. It remains the same story, but one's maturing perspectives and personal memories and associations allow it to be heard with ever greater layers of nuance and personal significance. Similarly, when first sung, the words of hymns may not have any personal association or significance. But as one repeats them over the years, they can gain greater meaning in light of life's inevitable joys, anxieties, successes, frustrations, friendships, betrayals, gratitude, guilt, losses, and the like. A hymn sung at one's wedding or the funeral of a friend cannot help but have greater personal meaning with every subsequent singing. Especially if hymns are "known by heart," they become ever more evocative, even as they grow in their ability to provide expressions of thankfulness, comfort, encouragement, or challenge. Likewise, the rituals of the liturgy take on greater significance as they are repeatedly heard and enacted in the context of personal and communal memory. Each new baptism offers members of a participating congregation the opportunity to rehearse their own baptismal vows, and to take stock of how well they have lived into the grace offered them. Each Christian funeral attended enables us to confront our own mortality, and also hear again the gospel of hope and resurrection.

I offer these examples of how one's life takes on layers of meaning to serve as an analogy for what I am proposing in this book. That is, through preaching and spiritual reflection, through counseling and catechism, through hymns and liturgy, the recognition of Christ's work as king, priest, and prophet can also grow over time in our memory and outlook such that each office in its connection to the Trinity gains an ever greater depth and resonance for Christian believers. In any given moment, one office may be emphasized, one aspect of Christ's saving work especially needed—yet the echoes and harmonies of the other offices and aspects will also be heard, felt, and understood. In one respect, the church year fosters this habit and outlook already. For example, the season of Lent typically brings out those aspects of Christ's work associated with his priestly office, and Easter certainly highlights his sovereign victory. Especially if one considers the hymns typically sung during these two seasons, evocation of at least these two aspects of Christ's manifold work is certainly present. Hymns especially, but also pastoral prayers, seasonal collects, and congregational litanies have great power to instill a deep and implicit sense of the faith, including Christ's atoning work. As one theologian notes, recognizing Christ's threefold office, and encouraging its archetypal function in and for the Christian life, means it must "retain or regain a living context in the devotional and liturgical life of the church, for it is in image and rite that archetypes dwell, persist, and exercise their power."[2]

Still, I believe the church would do well to be more conscientious and explicit in this regard, because an "implicit sense" does not necessarily translate into "a clear idea." Consider, for example, the doctrine of the Trinity. Many hymns refer to it in one manner or another, implicitly instilling a sense of its centrality and importance. And following Pentecost, the Trinity even has its own day of worship. But of the countless Christians who sing such hymns, or hear Trinity Sunday sermons, how many could actually offer even a basic explanation of the Trinity and why it is central to Christian belief? Presumably those who have been well catechized would be up to the task, but how many are, in fact, well catechized, especially in the modern North American context? A similar circumstance prevails, I believe, in peoples' understanding of the doctrine of the atonement. One may be very familiar with certain traditional titles or phrases ascribed to Christ and his work: he is the "Lord" or "King," the "Shepherd" or "Lamb of God," the "good Teacher," he "died for our sins," "gave himself as a ransom," and "triumphed over the grave." But having a clear sense of what these familiar terms and phrases mean, and especially how they relate to and interact with one another and the Christian life of faith, is quite another matter. How many Christians are, in fact, ready and able to give an explicit accounting for the hope that is in them,[3] when the subject is Christ's atoning work?

I have already suggested, in the closing sections of chapters 4, 5, and 6, some of the ways in which the particular offices of Christ might have a concrete impact and practical role in ministerial work and Christian living. In these concluding pages, I will offer some practical scenarios emphasizing more especially the ways in which Christ's threefold offices and work may be related, and presented in their triune integrity. As a preliminary to such scenarios, however, I should reiterate a point grounded in the exegetical work of chapter 3, namely, that each distinguishable aspect of Christ's work is already inherently trinitarian. Recall that the recurring scriptural pattern presents God's saving work in some variation of the following: initiated in and by the Father, accomplished

---

2. Geoffrey Wainwright, *For Our Salvation: Two Approaches to the Work of Christ* (Grand Rapids, Mich.: Eerdmans, 1997), 173.

3. As they are called to be prepared to do in 1 Pet 3:15.

in fact by Christ, and made available and effective through the power of the Holy Spirit. In this sense, each of the persons of the Trinity depends upon the agency of the other two in order to accomplish their common purpose of atonement. This point bears repeated emphasis, if for no other reason than to avoid all too common misunderstandings of God's saving work. Such mistakes may include an overly moralistic take on salvation, one that imagines Christ offering us an example or presenting us with rules of behavior, which we are then left to fulfill on our own rather than on the basis of our regeneration through the Holy Spirit. Or they may include a simplistic and almost tritheistic take on salvation, one that pictures the death of the selfless Son somehow changing the mind of an otherwise wrathful, vindictive Father. One must keep in mind the traditional dictum: "The external works of the Trinity are undivided." Whenever we discuss any particular aspect of Christ's atoning work, we should also always be able to specify the sense in which the Father and Holy Spirit are also always involved, in a complementary and enabling way, in that aspect.

With this admonition in mind, and returning to a more specific focus on the interrelations of Christ's threefold office, consider the following diverse scenarios. The first is a liturgical one, the most important and festive day of the church year, namely, Easter Sunday. As I suggested above, this holiday naturally emphasizes Christ's kingly victory over all that holds us in bondage, most especially death and the powers that serve death. The traditional liturgy and hymnody of this holiday resound with a sense of joy and triumph, and abound with images of light breaking the darkness, of Christ's triumph over the grave, of his defeat of enslaving evil, and the like. Moreover, the joy of Easter takes on a particular resonance and depth for those who celebrate it having also just commemorated Good Friday and Maundy Thursday. The liturgical and hymnic traditions of Good Friday will have emphasized Christ's priestly, sacrificial role, and the traditions of Maundy Thursday shape the way one should understand Christ's kingship: Easter's triumph is of the King who came not to be served, but to serve, and to call his disciples "friends."

Yet what of those for whom Easter is the sole occasion when they attend worship? Are they to hear only the word of Christ's triumphal reign? Does this risk presenting a one-sided picture of Christ's atoning work? As central as Christ's resurrection is, as central as his royal triumph over death is, the full significance of the Easter message will not be proclaimed without including reference to his priestly and prophetic roles. In one sense, such connections help broaden the "temporal horizons" of Easter. In Christ's sacrificial death, we are allowed to die to the past, freed from whatever bondage would begrudge us a new birth. In Christ's living, prophetic words, we recognize that our new birth and freedom is not simply a careless open-endedness, which we are to do with as we will, but a summons and empowering to God-given possibilities and fulfillment. In other words, Easter Sunday should not be celebrated simply as the timeless or static "day of resurrection," but as that day which serves as the threshold between a dead-end past and a living, life-giving future. Practically speaking, then, and depending upon the liturgical flexibility available within given traditions, this may mean that the hymns, litanies, prayers, homily, or sermon for Easter Sunday will exhibit both a trinitarian awareness and a "christological movement" that integrates references to all three offices and the diverse aspects of his atoning work. For example, one hymn might be used that focuses simply on the joy and blessing of the resurrection itself, that is, in straightforward glorification of Christ's royal victory. Another hymn might celebrate Easter, but as viewed through the lens of the cross, Christ's priestly role. A third hymn—perhaps the last of the service— might celebrate Easter as that transforming event that enables us to live with renewed faithfulness and service in the world, based on Christ's prophetic, life-giving role. Alternately, or perhaps as well, the preacher's sermon could make explicit connections linking the different aspects of Christ's threefold work, and the diverse ways these aspects transform Christian living. In sum, there are many ways one may highlight liturgically a particular facet of Christ's atoning work, even while interweaving its connection to the other facets of that work.

Consider next a common pastoral scenario, one in which a pastor, family, and friends are gathered beside the deathbed of a loved one. Clearly, the Christian hope of resurrection that is founded on Christ's own resurrection must be one aspect of the consolation offered, both to the dying and the grieving. In such a situation, Christians are called to rely upon the affirmation of Christ's kingship as a transcendent sovereignty that triumphs even over the natural inevitability of death. If this affirmation has been well taught and deeply imbibed prior to the actual confrontation with death, it will more likely offer a firmer support. But even if the affirmation of Christ's sovereign victory over death has not been so established in the dying or the grieving family members, a pastor is still called to reaffirm it. Why? Even if one rather flippantly replied, "because it's her job to say such things," this would not entirely miss the mark. A minister is not called simply to voice his or her opinions; rather, she or he is called to pronounce a message that has been entrusted to her or him, one given by God in the life, death, and resurrection of Jesus. But how is this to be done in a way that will allow this message to be heard? The question does not admit to one concrete answer, but only to two more general admonitions. On the one hand, to repeat the counsel offered above, the minister must give voice to the gospel in a way that displays pastoral sensitivity, wisdom, and spiritual discernment. On the other hand, the message must be voiced in such manner that it is recognized not as a personal conjecture but a proclaimed reality. That is, while being sensitive to the intersubjective dynamics of the situation, the pastor must nevertheless take care to present the gospel message of resurrection as an objective hope that acknowledges our fears and doubts even as it transcends them.

Yet it may well be that a sense of guilt or shame prevents the dying or the grieving from accepting this message of hope, based on some hindering sense that they do not deserve it. In such a case, a gentle urging of Christ's forgiving and reconciling priestly work may be the prerequisite for enabling acceptance of the promise of victory and resurrection. Alternately, it may be that a sense of life's ultimate futility and meaninglessness prevents the dying or the grieving from accepting this message of hope. In such a case, a gentle insistence that Christ does indeed prophetically proclaim that life has meaning and a transcendent goal may serve as a needed reorientation enabling the acceptance of the promise of victory and resurrection. Whatever the particulars of such a scenario, the pastor is called to bear witness to God's gracious sovereignty, his fiercely devoted and forbearing love, and his fulfilling final intentions for our existence that are greater than anything we might face in this life or even imagine for the next.

A more specific focus on the interrelations of Christ's threefold office might also be beneficial in another common pastoral scenario, namely, in the context of a new member class for those considering joining a congregation. This would be especially true if the class included anyone disillusioned with the "traditional" understanding of the atonement learned previously while he or she belonged to another congregation or denomination. To be sure, such disillusionment may have varying causes. It may be that this supposedly traditional understanding is not actually part of orthodox Christian tradition. Or it may stem from a one-sided, simplistic, or misguided presentation of certain elements that do in fact belong to the tradition. It may also arise less from the tradition itself and more from its idiosyncratic reception. That is, it may be that the personal experience or psychological makeup of the hearer makes a "mishearing" of what was taught almost inevitable. Whatever the particular case may be, it will clearly demand as much pastoral sensitivity and spiritual discernment as the minister can muster. Still, one should also recognize that a fluent understanding of Christ's threefold work may also give the pastor more practical options in presenting what Christ has accomplished, which may help dissipate the specific concerns of the disillusioned and skeptical prospective new member. For example, if such an individual remains dismissive because he assumes that a "penal substitutionary" understanding of the atonement is the only option, presenting a scriptural and theological exposition of the other forms of Christ's atoning work may open doors of understanding and acceptance that that person had not realized existed.

Similarly, if an over-emphasis on penal substitution has had such a guilt-producing psychological impact that it actually hinders a person's ability to receive the good news, one faithful and appropriate pastoral response may again be to emphasize these other understandings. But the best response may also be to broaden that person's understanding of Christ's sacrificial death. As I indicated in chapter 5, Scripture certainly recognizes Christ's death to be an expiating sacrifice for sin. But it also understands it as a sacrifice of "first fruits" and a means of redefining and reestablishing divine-human communion. In these understandings, the psychological emphasis is not on our guilt, it is not on a sense of our personal unworthiness, it is not on the sense of the indebtedness and obligation we should feel toward Christ for his sacrificial death. Rather, the emphasis should be on the manner in which, by means of his sacrifice, Christ claims us as his own, bestows us with his pledge of new and abundant life, and opens to us a gracious communion with God we would not otherwise have. In this understanding of Christ's death, we are encouraged not to look behind us in regret at our own shortcomings, but forward in joy and confidence on the basis of what becomes available to us in Christ, the firstborn from the dead, the firstborn of the new creation. For the discerning pastor, it should also be evident that Christ's royal victory complements and may help reinforce this understanding of Christ's priestly sacrifice.

Turn now to another practical scenario, one in which the pastor is counseling someone facing a "mid-life" crisis or a debilitating loss of meaning and purpose in his or her life. I have alluded to such a situation already, but let me say a few more words. Such a crisis may be particularly enervating to those who were raised with the encouragement that "they could become whatever they set their minds to" or the admonition that they "make something of their lives." In a cultural ethos—particularly prevalent among middle-class Christians in modern Western countries—that implies we create ourselves and our own reality, it can come as quite a blow to acknowledge that our lives have fallen far short of our earlier goals and dreams. Even more unsettling is to see how circumstances may have determined our lives in ways that have no discernible similarity to our earlier hopes. We may feel trapped by these circumstances that are beyond our control. Alternately, we may have actually achieved our goals, but come to view them as having no lasting or ultimate significance. In such a situation, conversation and counseling based on Christ's threefold office and work may offer a broader perspective, and a liberating way out of the dilemma. Once again, of course, the actual interactions with the person seeking help will require psychological skill and sensitivity and spiritual discernment. One should avoid above all a pedantic and abstract approach.

Still, true pastoral counseling is not generic. Rather, it operates on the assumption that the basic affirmations of the Christian faith are true, describing the real foundation and means for a fulfilled and fulfilling human life. So how might an understanding of Christ's threefold office actually help someone confronting the personal crisis just described? Consider first the way in which Christ the Prophet proclaims the true purpose and end of human living. Our lives and our "reality" are not something we make up, they are something God creates and offers to us. Life is not something we invent, it is something we receive through God's grace. And if it is to be put to its best and truest use, it must be lived in ways that correspond to the purposes God intends for it. To be sure, given our individual particularity, these ways will take myriad forms, corresponding to God's particular gifts to each individual, gifts that will help guide that person's particular path. Recognizing what these gifts are and acting upon them will certainly require faithful discernment and creative engagement—actions a pastor may help nurture. But concern for these particulars should not blind us to the larger theological point that an individual's sense of meaninglessness may be alleviated in part simply by having her or his life placed in the broader and more encompassing context of God's meaning and intentions. After all, Christ's prophetic teaching tells us that we may serve our God-given higher end even in seemingly trivial ways, for by serving even "the least"—the hungry, the thirsty, the stranger, the naked, the prisoner—we serve God (see Matt 10:42; cf. Mark 9:41 and Heb 6:10). As Protestant traditions on vocation recognize, real life rarely unfolds on a grand scale, but rather in the unexceptional opportunities of the everyday, and it is in them that we encounter our God-given calling to faithfulness.

In this regard, however, Christ's prophetic word may need to be reinforced with the assertion of Christ's sovereignty. Just as we are not in any original or ultimate sense the author of our own life, so, too, are we not its original or ultimate authority. God does not merely offer us a variety of options, among which we are left to choose according to our own idiosyncratic perspectives or impulses, for our own self-determined ends. Such an approach misses the fact that Christian faith reveals to us "a more excellent way,"[4] with ideals and norms that transcend our more limited standards and criteria, and that Christ summons us to act in ways we might not choose ourselves. In light of such revelation and calling, we can recognize that our own, more limited notions of "freedom of choice" may represent a bondage to a consumer mentality that can only in turn finally consume us. By contrast, recognizing Christ as king means we recognize him as sovereign over our lives and choices, knowing that only under this sovereignty will we truly fulfill our deepest human yearnings and desires. In a world of artificial meaning and ephemeral purposes, we long to be called to something beyond ourselves and greater than we are. The Christian counselor knows that this is exactly what Christ the King does.

Moreover, Christian faith at its truest displays what might be called an "incarnational realism." It takes seriously the "situatedness" of human life in time and place. It recognizes our limitations as creatures—the psychological and cultural constraints on our perspectives, the frailty of our bodies, the brevity of our lives—and calls us nevertheless to live our lives faithfully within these boundaries. It does not place demands upon us as if our lives were limitless and boundless. To be sure, it does offer, through the power of the Holy Spirit, a real and abiding hope in an eschatological future that will surpass our worldly dreams. But at the same time, indeed as a result of this realism and hope, Christian faith is also skeptical of all human fantasies and counterfeit utopias. In that sense, it is precisely *not* our task to "save" the world, our communities, our friends or family, or even ourselves—that is God's work alone.

---

4. The phrase is, of course, the Apostle Paul's, from 1 Cor 12:31, and serves to introduce his famous "hymn to love" in 1 Cor 13.

Perhaps in this regard we may invoke Christ's priestly sacrifice by suggesting that he enables each of us finally to surrender that which is often most precious to us, namely, our most deep-seated fantasies about ourselves and what we will achieve in our lives. Such fantasies are often rooted in childhood dreams and disconnected from the messiness and frequent intractability of real life, yet recognizing our union with Christ can allow us to give them up, indeed, offer them as sacrifices, thereby signifying the illusory life we have left behind. Christ's death enables us to die to our "old selves"—including any fantasized, ideal self—that we might truly live as new, God-given real selves. Letting such illusory images and hopes die on the cross with Christ represents both our resistance to conformity to this world and the beginning, through the renewal of our minds, of our spiritual transformation, that in Christ we might instead present ourselves as "living sacrifices" to God (Rom 12:1ff.). In sum, I suggest that knowing how to frame Christ's call more precisely in terms of his prophetic, royal, and priestly status and work will enable Christians to counsel more concretely and practically those confronted by a disappointing or seemingly fruitless or meaningless life.

Consider finally a scenario dealing with the meaning of the sacraments. Perhaps it arises in the context of parents who want their child baptized, or in the context of a catechism or adult education class addressing the role and significance of the Lord's Supper in Christian worship and life. How might a threefold understanding of Christ's atoning work help Christians understand the sacraments in a fuller, richer sense? Clearly, both baptism and the Lord's Supper have been, and may be, understood in multifaceted ways. The famous ecumenical document, *Baptism, Eucharist, and Ministry,* specifies five different meanings for each.[5] On the one hand, it describes baptism as signifying (1) a participation in Christ's death and resurrection, (2) an individual's conversion, pardoning, and cleansing, (3) the anointing and promising gift of the Holy Spirit, (4) incorporation into the Body of Christ, and (5) initiation into the kingdom of God.[6] On the other hand, it understands the Eucharist (communion or the Lord's Supper) as being (1) a thanksgiving to the Father, (2) an anamnesis or memorial of Christ, (3) an invocation of the Spirit, (4) a communion of the faithful, and (5) a meal of the kingdom.[7]

---

5. *Baptism, Eucharist, and Ministry* (Faith and Order Papers no. 111; Geneva: World Council of Churches, 1982).

6. Ibid., 2–3.

7. Ibid., 10–15.

As one may gather from these headings, the sacraments of baptism and the Lord's Supper are described with clearly trinitarian overtones and in ways that I could correlate with a number of my points regarding Christ's multivalent work of atonement. To undertake a full correlation here would, of course, take me too far afield at this point in my book. But I want to suggest a few ways that these sacraments may be more evocatively understood and grounded, when viewed through the lens of Christ's threefold office and work. First, baptism. Insofar as it is recognized as a participation in Christ's death and resurrection, it is also a participation in his royal victory. This is why it may also be understood as an initiation into the body of Christ and God's kingdom, because we have died to all old allegiances, and been born again to new life and new possibilities—even in this world—under the sole sovereignty of our divine Head. How can this be, given our manifest creaturely limitations? Because baptism also signifies our anointing by the Holy Spirit. Who we truly are, what our true purpose and end are, derives no longer from any mundane context or circumstance, for we are sealed in the Spirit and marked as God's own. Least of all does our own sin finally determine who we are, for we have been pardoned and cleansed by Christ's priestly sacrifice, that we may be prepared to fulfill the creaturely destiny he prophetically proclaimed and depicted, in word and deed.

In a similar and complementary manner, Christ's threefold office and work both explain and are explained by the host of meanings found in the Lord's Supper. In its presumably least controversial aspect, the Lord's Supper stands as a "memorial" of Christ and his saving work, on the basis of his own command: "Do this in remembrance of me" (1 Cor 11:25, Luke 22:19). Clearly, it includes an element of human commemoration not unlike that in any mundane memorial ceremony. Thus, Christians are enjoined to recall Christ's words and deeds, and to be inspired by his example. In this sense, we may say that we are enjoined to recall him in his prophetic role. His teachings and concrete actions are not to be forgotten, but remembered in order to serve as a continuing guide to Christian living. But it would grossly oversimplify matters to say that the Lord's Supper thereby memorializes something over and done with, something confined to the past. To the contrary, the church believes that the Lord's Supper is not merely, and certainly not primarily, a human ritual. Rather, it is an occasion in which the Christ is made living and present through the power of the Holy Spirit. Moreover, in light of this fact, it would also grossly oversimplify matters to take this as meaning that—apart from the way it moves our latter-day hearts—

our response to Christ's example is not based upon the ongoing sustenance and power of the Holy Spirit. This understanding of the Spirit's essential role is most clearly signified in the Orthodox prayer of *epiklesis*, or invocation of the Holy Spirit, said prior to the celebration of the Eucharist. It is a tradition that Reformed churches have tended to adopt prior to the reading of Scripture—a not inappropriate addition to this part of the liturgy, if it does not entail its subtraction at the commencement of the celebration of communion, or a masking of how it undergirds the whole of Christian life.

But even with a sense of the Spirit's role in making the Lord's Supper a matter not merely of our remembrance but of Christ's "real presence," it is crucial to recognize that the Lord's Supper also includes a forward-looking, eschatological element—an element that is likewise made not just future, but present, through the power of the Spirit. In the traditional words conveyed by the Apostle Paul, "For as often as you eat this bread and drink the cup, you proclaim the Lord's death until he comes" (1 Cor 11:26). The various gospel traditions reiterate this element, connecting it with the final revelation and consummation of the divine kingdom (see Matt 26:29, Mark 14:25, Luke 22:18; cf. John 6:54). In this regard, of course, the Supper serves as a sign of Jesus' status as "the once and future King," the Lord who sits at the right hand of the Father and will judge the nations on the last day. It also serves as a pledge of that coming kingdom and a foretaste of the messianic banquet, and as such, it also expands the communal circle beyond that of the original disciples to include the faithful of all the intervening ages. Additionally, a full understanding of the Lord's Supper also necessarily includes the recognition of its priestly, sacrificial element. The scriptural narrative explicitly connects the wine of communion with Christ's blood, the blood of the new covenant, poured out for many for the forgiveness of sins (Matt 26:28, Mark 14:24; cf. Luke 22:20, 1 Cor 11:25). Implicitly—given the narrative context of the Last Supper and what was soon to happen to him on the cross—Jesus symbolically reinforces the point by breaking the bread and saying, "This is my body, which is given for you."[8]

---

8. Only Luke 22:19 has this precise wording. Variations on these words implying the same basic point are found in 1 Cor 11:24, Matt 26:26, and Mark 14:22. John 6:48–58 also contains an interesting discourse on Jesus as "the bread of life," and while the context of this passage is not the Last Supper, the dialogue does imply a difference between the heavenly bread of the old covenant (the manna) and the "living" heavenly bread of the new covenant (Jesus himself).

In sum, any full and faithful conception of the church's sacraments of baptism and the Lord's Supper will necessarily be connected to Christ's threefold work and understood in living, trinitarian terms. Otherwise, they risk being presented in ways that will inevitably be insufficient, because they will have been sapped of their divine reality and power and made one dimensional.

With this observation, the time has come to conclude the presentation of my various scenarios. I hope these examples have offered a clearer sense of how my exegetical and theological work on Christ's triune and threefold status and work may be "cashed out" in practical, pastoral situations. All that remains to be said is to return to the hopes presented at the outset of this whole project. That is, I reiterate my fervent hope that this book has helped clarify why the church—her pastors and teachers, her deacons or presbyters, her laymen and women, her priests, her vestry and committee members, her confirmands and Sunday school students—should concern herself with a better theological understanding of the "triune Savior." I hope that I have made a convincing argument that such a theology helps illuminate the very source of her existence as church and elucidates the fundamental purpose to which God calls her, and through her witness, the whole world. I pray that these reflections will offer Christians of all sorts the spiritual and pastoral resources to deepen their own faith and extend a hand to those outside the church, offering them new hope, a new identity, a new sense of meaning, and new courage. We live in a world filled with uncertainty, coarseness, danger, and death—and in desperate need of such saving renewal. I hope that my work has helped explain in a multifaceted and nuanced, but also practical way, what it actually means to make the seemingly simple claim that "Jesus saves." As I suggested at the very outset, the rather awkward subtitle, "A Trinitarian Theology of Atonement," connects the God whom the church worships, invokes, and petitions with what it is that this God actually accomplishes for the reconciliation and restoration of the world. Without such a recognition of who God truly is and what he has done and continues to do, the church's sacraments will remain only human ceremonies, her prayers only human pleading, her preaching only human opinion and exhortation, her consolation only wishful thinking, and her service only human moralism and social work. But with a recognition of God's saving work in Jesus Christ through the power of the Holy Spirit, the church learns the world's God-given origin and end, and her own true purpose in fulfilling God's commission. With such a recognition, the church is given the means to escape the mundane banality that so often passes for a contemporary vision and reclaim its transcendent birthright: a powerful and multifaceted trinitarian imagination and life, serving her triune Lord and all those whom he loves, to God's greater glory and her own eternal fulfillment.

Gracious, holy, and almighty Father,
we praise and thank You for Your countless blessings of love and grace,
especially the work of Your Son our Savior, Jesus Christ.
By the power of Your Holy Spirit,
open our minds to You, we pray, and let our hearts cling to Your truth.
By Your holy strength, You free us from all that holds us in bondage;
confiding in that strength, help us learn true confidence.
By Your gracious mercy, You forgive us our faults and failings;
made new by that mercy, help us each day to live in You.
By Your righteous wisdom, You call us out of ourselves;
responding to that wisdom, help us become what You intend us to be.
To Your greater glory,
we ask these things in the name of our Lord and Savior Jesus Christ,
who with You and the Holy Spirit lives and reigns,
one God, now and forever. Amen.

Index

Note: Synoptic gospel parallels are cited typically only by their location in Matthew.